The Art of Denis Williams

The Art of Denis Williams

Evelyn A. Williams

PEEPAL TREE

First published in Great Britain in 2012
by Peepal Tree Press Ltd
17 Kings Avenue
Leeds LS6 1QS
England

ISBN 9781845231934

Supported by
ARTS COUNCIL
ENGLAND

Contents

For Katie Alice

FOREWORD

ANDREW JEFFERSON-MILES

THE FIRST PUBLICATION dedicated to the life and works of Denis Williams was *Denis Williams: A Life in Works, New and Collected Essays* (Amsterdam & New York: Rodopi, 2010), edited by his daughters Evelyn and Charlotte Williams. The fourteen contributors and their essays celebrate, describe and discuss Denis Williams' achievements in painting, art history, the novel, and in the anthropology of the Guianas. What emerges is the picture of a Proteus: a great artist whose unusual intellect and zest for life was in itself a singular gift.

This new book by Evelyn Williams focuses on the artist's journey: Denis Williams the painter; his origins, inspirations, and innovations in the painted arts. The accompanying overview by Louis James offers a concise and useful introduction to the range and scope of the life. I have enjoyed hearing Professor James speak on two occasions on the art of Denis Williams; once at a 1999 conference at the University of Dijon, and again at a 2002 conference at Newcastle University. The keen line of judgment demonstrated in these papers seemed to me at once astute as well as sympathetic. In this foreword I would like to extend that *élan* to questions surrounding the artist and his art, and something of the complexity connecting value to invention.

Evelyn Williams' book is a critical assessment that aims to initiate an extended conversation on art, for Denis Williams' paintings are the founding works of the National Collection of Guyana. The institution of a new collection is a significant event in the life of a nation, for it raises the following important considerations:

- How do we define the value of the new art?

- In a world of migratory populations, what explains why one nation will claim an artist for its own, while another nation, in which the artist has been equally active, overlooks him?

- If both acceptance and neglect hinge on premises that could be judged false, or misaligned, what could account for their perpetuation?

Let us begin with the condition of those who propose opinions on art and wish to promote them as potentially definitive statements. Documentaries, newspaper reviews of specific exhibitions, general art reviews, books, and monographs are means of propagating findings with attempts at judgments concerning worth. The conditioning in the mind of the participants in these initiatives is chiefly the exercise of received values. Such values require a body of knowledge to sustain them – a corpus of examples and their definitions – as the context for talking about what is being viewed. Thus to weigh Denis Williams the artist is to admit to the operation of a conditioned ground. We could define value in terms of factorials: from the nation, and not from the nation, *versus* the traditional, and the innovative. The artist who is recognised as being properly British and whose art is innovative would be contrasted with the artist who is defined as not being a British person, and whose art, almost by implication, is, contextually, innovative. In the early fifties, Denis Williams accepted a studio next door to the painter Francis Bacon. Bacon would be defined as British and innovative. Denis Williams, on the other hand, would be thought of as not from the British nation, and also innovative. In the conditioning of the British mind, these two artists occupy agonistic quadrants, distinguished by their nationality. In the second chapter of her book, Evelyn Williams cites how Wyndham Lewis, an early supporter of her father, described Denis Williams as "a Negro artist". Now, as a Guyanese artist born and raised in Guyana, I find this description jarring, for whilst it differentiates Denis Williams for Wyndham Lewis and his erstwhile correspondents, it in no way differentiates Denis Williams for me. In Lewis' eyes, Denis Williams' race, and hence, nationality, are self-evident signifiers. In my own eyes, to describe Denis Williams in these terms is genotypic tautology. Had I been born and raised under a colonial regime, I would still find Lewis' description undifferentiated, in that it intends a distinction which makes no sense outside the speaker's constrained frame of reference, and certainly is quite separate from the matter – namely, the discussion of artistic moment. It confuses, in that it appears to imply a particular style which, in actuality, might be wholly absent. An artist trained in the habits of a particular painting tradition is going to paint pictures influenced by that frame. If the Italian Renaissance is his dominant early training, as it was for Denis Williams, it becomes the referend in which he will start to paint. That the artist might have been born in Yemen, Tibet, Catalonia, or Canterbury would alter not one jot the evidencing of his initial training. Unless the artist's formative training can be ascertained, race, and its implications of nationality, is of little guide to artistic definition. Correctly then, one could better define the artist in terms of the artistic tradition that tutored him.

It is equally possible that Wyndham Lewis was being mischievous, with an ear to contention, and as an artist, one cannot help but feel a debt of gratitude that Wyndham Lewis took it upon himself to become involved with Denis Williams. The irony of a not-national painter out-painting born and bred English painters could not have escaped him, thus the epithet "a Negro artist" could have been Lewis' own stirring of the cauldron of controversy.

Admitting as much, nonetheless it could not be denied that entrenched habits of mind are notoriously difficult to alter for the better. The simplistic colour coding of the individual shields invulnerable judgments that barely lend themselves to question. In 2001, I questioned a gallery owner in London's Cork Street. I wished to gain some insight as to how buyers priced-in an artist's physical appearance and how this altered perception about the value of the art as a collector's item. The gallery owner cheerfully informed me that there was no such thing as black British art, only British art. Next, I perused his list of artists and noted that despite the relatively high media profile of artists who are black, brown, and yellow in the skin, none of his stable reflected it.

In his 1950 painting *Human World* Denis Williams began to reach for a new vocabulary of painting. He began to invent a new way of structuring his canvas that needs to be considered in terms of a break from his formative ground, his separation from what his contemporaries were doing, and his immediate inspiration in the Modernist painters in the Paris of the 1930s. What Evelyn Williams has succeeded in doing is to offer an extensive meditation on the nature, form, and force of her father's break from peers and recent antecedents. She arrives in many astute insights into the significance and potential value of Denis Williams' art. In doing so, she has managed to locate a new fulcrum, not just for the art of Denis Williams, but, in many ways, for newness in art itself. Understanding that the central discourse of European Modernism would be insufficient and misplaced in such an enterprise, Evelyn Williams is to be congratulated not just for deploying her own considerable intellect, but also for discovering in the deliberations of the Caribbean poet and thinker Kamau Brathwaite a diction much closer to home, and possessing the scope to receive without false distinction the originality and residual value of the art of Denis Williams. It is fitting that she should have been invited to deliver the thirteenth series of the Edgar Mittelholzer Memorial Lectures, in Guyana, in 2009 for which she chose the title "Art, Blood and Heritage" and in which she reappraised Williams' enduring legacy as an artist in the context of increasing globalisation.

Andrew Jefferson-Miles is a Guyanese-born artist and author. He edited the *Selected Essays of Wilson Harris* (1999), and has also published *The Timehrian* (novel, 2002), and *Art of Navigation* (poetry, 2003). He holds a doctorate in Creative and Critical Writing from the University of East Anglia. As an artist, he has exhibited at Tate Modern. He has contributed to *Denis Williams: A Life in Works. New and Collected Essays* (Amsterdam & New York: Rodopi, 2010).

OVERVIEW

LOUIS JAMES

THIS DENSELY RESEARCHED and generously illustrated study reveals previously hidden threads in the weave of modern cultural history. It traces Denis Williams' productive career across three continents, and shows how his accomplishments in literature, anthropology and archaeology were shaped and framed by the central discipline of his art, which informed everything that he did. But if the story is a global one, it begins and ends in Guyana, and roots his achievement in the land of his origin. It is relevant to begin with some comments on this context.

British Guiana, as the country was called when Denis Williams was born there in 1923, stands apart from the islands of the Caribbean basin with which it has been historically associated. The islands share a common denominator of tropical sun and sea, a sense of existing as an archipelago. But while Guyana is the third smallest nation on the South American mainland, the land stretches back for 83,000 square miles over five changing terrains, between seas embrowned by great river deltas, to the densely forested mountains of the Brazilian border. It is one the world's great natural landscapes, and awes the mind with a sense of brooding space. In contrast its population, in 1923 considerably smaller than today's 770,000, lives mainly in the narrow coastal strip, and is sharply fragmented. It includes descendants from across Africa, Europe and Asia. Perhaps most importantly, while on the islands the aboriginal inhabitants were virtually exterminated in the sixteenth century, Guyana's heartland holds the continuity with what Wilson Harris has called "the folk": the indigenous Amerindian tribes and cultures of the interior.

Denis Williams' career is both unique, and profoundly rooted in this background. The critic and dramatist Michael Gilkes, himself Guyanese, has argued that his country's combination of geographical space and a culturally fragmented people has created a psychic "syzygy" (simultaneous conjunction and opposition) in its artistic consciousness. This results in a tension between a heightened awareness of a defined external reality, set in contrast to that of fluid, fractured humanity. Denis Williams was to write three novels which similarly explored personal crises within increasingly austere structural frameworks, until in the last, *The Sperm of God*, the narrative faltered during experimental attempts to mathematically define human interactions, leaving the novel unfinished and unpublished. His visual art, more fruitfully, also grew out of a tension between personal and objective reality. His earliest surviving paintings are intensely individual, vividly realised family portraits, and the earliest of a line of searching self-portraits he was to develop throughout his lifetime. But his inquiring mind led him, increasingly, to intellectual explorations of external structures of physical and social reality.

Selected for a British Council Scholarship to London, his first exhibition at the Berkeley Gallery in 1948, two years after his arrival, brought him immediate recognition. He was "technically brilliant", enthused a reviewer. Wyndham Lewis, who was to become his active sponsor, commented "Mr Williams [...] possesses most remarkable gifts." These early paintings were associated with the "primitivism" of Picasso, but Williams rightly resented this association – he did not need a European artist to point him to his African heritage. More pertinently, on a brief visit to America, Williams was compared to the Cuban artist Wifredo Lam.

However Williams was following his own vision. Returning home in 1949, he mounted an exhibition of paintings on the theme of *Plantation Studies*, darkly envisioning the country's slave inheritance. It was meat too strong for his bourgeois colonial audience, and, smarting from their hostile reception, Williams turned back to London. Under the aegis of Wyndham Lewis, he presented his work at the Gimpel Fils Galleries in Mayfair, placing his British Guiana studies alongside powerful "symbolic realities", transforming scenes of contemporary London life into his own perspective of the *Human World*. This brought him the acclaim his homeland denied him – ironically prompting the British Guiana National History and Culture fund to purchase a sample of his work.

He studied at the innovative Camberwell School of Arts and Crafts, lectured at the Central School of Fine Art, and tutored at the prestigious Slade School of Fine Art; while his home at 21 Oxford Road became a meeting place for experimental artists. But meeting Denis Williams in 1954, Wilson Harris was startled to find Williams had turned his back on this earlier painting, and realism in any form, seeking to achieve abstract art of "a shining impassivity". He immersed himself in the artistic experiments of a London teeming with ideas.

As this book amply illustrates, Denis Williams earned a niche in the history of the Modernist Movement in London in the fifties. While much of this work remains to be traced, Evelyn Williams reproduces and discusses his extraordinary constructs of planes and colours and their relationships evident in surviving works like *Painting in Six Related Rhythms* (1954). Such work brought Williams international recognition, and he contributed to major art exhibitions in London and Paris, including the seminal 1954 Whitechapel Gallery exhibition, *This is Tomorrow*.

But Williams could never feel fully part of the London scene. A striking "black" artist in London's "white" art scene, at a time when interest in Picasso's African primitivism and Sartre's existential thesis of *négritude* were both fashionable, Williams was aware of the dangers of being taken as an exotic stereotype.

While Williams was in touch with contemporary art developments, he had his own agenda; his instincts were leading him towards the "objective" side of his national sensibility, a desire to inquire and define. For all his attempts to remain independent, Williams was touched by the surge of creativity in the Anglophone Caribbean. In the fifties Williams met up with the expatriate writers George Lamming from Barbados, and his own compatriots Jan Carew and Wilson Harris. All three were frequent visitors to the Williams home: Harris stayed there with the family for a period in 1954. Williams designed dust jackets for Caribbean novels, including Lamming's seminal *In the Castle of My Skin*. In 1957 he vividly illustrated a HMSO book *British Guiana: The Land of Six Peoples*. But that year Williams felt that he had pushed his own search for total objectivity to its limits, and for the second time in his life, his artistic quest dramatically changed tack.

West Indians seeking their cultural identity in the fifties were turning to Africa in search of their roots, but in general they made only brief visits. Williams, like his compatriot and friend O. R. Dathorne and (Edward) Kamau Brathwaite, was one of the few who stayed and immersed themselves in the African experience. Williams' first African landfall was significantly not the Slave Coast, but the Department of Fine and Applied Art at the Khartoum Technical Institute in the Sudan, "a geographical and cultural cross-roads at the heart of the continent", where he lectured in art. Contemporary opinion located the early migration of African civilization southwards from Egypt through the ancient civilization of Kush and its capital, Meroë. From 1959, Williams himself was to make his own explorations out into West and East Africa.

Africa did not lead Williams to the source of the Caribbean personality: his obsession with objective truth quickly led him to reject contemporary clichés of "the Negro identity". What his experience of Africa did was more profound: it totally transformed his Western-educated understanding of time, history and culture. Some of this epiphany he embodied in one of the most remarkable novels to emerge from the new wave of dialectical Anglophone Caribbean writing, *Other Leopards* (1963).

Williams abandoned the dialectical materialism of the European historians, and travelled south and westwards to lecture at the University of Ife, then located in Ibadan, Nigeria. Ibadan was at this time in a ferment of ideas. New concepts were emerging, based on the practice of local African cultures, challenging Western concepts of African art. Williams joined the committee of the Mbari Mbayo club of African writers and artists recently founded by Ulli Beier, and worked alongside the pioneers of a West African literary renaissance, including Amos Tutuola, Chinua Achebe, Wole Soyinka and Christopher Okigbo. As the co-organiser of the Oshogbo Art Workshops, he gave opportunities to local untrained artists, initiating a vigorous growth of contemporary art in the region. He painted murals, and designed book covers for Dennis Brutus and Wole Soyinka. He researched the relationship between Yoruba art and religion, forming the basis for a work challenging European responses to African art, *Icon and Image*. When the focus on West Africa widened eastwards to include Uganda and Kenya, Williams moved on too, and co-edited the seminal pan-African magazine *Transition*. He was now ready for the third and final move, back to his homeland, the newly independent Guyana.

In Africa, Williams had abandoned the Western concept of the solitary artist questing for illumination, and moved, through his study of archaeology and anthropology, to understand the traditional African rôle of art as a process at the heart of the social and religious practices of the community. From 1967 to 1974 he created a small farming homestead at Issano in the interior on the Upper Mazaruni. In this tranquil retreat he was to continue painting, and to write his important reflections on Guyanese identity and the rôle of the artist in the 1969 Mittelholzer Lectures. When British Guiana became the independent Cooperative Republic of Guyana in 1970, he was instrumental in inaugurating Carifesta – the celebration and exploration of Pan-Caribbean arts.

He was now a national figure, active on all major national committees for the preservation of history and culture, and, as the new republic's Director of Art, he played a vital part in enabling the emergence of a native "school" of Guyanese art through the foundation of the Burrowes School of Art. He also initiated the project that was to culminate in Philip Moore's *1763 Monument*, the huge bronze figure of Cuffy, the casting of which he personally supervised.

His mural *Memorabilia II* explored and celebrated his country's history. One particular work which reflects the fruitful resolution of the "syzygy" within the Guyanese context – the tension between private and external realities – is *Majestas* (1974). This is a massive image commissioned for the Anglican church at Kamarang, at once human and abstract, and a symbol of his nation's fragmentation and rebirth. Williams regarded it as his own finest achievement.

He remained Director of the Walter Roth Museum he had founded in 1974, which, with its academic periodical, gave international status to Guyanese archaeological studies, a discipline to which he became increasingly devoted. His skills as an artist were now deployed to produce paintings of an anthropological nature. His final work was a copiously illustrated academic text entitled *Prehistoric Guiana*, published posthumously in 2003. Yet, as that book abundantly illustrates, Denis Williams' concept of time never worked in one single direction: he turned to the past in order develop the national future he had done so much to establish and inspire.

Evelyn Williams has produced a book that clearly demonstrates how the varied skills of this most talented of individuals were united by his art, which lay at his creative centre. More than this, she has constructed a compelling account of the rôle of the artist in a developing society, and provided future students of Caribbean culture with a rich and detailed archival resource.

Louis James is Emeritus Professor of Victorian and Modern Literature at the University of Kent at Canterbury. His publications include *Fiction for the Working Man 1830-1850* (1963), *Print and the People* (1976) and *The Victorian Novel* (2006). He has recently contributed to *Denis Williams: A Life in Works. New and Collected Essays* (Amsterdam & New York: Rodopi, 2010).

Author's Note

The lines below are taken from *Caribbean Man in Space and Time* by Edward Kamau Brathwaite (in *Carifesta Forum: An Anthology of 20 Caribbean Writers*, edited by John Hearne, Institute of Jamaica, 1975). In this piece Brathwaite introduces the dual concept of the "outer plantation" and the "inner plantation" which provided me with a very useful point of departure in developing a context for this book.

archipelago: fragments: a geological plate being crushed by the pacific's curve, cracking open yucatan; the arctic/north american monolith: hence cuba, hispaniola, puerto rico: continental outriders and the dust of the bahamas. atlantic africa pushing up the beaches of our eastern seawards

the history reflects the pressure and passage of lava, storm, stone, earthquake, crack, coral: their rise and fall of landscapes: destructions, lost memories: atlantis, atahualpa, ashanti: creations: fragments

it would be better to begin with caribbean man: crouched: legitimate bastard: against space: dwarf, clenched fist of time

the unity is submarine

breathing air, the societies were successively amerindian, european, creole. the amerindian several; the european various; the creole plural

subsistent plantation maroon

multilingual multiethnic many ancestored

fragments

the unity is submarine

breathing air, our problem is how to study the fragments/whole

Introduction

DENIS WILLIAMS was the first black painter to win critical acclaim in Great Britain as defined by his reception by prominent figures of the art establishment, his peers, art critics and the curators of the new avant-garde art exhibition spaces in post-war London. Williams' presence is significant to the ongoing process of defining that decade. He was represented by Gimpel Fils of Mayfair, a prestigious international commercial gallery. He produced a body of work dating from the late 1940s which offers a much earlier art-historical reference than is widely documented.

His name is closely associated with the leading West Indian intellectuals, artists and writers of the post-World War II era and it is important to document and preserve the individual identities of those significant figures who might otherwise disappear from view or become subsumed in the narratives of political and social conflict.

His encounter with the privileged preserve of the western art world provides an opportunity to examine and acknowledge the implications of its power, and the authority of its chorus in selecting and determining visibility and inclusion. A study such as this may well support the evidence of those who question and examine the consensus and reign of "the canon". The circumstances that led to his paintings being exhibited and purchased for private and public collections is examined. There was an intellectual acknowledgement, at least, that the work of a successful colonial artist would require representation in London; his presence could not be ignored. The contents of this study are offered in order to enrich Caribbean art-historical memory and to underline the complex, nuanced narrative of what is, after all, a shared history.

Williams was brought up in a society in which you were expected to have no image of yourself other than as a British colonial subject working within a colonial system. British Guiana (colloquially known as "BG") had been exclusively a colony of slave plantations, a plantocracy lacking the buffer of a resident middle class. This created its own distinct issues in the relationship with Great Britain which inevitably had its effect on the practice and appreciation of art.

Art research materials relating to Guyana's historical past continue to be discovered. The "masters" brought with them their own culture of art and created the official posts of Colonial Artist and Colonial Architect. There was the work of colonial civil servants and that of those wealthy business classes who were hobbyist watercolourists. Their subject matter included scenes of the plantations – viewed from a distance – and other novel local sketches. There was the work of professional artists engaged in pictorial journalism, and those who took part in expeditions into the interior, rather in the manner of the artists who accompanied the wealthy on the European Grand Tour, making ethnographic, topographic and botanical records. The repertoire of the colonisers, its subject matter and its long-established ancillary associations established a visual imprint which reinforced the transmission of imperial values to combine in a legacy which inevitably influenced the early pioneers of Guyanese art.

The chapter entitled "The European Imprimatur" considers to what extent this view is validated by tracing the indelible marks of its pervasive bias on Williams as a young artist. Through an examination of the published accounts of a wide variety of contemporary figures in British Guiana, this study also references the scope of that imprint against a background of ethnic diversity. The evidence gives a sense of the uneasiness and the counter-responses emerging among the colony's artists.

Williams' experiences as a young painter offer an account of what was at stake in organising and grouping for art display and in fostering an interest and participation in art. In an environment where there were conflicting ideologies at work, the study traces the assumptions that were endorsed and subscribed to, and directs attention to what was being exchanged and guaranteed to those who were deemed worthy of inclusion in the community of art. Williams believed that the vacuum created by the absence of a direct cultural lineage for those of African descent was a primary factor in the early development of Guyanese art which can partly explain the predominance of black artists in Guyana.

The art of the Caribbean region has been characterised as conservative in both subject and approach, founded as it is on a heritage of Western models emphasising pictorial realism. Such observations would certainly have been true of British Guiana in the early 1940s where this tentativeness and absence of a climate of experimentation can further be directly related to its isolation. But Caribbean credentials and credibility are typically over-generalised. For example, in Guyana, conservatism can be seen to be equally indicative of the degraded self-image associated with the particularly brutal slave regime of a very long-standing plantocracy, and to the power relationships in the subsequent transmission of values.

There are many good reasons why it is appropriate to approach Williams' contribution through an art-historical dialogue. This study demonstrates how he explored his own intellectual dilemmas through the creative experience and used his art to confront the world. It presents the case that art was central to the development of his theories of culture and to his activities in cultural nation-building. The absence of a comprehensive overview of Williams' art can be explained, in part, by the difficulty of accessing primary sources. Paintings such as *Human World* have been expertly conserved and curated, whereas other surviving paintings are in a precarious condition and many remain unlocated. My approach has been founded on a direct study of as many of the drawings and paintings as I have been able to trace and reproduce and I provide a frame of reference by giving working titles for those that are uncurated. The study is firmly based on a wide range of unique primary sources and published texts by Williams and distinguished contemporary figures, and on Williams' personal handwritten documents – charged as they are with their own dynamic.

The developing and overwhelming aspiration of Williams' generation – the reformers, the patriots, politicians, intellectuals, writers and artists – was for independence. Men and women from all walks of life and with widely varied ideologies became united in their view that independence was a necessity for the well-being of the West Indian psyche.

In post-war London, Williams was labelled "A Negro Artist" and this chapter of the study examines Williams' experiences of the cultural encounters in the transatlantic exchanges of the early post-war era when his large powerful canvases attracted considerable comment. It offers a first-hand account of the dynamics at play in creating constructs of difference. The study examines the historical, social and political imperatives that measured, shaped and sought to place Williams as an artist. A *Time* magazine article of 1950 with its vocabulary of racism signals those attitudes of the era that could only frame Williams in terms of a racial stereotype. The study examines this public positioning and the terms of his acceptance within the metropolitan art world with particular reference to Williams' own statements. It considers the extent to which the progression of his career was a conscious negotiation of the space in which he could determine his own identity.

The measure to which Denis Williams' achievements were circumscribed as "a Negro artist", the burden he felt and his attempts to transcend his situation are further investigated in "The Restless Course of Experiment". In art-historical terms Williams' most powerful paintings of the early post-war period call for inclusion in an analysis of the iconography of modern primitivism. In the documentation of the celebrated abstract works that followed, notable figures including Salvador Dalí suggested resonances of a distinctive cultural memory embedded in Williams' non-European synthesis of modernism. These works have their part to play in an appreciation of the early process of transition in art from its Eurocentric focus to an increasingly international one.

In the post-war era Williams had struggled to secure a validity that was not coupled to his status as a colonial subject, a status that he may have felt had become integral to the appeal of his work. Williams' success conferred intellectual and artistic distinction but this success also raised issues that subsequent black artists would also face. His heroic effort to sustain a career wholly as a painter is relevant to any consideration of how black artists have gained their presence and visibility and he can be seen as a pioneer in the process of negotiating a dignified space for the black artist in Britain. His dilemma was that if he rejected the terms of acceptance, what continuing patronage would be likely, given that Europe was the economic centre of the art world?

From Williams' documented statements we can surmise that he was, in fact, ultimately dissatisfied with the nature of the patronage he received in London. His work had become located within a cultural milieu which he came to reject for a number of reasons, not least because his presence provided ready evidence of its polite, liberal "tolerance". Other views he articulated only much later in his life. He came to spurn those complicit in the art commodities market place whilst his own power and that of his compatriots remained restricted and qualified. The subtext presents the terms of Williams' reception by the self-elected élites through reference to material from many direct sources. It is the story of a person faced with uncomfortable and unsettling issues. For Williams, it raised the questions of underlying human integrity as well as his own artistic integrity. So where in fact did all this leave him?

Following his participation in the exhibition *This is Tomorrow* in 1956 he made the dramatic decision to turn his back on the artistic establishment that had elevated him to the status of a celebrated painter working as a tutor at the most prestigious of the London art schools.

In "A Triangular Dialogue" this study turns its attention on the artist's mapping of the dimensions between Europe, Africa and the West Indies. His art is focused on the quest for authenticity, specificity and universality. Using diverse sources – literary reviews, published academic and experimental writing and art appreciation as well as material from early Guianese periodicals – the study examines Williams as a creative individual engaging with historiography. He explored the relationship of the West Indian to an African heritage at a time when perceptions of Africa were largely spiritual and romantic.

His experiences led him to explore the possibilities of the future rôle of the West Indian artist in a post-colonial context. Williams saw the artist as "an integrating cultural agent". Despite a common heritage in the transatlantic Slave Trade, the English-speaking countries of the Caribbean did not forge the unity of purpose that many seemed to expect. From the signal event of the first West Indian Art Exhibition, which was held by the Guianese Art Group – founded in 1944 – to the first Caribbean Festival of the Arts (Carifesta) – which was initiated and first held in Georgetown in 1972 – the process of grouping for art display may well have exposed the harsh realities of what was at stake in mediating a sense of regional identity from the plurality of approaches to nationalism.

There is a creative dynamism in any society drawing from so many different strains, each with distinct experience and distinct styles of worship, performance, verbal and literary expression. In the Caribbean this is evidenced very visually in manners, dress, architecture and lifestyles, and the vibrancy of its artistic genres. It presents a social surrealism of curious shifting complexity in the carnivalesque course of everyday life. This is invariably viewed in a positive manner, as a demonstration of a strong instinct and spirit of survival that has been cast as a mainstream hallmark of the peoples of the Caribbean region.

The art of the region is often characterised by its hybrid nature, its cut-and-paste appropriations born of impulse and necessity, in the manner of a New World patchwork quilt. Labels are applied with authoritative judgement that would nevertheless still seem to require metropolitan endorsement. Inclusion in the global story at that time meant following the rules and principles of the western art tradition. Its criteria demanded evidence of a chronological timeline and a distinct and readily attributable style. The absence of such immediate clarity characterises the conversation surrounding perceptions of an "authentic" Caribbean aesthetic. Williams coined the term the "Guyana School" in an attempt to address this issue of cultural definition and to eschew preconceptions inherent in such labels as "naïve", "primitive", "unschooled"or "intuitive".

Majestas was described by the artist as the best painting he had ever done. Self-evidently autobiographical, it provides a fresh context for examining his continuing engagement with the complexities of personal, national and regional identity. *Majestas* attests to the challenge Williams set himself as an artist, in symbolically throwing off any prescribed identity: imagining alternative outlooks, and whether cultural identities are capable of being reinvented. Guyana, in its ancient, historical and contemporary manifestations, became his central artistic preoccupation.

In this study the intention behind his work is substantiated by supporting documentation which immediately references the presence of a holistic theory of culture. It is a sophisticated exploration of cultural discourse outwith a political rhetoric: an idealistic vision in which the artist focuses on the filialistic relationship of all Guyanese to their South American heritage.

The desire to frame something as positive as a Caribbean identity, and as distinct and authentic as a Caribbean aesthetic, has to a large extent been grounded in artificial constructs of post-emancipation, post-colonial, post-independence identity which are blind to the plurality within the region. It is a desire of wide currency for the Caribbean region to be viewed as a harmonious cultural entity. National and economic ideologies have invested in refashioning the landscape of plantation culture as an idyllic tourist paradise and in tagging its art forms as a cultural commodity. Guyana sits uncomfortably with such Caribbean characterisation as its location and profile are relatively peripheral; it does not have the critical demographic numbers required to make easy claims of commonality, and the schisms of race politics have created cultural forces at odds with a climate in which art can readily flourish.

The large mural *Memorabilia II,* sited in the National Cultural Centre in Georgetown, provides us with an opportunity to consider Williams' contribution to the national reconstruction project in Guyana following independence. He eventually found himself in a position similar to that of many of the intellectuals, radical thinkers and "revolutionaries" of his generation: he became an advisor at the highest levels of government. This chapter focuses on the seamless link between Williams' philosophical theory of culture, his art and his archaeology of Guyana and provides a key to the complexity of his creative imagination.

The Caribbean experience exemplifies many of the broader dynamics of cultural encounter. Its historical and contemporary realities focus on this commonality of experience in the constant repositioning of the particular and the universal. Williams witnessed the shift of the Caribbean nexus away from its relation to Old World cultures to one that has adjusted to take its place with nations of the Americas, identified with New World credentials. He produced a body of work that helps to illuminate the psychological landscape of the early migrations to the metropolitan centres through themes such as displacement, exile and transcendence that have since become almost commonplace.

Denis Williams' contribution to art history should be examined against this wider background of signal events and strategies that came to typify the experience of emergent Third World countries in the post-World War II era. It was a period of radical transition and dramatic worldwide challenges to authoritarian systems of the kinds based in long-held perceptions of natural hierarchies amongst human beings: in systems predicated on superiority and difference.

Williams' works can be seen as statements with recognisable social content, as disclosures of a life that gives meaning to Brathwaite's notion of "the inner plantation" and the resonances of the dramatic psychological journey from an ancestral base which is central to the Caribbean experience. Through his art Williams made the intellectual journey from revolution to redemption. He was, as Guyana's former President Desmond Hoyte concluded in his introduction to Williams' 1984 Mittelholzer Lecture Series, "an artist in all the many-splendoured meanings of that word."

ACKNOWLEDGEMENTS

MANY PEOPLE have been involved in the creation of this book. I would particularly like to thank Jeremy Poynting and Hannah Bannister at Peepal Tree Press who appreciated the importance of the study. Elfrieda Bissember, curator of Guyana's National Collection and Director of the National Gallery at Castellani House, was encouraging in many ways, and I am pleased to have this opportunity of recording my gratitude to her. Dr William Housley, Dr Andrew Jefferson-Miles and Dr Leon Wainwright were kind enough to review my initial draft, and provided me with critical observations and suggestions which enabled me to reach beyond the initial scope of my manuscript. I am very grateful to Andrew Jefferson-Miles and Louis James for their perceptive and generous forewords.

Any book of this kind relies on its images, and from New York Arlington Weithers directed the initial preparation of the photographed artwork. Alan Lindsay carefully restored a number of family photographs which I had thought were damaged beyond repair, but which are now included in the Chronology. All of the original photography of the artwork is my own unless otherwise stated.

Among those individuals who shared materials and information are Vibert Cambridge, Jan Cox, Sarah Dick, Philbert Gajadhar, Stanley Greaves, Ana Guimaraes, Wilson Harris, Martin Harrison, Carl Hazlewood, Janice Lamar-Jones, Marjory Lobban, Donald Locke, Betty Meggers, George Mentore, Doris Rogers, George Simon, Janet Stanley, Anne Walmsley, Ras Camo Williams, Charlotte Williams and Jennifer Wishart.

I am grateful to the Whitechapel Gallery Archive for permission to reproduce images from the catalogue for the exhibition *This is Tomorrow*; to Ras Camo Williams for permission to reproduce *Williams by Williams,* the Beaverbrook Art Gallery for permission to reproduce *Painting in Six Related Rhythms*, and *The Times* / NI Syndication for permission to reproduce the photograph of Williams at the Morris Singer foundry. I am indebted to Kamau Brathwaite for the insights expressed in *Caribbean Man in Space and Time.* I also acknowledge my debt to all the other institutions and collectors who have permitted reproduction of their paintings or arranged for special photography. This has been acknowledged in the image captions.

I must pay tribute to the staff of the public galleries and institutions in the UK whose consistent professionalism was so encouraging: the British Library Newspaper Archive; the Whitechapel Gallery; Gimpel Fils of Mayfair and the Tate Gallery Archive. In the USA and Canada, Cornell University Library and the Beaverbrook Art Gallery provided prompt and helpful assistance. In Guyana, my access to materials was facilitated by the generous cooperation of staff at the Caribbean Research Library of the University of Guyana; the National Archive; the National Trust; the National Museum of Guyana and the National Collection, Castellani House. In Barbados I was ably assisted by staff at the Shilstone Memorial Library in the Barbados Museum and Historical Society.

Most of all, I thank my partner Andrew Lindsay who assisted with research; took photographs; compiled the Index, the Chronology and the Bibliography; provided an exhaustive editorial and technical overview of the manuscript at all stages, and finally prepared the camera-ready version. This study would not have been presented without him.

Evelyn A. Williams

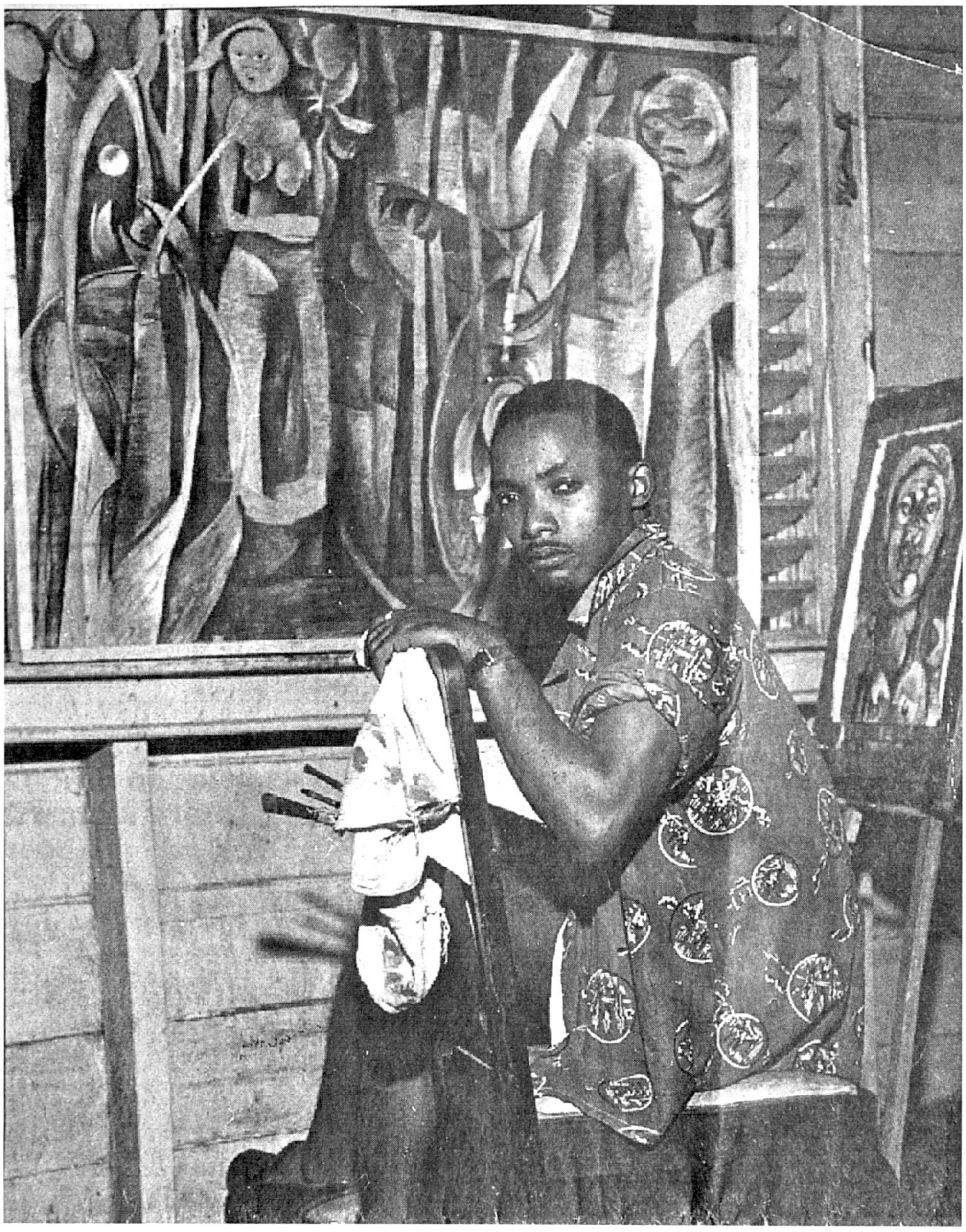

At work on *Plantation No. 1* (1949). Georgetown.
Retrieved image. Courtesy Gimpel Fils.

Chapter 1

The European Imprimatur

The new Creole household emerged on the cluttered but cosy Victorian model of fruity wallpapers and dark, polished interiors accented with pewter, brass and ceramic *bric-à-brac*. Furniture, furnishings, tableware and personal items, everything in a word which tended to the enhancement of "dignity", were imported from Europe and America. Along with these came paintings, prints and books for the discerning.[1]

DENIS JOSEPH IVAN WILLIAMS was born in 1923 and grew up against a background of this type of West Indian environment, in a highly controlled society. It had a historically inbuilt dependence for its existence on the imperial economy in which the dynamics of its supply and demand lay beyond local control. The natural landscape of the tropical lowland area of British Guiana was – and still is – at the mercy of dramatic climatic fluctuation. Add to this the endemic unemployment arising from the insecurities of seasonal labour dominated by sugar-cane cultivation and the picture was always one of unstable economic production with a significant proportion of the society to be found subsisting outwith the cash economy.

From the narrow coastal strip between the Atlantic Ocean and the densely forested backdrop of the vast South American continent people looked outwards. Migration was outwards to the islands for work and family ties; outwards to the Atlantic beyond which lay the mother country. This meant that the local population evolved with an expectation of displacement as a constant in life; a mixed people who had to find a pathway with no certainties about their lifestyle, the security of their family and the future a constant worry. Major concerns included food shortages, poor health care, disease and lack of employment.

The Caribbean of the 1930s was restless and uneasy as it sought reform of its political and economic organisations, the removal of unjust social structures, and above all it looked towards the prospect of self-government and independence.

Life in the Caribbean was characterised by a rumbling discontent over exploitation and the inadequate social provision made for its people. There was a paucity of resources causing desperate poverty, squalor and deprivation. Williams recalled:

> It's the end of 1936. The world economic depression had left its mark on the fortunes of Guyana sugar; the colony's budget had been bolstered by dispensations for the past several years; unemployment everywhere added to a discouraging situation. As though all this wasn't enough, our population universally suffered from the scourge of malaria and the many disabilities flowing from it. Those of us at school then will remember the effects of its ravages: the gaps in the school benches, especially during afternoon sessions, where friends had stayed home with "fever"; the taste of quinine dispensed at cost price from the nearest post-office [...].[2]

An inappropriate educational system compounded the legacy of cultural destruction: primary school accommodation was organised by the government, church missions, sugar estates and mining companies, but it was in short supply, and the buildings were in poor condition. Only in 1945 was a start made on a programme of building new primary schools.

The colony, in the most southerly, far-flung reaches of the Caribbean, was under the authority of a Governor whose rôle was to ensure that the British Crown was able to control its economic interests from Whitehall in London. The Governor headed an appointed Executive Council, which in turn had the power to veto or pass laws, overriding the wishes of the local, unrepresentative Legislative Council. The local political agenda at the time centred on the economic and social conditions of labour and the pressing need for constitutional reform of the Legislative Council towards a greater representation of the people.

National identity would become an intractable issue when so many felt no genuine stake in a country where the land and means of production were not their own; where organisation around ethnic identity segmented any idea of nation, where the main challenge was in gaining an economic foothold without ownership of territory; where the distance from one's own cultural legacy was compounded by the profound recasting of the self-image that took place under the colonial system.

The social classification of the local colonial subject peoples was a complex matter of race, class, hair texture and skin-tones which had its origins in the practices inherited from plantation culture and remnants of the embedded Indian caste structure surviving from the system of indentured labour. From the 1940s onwards the Indians were the largest ethnic group and became dominant in argicultural production in rural areas of the country. The African peoples largely populated the urban areas. There were some Chinese and Portuguese. Despite being long-standing inhabitants of the Guianas, the Amerindian peoples were next to invisible and their social identification remained tribal. Social deformity was embodied in the *status quo* and this peculiar ethnic diversity lay at the heart of the particular difficulties that cultural nationalism would face in British Guiana.

Denis Williams was a Georgetown boy, which meant he had little experience of the country outside of the city. The lushly forested hinterland was barely known to him. His immediate landscape revolved around the distinctive markers of the city – Stabroek Market, St George's Cathedral, the Victoria Law Courts, Old City Hall – all boasting gardens with ornamental palms and colourful hibiscus. Leisure and special events might include walks along the sea wall that protected the city, or a cycle ride to the Botanic Gardens with its manicured lawns and specimen plants.

The European imprimatur cast a long shadow as it was promulgated through the system of administration. It effectively had an assimilationist influence within a large section of urban society in particular and consequently on the development of its art. Few would have been in a position to resist or reject its control, where the values of absolutely ruptured peoples had been overlaid and where there was little occasion to reference one's own culture.

On one level there must have been an air of quiet amnesia in which the perceived shame of slavery was seldom mentioned. The prevailing cultural heritage was one in which few of African ancestry were able to take pride because there were few positive references. For many, that shame brought about a determination to rise above the slave side of their history and culture through rejection of work on the land and its associations. The African urban classes monopolised to a substantial degree the opportunities provided by education. English was the official language of the colony and it was used exclusively in schools and to gain access to advantage and upward mobility in employment, particularly in the civil services. Each language speaks for a world of its own and clear distinctions developed between Indian and African Creole.

Georgetown had developed as a rather beautiful city at the mouth of the Demerara river, laid out on a grid pattern by the Dutch with a complex of irrigation canals, bridges, paaling, kokers, dams and levées to control the swamp waters. Colonnades of flamboyant trees with white-painted trunks shaded the main streets, and the dramatic Victoria Regia lilies were cultivated in the wider canals. There was a mix of elegant wooden architecture, neat houses, churches and a handsome cathedral. On the surface everything suggested a well-ordered colony.

Everyone regarded England as the mother country and the Union Jack was dominant on the flag of the colony until 1955. Williams would have grown up listening to the BBC World Service, following the progress of World War II on the radio and backing England. Life was controlled from London. The systems of civil life were laid out along English lines: the Westminster administration of the civil service, the European, knowledge-based education system, traffic on the left, trams, polite queues for cricket at Bourda Pavilion, horseracing at the Demerara Turf Club in D'Urban Park, the bandstand in the Promenade Gardens.

Williams' father Joseph Alexander Williams was born in 1881; his grandfather probably in the late 1850s or 1860s in the old African town of Ithaca in the ancient county of Berbice. People from there were the direct descendants of the slaves.

> The half of the family behind my father is the real stock. These are the people who come from slavery. [...] These people were Africans in culture – their food, their way of being etc. Their families were my interface with my ancestry; my people. We grew up together. Through them I would see into the past.[3]

His father had two sisters who lived in Agricola, a village just outside Georgetown. It was a "Negro" village on the main public road that ran to the south. Roy Heath has described it at that time as being "the most tranquil village in the country, [...] I never once heard a raised voice, except that of a child being flogged for some misdeed."[4] Many of the freed slaves had established themselves in such village communities as peasant proprietors though considerable numbers still depended on the sugar plantations for part-time employment.

The further from the public road you lived, the more free from constraints you might have found your life. There was a reckoning that it was in the back-land villages where a marginal life of subsistence provision-beds met with sugar cane, rice paddies and colourful jhandi flags beyond the gaze of the colonial administration, that the remnants of African cultures had any chance of survival, in ceremonial foods, in Queh-Queh songs and dances, in Cumfa dancing and the Oku drums.

Unlike most colonies of the West Indies other than Trinidad, British Guiana was home to the significant and distinct culture of a large population of Indian immigrants. They brought to the colony a very highly developed and predominantly Hindu culture which, within limits, was allowed space for survival by the colonial authorities and estate managers in a way that the African culture of the enslaved was not. In time it evolved its distinctive creole forms particularly in its sacred architecture and the related styles of dance and performance, with the attendant costume and cosmetic arts of its religious festivals. They brought with them enough elements to enable them to continue to hold together as a community of people. Those of African descent had little such cultural cohesion to cultivate.

The cultural lacuna was efficiently managed using the tools of formal acculturation: education and the Christian religion. Some measure of redemption could be found in the affirmation of the "religious character" possible as a willing Christian. As Williams observed: "Since dignity could no longer be won in terms of the antique model, it therefore had to be sought in terms of the European."[5] This view implies a historical correlation between the thorough erasure of the African ancestral cultures and their subsequent compliance as colonised subjects.

There is a historic divide between the sacred and the secular in the canon of European art which may go some way to explain the relative invisibility of Indian artists and the predominance of Africans who, as disinherited and degraded subjects quickly needed to acquire a language of symbols, concepts and attitudes with which to shape their creative outlook and to accommodate new values and new circumstances:

> [...] during the first decades of the nineteenth century the Africans of Demerara, Essequibo and Berbice were willing enough, indeed notably eager, to receive Christian teaching, baptism and a new name. This *volte face* in cultural identity had occurred within half a century of the war of 1763. The uncompromising pagan of antique times had been transformed into the pliant Christian of the Creole period. [...] Whereas commentators of the thirties and forties unanimously note a rush to Christianity amongst the Africans, the Hindu and Moslem immigrants had no need at all of conversion, whatever missionary pressures were brought to bear upon them. As we know, they do not to the present time. This fact coloured the African sense of identity throughout the Creole period and into the revolutionary period; for in assuming the Christian faith the African also assumed corresponding social and cultural practices which caused him to look down upon the culture and beliefs of East Indian and later immigrants. [...] The spiritual needs of the Creole Africans were now met quite effortlessly by the missionaries. Christianity would, however, prove a desperate refuge for it introduced to the Creole African a notion not conceivable in antique times – that of a white Saviour.[6]

Williams' father had secure employment as a seaman: a purser on a local ship that carried merchandise along the main rivers of Berbice, Demerara and Essequibo. He was a gentle man, a Jehovah's Witness with passive religious manners. Williams' Barbadian mother replicated European niceties in the household and "proper" English was spoken at home. Her own fine manners were required for her work as a ladies' dressmaker and companion to the expatriate wives who lived in the large houses in the Kingston area of Georgetown. She was at one time a lady's maid to the wife of the colony's Minister of Education, Major Bain Gray.[7] Her female clientele would come to the family home from time to time for their dress fittings. The etiquette of the table, the afternoon tea-and-cake ceremony and many of the household graces and courtesies, redolent of the fading manners of Empire, were routine. Unlike most colonies of the West Indies British Guiana had not been permanently settled by Europeans and their families in numbers significant enough to support an élitist culture of art. Indeed, there was little evidence of a visual arts culture to develop, confront or challenge, little save the deadening influence of the colonial circumstance.

You did not have to be a particularly wealthy household to have domestic help as the Williams

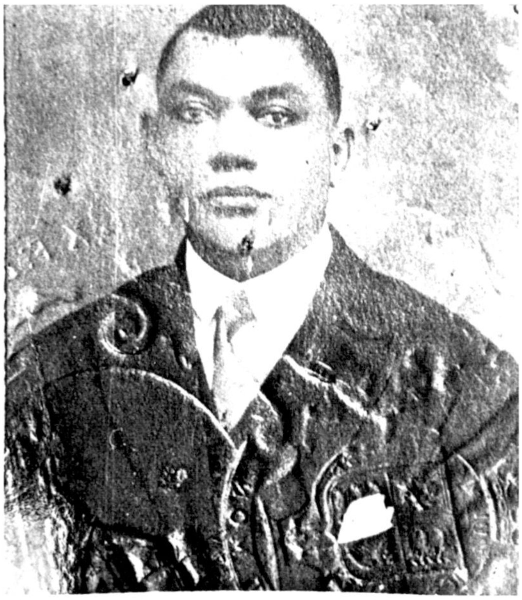

Father, Joseph Williams, *circa* 1910.

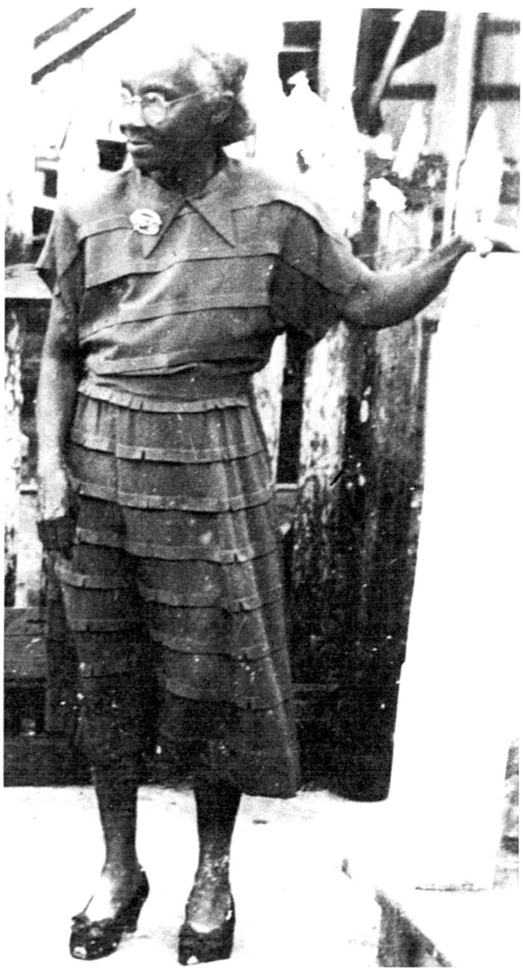

Mother, Isabella Adonis, *circa* 1945.

family did; rather it spoke of the breadth of poverty in the country as a shared experience. Williams did not come from that type of middle-class West Indian family that adopts a position of contempt towards its own and denies any relationship with them. His family was more typically traditional with the strong maternal figure central to all decisions and activities.

His younger brother Everard had died and so Denis seems to have been well protected by his sisters. It was a cloistered home life that was very secure and supportive though he was conscious that his own family's lifestyle bore no immediate similarity to that of other local black families. His mother called him "paper man", "because I was so sensitive, scared easily – you know, paper, because you blow over easily."[8] He was known as "Sonny" to most. From an early age he appears to have been self-driven. "He often related his recurring dream at about age six, having to consume – before daylight – a granite mountain which stood outside his bedroom window. He would awake, he explained, to the feel of gravel in his mouth only to fall asleep again and continue this somewhat haunting dream."[9] But Williams was perhaps more than unconventional in his private view of himself. He recalls always challenging his mother, saying: "You'll see, I am going to be something. My mum used to twist my ears and say 'Why don't you hear, boy?' and I would be saying 'one day, when I grow big [...]'."[10]

The British educational system, with its ingrained world-view and imperialist attitudes, dominated school life. His parents were enlightened in allowing him to opt out of school for a period when he was eleven to pursue self-study, particularly because education was the only thing that aspiring Africans had at that time.

> I always knew I was different, something special. The business of staying home from school for a year was the acme of this. I wasn't like the other chaps in the playground. I never felt like them. I always knew I was more worthy than people perceived me to be – somehow destined for greater things. I could find no one like myself, no reference point to tell me who I am and always I know I am different. As a consequence I didn't have many friends amongst the boys at school. I couldn't relate to them and their concerns. Even though they were bright chaps I could never look up to anybody or envy them.[11]

His sister Verna Williams relates how Denis was obsessed with drawing and painting. "He was an observer by nature, always at the margins of society, even in the family home. Irrespective of where he was or what he was doing, he was always observing and sketching [...]." Such observations underline an early determination to pursue his own interests and to find his own pathway.

His father was proud of his son's abilities and would show off his sketches and drawings to visitors and family friends. Books were not typically a part of a Guianese home, as Williams was to recall later:

> The *Awake* magazine and my mother's crochet books were the only literature readily available in the house and I read them all. Later Eileen [his elder sister] was to make available to me a whole number of books [...]. At 16 she left home to work to bring in money for the family. She worked in a newspaper office and when consignments of books came in she would let me choose from them freely. She would then have to work to pay for these books. It was therefore due to her that I had access to Milton, Keats etc. and to a five-volume history of Art by Élie Faure – these must have cost an immense amount.[12]

He attended private schools, as did Forbes Burnham, Desmond Hoyte and Shridath "Sonny" Ramphal. Only a very few had the privilege of a higher education, depending on whether their parents had money. At the age of eleven he had taken part in the *ad hoc* art classes in drawing and painting held at Bishops' High School,[13] organised by Golde White (Mrs Monty White) and Mary Heron-Bruce, who contributed to the development of Guianese artists by promoting their work in exhibitions and stimulating a culture of critical appreciation. Williams completed his Senior Cambridge School Certificate and was sixteen at the outbreak of World War II when he began his own short spell as a teacher.

Writing years later about Giglioli's work on endemic malaria in British Guiana he remembered:

> Those of us who were teachers before the war could have constructed graphs, had we thought of it, of malaria periodicity in our areas from the pattern of noughts [...] in the daily attendance registers of the country. In short, the people of the coastlands just about survived their environment of man-made swamps and canals, trenches, ponds, rice padis and flood fallows with no more hope of doing anything about it than the dying Babylonians.[14]

Severe hardship was experienced as a direct result of the war: the products of the colony were taken for export and scant attention was given to the organisation of the needs of local consumption. There was a dependency on imported products from Europe and the shipping supply lines were often disrupted. There had been enemy submarines in the Atlantic Ocean off the coast of British Guiana and bauxite ships from the colony had been sunk by German U-boats. The consequent reduction in imports caused shortages and increased the costs of living. For example, between 1938 and 1944 the cost of food rose by fifty-four per cent in Georgetown and sixty-eight per cent on the sugar estates in the rural areas.[15] Shopkeepers hoarded goods and demanded higher prices; black-marketing became common. There had been civil and labour disturbances in Georgetown in the 1930s and so the colonial administration took measures to provide relief to the people through subsidisation of essential commodities and subsistence goods. Many families were in receipt of cost-of-living allowances or the war relief payments which were granted throughout the British Caribbean.

Williams developed clear interests in both writing and painting. He paid tribute to his mother's part in developing and nurturing those interests. Guianese women played a formative rôle in the development of a culture of art in British Guiana and we know his mother had been involved in decorative arts. The Women's Self Help Association, started in 1912–1913, though run by expatriates, had involved local women and they held their own art and craft exhibitions.

> My mother [...] was the artist and painter from whom I drew my skill. I have memories of the smell of pigment, the colours, two pictures that she had painted in the house and a table painted with a special technique that gave the flowers she painted an embossed feel. She had a beautiful mahogany box of paints with brass clasps. This and her jewel box are the two visual markers of her in my life. The jewel box was a casket, lined with velvet in which she kept her chains, her gold [...] rubies, turquoise, glittering colours. These are the vibrant colours that stick in my mind. When I was about 15 and studying [...] under our pioneer art teacher, E. R. Burrowes, she gave me the paint box and this is how I began my career [...].[16]

By the early 1930s certain pioneer sign painters in Georgetown had also been working in oil on canvas and in 1930 Golde White was instrumental in organising a historic exhibition of local talent. As she wrote in a letter to Dorothy King: "There has been no Art exhibition for some years in this colony."[17] This exhibition was to be organised along the professional lines Golde White demanded, with a catalogue and prizes and a committee selecting and judging on quality and merit.

The British Guiana Arts and Crafts Society was initiated in 1931 by a group of British expatriates assisted by Golde White and it worked to stimulate and support the visual arts.[18] Among the figures to emerge from this early group had been Edward Rupert Burrowes, Hubert Moshett, Richard Gui Sharples, Reggie Phang, Vivian Antrobus and Sam Cummings – a group of talented local artists. Membership of this group was essentially proletarian, and it held its first exhibition in 1931 under the auspices of the Governor. As Burrowes acknowledged: "[…] the stimulus given it by the energetic and invaluable control of Mrs Golde White implemented and set for local artists the vision of new horizons."[19] The A&C was instrumental to the dynamics of control in the development of artistic aspiration and the idea of a community of art in the colony. It exhibited a range of arts and crafts as well as paintings: no copies were allowed. The 1931 exhibition was reviewed in the *Daily Argosy* newspaper and was reported to have included subjects from a wide range of genres in oil, watercolour and pastel. Williams himself had attended that first exhibition when he was eight years old. He later said: "That was a tremendous event in my life and that anchored my whole future, seeing those works."[20] Williams would later make his debut at these annual group exhibitions. The A&C in Georgetown clearly provided an influential precedent and model for the British Council, which was present in the colony from 1944. As Cummins, Thompson and Whittle have noted: "The establishment of the Barbados Arts and Crafts Society in 1944 […] was significantly influenced by the work of the Council. The symbiotic relationship between the Council and the Society at this time cannot be too heavily stressed."[21] As in British Guiana it was Golde White who was instrumental in the formation of the Barbados Society.

In his earlier years E. R. Burrowes, working under the supervision of the literary painters, deferred to the traditional models of sound if conservative standards of good taste. As Williams noted: "The authority of the art forms transmitted by the artist-amateurs and the Arts and Crafts Society was obviously immense. The prevailing idioms were those of the British Royal Academy of the twenties or even earlier."[22]

It is of more than academic interest to note the varied nuances of the closeness of the master-slave relationship in the canon of the art of the colonial "masters", not least in the work of academicians Sir Joshua Reynolds and Thomas Gainsborough.

This authority was, like the administrative authority of the colony itself, a controlling force. Like other subject colonials practising an intrusive art, Guianese early acceptance of these art forms was largely, though not wholly, uncritical. In those days the colonial authority both contextualised and controlled the models of cultural expression in the perpetuation of the systematic self-interest that sought to wipe out any continuity of cultural heritage, imposing instead the imprints of a European consciousness. The deliberate acts of cultural destruction in the banning of African social and cultural expressions were part of the control mechanisms of power. Within the degraded society there was a selective tolerance of fragments of antique cultures, most notably in the practice of the Hindu religion.

This gives a sense of the complexity of the issues confronting local artists, but acceptance was not wholesale. There seems to have been some early resistance to the assertion of this influence and control in the practice of art. In a revealing article Burrowes appears to be making a clear statement about the competing forces of aesthetic and economic judgement. He implies a knowing subjection to a prescriptive framework of subject and style:

> The birth of a definitely British Guiana Art can be traced back to the year 1934 when the British Guiana Arts and Crafts Society held its Fourth Annual Exhibition at the Carnegie Building. This Exhibition unlike the three previous ones provoked much argument among our art critics. The most controversial of the paintings were Gui Sharples' illustration of a stanza from the Rubaiyat of Omar Khayam, Hubert Moshett's portrait of his two sons, Reggie Phang's self-portrait and my symbolic study of a Chinese girl entitled "Child of Destiny". But the movement towards this new outlook did not gain momentum as most of us were at that time still concerned with the necessity of selling our work and so the old uninspired forms of naturalism continued with sometimes a flare of Guianese modernism from the brush of Moshett, Phang or myself.[23]

For a further balance of historical perspective Dr Nesha Z. Haniff has given an account of the significant rôle women played in the development of art in British Guiana:

> Perhaps the most interesting exhibition for these years was the 1942 exhibition. More than half – 80 of the 156-piece exhibition – were done by women. In this exhibition some of the women were Winnie da Silva, Marjorie Broodhagen, Irene Bennett, Mary Heron-Bruce, Golde White and Edna Harte, exhibiting along with E. R. Burrowes, Basil Hinds, Denis Williams and Hubert Moshett.[24]

The central presence that the British Council assumed in the process of acculturation saw visiting professionals giving lectures in the Town Hall in Georgetown to crowded audiences. For example in March and April of 1948 "a young English artist, John Harrison, was lecturing weekly to a small group of practising artists and other interested, on the origins of modern art, the work of Picasso and Gauguin, and the painting now being done in England."[25] Harrison was Arts and Exhibitions Officer of the British Council, and in the 1950s gave a course of lectures in Barbados to schoolchildren on "Looking at Pictures". He was appointed to give expert information to artists in British Guiana.

Writing in 1976, Frank Pilgrim recorded:

> [...] in days when the definition of culture was narrowly limited to representations with a European bias there was a multiplicity of cultural societies, and groups like the "Athenaeum", the "Amateur Dramatic Society", the "Philharmonic Musical Society" [and] the "Histrionics" feature prominently in the social life of our country during the 19th and early years of the 20th century. [...] In the 1940s and 50s Georgetown could boast of two classical symphony orchestras – the Georgetown Philharmonic and the Princessville Symphony Orchestra.[26]

Further referring to the extent of this acculturation, Williams recalled:

> I used to go every Thursday night to listen to Elgar and such things at the British Council. It's only that culture that existed at that time and every Thursday night I used to go listen to T. S. Eliot's poems and all this kind of culture.[27]

For a wider sense of what was at stake in nurturing the "European bias", it is worth remembering that local cultural practices like Cumfa dancing and drumming were still restricted in the late 1930s. Dance and drumming were viewed as being too close to antique religions; and there were attempts to suppress the African drum from the legacy of the fear it aroused of the threat posed by runaway slaves. But if the erasure of African culture was most thorough in African languages, African drumming and music survived in submerged and creolised forms. As Martin Carter has written: "It is because music is the very language of the inner life that we can so easily find such expressions of the life of the people in it. Torture and hope is a furious tension."[28]

The British Guiana Arts and Crafts Society was superseded by the nationalist Guianese Art Group, with R. G. Sharples as its first president. This was ideologically part of a growing region-wide consciousness in the referencing of culture with national development. Significantly it was founded in 1944, the same year the British Council was established in Georgetown. Equally significantly, it was founded by and for Guianese artists. The group's regular annual exhibitions afforded a greater opportunity for public recognition and elevated the practice of art and the rôle of the artist by "non-European" agents. There was a distancing from craft activities and D. L. Bourne[29] noted that artists were becoming more active throughout the whole year rather than working only for exhibitions. "One of the achievements of this group was the holding, for the first time in British Guiana, of a West Indian Art Exhibition. Although the pieces exhibited were not fully representative of all the colonies taking part, the exhibition helped to convey an impression of the style, spirit and general upsurge of art in the Caribbean area."[30] This group was distinguished by an approach to nationalism that was sympathetically pan-Caribbean. Its attitude was progressive and outward-looking, distinctly reaching beyond the prescriptive local framework, and Bourne hoped "[...] that future exhibitions of this nature will embrace a greater number of colonies and examples of painting by their best artists."[31]

Williams wrote that the activities of the group alerted public awareness to the possibility of the artist as "an integrating cultural agent". The impression persists of mulatto dominance in these cultural activities. But we can also note Williams' point: "Amongst its noted members were Africans, East Indians, Portuguese, Chinese, British and persons of mixed origin. This fact acquires an importance in retrospect which was by no means evident at the time."[32] Bourne lists E. R. Burrowes (1903–1966), H. Moshett (1901–2002), G. Sharples, A. Vanier, and R. Phang amongst the pioneers of the period with young artists like C. Gomes, D. Williams, Hinds and himself as those who would follow. Several women artists were active in this group, including M. Broodhagen (d. 2000) and E. Cadogan. It should also be noted that membership of the Guianese Art Group comprised "recognised" artists, a distinction which implied a degree of gravitas and professionalism, and possibly even élitism but, definitively, a new sense of itself.

Williams was to observe:

> A degree of conceptual liberation from the European absolutes of the Arts and Crafts Society of the preceding era was to be expected in the Guianese Art group. This was stimulated in several ways. In the first place there was an expanding awareness of the Caribbean as a cultural sphere. [...] Characterising the period, also, was the emergence of an informed criticism and consequently the development of a didactic dimension in the practice of art.[33]

Subject matter was far more experimental as evidenced in the titles of works: Dudley Charles' "evocations of the world of magic animality" in *Palings* (1946) worked in acrylics and Michael Cox's "interpretations of exotic landscape through manipulation of surface texture" are seen in *Tramen Pool* (1945).[34] Both paintings are in the National Collection.

Between 1943 and 1950 a great variety of clubs became reorganised as the British Guiana Union of Cultural Clubs. A. J. Seymour noted that "[...] after seven years, the Union ceased to meet, since other bodies like the British Council and the Extramural Department of the University of the West Indies had emerged to carry out on a professional basis what had previously been done on an amateur level."[35]

Seymour had earlier made the point:

> [...] there is no recipe for planning a culture.[...] I wish I had time to contradict Eliot and argue that no new culture can grow naturally in our present artificial civilisation, but to those of us in the West Indies who wish to push ahead too rapidly Eliot has the restraining word of wisdom. He writes: "You must wait for the grass to grow, to feed the sheep to give the wool, out of which your new coat will be made."[36]

Seymour was writing as the Chief Government Information Officer of the colonial administration and he was also a respected intellectual, critic and poet. in 1945 he had founded the literary journal *Kyk-over-al*[37] to support and develop West Indian cultural growth. His architecture of "cultural self-sufficiency" inevitably deferred to a definition of cultural authority imbued with the prescriptive, élitist values of the European imprimatur. In his essay "The Creation of Quality in the West Indies"[38] he offers a view of West Indian society as a "[...] pyramid with an élite, in the Eliot sense, people with an understanding of true quality." In the words of Michael Swan, commissioned by HMSO to write about British Guiana, this viewpoint had wide currency amongst "[...] the large section of reasonable, moderate Guianese who understood the dangers of precipitate action."[39] But it was a contradictory approach that could only present difficulties for the peculiar "artificial" racial context of Guianese society.

Elseswhere Williams gives further insights into the cultural life of Georgetown:

> In 1944, Forbes Burnham was 21, Cheddi Jagan 26, Wilson Harris an obscure civil servant writing poems later to be collected as "An Epoch of Homelessness", Mittelholzer, after a calamitous flirtation with naval life, was writing in Trinidad, and A. J. Seymour was at the Bureau of Publicity and Information. In that year all fashionable Georgetown went to the première performance of "The Legend of Kaieteur", Philip Pilgrim's modernistic choral rhapsody (I'd call it) on Seymour's epic poem, at the Assembly Rooms – a blunt straddling bit of Old Georgetown embowered in flamboyant splendour at the head of Main Street. Within days our first composer was dead – of typhoid contracted whilst touring the "Legend" to New Amsterdam. The world of sport had recently lost the dashing gifts of Robert Christiani. These two deaths brought Georgetown to its knees. But in 1944 it could have been any of us; the public health environment remained sovereign and capricious master of all our destinies.[40]

It was E. R. Burrowes' Working People's Art Class, founded in 1948, which took over the lead in democratising the art community and producing the next generation of artists. Burrowes had been a skilled tailor, and both he and Moshett had been sign painters at some point in their journey, significantly underlining the importance of working people as originators in the development of the visual arts of British Guiana.

Taking art to "the man in the street", the Working People's Art Class saw Burrowes addressing the cultural anachronisms of subject and style in his own painting and in those he influenced.

Marjorie Broodhagen was among those first artists who focused on the way of life of their own people as suitable subjects for painting. The work of Donald Locke, Basil Walcott, Rex Walcott, Patrick Barrington and Emerson Samuels was well represented in the Third Art Exhibition of the Working People's Art Class in April 1952. "Their works are not imitations of any style, either European or African, but original expressions of the basic subjectivity of our mixed origin and cultural aspects."[41] In developing notions of national consciousness Burrowes moved away from his earlier approaches and nurtured this appreciation of local style and content. He was the first to institutionalise art teaching and his instruction extended to lectures on aesthetics, historical art studies and critical appreciation. The Working People's Art Class was funded by businesses and institutions including the British Council.

Writing with the assumed authority of the era Michael Swan observed:

> During the last decade or so Guianese interest in the practice of painting [...] has greatly increased. This is largely due to the excellent and inspiring work of Mr. E. R. Burrowes at the Working People's Art Society, which he founded – work for which he has been honoured with an M.B.E. [...] Most of the painters appeared to be of African origin, and although their immediate inspiration was European, the uninhibited statements of the paintings, often frankly sensual [...] seemed to have their origin in the atavisms of race.[42]

Williams himself recorded changes in the direction that art was taking:

> For reasons which remain as yet poorly understood, the dominant expression of the pioneer painters of the twenties and thirties had been landscape. Now, in the forties, the human figure acquired expressive importance as its powerful emotive potentials were suddenly realised. Concurrently, the portrait as an independent study emerged. Painting thereby achieved a novel richness [...].[43]

The surviving record of works shows that portraiture had indeed occupied Williams' attention. At this time he was working as a clerk in Georgetown, a post opened through education. In 1943, government civil servants were given pay rises and his position may well have attracted a good salary in relative terms, enabling him to pursue his art interests.

In the catalogue of the Exhibition of West Indian Paintings, held at The Institute of Jamaica in 1945, Williams' work appears alongside that of Golde White, whose "[...] influence on newly emerging artists should not be underestimated" and who at this time in the early 1940s was producing "striking portrait heads".[44] For Williams, the use of his own family members as fitting subjects of his early art indicates an unselfconscious and dignified social confidence in a secure family legacy in which the importance of manners is evident.

Of these early works, *Portrait of Peter* was purchased for a national collection. The close family resemblance and links in its composition to *Self-portrait* (1945) are clear, and suggest that this is in fact an early self-portrait. Williams may have deliberately chosen titles that obscured the fact that he had limited opportunity of varied portrait subjects; we see this in his portraits of his sisters. But an ambiguity is created that is revisited in later works to become one that hovers over the particulars of personal identity. The self-portrait certainly became a significant autobiographical element of Williams' output. It allowed him the means of accessing the common ground of universal understanding.

In 1944 Williams was 21, a young man. He developed as an intellectual artist and this early work stands out through the striking resonance of an inner reflective process. The artist has perhaps made an unconsciously revealing statement of his inner emotional workings at that time. His other self-portraits of this period are altogether more objective, outwardly conveying serious attitudes of dignity and composure. *Portrait of Peter* is therefore important for what it might additionally tell us of the artist. So what does the painting capture? Unlike the other works, in this self-portrait the eyes are side turned and deliberately disengaged, raising an immediate question for the viewer. In this period of coming of age before Williams left for London can we detect a diffidence; a self-questioning psychological dimension; prescient misgivings?

The development of his art, the form of painting in oil on canvas, employing a vocabulary and visual language which was directly influenced by the European legacies was founded in the unlikely opportunities he found locally, in his immediate rôle-models and the supportive community of art which allowed him to be an artist. But Williams was questioning and experimenting. He was looking elsewhere. He had naturally outgrown what was available locally. He was now seeking to develop his inventory of skills. In this small painting we can see that the artist was moving away from strict representation and was employing expressive treatments. The apparent casual looseness of the brushwork belies the mature technical control of the artist. The harmony of colour is achieved through a severely restricted palette of blue and yellow ochre. White highlights and dramatic tonal and textural contrasts are used to emphasise the dimensions of the fall of light. This control of colour and light allows the artist a great freedom to explore the brushwork that ties the whole work into a cohesive entity. What the young artist conveys is a sense of sharing a heightened personal psychological awareness. The suggestion of unease in his facial expression is supported by the treatment of the shifting brushwork of the background. The image conveys an emotional anxiety beneath the pictorial content through the blue chiaroscuro and the swirling unsettling treatment. If any intellectual doubt existed, could it be that the artist found himself looking into a painting in which he realises he has assimilated his own image in ways that were disquieting? Did he capture his own psychological and emotional tension, only to find his identity somehow compromised? Against the immediate colonial context, however faintly sketched, is it possible to detect the roots of an inevitable artistic crisis? Given the circumstances of his world, there seems a fateful logic to the idea.

One of Georgetown's landmark buildings was the British Guiana Museum, largely destroyed in the 1945 Great Fire when some of the city's oldest and most beautiful wooden buildings were lost or damaged. The Royal Agricultural and Commercial Society (RACS) was the parent body of the Museum. It operated the Zoo collection and the Museum collection, and there was a healthy membership by subscription. In conjunction with the British Council, the Combined Cultural Committee of the RACS organised films, musical evenings, lectures and exhibitions that were often held in the Reading Rooms. There was a separate exhibition committee that organised children's art exhibitions, competitions and photographic displays. The Museum would receive gifts and donations of paintings and ceramics, and the proceedings of the Society were published in the *Timehri* journal. From there we learn that a School of Art had been proposed as early as 1886.[45] It was here in the Museum that Stanley Greaves had seen *Portrait of Peter*. Greaves recently wrote:

> My first meeting with Dennis Williams took place in the British Guiana Museum of the 1940s – destroyed by fire in 1945, rebuilt before Independence in 1966 and renamed the Guyana Museum. This "meeting" took the form of looking at a small oil painting of a boy. [...] I visited it [...] and often wondered what kind of a person the artist [...] was. [46]

Greaves states that by his early twenties Williams had already "exhibited work and gained a reputation as a figure painter" and that *Portrait of Peter* was the work that earned him the first-ever British Council scholarship in art in British Guiana. The award was made in 1945, although Williams was unable to take up the offer until the following year because of hostilities in Europe. The decision to confer this award was made by Alan D. Steward, who left the colony in 1946. D. L. Bourne pays tribute to "[...] the assistance and encouragement that has been afforded artists by the British Council. Books and periodicals on Art are made available from the small but valuable collection in the British Council Library, and sound advice and encouragement is given by the Representative himself, Mr Steward, to the artists with whom he comes into contact."[47] Williams recollects that year:

> In 1945, symbolically enough, the heart of Georgetown was burnt out in one of our several spectacular fires, and symbolically too the Assembly rooms infected as it were by airborne sparks and the heat and its own imperial rot, burned. It burned as eternally as Orozco's "Man Aflame" under equally eternal Guyana clouds. That year our great national poet, Arthur Seymour founded a literary magazine named KYKOVERAL. Young men in strange uniforms with strange decorations were returning from far-flung theatres of war: others had put off uniforms for academic robes in various universities in Europe and America; yet others had been stricken in these strange uniforms, never to come back. [...] On very many levels an epoch of homelessness was slipping, unnoticed, into the past.[48]

At this time we know of seven recorded

Retrieved images

Right: *Portrait of Peter*. Oil on canvas.
Purchased by RACS for a
British Guiana National Art Gallery.
Selected as "Picture of the Year" by the Judging Committee
at the Exhibition of West Indian Art held in Georgetown
in November 1946.

Below left: *Self-portrait with a Military Helmet* (1945).
Purchased by RACS for a
British Guiana National Art Gallery.

Below right: *Self-portrait with a Towel* (1945).
Purchased by RACS for a
British Guiana National Art Gallery.

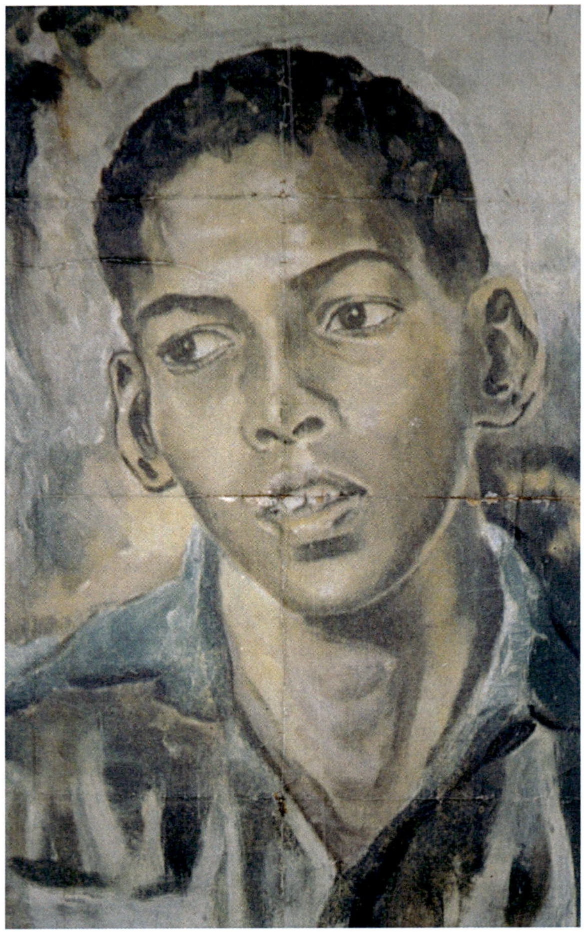

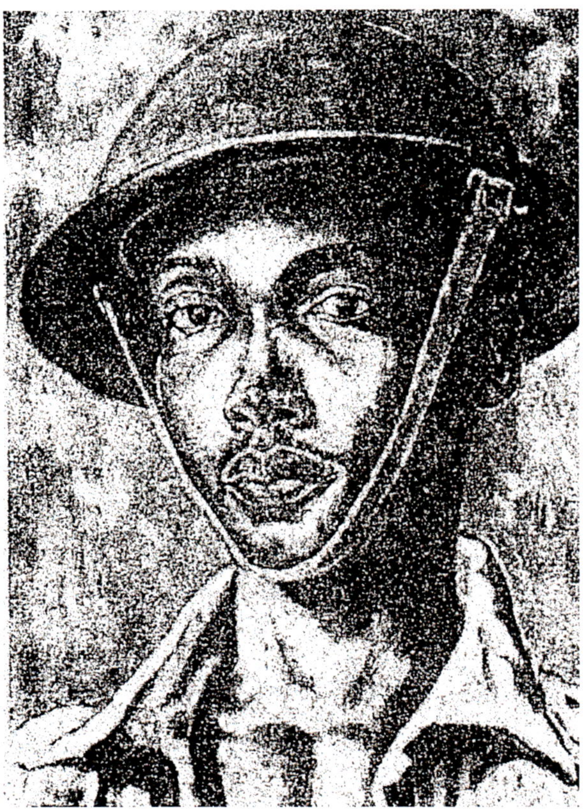

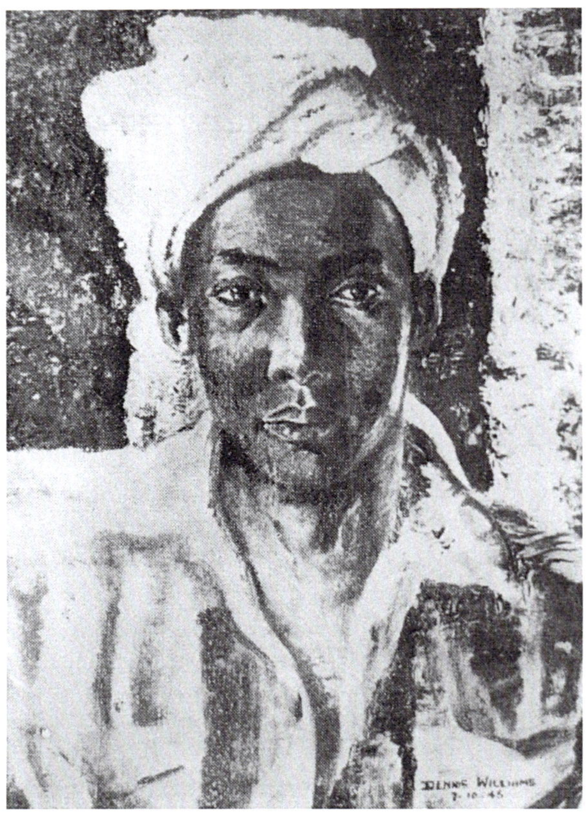

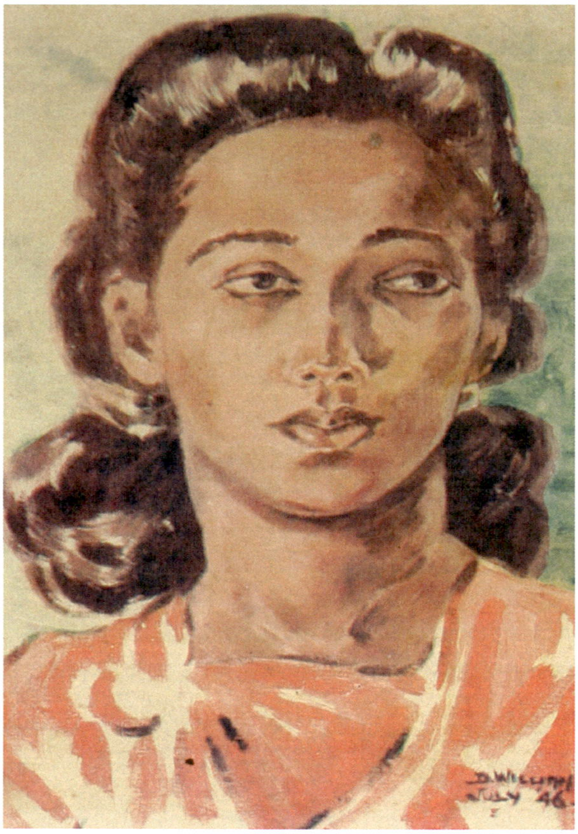

Head in Oils (1946). Oil on canvas. National Collection.

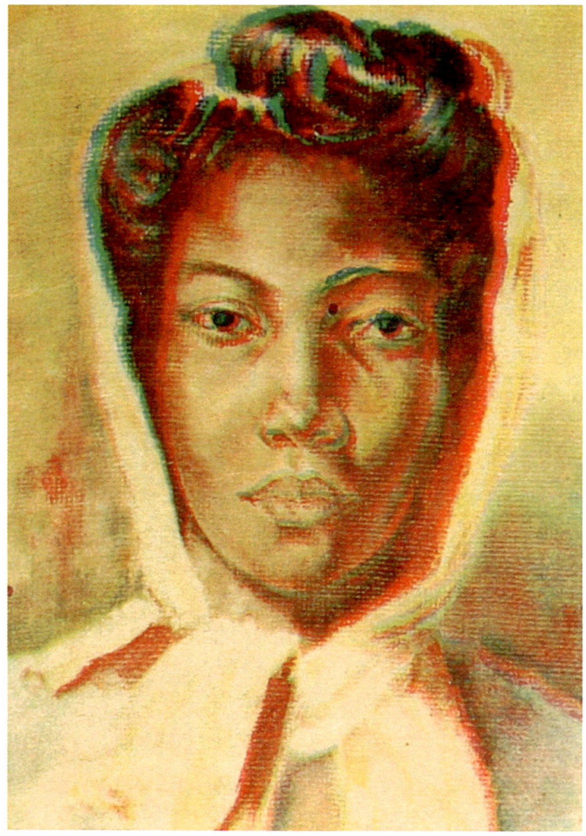

Janie (1946). Oil on canvas. National Collection.

portraits that were produced shortly before Williams' departure for London to study at the Camberwell School of Art. *Self-portrait with a Towel* (1945)[49] was purchased by the Joint Committee of the RACS of British Guiana and the British Guiana Museum. This was a remarkable group of people who became the custodians of art, having the foresight to make collections on behalf of the people of British Guiana in order to form the nucleus of a British Guiana National Art Gallery.[50] This portrait may well have been purchased on the back of Williams' success in winning his scholarship. In it we certainly see a confident and committed young artist at the age of twenty-two. The flamboyant towel over the head and the loose folds of his shirt belie a serious-minded expression. *Janie* (1946) wearing a pale headscarf has been identified as Williams' sister Verna, otherwise known as "Pinksy". The family likeness and the familiar coral blouse suggest that *Head in Oils* (1946) is a sketch study for his portrait of Leila. Hubert Moshett's signature appears in the margin of this reproduction and the caption reads: "A delightfully charming study that brings out the spontaneity and skill of the artist."

Leila[51] is dated 12 May 1946. His sister's likeness is most economically worked with a restricted complementary palette and dramatic white highlighting. The initial impact of colour is achieved through the loose working of the silky blouse, and the light emanating from the creamy vermilion tints and hues suffusing the skin tones. The head is set against a simple supportive background that engages the whole palette in its brushwork. The composition is well balanced and the artist's three-quarters view down towards Leila's slightly tilted head is assured. The solidity of form rests in the artist's easy use of a vibrant yellow chiaroscuro. The command of technique is further emphasised in the treatment of Leila's hair where brushstrokes follow the directions of the stylishly dressed waves of hair, pressed and pinned high off the brow. The portrait speaks of his closeness to his sister; it captures her eyes engaged in a reflective, thoughtful expression.

This small portrait is one of the finest examples

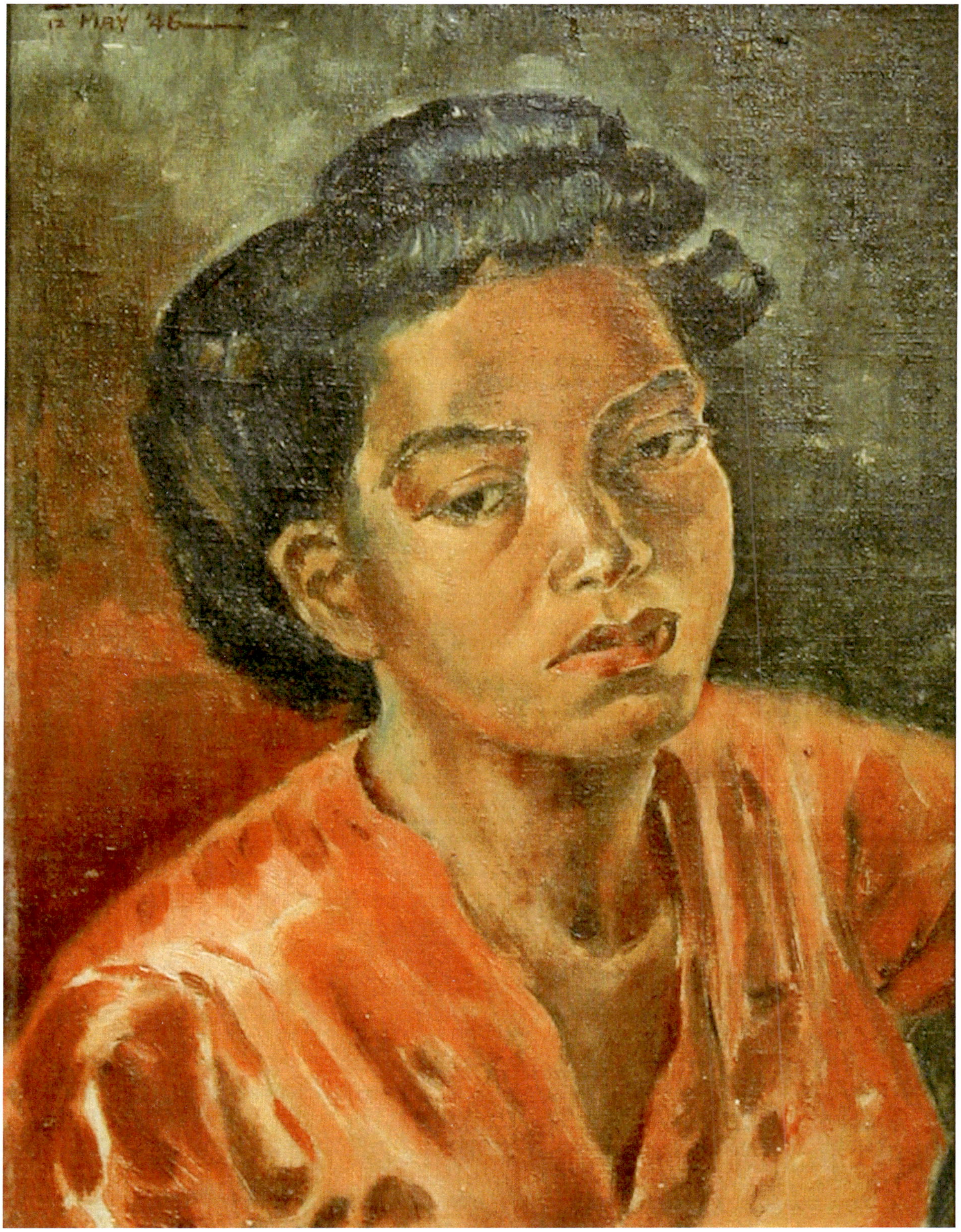

Leila (1946). Oil on canvas. 35.5×25.5 cms. National Collection.

of Williams' work prior to leaving British Guiana to pursue his studies in London. He recalls his mother's reaction to it, and again acknowledges her part in his development as an artist: "As I grew up she was my most ardent critic and supporter. When I painted Leila she studied the portrait with her hand funnelled over one eye to produce the three-dimensional effect. She taught me that."[52] These early portraits celebrate the advanced formal skills Williams was able to achieve through exposure to a range of experience. This combined knowledge was founded on an acquaintance with art through clubs, demonstrations, instruction, journals, books, exhibitions and the acquired knowledge of his teachers. The portraits demonstrate an easy understanding of the visual elements: three-dimensional form, the dynamics of composition and the drama of chiaroscuro and colour. His achievement also owes a debt both to supportive groups and pioneering individuals like Golde White and E. R. Burrowes.

The dignified, overall restrained approach shown in the majority of Williams' portraits can be contrasted with *Two Figures in Gouache* (1946), which gives a further glimpse of broader influences. This work is evidence that Williams was beginning to experiment with different approaches and techniques before he left Georgetown to take up his formal studies. The younger artists were also looking to the Cuban, Mexican and Latin-American canons for closer affinities. As he later wrote:

> In this broadening of the artistic horizon, publication of Cuban contemporary art in the review *Pintura Cubana de Hoy* created a degree of interest among the younger Guianese painters, particularly through the expressionist treatment of the human figure.[53]

But it is certain that before ever setting foot on the *Marine Marlin*[54] on his transatlantic journey in 1946, Williams had intellectually engaged with Europe and with the weight of its established authority on the history of art and learning. This is demonstrated in his paintings but he also had access to art books and we know he had studied the five-volume *History of Art* by Élie Faure. From the fact that Williams refers to these volumes on several occasions in later interviews, we can surmise that it was a formative influence.

The approach of the Faure volumes is to trace the history of art in a chronological structure down the centuries. The artistic achievements of great civilisations are sketched with great sweeping brushstrokes across cultures and vast continents. This type of imprint may well have laid the basis of Williams' later questioning of Eurocentrism, but it was Faure's essay *The Spirit of Forms* (1927), contained in the final volume, which would have most excited Williams as an artist. Here the chronicle departs from its "order" and in a lyrical style, points to the potency at the heart of artistic creation. Faure's position validates the special status of art and artists. Art is placed at the motivational centre of life, present from the beginning. Faure sees the work of art both as an aesthetic creation and also as an instant of a given civilisation.

> Universal form is built on a single basis. It can be discovered anywhere. Poor indeed is the one who, for example, fails to see in a human or animal skull not only a well-ordered countryside with hills and valleys, rivers, internal movements, geological unity, and rhythm, but also a perfect sculpture with its asymmetrical balance, its silent planes, its fleeting lines, its expressive projections, and its sinuous and pure profiles.[55]

Faure sees the same forms and proportions at work in the functional logic of nature and in art. It was a novel and compelling vision that demonstrably affected the young Williams and we can trace its lingering effect in his developing aesthetic outlook.

A photograph of "Sonny" taken in 1945 shows him in full pin-stripe serge suit, tie and kerchief; he would have been wearing highly polished, closed shoes. Typically, these were outward symbols of dignity and worth. His expression is proud and confident. Many of his compatriots had joined the British Forces as a matter of patriotic duty. He had been born British, and was not yet fully aware of being West Indian. He was not fully aware of being black for that matter – until he went to England. One of his ambitions was to paint royalty. He was young, talented and articulate. He was already a highly accomplished draughtsman. A keen and thoughtful observer, he maintained a certain aloofness from others. He had confidence in his own opinions and abilities. He had grown up understanding that for the future to be anything it would mean stepping out into the wider world, and now London awaited him. This was the nature of the European imprimatur.

NOTES TO CHAPTER 1

1 Denis Williams, "The Cultural Heritage". (1976). Unpublished typescript, later published as "The Visual Arts in the Cultural Evolution of the People of Guyana", in *UNESCO Courier* (Vol. 1, No. 7, 1987), pp. 2–4. It was also used as the text for an exhibition in Caracas, Venezuela, in March 1987.
2 Denis Williams, *Giglioli in Guyana (1922–1972)* (Georgetown: The National History and Arts Council, 1973), p. 45.
3 Charlotte Williams, interview with Denis Williams (1998).
4 Roy Heath, *Shadows Round the Moon* (London: Collins, 1990).
5 Denis Williams, "The Cultural Heritage". Quotation only in the typescript version (1976), p. 9.
6 Denis Williams, "Identity in Guyanese Plastic Art", in John Hearne (ed.), *Carifesta Forum: An Anthology of 20 Caribbean Voices* (Jamaica: Institute of Jamaica, 1976), pp. 181–183.
7 Major Gray was the first Principal of the Teacher Training Centre, founded in 1928. In 1973 it was re-named the Cyril Potter College of Education, after its first Guyanese Principal.
8 Charlotte Williams (1998).
9 Jennifer Wishart (with E. Williams), "The Island of Guiana", in C. & E. Williams (eds.), *Denis Williams: A Life in Works. New and Collected Essays* (Cross/Cultures; Amsterdam & New York: Rodopi, 2010), pp. 187–199. This image recurs in his second novel *The Third Temptation*.
10 Charlotte Williams (1998).
11 *Ibid.*
12 *Ibid.*
13 "The institutions responsible for teaching and promoting art were the Teachers' Training Centre, the Bishops' High School and the two convents – Ursuline and Mercy Orders." Recollected by Marjorie Broodhagen in Nesha Z. Haniff (ed.), *60 Years of Women Artists in Guyana 1928-1988: A Historical Perspective* (Sponsored by the Guyana Women Artists' Association, 1988), p. 15.
14 Denis Williams, *Giglioli in Guyana*, p. 45.
15 Munro, Arlene, "British Guiana's contribution to the war effort, 1930-1945: A preliminary investigation", in *Stabroek News*, 9 October 2003.
16 Charlotte Williams (1998).
17 Reproduced in *60 Years of Women Artists in Guyana*, p. 9.
18 See D. L. Bourne, "Painting in British Guiana", in *Kyk-over-al* (Vol. 1, No. 2, June 1946, and Vol. 1, No. 3, December, 1946), pp. 26–27.
19 E. R. Burrowes, "Art in British Guiana", in *Kyk-over-al* (Vol. 5, No. 15, Year end 1952), pp. 41–44.
20 Anne Walmsley, interview with Denis Williams (November 1993).
21 Alissandra Cummins, Alison Thompson, and Nick Whittle (eds), *Art in Barbados: What Kind of Mirror Image?* (Kingston, Jamaica: Ian Randle Publishers, with Barbados Museum and Historical Society, 1999), p. 38.
22 Denis Williams, "The Visual Arts in the Cultural Evolution of the People of Guyana", p. 2.
23 E. R. Burrowes, "Art in British Guiana", p. 42.
24 In *60 Years of Women Artists in Guyana*, p. 11.
25 Reported in *Kyk-over-a*l (Vol. 2, No. 8, June 1948).
26 Frank Pilgrim, notes in the Souvenir Programme for the opening of the National Cultural Centre in May 1976.
27 Spencer Richards, interview with Denis Williams (1997).
28 Martin Carter, "Is there a West Indian Way of Life?" Symposium in *Kyk-over-al* (Vol. 6, No. 20, 1980), pp. 193–194.
29 Bourne was secretary of the Guianese Art Group.
30 D. L. Bourne "Painting in British Guiana", p. 27.
31 *Ibid.*
32 Denis Williams, "The Cultural Heritage", *UNESCO Courier*, p. 13.
33 *Ibid.*
34 Captions in the Exhibition Catalogue accompanying items from the National Collection of Guyana exhibited in Caracas, Venezuela, in March 1987, pp. 7, 8.
35 A. J. Seymour, *Cultural Policy in Guyana* (UNESCO, Paris: Imprimerie des Presses Universitaires de France, 1977), pp. 27–28.
36 A. J. Seymour, "Notes Towards the Definition of Culture", in *Kyk-over-al* (Vol. 2, No. 8, June 1949), p. 33.
37 Dutch, meaning "View over everything". The periodical was named after the small island near the confluence of the Mazaruni and Cuyuni rivers just before they merge with the Essequibo.
38 *Kyk-over-al* (Vol. 6, No. 18, mid-year 1954), pp. 43–53.
39 Michael Swan, *British Guiana: The Land of Six Peoples* (London: HMSO, 1957), pp. 123. [The foreword is by Winston Churchill. Denis Williams was commissioned to provide the book jacket and illustrations].
40 Denis Williams, *Giglioli in Guyana*, p. 59.
41 E. R. Burrowes, "Art in British Guiana", p. 42.
42 Michael Swan, *British Guiana: The Land of Six Peoples*, pp. 129–130.
43 Denis Williams, "The Cultural Heritage", *UNESCO Courier*, p. 4.
44 Cummins, Thompson and Whittle, *op. cit.*, p. 39.
45 *Timehri* (Vol. 5), p. 134. Edited by E. F. im Thurn.
46 Stanley Greaves, "Meeting Denis: A Mind Engaged", in C. & E. Williams (eds), *Denis Williams: A Life in Works* (2010), pp. 163–180. [See note 49].
47 D. L. Bourne (1946), p. 27. The British Council also organised exchange exhibitions with British Guiana and neighbouring colonies. An account of Alan D. Steward's farewell party appears in the same issue of *Kyk-over-al*.
48 Denis Williams, *Giglioli in Guyana*, p. 59.
49 The portrait is signed "Dennis Williams". The spelling "Denis" appears on his birth certificate, but this variant is frequently encountered.
50 The early collection for a British Guiana National Art Gallery was housed in the Georgetown Public Free Library. See the Foreword by Vincent Roth in the *Guiana Edition* No. 14: "Graphic Art in British Guiana: A Collection of

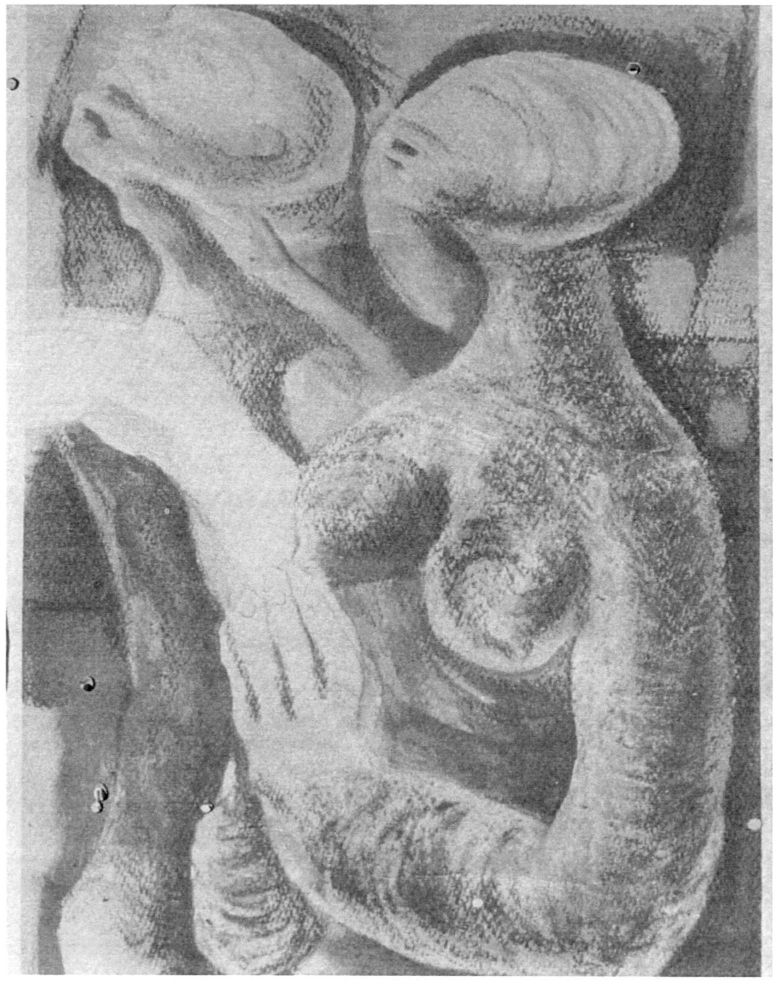

Two Figures in Gouache (1946). National Collection.

Works by Local Artists 1944–1948", published by the *Daily Chronicle* Ltd., Georgetown, British Guiana, 1949.
51 A newspaper cutting from 1978 shows Education Minister Vincent Teekah receiving *Portrait of Leila* from Eric Stoby, the managing director of Wieting and Richter Ltd.. Also pictured are Denis Williams and A. J. Seymour.
52 Charlotte Williams (1998).
53 Denis Williams, "The Cultural Heritage", *UNESCO Courier*, p. 4.
54 An interesting account of this voyage is given by A. J. Seymour in "Voyage from the West Indies" in *Pilgrim Memories* (Georgetown: Labour Advocate Printers, 1978), pp. 1–22. He describes how "Denis Williams did a fine study in pencil of men playing dominoes in the lounge." (p. 13).
55 Quoted in Ferrier, Le Pichon and Glanze, *Art of our Century* (New York, 1988).

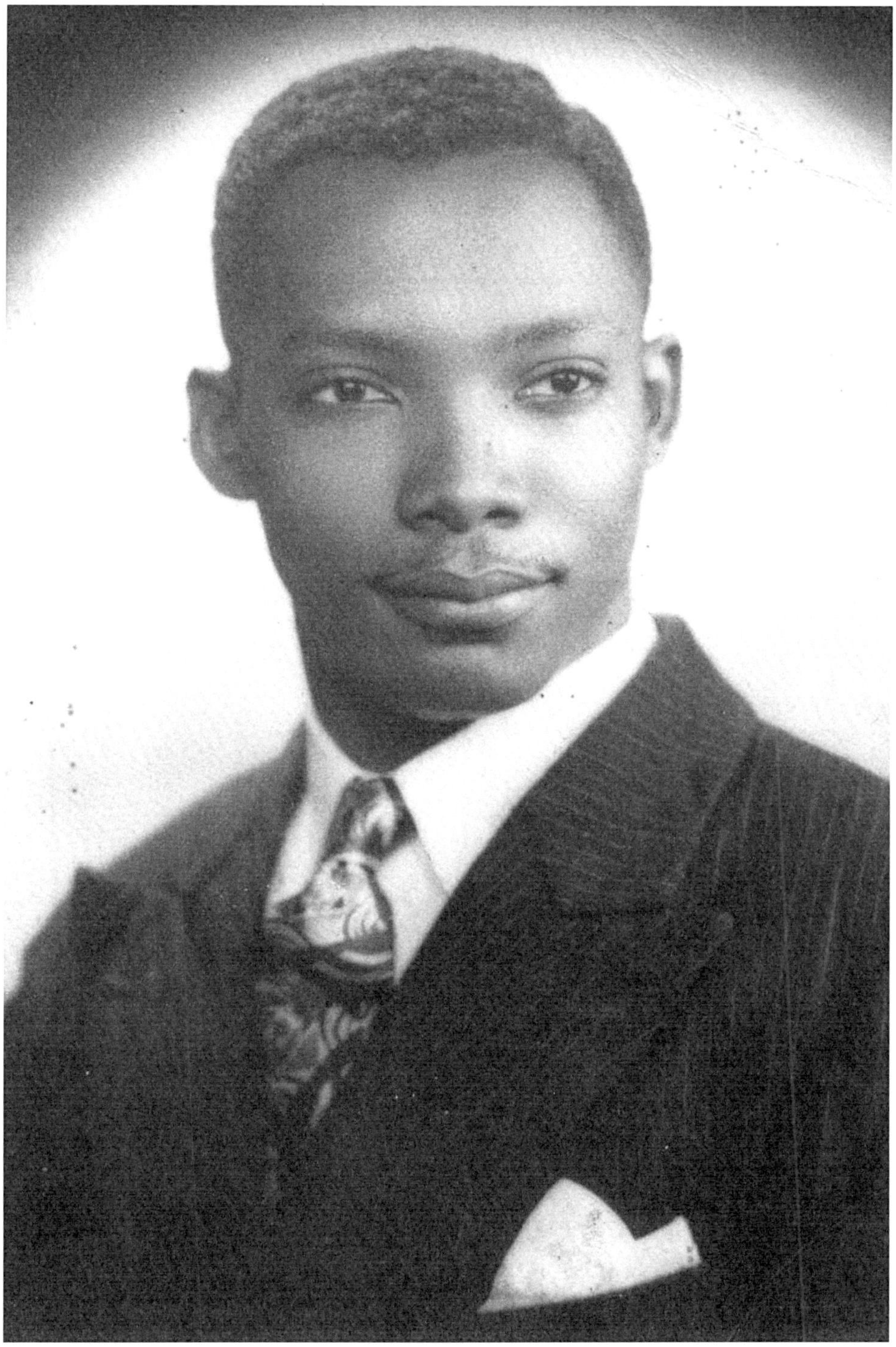

Denis Williams in 1945.

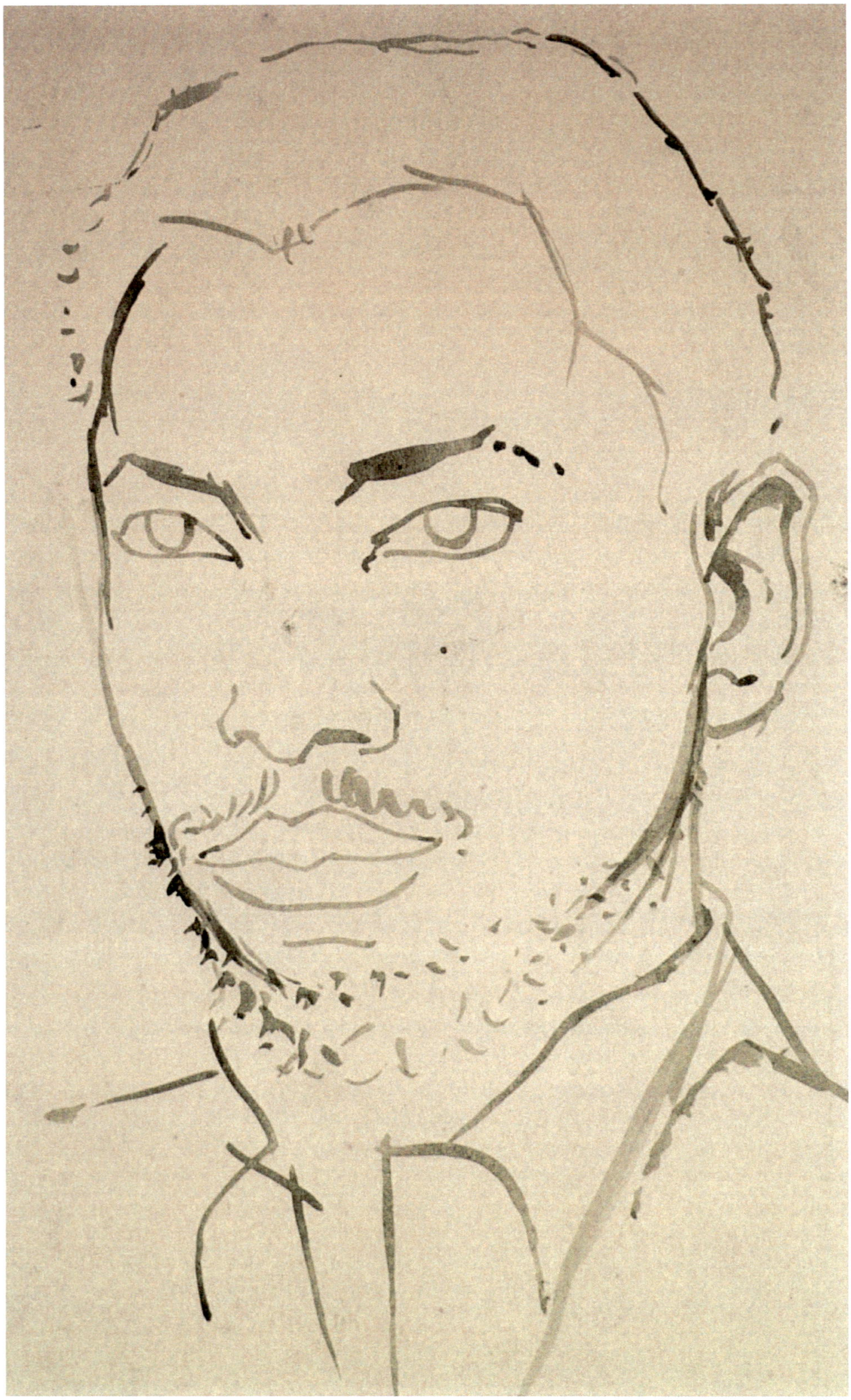

Self-portrait (1952). Brushline on paper. Williams estate.

CHAPTER 2

"A NEGRO ARTIST"

WILLIAMS FOLLOWED A FAMILIAR path for a talented young man in the late colonial period – he travelled abroad. In his case it was to take up the British Council Art Scholarship he had won in 1945. For many colonial subjects at that time, study abroad was a route to freedom from the destructive social and economic tethers of dependency. The generation of very early migrants to the metropolitan centres after World War II identify as a group whose anti-colonial sentiments forged the intelligentsia of the post-independence period, but as a general rule those who found success abroad did not return. For his part, the British Council scholarship allowed the young Williams to pursue the advanced studies in drawing and painting which at that time were available nowhere in the British West Indies.

His training at Camberwell would have exposed him to extremes. We know that life classes, for example, were an important part of the curriculum and that the student was faced at once with the complexities of the living model in the academic study of its anatomy and perspective. Williams would have relished this opportunity. But it was also the case that experimental courses in the Bauhaus manner had been introduced. Claude Rogers, William Coldstream and Lawrence Golding were Williams' tutors and he was highly enthusiastic.

Post-war London made a huge impact. In 1945 Churchill had lost the General Election to Clement Atlee. Great Britain had heavy war debts including the $4 billion war loan from the US, and some quarter of a million homes lay destroyed in bombed rubble. Atlee's austere Britain of "make-do-and-mend" was a grey era of shabby optimism. Good times were anticipated but postponed as Atlee prepared a famine plan. In 1947 there was a fuel crisis; rationing was the order of the day and people turned to the black market economy. Everyday life was grim. The country was riven with regional and class divisions locked into a narrow cultural nationalism: few had been abroad. Interracial marriages, romances and liaisons were met with negative reactions.

The pioneering wave of West Indian intellectuals, artists and writers who were in Europe in the 1940s and early 1950s were compelled to rehearse the deep psycho-social repertoire of exile and experience of homelessness once they oriented themselves within their new but hostile arena. For many their "native" background now became transformed into an exotic map – a material resource to explore. There were imaginative charades and guises to enact and a reluctant audience to confront. There were protestations of loss and neglect by being marginalised, and calls for liberation. Like most West Indian intellectuals Williams had to make his own sense of the complex and wide-ranging decolonising discourses. As Cy Grant remarked:

> [...] I didn't have any strong great feeling for Guyana. But, at that time. you know, one didn't confront issues of identity. That came later in one's life. At that time you just accepted that you were slightly privileged but, at the same time, underprivileged.[1]

Blackness took on new dimensions for West Indians. Andrew Salkey explained: "For what it's worth, London made me Black, long before Malcolm, long before the Black Revolution in America."[2] The theatre of Empire had established its cast of characters and there were great challenges. Political and economic imperatives aside, street-level experiences were profound and new, challenging politics of race had to be negotiated in the post-war reconstruction of identities. Expatriate communities found each other. This was Williams' experience: he met others from St Lucia, Trinidad and Jamaica, and recognised that they were all West Indians.

Following his short training he spent two years working in London as a clerk in the Colonial Ministry in order to support himself. His first recorded London exhibition was with Kofi Antubam at the Berkeley Gallery in 1949. Williams' work was singled out as possessing a "strange and rather ominous sympathy between the urgently primitive and the most sophisticated eroticism of the School of Paris." The reviewer continued:

> As a painter he is technically brilliant with a lovely appreciation, and power over, the texture of pigment. His confident sense of tonal values is more apparent than his powers as a colourist, and he is very sure of himself as a balanced draughtsman with an understanding of the confines of his picture space. The present affinity of some of his work with that of modern European masters is more apparent than real, and there should be little doubt that immediately he re-subjects himself to his native inspiration his great talent will transcend extraneous circumstances and find its natural expression.[3]

This was the exhibition that attracted the enthusiastic attention of Wyndham Lewis[4] who declared: "Mr Williams [...] possesses most remarkable gifts" and commented in particular on

> [...] *Monolith*, which has a look of Picasso, and *Figure* with a lemonish illumination reminiscent of Vaughan [...] though when I mentioned Picasso, he [Williams] answered "It is not a case of my going to Picasso, Picasso came to Africa and to me."[5]

Yet there is no doubt that close at hand throughout the period is a debt to the liberating legacy of Picasso in modern primitivism and there had been an important post-war Picasso exhibition at the Victoria and Albert Museum, which had taken London by storm. Lewis' review continued: "The 'dark unconscious', as Lawrence would have it, staring at itself in the Picassoan mirror, is unquestionably a fascinating spectacle."

Lewis notes that Williams also had work on show in the *Colonial Exhibition* at Marble Arch, London, organised by the Central Office of Information. The Colonial Month had been opened by the King in June 1949. It was a nationwide initiative with its centre in London. There were special displays at all the main institutions and museums; there were art shows and films and ethnographic exhibitions. The British Nationality Act of 1948 suggested that a new relationship was being sought with its colonies in the winding-up of Empire and through the new Labour government's democratising agenda. This type of initiative seems to have been part of wider yet uncertain efforts to modernise the colonial relationship and move attitudes towards dismantling the more pretentious myths of Empire. For example, the Annual Colonial Report for 1948–1949 and two debates held in the Commons were described at

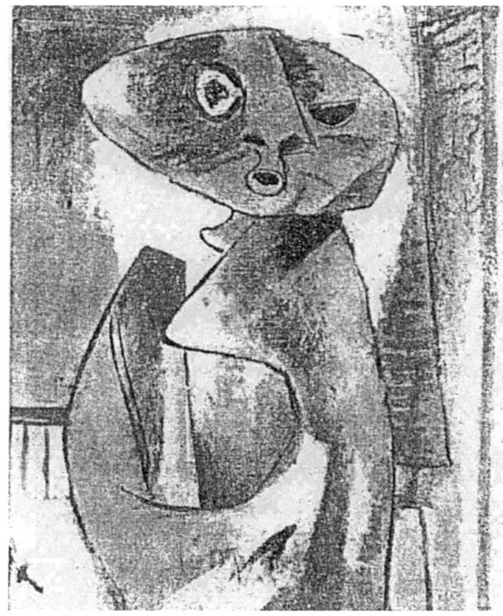

Figure (1949). Reproduced in *The Listener.*

the time as "remarkable, for a deeper and more informed approach than hitherto."[6]

In July 1949, on his way to visit his family in Georgetown, Williams spent just over a week in New York on a transit visa. Lewis and Keith Vaughan (1912–1977) had provided him with a number of helpful introductions. Paul O'Keeffe writes: "Rarely did Lewis act in anybody's exclusive interest but his own. His generosity towards a 26-year-old black painter from Georgetown, British Guiana, therefore, was noteworthy."[7] So what was Lewis' rationale in promoting Williams? His work was governed by a sharp intelligence: did this talent and intelligence confound him? Lewis had spent the war years in North America, where he experienced severe financial problems and felt that he had been badly treated. He had formed the opinion that Canadians took "a sort of pride in being repellent, rather than attractive, to the stranger within-the-gate."[8] However the artist Alex Jackson gave Lewis "a royal welcome" and received him, "coming from a foreign milieu, like a brother."[9] It may be that the memory of that welcome kindness inclined him to champion Williams.[10]

Alfred H. Barr Jr. was the Director of Museum Collections at the Museum of Modern Art, New York. Lewis wrote to say: "I am writing you this letter because (1) I regard him as a young man of very unusual talent: and (2) it is obvious that that talent will be wasted unless he can somehow, at this juncture, arrange his life in such a way as to enable him to paint [...] Caribbean people, technically "British", are in fact culturally Americans. Mexico City, New York, are for him the centres of his world

– not London."[11] He also wrote to the art historian and collector James Thrall Soby and to his friend Professor Felix Giovanelli of the University of St Louis who had connections in the art world.

The letter from Lewis to Giovanelli gives a flavour of the attitudes of the era:

> [...] I discovered a young Negro of great talent as a painter [...] What the position as regards Negroes is in New York I do not know: but I have taken the great liberty of giving him your address [...] Denis Williams is an extremely intelligent young man [...] He will not be a disagreeable contact (though I hope he will not be a socially embarrassing one) [...] Guiana is no place in which to be a painter. It would be wonderful if he could stay in New York [...] The main fact in all this is that he is a very unusually promising artist.[12]

O'Keeffe notes: "When Williams reached New York he found Giovanelli 'urbane and charming, but [...] less than optimistic [...], for racial reasons, of (his) contemplating a career in New York.'" Despite his best efforts, Giovanelli was unable to procure an extension to Williams' visa, or to raise sponsorship which would have allowed him to stay. Soby and Barr were both "out of town". "At the Museum of Modern Art his work was thought to be immature and over-influenced by the Cuban painter Wifredo Lam. Finding New York an alienating environment in which to paint, Williams abandoned the idea of making it a permanent base and continued his journey to Georgetown."[13] He clearly appreciated what had been done to help him, and in a letter of 27 July he wrote to Lewis: "I am truly very very proud to be recognised by you and shall always be grateful for the kind help you've extended to me."

He arrived in Georgetown in the summer of 1949 and remained there until May of the following year. He wrote to Lewis saying that he was enjoying the sun and the heat, but missing the intellectual life of London. The tropics provided a visual stimulus. "I spend a lot of time contemplating Nature in these Southern parts, but she's very stubborn and of course one 'sees' only with great difficulty. There is a greater mystery here, a stubborn triumphant remoteness which defies intimacy. I spent two days in the country last weekend and I came back afraid to begin painting."[14]

He fully intended to explore the possibility of his future in an environment that was outwardly multi-racial and to participate actively in advancing the visual arts in British Guiana.

> Every Guianese who leaves his country for higher education should be considered a precious commodity to return equipped for a key place in Guianese society. [...] The leading intellectual in British Guiana today is Mr A. J. Seymour, a poet and critic [...], and editor of a literary magazine, *Kyk-over-al*. He is typical of those West Indians who, having absorbed European culture by education, believe that the West Indian writer's duty is to remain in his home area and create its literature there, however discouraging the conditions.[15]

This was the opinion of the British Government implicit in the words of Michael Swan, and O'Keeffe writes: "Lewis, meanwhile, was making enquiries of the Foreign Office [...] He learned that the policy laid down by the Colonial Administration could be summed up in one phrase: 'to educate here for use in the Colonies.'[...] so that he may go back and promote Culture in British Guiana."[16] This was also a widespread view amongst West Indian intellectuals and clearly Williams' personal ambition. In the event, he was pulled up sharply by some unwelcome realities. He faced a vacuum in Georgetown where he realised there was little opportunity for him to support his own art; where his career opportunities under the colonial administration remained bleak;[17] where there seemed to be no centre of gravity for a specifically West Indian art. He wrote to Lewis:

> It is highly desirable that colonial young men return to their people [...] but to return to the West Indies now to make music or to paint pictures simply amounts to artistic suicide. I had hoped that things would be better after three years but here in Guiana I see only smugness and a dull contentment with what goes. I couldn't sell a thing here, though my work would be treated with profound respect because it has obtained the blessing of Europe – and so on. [...] But as I've told you before, I'm much more interested in the New World – and the sun. The cultural influence of Europe I find very dominating and a bit alien, despite my rather "English" education – Shakespeare, British Empire history and all that. [...] If my New World plans fail I should most certainly prefer to paint in Eng[land] to some audience, than here to none at all.[18]

He expanded on this in a critical polemic published in *Kyk-over-al*:

> There is no vision [...] we cling to a dream of a very negative quality. The person in Guiana looks

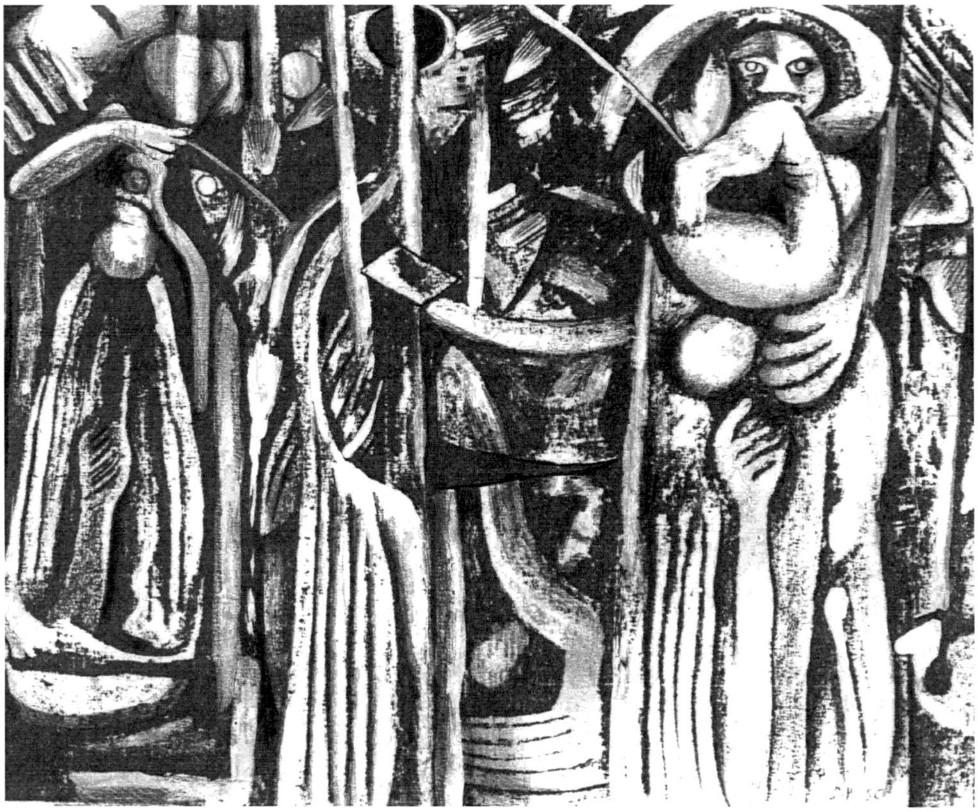

Plantation No. 3 (1950). Retrieved image. Courtesy Gimpel Fils.

> outward. Naturally. But the aggressive European pattern is always strange, aloof and unfriendly. There is no substantial link. Here we are up against history, race and culture [...] so we create a myth – an edifice which is nearly secure enough to make us forget our troubled yesterdays in the accomplishments of those most like us. [...] Our heroes function in a purely decorative way, showpieces of our different and differing races, brilliant enough to cast the sharp reflections in which we bask.[19]

His early hopes of returning to settle in British Guiana were therefore unrealised and the subtext of his early writing speaks of a deeply-felt frustration. "The prophets are beginning to arise," he wrote. "They will of course suffer the common fate of the breed. But the question is, does Guiana really want these men?"[20] In another letter to Lewis he suggested that he had not ruled out the option of moving away from Guiana altogether. "Even if I get a chance to return to New York, I'm still in love with the idea of working in Mexico or Brazil." He felt that he "should work in some capital of the Americas (race, cultural inclination etc) rather than in Europe" and lamented the "[...] hopelessness of trying to paint to such an unreceptive audience as West Indians at present generally are." He still recognised the need for European endorsement: "Mr de Bethel[21] tells me you are trying to get something done for me in *Studio*. That would be an *excellent* international letter of introduction from England, and would be priceless to me at this stage."[22]

He exhibited in Georgetown in 1949 under the aegis of the Guianese Art Group. He had begun work on *The Plantations*, which he described as "a suite of paintings". They explored the human impact of the legacy of plantation culture. They developed subject matter through which he positioned himself as an artist, and which was to culminate in the *Human World* series on his eventual return to London. *The Plantations* were large-scale pieces on a theme which he referred to as "the material at my own back door [...] candidly African in their language, though the subjects were very much the Guianese environment of mud and sugar-cane and jungle and black people."[23]

This harsh Guianese subject matter was presented in a rhythmic spatial arrangement of interlacing curves and interlocking planes which revealed a range of symbolic motifs: human limbs, branching vegetation, human and animal heads, foliage and plantation cane. All recede into an unknown, impenetrable space without parameters, boundaries or horizon. For Williams the visual possibilities of forest and cane-field in symbiotic relationship with human form provided the unavoidable iconography for the painful content of *The Plantations*. The space is filled in the imagination not with a relationship to vaguely remembered ancestral gods and romantic jungle mythologies but with the proximity of immediate and ominous threat whilst the potential of revelation is reserved. The sum of this iconography brings to mind Kamau Brathwaite's potent reference to the "inner plantation" where "[...] we are concerned with cores and kernels; resistant local forms; roots, stumps, survival rhythms; growing points [...].[24]

Williams was consciously pursuing a Guianese aesthetic through his subject matter and style. Wilson Harris recorded that *The Plantations* were four large studies in gouache on sheets of thick brown paper in which Williams evoked figures of plantation life. "They appear like mythical figures whose mutilation in the past have succeeded finally in cutting to the bone their sentient anguish. The huge moon face of seer or saint or rapist rises to overwhelm in abstraction the peculiar anguish of the women of the plantation."[25] He also exhibited two large-scale works in oils, *Origins* and *Burden or Release*, the latter described by Harris as "one of the most powerful and successful paintings of the *Human World* period."[26] These paintings were made on jute sackcloth, which was cheap and readily available, its loose weave sympathetic to broad expressive treatment.

This suite of paintings established the conceptual baseline of Williams' work. Swan gives the flavour of conservative contemporary responses: "In Georgetown I saw some of the work of his early Guianese period; it is startling, frightening, violent in mood; drawn, it seems, out of the darkness of Africa."[27] Harris records that these huge paintings "aroused considerable comment that bordered in some instances on hostility." Williams himself later recalled this contemptuous public reaction:

> These paintings were exhibited. They were instantly denounced. Concerning one in particular, *Origins*, a local newspaper informed the public that precious scholarship money had been wasted on a man who only wished to take Guianese back to Africa.[28]

Writing four years later, Gloria Escoffery recalled:

> When Denis Williams returned to British Guiana after his period of study abroad his new work found no favour in the eyes of his former patrons. According to one source of information he had become "very silly". Others say that the response which greeted him was insulting, approximating to persecution.[29]

His respectable Guianese audience – referred to by Swan as "the small, integrated intelligentsia of Georgetown" – was not receptive to the powerfully cathartic emphasis in the paintings on "ugly passages and aspects of personal and social experience of the artist and his people. They pictured and expressed the monstrous imagery of the past." They were also described as "aesthetic collisions which followed his contact with the screaming canvases of Wifredo Lam and René Portocarrero of Cuba."[30]

We can bring to mind Wifredo Lam's *Jungle* (1942–43). At that time there was widespread interest in Cuban art both in the Caribbean and in Europe, and the Musée Nationale de l'Art Moderne in Paris was to hold a major exhibition of Cuban art in 1951. Wilson Harris had also observed that: "The closest parallel to Denis Williams' painting in the West Indies is in the work of Wifredo Lam, the great Cuban painter. Williams' work is, like his, an amazing compression of the mystical, the tragic and the beautiful. And both artists are vitally concerned in their work with the approach to the particular and the universal."[31]

The outrage Williams' paintings were met with in his own country was bitterly felt. He saw that a prevailing orthodoxy was still largely underpinned by colonial values and that it was circumscribing the growth of Guianese art. The colonial influence still permeated the country's outlook and shaped the scope of the nation's artistic approach and vision.

E. R. Burrowes' Working People's Art Class was producing a generation of artists who were moving towards an alternative perspective, one that presented an intrinsic local dimension to its exposure to international movements and styles. To some extent they were encouraged by the handful of people like Denis Williams who were to gain recognition in the metropolitan centres and whose presence created a transitional bridge that then helped to elevate the whole concept of the artist in the colony.

In an article entitled "Old Wine in New Wine-skins" Burrowes had argued that masters such as Signorelli, Ucello, Breughel, El Greco, Velázquez and Goya were "all brewers of the various vintages of art which we now call Modern. So modern art can be referred to as 'Old Wine in New Wine-skins'." He goes on:

> The art of British Guiana is the art of the Caribs[32] [...] whose Timehri truly represent the primitive source without which no country can claim an art of its own. Apart from these, we who practise art, being merely the offspring of aliens from other parts of the earth, have gone awhoring after the strange "gods" of the three European countries that have in turn guided the destinies of this colony. The result of our efforts has been the giving birth to an illegitimate hybrid which has neither the virility nor the aesthetic virtue of its mixed parentage. A gloomy picture, but not altogether without hope. [...] But the Working People's Art Class first exhibition in April of this year [1949] was an outstanding example of the aesthetic progress being made in British Guiana. The work [...] was of an unspoiled freshness, in which modern primitivism and even intellectual abstraction were pleasingly demonstrated, and therein lies the hope of a future development of a typically Guianese Art, [...] our own wineskin.[33]

Times were changing and in a review of an exhibition by the emerging local artists of the WPAC, the tensions are evident:

> Not unexpectedly, an extraordinary amount of comment and criticism has been aroused by the venturesome adventure into modern art by both Dennis Williams and the students of the Working People's Free Art Class. [...] And *Chronicle* columnist Frank "Art My Foot" Pilgrim levelled a broadside attack on the budding Picassos of the Art Class in his review [of their recent exhibition]. [...] "Probably because of the fact that the great English art critic Wyndham Lewis eulogised the former, local critics showed inclination to be somewhat less outspoken in their condemnation of his work. The members of the WPAC, however, could not hope to escape the caustic comments of several visitors who attended their exhibition."[34]

In a British Council half-hour broadcast in 1951 on the Commonwealth radio station ZFY, Burrowes makes the familiar point that "from time immemorial artists who have had the courage to express their personal inspirations have been faced with unsympathetic antagonism." He stressed: "This antagonism emanated not only from the ordinary layman but also found expression in their intellectual contemporaries."[35]

George Lamming more pointedly emphasised his experience of this reaction from Caribbean audiences to any radical departures in art and literature:

> This was the kind of atmosphere in which all of us grew up. On the one hand a mass of people who were either illiterate or if not, had no connection whatever to literature since they were too poor or too tired to read; and on the other hand a colonial middle class educated, it seemed, for the specific purpose of sneering at anything that grew or was made on native soil.[36]

These attitudes are further confirmed by the strength of opposition to a proposed sculpture for the new Post Office building in Georgetown, the original structure having been lost in the fire of 1945. This was expressed in an editorial headed "Wrong Thing, Wrong Place" in the Georgetown *Daily Argosy* of 30 June 1950, which concluded: "we cannot regard it, whatever it is, as money well spent." The commissioned artist was Frank Dobson, then Professor of Sculpture at the Royal College of Art.[37] A full-scale clay model of the proposed artwork was described in *The Times* of London (24 July 1950) as a "remarkable bas-relief". In a letter to the Colonial Secretary,[38] Mr Costello, the Planning Officer of Georgetown, made an impassioned plea in support of Dobson's work. Costello accused the *Daily Argosy* of being "prepared to have this Colony preserved as a backwater in matters pertaining to art." However the Governor dismissed it as "utterly unsuitable" and hoped that "some less advanced sculptor can produce a suitably elaborate edition of the Colony's Arms." The Executive Committee of the Colony met to discuss the Dobson work and decided that the Secretary of State be advised that the Colony was unanimously opposed to the proposal.

Mention has already been made of *Two Figures in Gouache* (1946). This work is most interesting, as it stands alone as a surviving record of Williams' early treatment of the figure and it can be directly related to the general widening of the repertoire of Guianese painting that occurred in the 1940s. It can also readily be compared with the treatment of figures in the *Plantations* suite and to later works he exhibited in London. These comparisons are made because they point to similarities in specific aspects of style that are present both before and after his formal training.

The comparisons also raise a question concerning the possibility and nature of any "survival rhythms" in the art of a ruptured people. Can we defend the uncomfortable language in Swan's observation that the "uninhibited statements of the paintings [...] seemed to have their origins in the atavisms of race" when we compare it with Williams' own words: "Obviously the heritage survives [...] that heritage is no longer pinned to the antique forms [...] that heritage remains there just the same."?[39] When released from clumsy language, both views are suggesting that in some way art can be infused with affinities that resonate beyond what was clearly physically irretrievable.

In the event, the critical setback of the 1949 exhibition in Georgetown and the impossibility of advancement in British Guiana saw a disillusioned Williams leave his homeland to pursue his art in London. Basil Hinds later described him as an "aesthetic exile"[40] and Wilson Harris indicates that much of the work dating from this period was subsequently destroyed.[41]

On his return to London Williams was challenged to explore the genesis of an appropriate idiom which his quest to establish himself as an artist was bound to include. The "inner plantation" landscape of his South American homeland now became his springboard. The dark forest backdrop becomes an inner construct of memory and identity and the location of the spirit of the artist. This inner presence of the forest in the memory and imagination can be seen as a distinct feature in the work of many artists and writers from the region. It is a manifestation of the process that transforms the estranged homeland into an idyllic landscape. It provides a blank canvas for a world realigned in the memory of those artists who first looked inwards to create a mythology of the hinterlands of the Guianas:[42] a new-found, newly-realised mythology as rich as that of El Dorado. We can characterise a number of elements in his works of this period as he contextualises the notion of the "inner plantation". The local reality contained in *The Plantations* is sustained and transformed by the figures Williams found on the move on the streets of London: figures in close proximity; figures massing in the underground network. The plantation and rainforest settings become transformed into "the asphalt jungle". Diverse ideas conflate in this process of negotiating his own space as an artist. There are elements that acknowledge his exposure to contemporary European intellectual ideas; that testify to but do not rely on his European training. And inevitably there are the oblique references to the influence of Picasso that were widely applied to the work of artists of the era. The most striking marker here is the artist's exploitation of the relationship to audience through the treatment of space. It is insistent and overwhelming. This is achieved through the presence of the impenetrable backdrop and the drama of simplified sculptural forms compressing and overwhelming the two-dimensional space. The dense structure of bold, energetic lines forces the eye in a radically cropped perspective supported by the abstracted chiaroscuro patterns and play of contrasts. Williams had been working furiously and he was now anxious to mount an exhibition:

> I rang Wyndham Lewis who had in 1949 written the first review of my work (on a small exhibition I shared with a man from Ghana). I told him I had done a lot more work and he invited me to bring my paintings over to his home. He was painting his now famous T. S. Eliot. The finished portrait of Dame Edith Sitwell was in the room. Lewis arranged viewings of my paintings and within a week I had as many as three offers of exhibitions.[43]

O'Keeffe describes how Lewis attempted to organise a consensus to promote his *protégé* by "[...] bringing it to the attention of certain key people, notably, Henry Moore and, in hectoring terms, Herbert Read."[44]

In a letter to Read he pointed out that:

> [...] the British Council has been helpful with regard to this young Negro, but if he is to survive he must be found a job. Because of his colour this presents great difficulties. It is a pity that all this talent should be lost for no better reason than that its possessor's skin is controversial. I understand, for instance, that it is going to be exceedingly difficult to find a school prepared to engage a Negro teacher. [...] At this juncture, Committeeman Read, your vigorous action might be decisive.[45]

He exhibited at the prestigious Gimpel Fils gallery in London's Mayfair in December 1950, and it was this that would bring the validation that his homeland had denied him. This exhibition was the subject of Wyndham Lewis' enthusiastic review "A Negro Artist" in *The Listener*.

The Gimpel Fils exhibition catalogue of December 1950 records that he exhibited a group of large oil paintings which were developments from his Georgetown studies and likewise called *The Plantations*. The works of this phase were characterised by Lewis as less naturalistic and more detached evocations of the forest in abstract magical terms. He contrasted these works

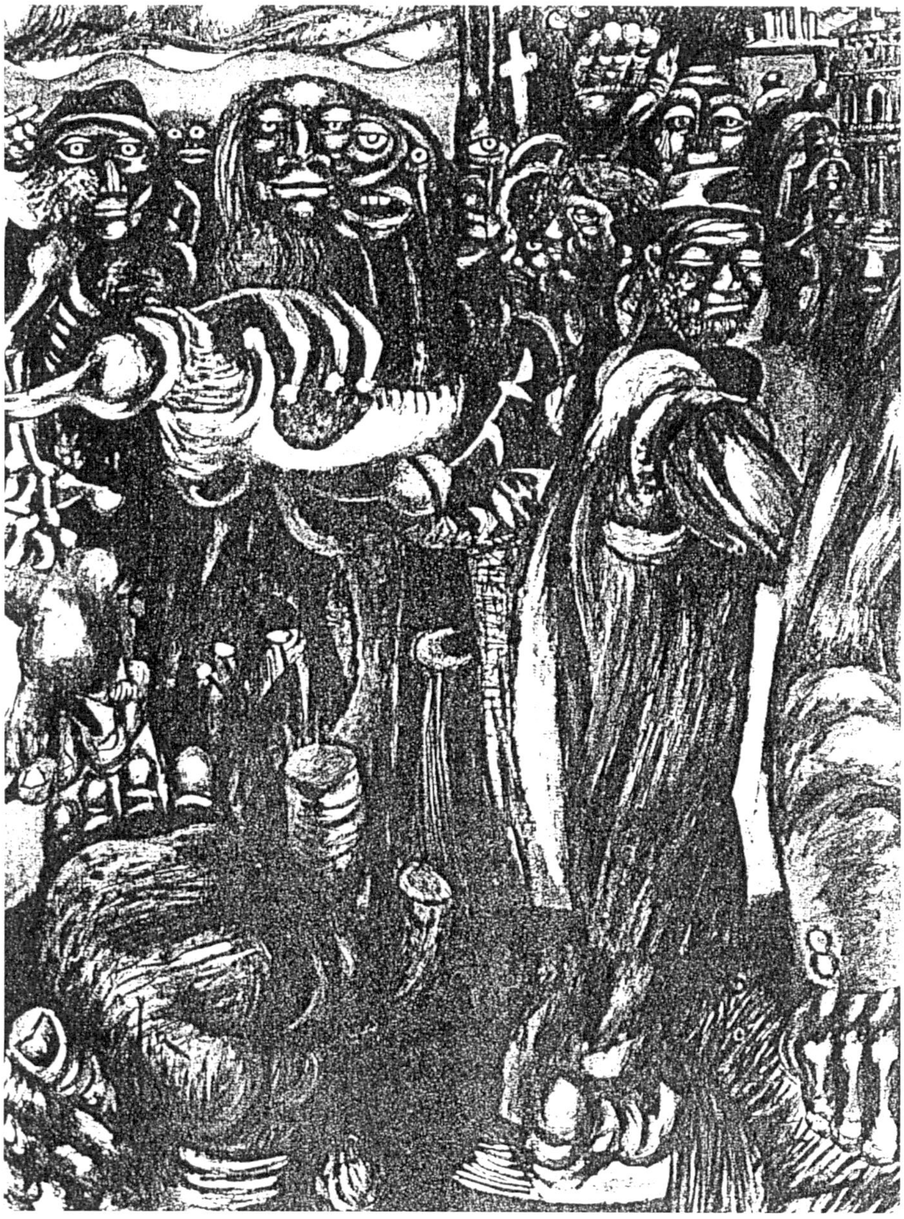

Human World series (1950). Tempera and oil on canvas.
Retrieved image. Courtesy Gimpel Fils.

with the four large paintings in tempera and oil which Williams had grouped under the title *Four Dimensions of Anguish*. This series included *Hysteria*, *Securities*, *Human World* and *The Subway World* which Lewis refers to as "symbolic moralities". Other works – *Origins* and *Burden or Release* – were both large oils painted at the same time which were exhibited with *The Mystic Marriage* as well as a body of supporting studies and drawings. The evidence of the surviving works; the evidence of the exhibition catalogue containing the unequivocal titles of the paintings – these, together with the contemporary statements and reviews, confirm a view of Williams' inner nature as an outsider, an observer. A door had opened – he was inside, but not an insider.

The themes of his work now emphasised the universality of his experience. In these paintings there is a dramatic, all-embracing metropolitan reality in the visibility, plurality, hybridity and levelling on the streets of London. He was employing techniques and synthesising his responses through his own very particular and individual cultural lens. His subject matter was original and contemporary to the wider reality of his own experience; his style distinctive. He occupied and commanded a unique space. As Henry Moore remarked of this exhibition: "He has power, and he has ambition."[46]

Lewis' review of these paintings – contained in the penultimate article he was ever to contribute to *The Listener* – begins: "I do not wish to be guilty of what is called overpraising [...] but I consider Dennis Williams a young man of very remarkable talent" and ends: "No one interested in what is being done in London today should fail to see them [the paintings]."[47]

Human World (1950) was met with particular acclaim. Any present-day assessment of this painting needs to take into account the sources of its imagery and the specific context of the austere environment and rapidly changing social climate of late 1940s London, where it was painted. As we have seen, World War II was a raw feature of the collective consciousness and the European art world experienced all the tensions of the New Age. Many artists were beginning to pick up on the directions abstract art had indicated before the war. Many had begun using the figure in new ways to express their experience of war, distress and alienation. Received concepts and old values were challenged amongst which were the niceties of "beauty" and "good taste". Some responded with more expressive approaches, some used the figure more symbolically and the interaction between abstraction and realism was typical of the era. There was a shifting political emphasis in the use of the term "realism" in art. In the Western tradition, realism had resonances in both conventional, conservative subject matter and in radical utilitarian socialism. Now it took on new

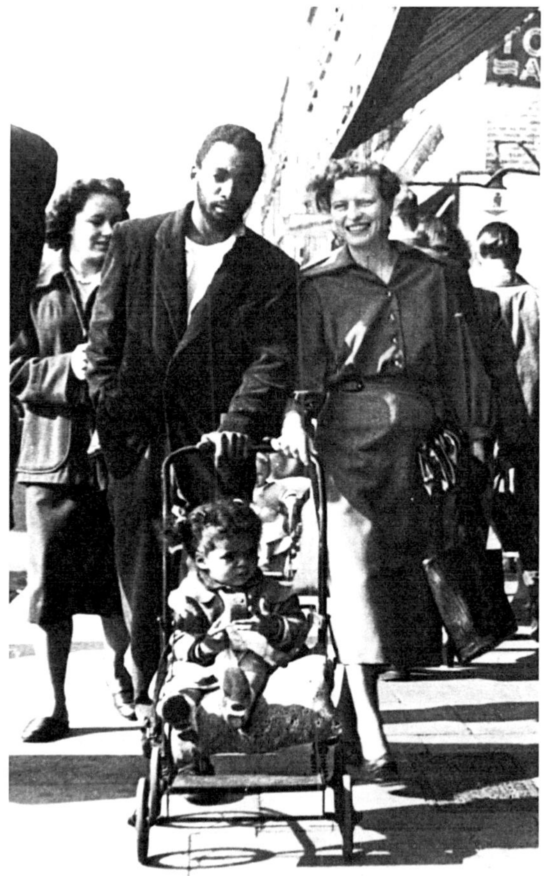

Street photograph with Katie Alice, London.

meanings. There was a new "real" to be explored, often through such themes as angst and alienation, and the landmark social changes of upheaval and migration. Lewis noted that Williams frequently used the word "anxiety" in conversation.

From our current shockproof viewpoint it requires a significant mental shift to appreciate fully the visual and sensory power the images in a painting could have had. The context of the time in which *Human World* was created is necessary for a full understanding of its content and meaning, and also its continuing relevance. It identifies a visual metaphor of West Indian migration. But the symbolism can also be seen as a portent of migration as an issue never specific either to Britain or the West Indies. The metropolitan vision suggested in the painting relates to economic, social and political demographics of migration through the widening evidence of miscegenation. From America came a new era in approaches to race. Following World War II we see the disintegration of segregation; and in 1948 the statute forbidding miscegenation was held to be unconstitutional. These changes were expressed in a wave of liberal assimilationist sentiments. These remain significant global issues.

The angst of the alienated spirit in the diaspora is not the sole preserve of a legacy of colonialism. It is worth remembering that not every immigrant in the Britain of the 1940s and 1950s was an economic migrant. Not every black face was Windrush. People like Williams and his West Indian cohort regarded themselves as an intellectual élite. Street-level British race politics was not their agenda. They were debating independence, not planning to remain in the UK.

The street photograph is clearly significant to the final composition where we can see that the figures and background relate to those of the photograph. The experimental use of photographs as a source in art has a lineage that goes back to the era of the Impressionists. Picasso had frequently worked directly from photographs, as did Francis Bacon. We may argue that the prior organisation of mass and scale of the photograph allows the artist a method of rapid vigorous working leading to the seemingly unstudied, spontaneous effects achieved in *Human World*. The figure on the right-hand side, with curled gold and ginger hair, wearing a stylish outfit of the day, is Katie Alice with her daughter in the pushchair. The central portrait was originally that of the artist himself and this figure is therefore ambiguous. It retains its likeness to the artist in terms of height, colouring, shape of head, and the treatment of the brow, but the artist has in fact painted himself out of the composition and his reason for doing so remains a curious enigma in the context of identity. Perhaps he was signalling that he did not wish to be pigeonholed or patronised as "a Negro artist", and that he may have wanted to explore alternatives to the prevailing discourses.

What the artist captures in his painting is the electric street atmosphere that literally was the "human world" in these post-war years of displacement. There is a positive aura in the movement and vibrant mingling of worlds. The atmosphere surrounding the figures is one of optimism, momentum and life. The composition of the main figures creates an insistent, monumental presence in the foreground. The supporting hosts of spectral figures are folded in fabric, emphasising their forms and their movement, their faces capturing an eternal moment. They occupy the middle ground, evoking a hypnotic, subliminal response – an arresting portent of the future.

The figure composition is set in an elevated metropolitan backdrop made up of composite aspects of the Thames Embankment: a tower, warehouses and a wharf. Williams' first impressions of the metropolitan environment must have been of the huge scale of its backdrop: the high density of buildings; the tall threatening chimneys on rooftops, houses and factories, belching out smoke and filth beneath a low-hanging fog. British writing of the nineteeth century had compared the overwhelming aspect of the industrial landscape of London to that of a jungle. But it is summer and the skyline is detailed against patches of high blue sky. The development of a simplified background defines the space in relation to the mass of moving figures. This great surge of humanity suffuses the man-made environment with its life.

The artist has exaggerated the muscularity of form to increase the dramatic reality. Broad brush strokes balance the weight and force of the mass. The colours are tertiary greens and browns in muted tonal values, giving an overall cohesion to the figures and buildings. The high modelling is worked with yellow ochre light, picking out the forms in a pattern that unifies all elements. Throughout, flicks of zinc white create textural scumbling that highlights the movement of the mass. Accents of colour keep the eyes moving and focusing on the images from foreground to far distance. The energy and assurance of application contribute to the overall liveliness of the work. Brush marks, rapid strokes and textural paint effects create a dynamic surface quality. Typically it relies on Williams' consummate draughtsmanship and innate tonal command. As Lewis remarked: "Dennis Williams is a very fine draughtsman, as, being a figure-painter, he is bound to be. People do not become figure-painters if their draughtsmanship is defective."[48] Bold and original, it is an imaginative visual statement that acknowledges the broad colonial context of the time but seeks to define that experience at the universal level of the title.

Williams recalled that at the outbreak of the Korean War in 1950 he had narrowly escaped being called up by Britain and this brought him face to face with the impending existential

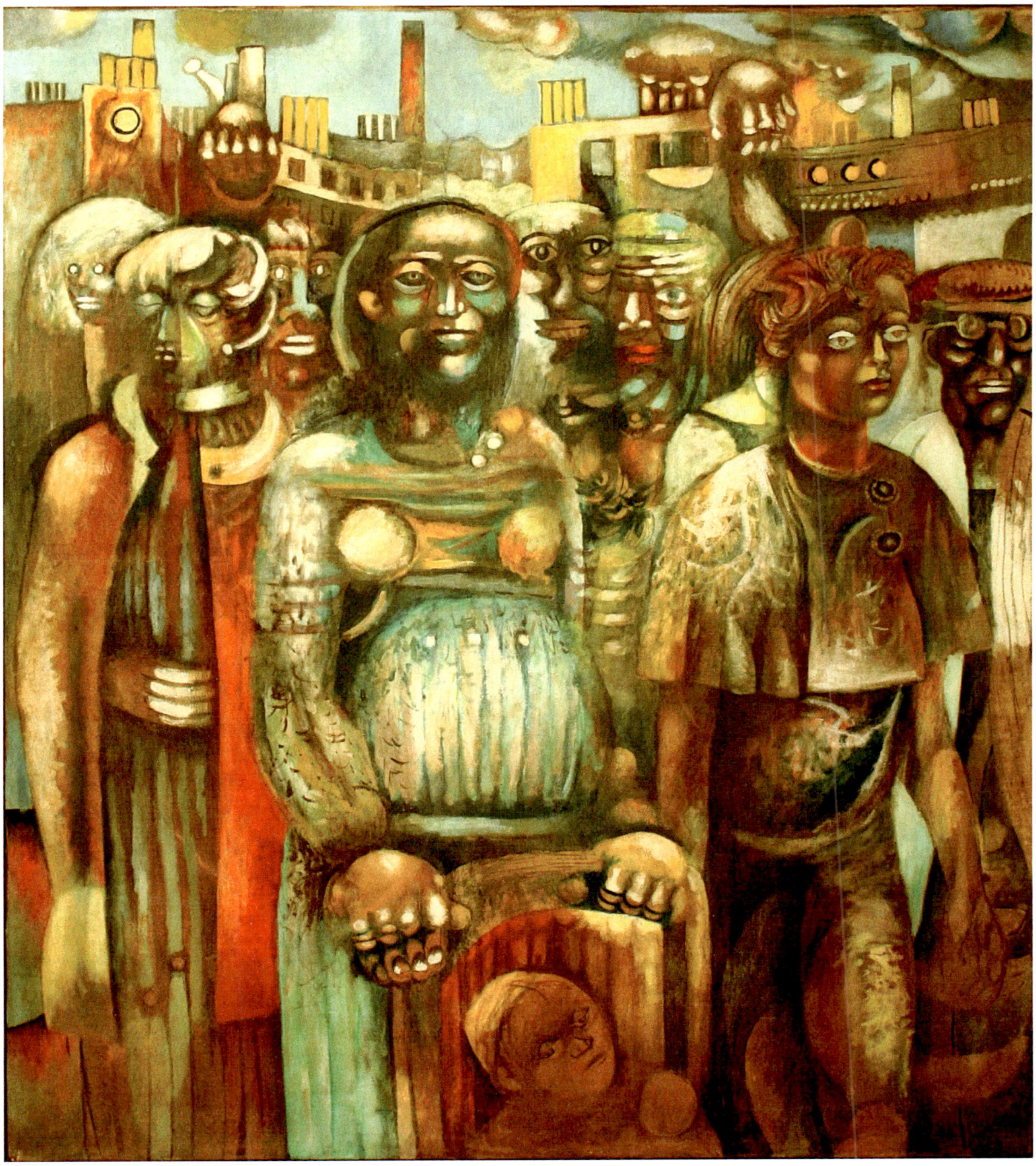

Human World (1950). Tempera and oil on canvas 152×132 cms. National Collection.
Photograph by Ohene Koama.

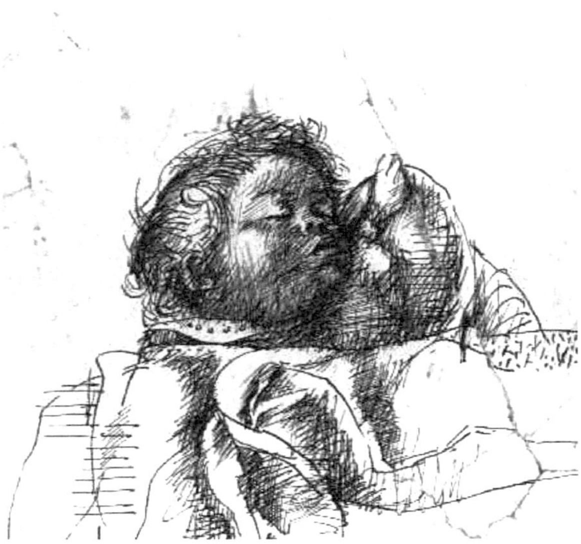

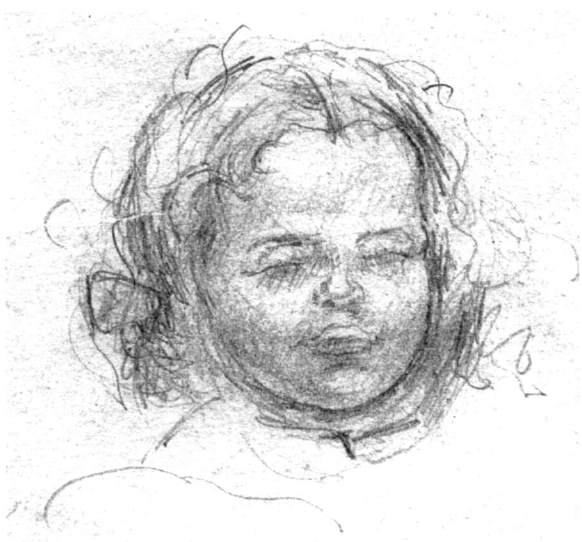

Family sketches, early 1950s.

angst. Reading between the lines of the review of the exhibition, Lewis seems to suggest that a theoretical complication existed whereby Williams' wearying anxiety became conflated with his social symbolism and metaphysical theory.

Williams recollected:

> I used to go and stand at this time in the morning on the pavement to look at all this mass of people in this panorama of threat. That's what that was about. You know, the sense of something impending which was what he [Sartre] picked up in existentialism: this "nausea". Well, that was very much with me in those early days of forming myself in an alien culture. And pictures like this [*Human World*] resulted.[49]

Wyndham Lewis considered Williams to be greatly influenced by Jean-Paul Sartre who was involved in several revolutionary intellectual movements in France in the 1940s and 1950s including *La Négritude*. In 1948 Sartre wrote an introductory essay for an anthology of poetry compiled by Léopold Sédar Senghor, the first president of Senegal. It was an analysis of his thoughts on black culture to which he gave the title *Black Orpheus*. Many black migrants in the London of the late 1940s identified with the ideas and expressions of Pan-Africanism[50] that had developed from the socio-political concern surrounding the stark fact of black people occupying the bottom echelons of every society in which they found themselves. People sought solidarity in the notion of "African brotherhood" and of an "African personality". Such ideas contributed to discussions of race, identity, and aspiration for wholesale societal change. Among the West Indian migrants there was much excitement about the prospect of independence and the possibilities of a West Indian Federation. Williams' generation was all but forced into the politics of identity.

Like his West Indian cohort Williams would have been exposed to the Africa of his origins largely through the imprints of a European consciousness. It was a devalued heritage. However Williams became a regular visitor at the British Museum where he was able to seek out the art of Africa. In London, many of the prevailing discourses on race were focusing on an intense reappraisal of Africa and we see the emergence of radically revised views and approaches by Europe towards African history and a new recognition of the plurality of its cultures.

Williams' work explored the possibilities of subject matter that addressed race issues in a universal context but which did not pursue a protest-conflict. This had not been a formative part of his own West Indian experience:

> Mr Williams has chosen to live in Britain and to do his work here. As an artist he sees himself as set four-square in the traditions of western culture; and yet he carries other strains within himself. It is his belief that he has a duty to bridge the different societies to which he belongs, the West Indies on the one hand, Britain on the other: a duty, moreover, not to preach nationalism, not to break away or cut asunder, but rather to reconcile those societies to each other.[51]

While his subject matter includes references to the racial past, it is framed in a context that attempts to strike out in a contemporary and inclusive direction as the titles of his paintings suggest. He portrays his black people as ordinary human beings rather than protagonists in a racial struggle.

In those days, part of the critical acclaim of Williams' work was no doubt due to the novelty of his colonial status. Critical reaction to his "alien", "exotic" or "foreign" presence in the art scene was ambiguous and sometimes inept. In a *Time* magazine article, Williams was further characterised using the following words in sequence: "Negro", "threatening", "jungle", "loin-cloth", "primitive" and "savagery". Even for its era the article had patronising overtones.[52] But it is also the case that the unfamiliar in his work – its powerful, heavy-limbed aesthetic; its stark, dominating frontality and confident ownership of the gaze – was eagerly celebrated in contemporary London.[53] News of Williams' success quickly reached Georgetown. An article in the *British Guiana Chronicle* reports:

> The titles of these thought-provoking pictures – *Origins*, *The Shock of Eternities*, *Human World* – have a literary flavour, and Williams combines his wonderful power of expression with a philosophical turn of mind. [...] It is probably too much to expect that the municipality of Georgetown would wish to purchase any of Denis Williams' latest pictures, since he is only a Guianese, and the saying " a prophet is not without honour etc." is only too true of British Guiana; but if any private collectors are anxious to obtain examples of his work, now would be the time to do so, as prices of subsequent pictures will be very much higher due to the brilliant success he has now achieved.[54]

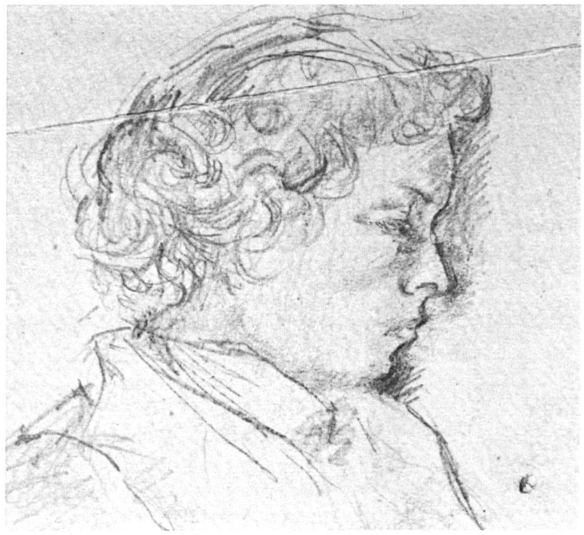

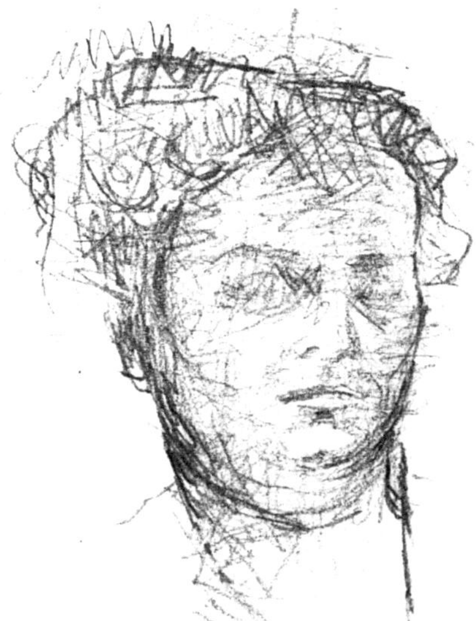

Katie Alice (early 1950s).

Such newspaper articles may well have prompted local organisations in British Guiana to purchase *Human World*. Wilson Harris writes: "When I returned to Guyana I launched a programme designed to purchase *Human World*. This was achieved eventually."[55] Dr Frank Williams set up a fund to buy the painting through public subscription and it was stored in the Guiana Museum as part of the national collection. Its arrival in 1956 was most significant; its size and metropolitan status raised immediate questions.

> In the first place it introduced the problem of State patronage in the visual arts, an issue that was unlikely to have arisen spontaneously in a colonial context, while the question was to arise later of professional curation of a growing national collection.[56]

There was great excitement and an enthusiastic desire to claim the work for British Guiana, though there was also some puzzlement – the content seemed familiar, but it was not BG. There is certainly a striking irony in the fact that his art was not appreciated or accepted in British Guiana until it had been "validated" in London.

It is clear that the British art establishment displayed paternalism towards its "exotic" artists. It was Wyndham Lewis who had categorised Williams as "A Negro Artist". Williams was contemptuous of two incidents that made him particularly conscious of the difference between his image of himself and the way others saw him:

> Once, whilst looking at the artists of the Louis XV court, this pukkah fellow said to me, "What is

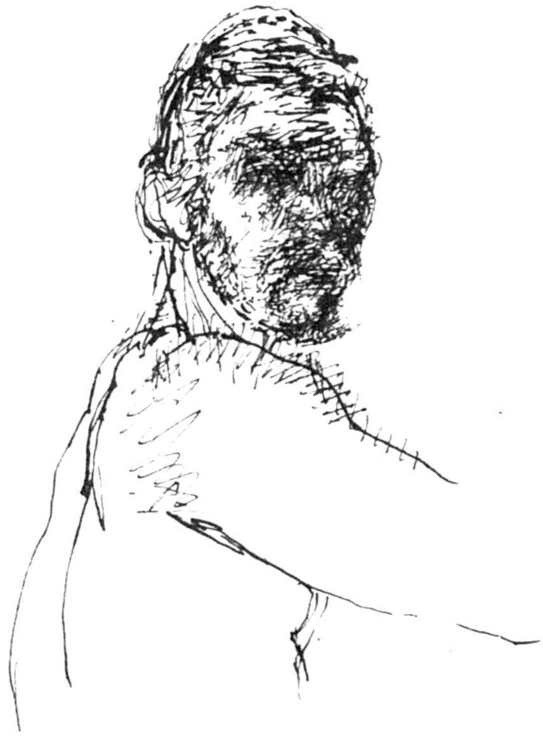

Self-portrait sketches (1952). Pen and ink. 29×23 cms. Collection E. Williams.

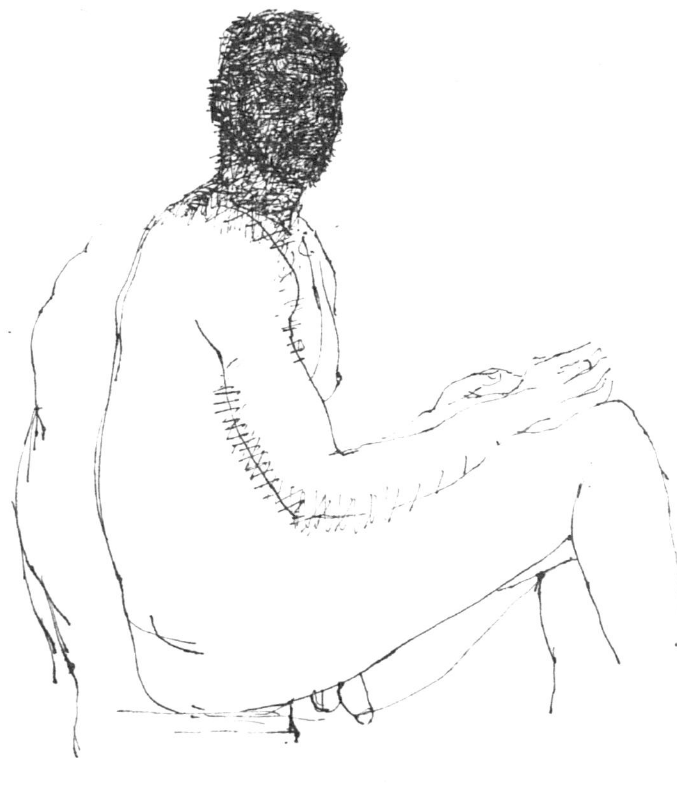

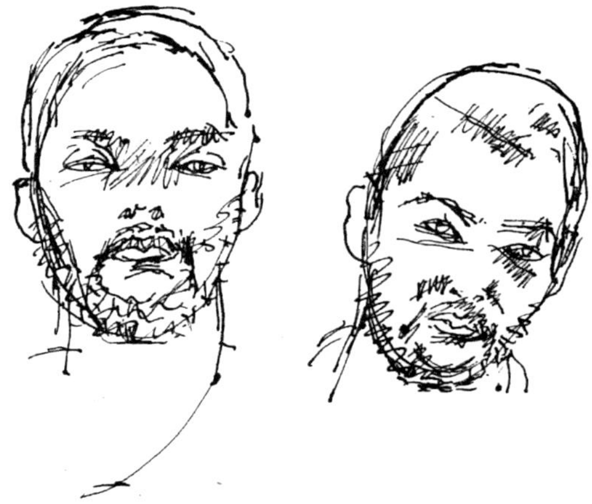

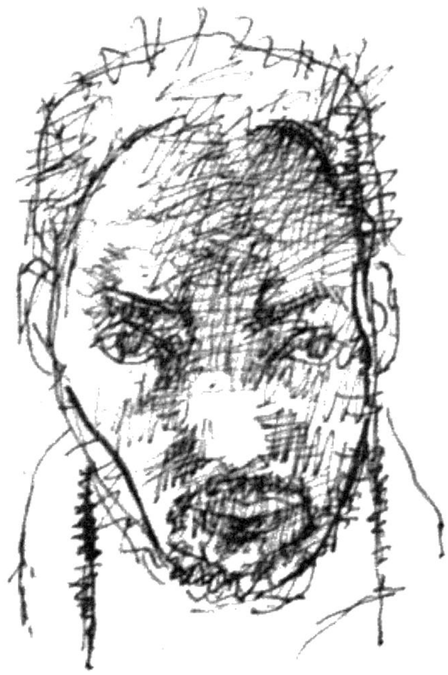

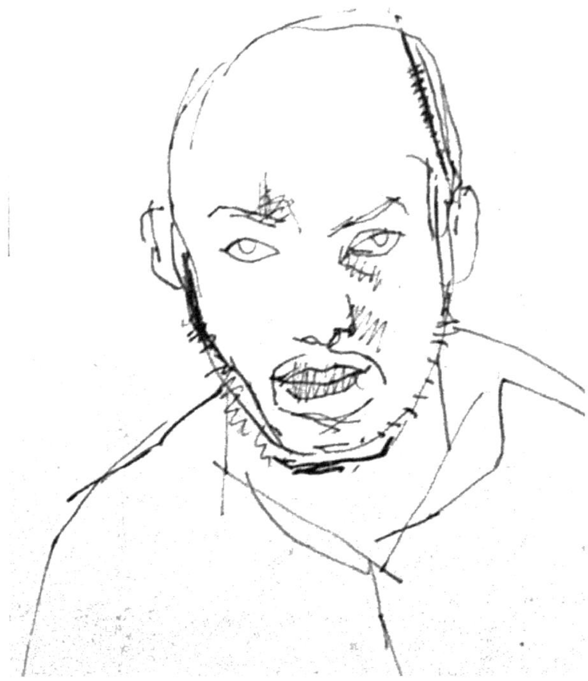

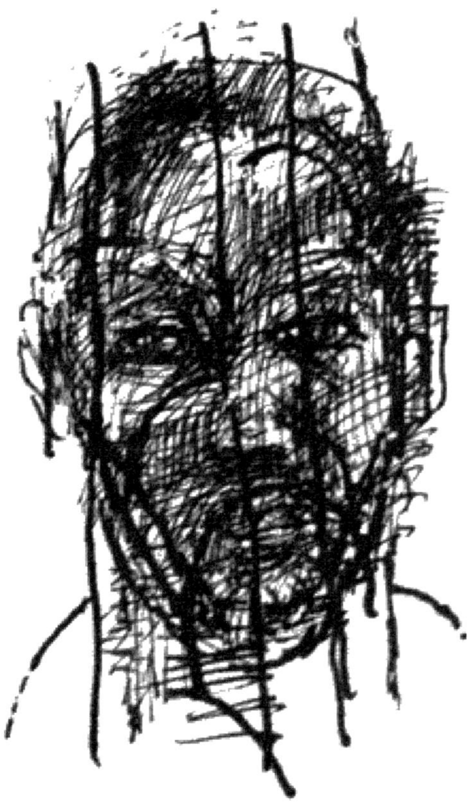

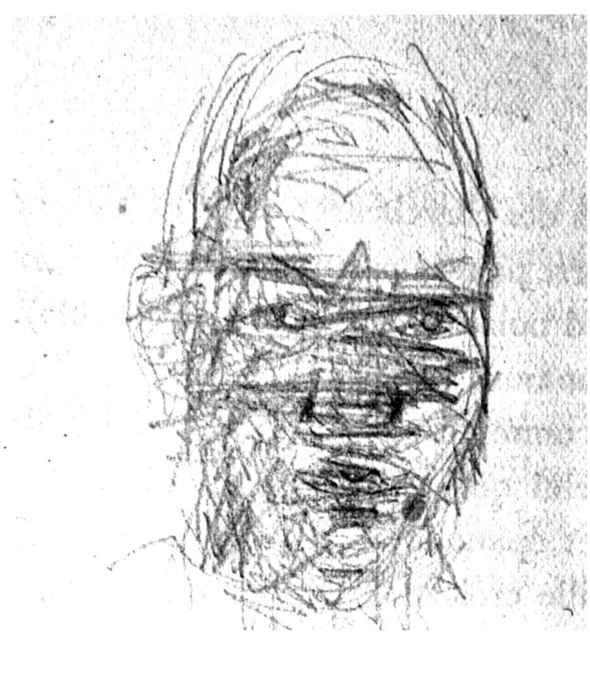

Self-portrait sketches (1952).

> this to you? What does Fragonard mean to you? What does Watteau mean to you?" I gave him the academic answer. [...] But in my own evolution this was a watershed. It helped me to see myself and my place in this society as I was seen by him, not as I saw myself, in this élite gentlemen's club. An impromptu party at Francis Bacon's place hammered this home. It was a group of Royal College of Art types, they used to be drunk at lunchtime, men kissing each other, raucous behaviour [...] One guy, John Davenport, art critic of the *Observer* said, "this must make you feel very uncomfortable." He was suggesting the same thing.[57]

Paternalism and exoticism aside, there was also a prevailing enthusiasm for original and compelling art that placed itself at the margins of official culture, like that labelled "Art Brut". After several years in London Williams had experienced prolonged personal exposure to labelling. He had witnessed the fondness for the "modern primitive" in the arts that came close to cultism. He had also recognised the limitations assumed in the explicit label "social realism". There were dangers in a constraining political or social agenda that defined and narrowed subject matter within a particular context of time – it could be too readily misappropriated. He was aware of becoming caught up with the expectations implied in labelling and his response to this success was ultimately negative. He later wrote:

> Paradoxically, however, as Fanon has so perceptively shown, given the circumstances of the day, acceptance on this level was in fact far the most unacceptable, indeed probably the most humiliating of choices open to the Colonial artist.[58]

Although western influences had inevitably left their mark it would be wrong to deny Williams' innate talent, his sensitive awareness of his heritage and his own originality as an artist. He understood the powerful influence of non-European art in the early twentieth century: "He [the European painter] absorbed the influence of the Japanese print. Then he discovered the primitive African Negro, pre-Colombian, Oceanic sculpture; the art of Siberia, cave paintings. These influences were profound, infused European art with red blood."[59]

Whatever his own agenda in his ready promotion of his *protégé*, Wyndham Lewis was certainly instrumental in Williams' progress. At the Central, Williams worked alongside Alan Davie, William Turnbull, Keith Vaughan and Victor Pasmore. Roger Hilton became an associate. Now regarded as something of a *bête noire* of British abstract art, from Williams' perspective he appeared to be a model of a British middle-class artist; he gave introductions to Patrick Heron and Lucian Freud.

In an article in *Apollo*, one critic, writing of Williams' painting *Hysteria*, describes it as being a large canvas loaned to a contemporary exhibition at the new premises of the ICA (Institute of Contemporary Arts)[60] where coincidentally it was hung next to one of Victor Pasmore's earliest abstract works. Of Denis Williams and his work the article states:

> Twenty-six, a Negro who has lived in British Guiana, Williams is now in London. His work is virile, horrific. He can depict humanity surging forward glaring through spectacles and surrounded by urban architecture, so that the jungle comes to our nostrils. *The Asphalt Jungle* might be the title of most of his work. It is at present not completely organised and is therefore rather incoherent. It is grotesquely ugly and bitterly satirical. But it has power and promise. It links in spirit with that of Edward Burra, though it is entirely different.[61]

Wyndham Lewis had written of *Hysteria*:

> The main figures are a pregnant woman, a hysterical man, and a newspaper seller. The man convulsed by hysteria is mankind today. The role of the newspaper seller is to be an intermediary; it is through this shouting man that all the violent news from everywhere reaches us, the news responsible for our condition. The pregnant woman stands for man's hope. The future lies in her belly: a millennial hope of a future when men will no longer exploit, torture, and kill one another. For Williams is, among other things, a millennial politician.[62]

Denis Williams was now living at 21 Oxford Road in London's Kilburn with Katie Alice and his young family. Something of the atmosphere of the period is captured in this recollection by his daughter Janice:

> I don't know if the building is still standing but the atmosphere generated in our small flat on the first floor was electric. It became a meeting place for new artists of every persuasion: painters, potters, poets, writers, sculptors, theatricals, post-war "New Order" café society, right there in our home.
>
> Dad was an extremely charismatic man, you felt his energy the minute he walked into a room. The vibrancy of his presence ensured that he

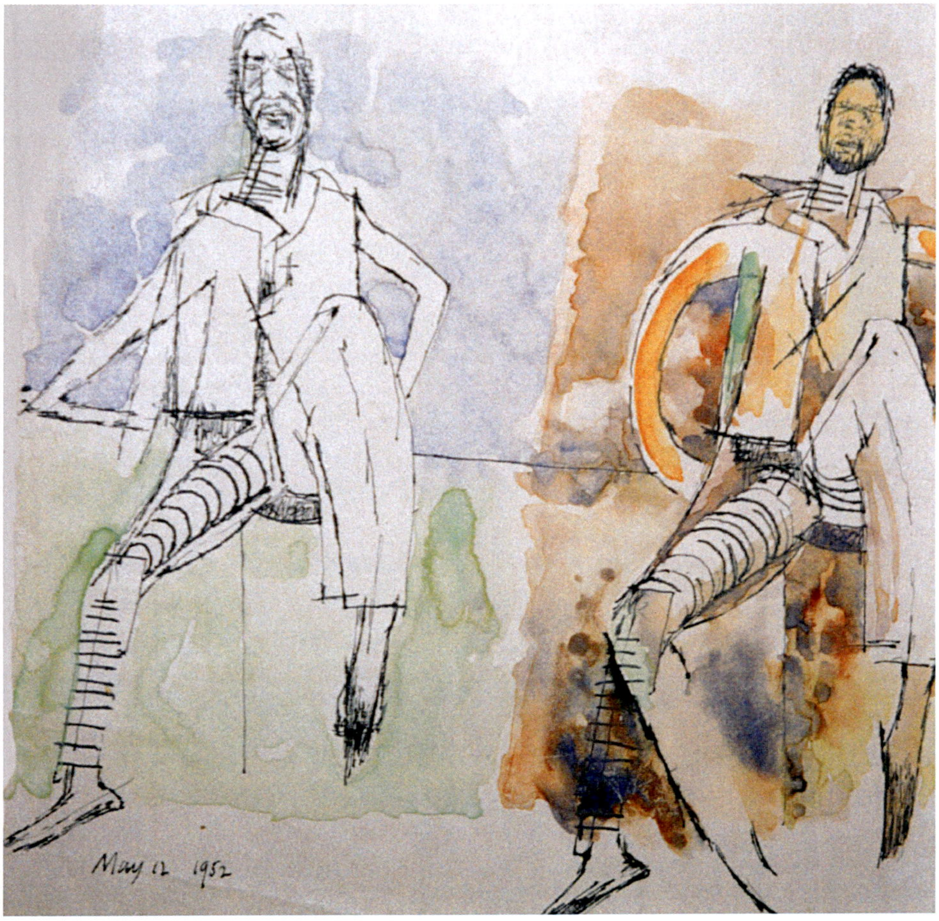

Figure sketches (1952). Pen, ink, watercolour. 20×20 cms. Williams estate.

always attracted a following of creative people. He encouraged and enthused them; debated, and shared ideas. Patrick Heron, John Watson, Alan Davie, Wilson Harris, Jan Carew, John Holness, Tommy Baptiste, David de Bethel, Keith Vaughan, Roger Hilton – these are some of the characters I remember having met as a child. The cultural environment experienced by us as Denis' and Catherine's family at the time had far-reaching results. We are now all artists in our own way and feel privileged to have been at the centre of these unique times.

Debates about trends in the early fifties went on until the early hours; even as a child I could sense the buzz in the room, long after I had been sent to bed. I would be allowed to stay up if it was not too late and be fascinated by the spirited atmosphere. It felt exciting; they were excited. The war was over and liberation was in the air. Refugees, rebels, reactionaries, revolutionaries: they all wanted to express their freedom. Times were changing. The confines and rigours of the traditionalists were giving way to creativity. The militaristic shadow of the Nazi years along with its regimes and discipline had folded.

Out of death, destruction and pent-up frustration came new ideas, a new order; rejuvenation and renovation were necessary. Dad was involved in developing a new approach, a different painter's perception, seeing subject-matter in terms of shapes, colours and synthetic lines but within a disciplined form: freedom but with foundation. Abstract art provided an opportunity for different perceptions other than figurative realism.

Denis shared a studio with Francis Bacon. From my earliest memories it appeared to be in a derelict building, bombed during the war, a wrecked shop front on the ground floor served as an entrance. Upstairs Denis had a room on one side of the landing, Francis on the other. Art materials and canvases were interchanged across the hall. A ray of light from a small window breached the dilapidated interior of Denis' work space whilst Francis had metamorphosed his into a cavernous enclosure, blacked out and ominous. I can feel it now, being overwhelmed with the smell of turpentine and a dark foreboding. Denis was appreciative of canvases discarded by Francis, and would reverse them thus creating a clean serviceable area on which to paint. Francis didn't have much patience with disappointing or unsatisfactory work. It would be quickly scrapped, a luxury most struggling artists could ill afford.

It's like theatre in my head; the imagery and drama of such visits have remained with me forever. A highly charged tense atmosphere pervaded the studio emanating from both Francis and the décor. As a young child it was overpowering, seated on a rumple of bedding on the floor watching him paint on a large canvas hanging on the wall. He turned to check on me every now and then. "Don't move and don't talk to me," he pronounced. Clutching my crayons and paper I was dumbstruck. "Draw!" he yelled. I gazed up at his face and black-attired body. He was always in a black shirt, black trousers and sandaled feet. At any given moment he could start shouting and swearing at himself if things weren't going well on the canvas. He was bold, intimidating and impatient; a big personality with big paintings. My memory tells me Francis had inherited family money from Anglo-Irish landed gentry connections. He didn't visit our home more than a few times but I remember he was very fond of Catherine my mother. He gave her some beautiful cut glass dessert dishes, part of his inheritance which I now treasure, passed on to me in memory of the times Francis babysat me.

They were all big personalities who visited 21 Oxford Road. Alan Davie was a colourful character, etched in my memory partly due to his brightly coloured clothes and partly the sparkly jewels he'd bring me to "ooh and ah" over. He would call me over and sit me on his knee and open a Bryant and May matchbox full of gems. A tiny Aladdin's cave. A jeweller by trade before becoming a painter, as far as my memory tells me. He was a great storyteller too, and as a child I looked forward to his visits.

Either Roger Hilton or William Turnbull would bring us Swiss chocolate. It was a "yummy" treat, when food was still being rationed. They used to dress in black too. I can see Roger now, dark hair parted on one side; bespectacled with a wide forehead, always in ardent discussion. An intellectual, I now know.

Against the backdrop of post-war frugality the richness of ideas generated in our small sitting room gave me the sense that this was the hub of the universe. They were multicultural gatherings – of European refugees, "Nicky" from Hungary, homeless Barry who sometimes slept on our floor and compatriots from the West Indies. It was the world in our kitchen! Mother with her Celtic heritage of Welsh language, poetry and song contributed to the atmosphere: beautiful and feisty, her metaphysical mind was inspiring.

We danced too. The West Indian "boys" brought records of much loved calypso music played to quell longings for "home". I remember a character from Trinidad – "Prince Gordon" we called him because he could tell the most exciting bedtime stories about princesses and their princes: we loved him. There was Tommy Baptiste training to be an opera singer who would perform. It was wonderful to hear Jan Carew, Wilson Harris and George Lamming earnestly arguing their differences.

The cultural exchange was dynamic, a reflection of who Denis was.[63]

From this period there are numerous spontaneous drawings of family and friends. There is a drawing of George Lamming, on which he notes:

> My mind must have recorded more than the pencil could put down. For I did this very easily in an elegant ink line to submit to Michael Joseph. This is a tracing paper copy for you. I hope Nina will be a bit more pleased. Denis.

Wilson Harris spent some time staying with Williams at 21 Oxford Road, and George Lamming and Cy Grant were among frequent visitors. It was Harris who observed:

> When I met him again in England in 1954 I was inclined to criticise him rather too bitterly for renouncing the invaluable experiments that I thought still possible in the *Human World* theme. But for Denis Williams, art was not a branch of politics.[64]

So what was Denis Williams renouncing? By 1952 he was already seeking to purge himself stylistically; perhaps he was already subconsciously challenging Sartre's celebration of racial essentialism. He felt under great pressure to commit to themes in his work that embodied the epic, unending struggle at the periphery. He felt the pressure to meet certain expectations of subject matter which would have effectively marginalised him to being a "Negro artist". He later recalled: "Because I was the first black teacher, I had very special clothes made and all that kind of presentation business. And after a while, I realised that really I'm working myself into a straight jacket. The image of myself."[65] He had reached a turning point where his impulse was to attempt to transcend any parochial characterisation of the "Negro experience", and instead to engage with contemporary aesthetics and embark on the restless course of experiment.

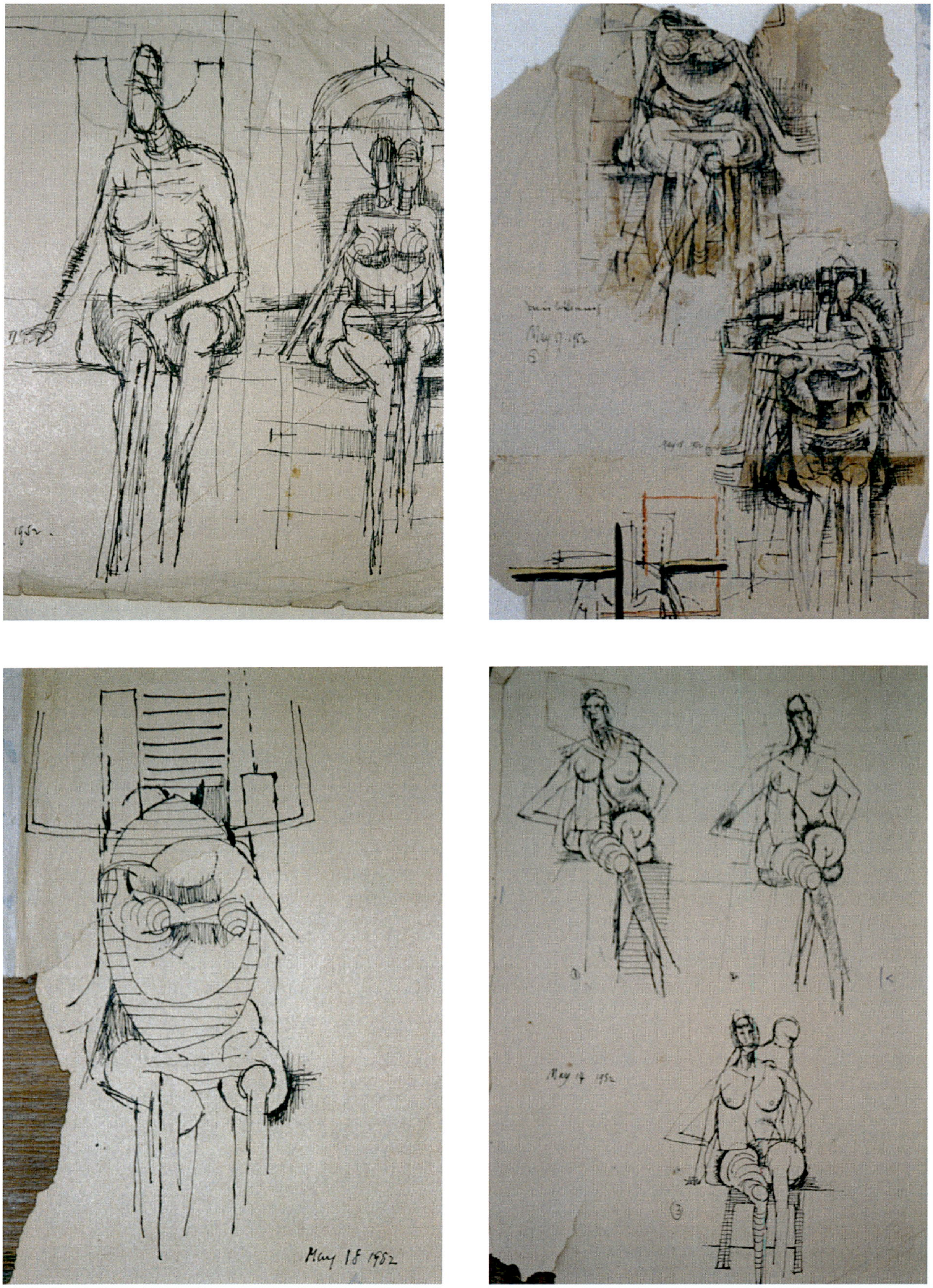

Figure studies (1952). Pen and ink, watercolour. Williams estate.

NOTES TO CHAPTER 2

1 Quoted in Mike and Trevor Phillips, *Windrush: The Irresistible Rise of Multi-racial Britain* (London: HarperCollins, 1998), pp. 12–13.
2 Andrew Salkey, *Georgetown Journal: A Caribbean Writer's Journey from London via Port of Spain to Georgetown, Guyana*, 1970 (Trinidad, Port of Spain: New Beacon Books, 1972), p. 124.
3 Kenneth Romney-Towndrow, "Kofi Antubam and Denis Williams at the Berkeley Galleries", in *Venture: Journal of the Fabian Colonial Bureau* (Vol. 1, No. 7, August 1949), p. 11.
4 Wyndham Lewis (1882–1957). "In 1946 Lewis became art critic for *The Listener*, under the inspired regime of Joe Ackerley. He held that influential post, which reinforced his authority and reputation as a theorist and painter, for the next five years and wrote nearly fifty reviews." [Jeffrey Meyers, *The Enemy: A Biography of Wyndham Lewis* (London: Routledge & Kegan Paul, 1980), p. 291].
5 Wyndham Lewis, "The London Galleries", in *The Listener* (British Broadcasting Corporation, 14 July 1949), p. 68.
6 *Journal of the Royal African Society* (Vol. 48, No. 193, October 1949).
7 Paul O'Keeffe, *Some Sort of Genius: A Life of Wyndham Lewis* (UK: Pimlico, 2003), p. 547.
8 Lewis, Wyndham. "On Canada", in George Woodcock (ed.), *Wyndham Lewis in Canada*, (Vancouver: University of British Columbia, 1971), p. 28.
9 *Op. cit.*, p. 27.
10 David Trotter has observed: "He [Lewis] was capable of spontaneous acts of generosity, such as the unstinting support he offered Denis Williams, a 26-year-old Guyanese painter, in 1949–1950. [...] He wrote admiringly about Williams's work and found him a job at the Central School of Arts and Crafts in Southampton Row." ["A most modern misanthrope: Wyndham Lewis and the pursuit of anti-pathos", in *London Review of Books* (January 2001)].
11 W. K. Rose (ed.), *The Letters of Wyndham Lewis* (London: Methuen & Co. Ltd., 1963), p. 500 [Letter of 10July 1949]. A copy was also sent to James Thrall Soby, a private collector of contemporary art and a Trustee of the Museum of Modern Art.
12 *Op.cit.*, pp. 500–501.
13 Paul O'Keeffe, *Some Sort of Genius*, p. 547.
14 Letter to Wyndham Lewis dated 9 August 1949, written from 19–19 Durban and Haley Street Georgetown. Courtesy Cornell University Library.
15 Michael Swan, *British Guiana: The Land of Six Peoples*, pp. 121–122.
16 Paul O'Keeffe, *Some Sort of Genius*, pp. 547–548.
17 Williams returned to his old job as a clerk in the accounts department of the Georgetown Post Office..
18 Letter to Wyndham Lewis from Georgetown dated September 1949. Courtesy Cornell University Library.
19 "Guiana Today", in *Kyk-over-al* (Vol. 2, No. 9, December 1949), pp. 9–10. [Twice reprinted: see Bibliography].
20 *Ibid.*
21 Designers David and Joan de Bethel were both supportive friends. David was best man at the wedding of Denis Williams and Katie Alice.
22 Letter to Wyndham Lewis from Georgetown dated 19 August 1949. Courtesy Cornell University Library.
23 Denis Williams, "1763, Carl Blackman and all that..." in *Kaie* (No. 14, July 1976), pp. 52–55: p. 52.
24 Edward Kamau Brathwaite, "Caribbean Man in Space and Time", (1974) in John Hearne (ed.), *Carifesta Forum: An Anthology of 20 Caribbean Voices* (Jamaica: Institute of Jamaica, 1976), pp. 199–208: p. 204.
25 Wilson Harris, "Review", in *Kyk-over-al* (Vol. 2, No. 9, December 1949), p. 32.
26 Wilson Harris, "Two Periods in the Work of a West Indian Artist", in *Kyk-over-al* (Vol. 6, No. 20, 1955).
27 Michael Swan, *British Guiana: The Land of Six Peoples*, p. 130.
28 "1763, Carl Blackman and all that...", p. 52.
29 *Barbados Advocate*, 16 August 1953. Ms Escoffery (1923–2002), Jamaica-born artist and poet, was an exact contemporary of Williams, and had studied at the Slade while he was a tutor there.
30 A. J. Seymour, *Art in Guyana* (Georgetown: National History and Arts Council, 1971).
31 Wilson Harris, "Review".
32 He may well have been referring to the recent discovery of rock-painting near Imbaimadai.
33 In *Kyk-over-al* (Vol. 2, No. 8, June 1949), pp. 18–19.
34 Philip Vieira, "Adventure in Art", in *Kyk-over-al* (Vol. 3, No. 12, 1951), p. 166.
35 *Ibid.*
36 George Lamming, *The Pleasures of Exile* (1960) quoted in Kenneth Ramchand, *The West Indian Novel and its Background* (London: Faber & Faber, 1970), p. 40.
37 Frank Dobson was elected to the Royal Academy in 1953. His sculpture, *London Pride*, was a major feature at the Festival of Britain and was subsequently bequeathed to the nation.
38 File CO 111\818\8. The same Mr Costello's name appears as purchaser of Williams' *Plantation No.1* (1949) from the Gimpel Fils exhibition of 1950.
39 Errol R. Brewster, "'A Given Dream' – Dr Denis Williams CCH in his own words". Transcript of a series of interviews, dated 14 July 1998. It formed the basis of a video documentary.
40 Basil Hinds, "Retrospect of Art in the Sixties", in *Kaie* (No. 6, December 1970).
41 Wilson Harris, "Two Periods in the Work of a West Indian Artist", pp. 183–187. "The paintings that survived included *Burden or Release*, *Mystic Marriage*, *Umbrellas*, *Securities*, and of course the greatest of them all in that period – *Human World*. Some of these paintings hang today in national and private collections in Europe."
42 These might include Edgar Mittelholzer, Wilson Harris, Denis Williams, Jan Carew and Aubrey Williams.
43 Charlotte Williams, interview with Denis Williams (1998).

44 Paul O'Keeffe, *Some Sort of Genius*, p. 566.
45 W. K. Rose (ed.), *The Letters of Wyndham Lewis*, pp. 527–528 [Letter of 17 November 1950].
46 Quoted by Wyndham Lewis in the exhibition notes (1950).
47 "A Negro Artist", in *The Listener* (British Broadcasting Corporation, 7 December 1950), p. 696.
48 *Ibid.*
49 Anne Walmsley, transcript of interview with Denis Williams (1993), p. 12.
50 The last Pan-African Congress was held in Manchester in 1945.
51 "Colonials in Britain: West Indians as University Teachers", in *The Times British Colonies Review* (Spring 1955), p. 45.
52 Anonymous, "Newcomer from Guiana", in *Time* magazine (18 December 1950), p. 46.
53 The sales record in the Gimpel Fils archive shows that *Human World*, *Burden or Release* and *Hysteria* were initially reserved by the Tate Gallery but subsequently not purchased due to lack of funds. *Plantation No. 3*, oil, was bought by Fernandes. *The Mystic Marriage*, gouache, was reserved by Board of Fernandes. *Study*, pastel, was bought by Dodgson of Edith Grove, SW10. *Study of a hand* was bought by J. P. Cooper of All Souls' College, Oxford.
54 "Denis Williams of B.G. Styled 'Artist of Genius'", in *British Guiana Chronicle* (7 January 1951). Also mentioned in the article is *The Subway World* in tempera, purchased by Mrs Hewer for Vine House, Henbury, Bristol.
55 Personal communication from Wilson Harris (January 2010).
56 Denis Williams, text of the catalogue for *Castellani House – The Inaugural Exhibition of the National Collection* (Georgetown: Department of Culture, April 1993). Williams notes: "In the matter of the world's art, the collection includes *The Fall of Troy*, attributed to the great British Romantic painter J. M. W. Turner and *Grantley Hall, Yorkshire* by his countryman, Professor Carel Weight of the Royal College of Art."
57 Charlotte Williams (1998).
58 Frances C. Locher (ed.), "Williams, Denis Joseph Ivan", in *Contemporary Authors, A Biobibliographical Guide to Current Writers in Fiction, General Nonfiction, Poetry, Journalism, Drama, Motion Pictures, Television, and Other Fields* (Detroit, Michigan: Gale Research Company, 1980). Vols 93–96: p. 557.
59 Denis Williams, "Guiana Today".
60 The ICA from its inception was involved in a wide range of arts activities focused on contemporary movements, experiments and developments in art. It was originally headed by Roland Penrose, Herbert Read and others before it moved to Dover Street in 1950. Williams took part in several mixed exhibitions at the ICA, including *Eleven British Painters: Recent Work*, July to August 1953.
61 *Apollo*, January 1951.
62 "A Negro Artist", *loc. cit.*
63 Personal communication from Janice Lamar Jones (May 2008).
64 Wilson Harris, "Two Periods in the Work of a West Indian Artist".
65 Anne Walmsley, *op.cit.*, (1993).

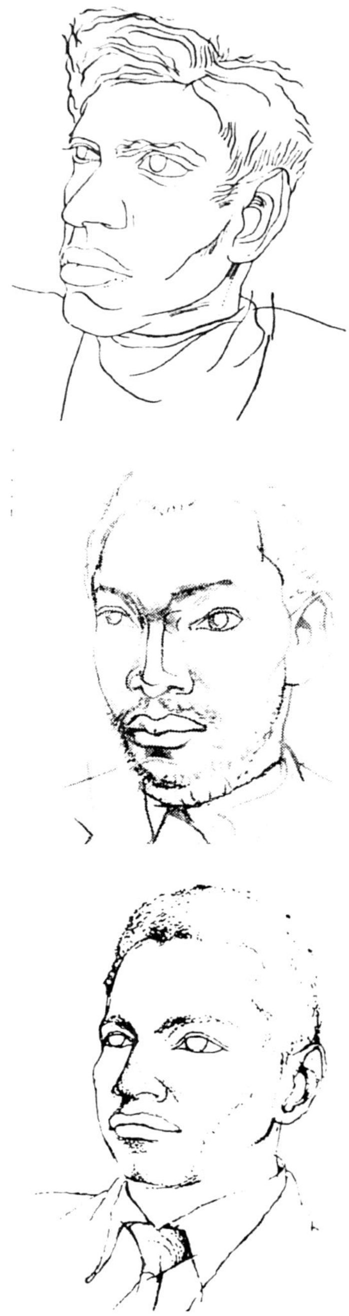

From top: flyleaf for *In the Castle of my Skin* by George Lamming; Denis Williams and Jan Carew, from *The Times British Colonies Review*, Spring 1955.

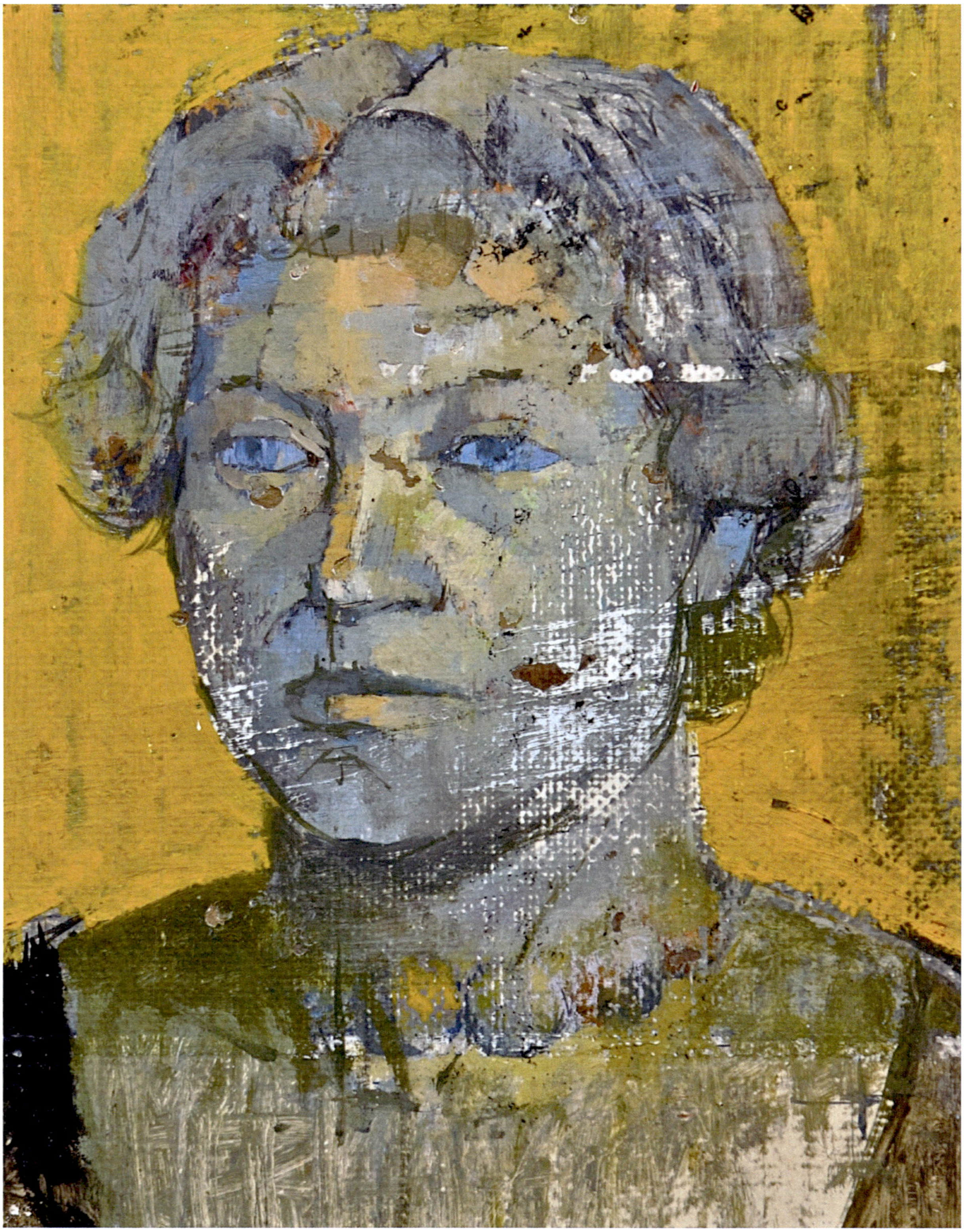

Portrait of Katie Alice (1955). Tempera on board. Collection C. Williams. Photograph by Arlington Weithers.

Chapter 3

"The Restless Course of Experiment"

Williams was embarking on what he would retrospectively refer to as "the restless course of experiment,"[1] exploring the various languages of the new abstract. His folio of work is revealing of the era. As a whole it can be seen to confirm the transitional uncertainty of the new age and to illuminate the post-war battleground between figurative art and abstraction.

Between 1946 and 1948 he had studied painting at the Camberwell School of Arts and Crafts where, significantly, Victor Pasmore (1908–1998) and Kenneth Martin (1905–1984) were tutors. He then taught at The Central School of Art from 1950 and was visiting tutor at The Slade School of Fine Art, London. During this period, Camberwell and the Central produced a remarkable number of innovative artists and art theorists. Many artists were turning from figurative and narrative subject matter and reassessing the pre-war advances into abstraction. Victor Pasmore had embraced abstract art and his influence permeated a wide circle.[2]

These art schools became the workshops of the new abstract art in post-war London. This was also a time of ground-breaking and rousing exhibitions. In 1951, the ICA staged *40,000 Years of Modern Art*, regarded as

> [...] the most brilliantly staged exhibition in London since the war.[...] It exposed cubist, abstract, expressionist and surrealist works in juxtaposition with tribal masks and figures from Africa and the South Seas, to demonstrate that when a creative artist draws inspiration from an alien culture the result is a complete transformation. The position of honour was given to Picasso's Les Demoiselles d'Avignon, the most famous of all modern pictures, and the first to widely disclose the cubist manner and the influence of African masks. It had never been seen in London before and was on loan from the Museum of Modern Art.[3]

This was the same year as the Festival of Britain, which Herbert Morrison called "a tonic for the Nation". It was a period of great energy and innovation in art and a new optimism symbolised in the possibilities of International Modernism in architecture. It is interesting to note that Williams himself held a lifelong interest in the possibilities of architecture and there are novel ideas and sketches for tropical housing in his portfolio.

Contemporary artists were discussing entirely fresh sources of reference in their work. For example, the ICA held an exhibition inspired by the drawings of D'Arcy Wentworth Thompson, drawings based on the relationships of principles of proportion contained in his book *On Growth and Form*. William Fagg had drawn a tentative link between these principles and the proportional relationships at work in tribal sculptural forms. He described an exhibition of "Traditional Art from the Colonies" held recently at the Imperial Institute, London, as "the best display of tribal art, selected and arranged as 'art' that has ever been held in Great Britain."[4] It is interesting in the context of the later unfolding of Williams' interests that this exhibition had included some of the most important of the famous antique bronze heads from Ife and examples of all periods of the related work from Benin, specially flown to London from Nigeria. There was a growing tendency to select and elevate "tribal" art and objects of material culture as art exhibits but this practice was uneven. Wyndham Lewis, commenting on the Colonial Exhibition at Marble Arch, notes that Williams' paintings seem to have been hung "as anthropological curiosities."[5] In some quarters the response to this new appreciation within art was less than enthusiastic. In March 1951 the *Glasgow Herald* described an exhibition of Haitian paintings as "Voodoo on canvas", and referred condescendingly to these works as "the first to be produced in the little Negro republic." A review of Wifredo Lam in the *New Statesman* complains that:

> [...] whereas Picasso's painting was made up of formalisations which originated in complete, logical structures, [...] Lam's paintings are made up of fragmentary, illogical juxtaposed symbols. [...] but, finally, the works remain foreign, remain weird; either because we are ignorant of the special meaning of their original context, or because they are, in fact, incoherent. [...] In art there is always a danger for both painter and spectator, of international vulgarisation.[6]

Many artists were abandoning the constraints of figurative art. Many rejected nature as a starting point and were contemptuous of "abstractions"or "improvisations" from nature. There was critical resistance to the new directions of non-representational abstract art and the arguments for and against were often very heated. Wyndham Lewis, for example, was emphatically opposed to abstract art, as were many key figures of the art establishment. There were important distinctions to be wrestled with and defended in the application of the label "abstract". There was rivalry and conflict surrounding the very concept of a new abstract art.

Pasmore emphasised that he constructed from within, that he did not abstract from the outward appearances of nature but from a free construction of visual elements composed in the manner of music. Some challenged the use of mathematical ideas as source material. Others rejected literary referencing, or imitation of any kind. There were disagreements about the implications of the use of colour in abstract art and any kind of association with the functions of decoration. These tensions were typical among Western artists of the post-war era as they engaged with the challenge of defining new directions.

Francis Bacon was acutely aware that in Europe artists in the 1950s were "trapped between the rising tide of abstract art" and the pressing need to "portray human emotion."[7] Williams had occupied and worked in a studio alongside Bacon in the early 1950s: a couple of dilapidated upstairs rooms of a vacated building in a bombed-out London street. This was during the *Human World* period. Williams remembered Bacon as "a dominating if not overpowering figure."[8] In a frank letter to Keith Vaughan, he noted that Bacon " [...] sees people as mountains of flesh. He is obsessed by this extraordinary capacity for flesh to breathe, walk, talk." Vaughan himself wrote:

> 27 January 1955. Interesting account this morning from Dennis Williams of the time he lived and worked in a small room adjoining Francis Bacon's studio; idolising Francis at the time, longing to be of service to him and ending up by becoming so wholly enslaved to his personality that he was incapable of any independent action [...] "as though my personality had been wiped out." I felt how easily I [Vaughan] could occupy the same rôle in relation to him.[9]

So what new directions was Williams investigating in his quest to purge himself? What was the nature of the restless course of experiment? He was deliberately avoiding any exploitation of narrative cliché or easy association with the success of the earlier *Human World* series of paintings. He was seeking to engage with artistic solutions other than those that overpowered and compelled the audience: solutions that allowed a different experience of compositional space. His new approach demonstrates that he was abandoning the overt limitations of illusionistic space in order to attain a greater spiritual liberation which would import a new dimension of transcendent contemplation into his work.

Family papers include an exhibition catalogue[10] which shows that Williams was familiar with the work of Roberto Matta, the Chilean-born painter of non-Euclidean space associated with the surrealist group led by André Breton. Matta painted what were described as "inscapes" – explorations or maps of the unconscious mind. It was the contact between André Breton and Aimé Césaire in Martinique in the 1940s that led to what is termed "black surrealism". On one of the pages of the exhibition catalogue Williams has made a small self-portrait sketch, dated 1952, which stylistically places it with his many other small portraits of the same date.

In his study *The Inner Plantation* (1952) we can see that Williams pays homage to the directions indicated by surrealism and its legacy. This large study provides a significant insight into the development of his conceptual baseline as it is dated just two years after *Human World*. The landscape of the "inner plantation" is clearly present in the entangled curvilinear dynamic. But he has taken intellectual control of his subject matter, and the plantation iconography is being subordinated to a controlling logic. These experimental works, the folio sketches and watercolour studies demonstrate the further development of the subject. Giant leaf and sugar-cane motifs; tangled vegetation; organic, umbilical forms; symbolic screaming heads, reminiscent of Bacon; of humans and beasts reduced to arcs and spheres are all used to establish an ambiguous internal environment. It is the subjective, psychic space of blood-red pools and purple shadows; it is an inner, wrap-around space of reverberating sounds. There are resonances of Matta's vocabulary of forms in the stretched tendons, tubes, valves, transparent membranes and tensile skin.

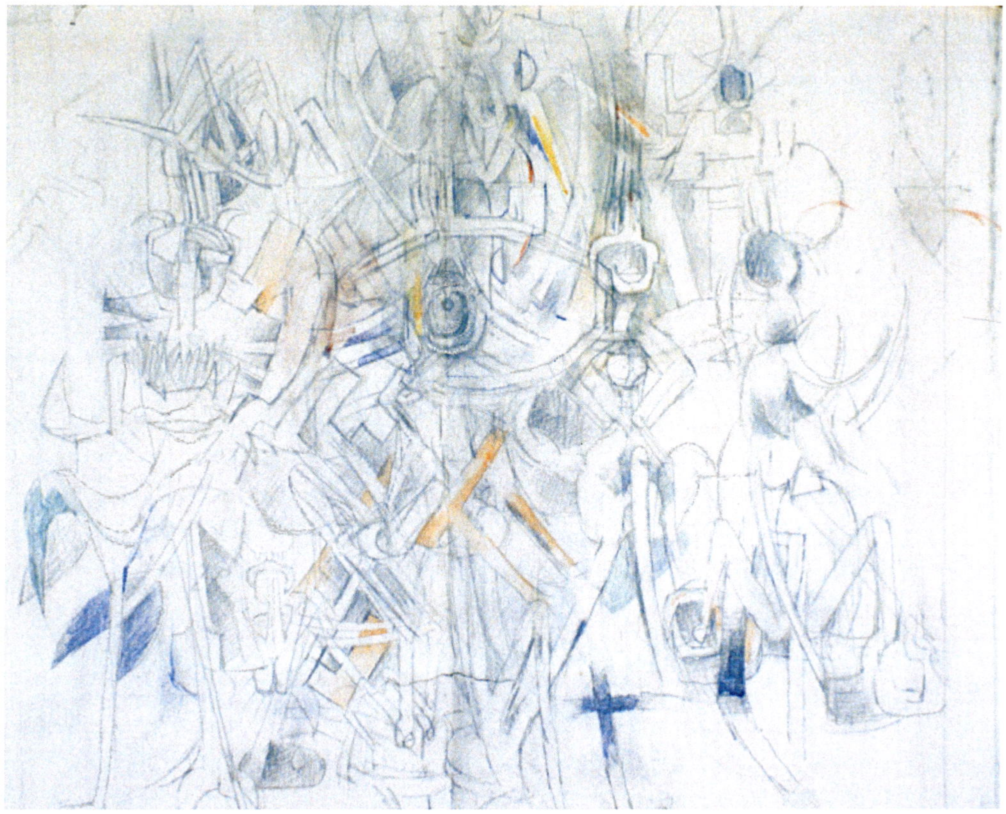

The Inner Plantation (1952). Study. Pencil, watercolour.
52×45 cms. Williams estate.

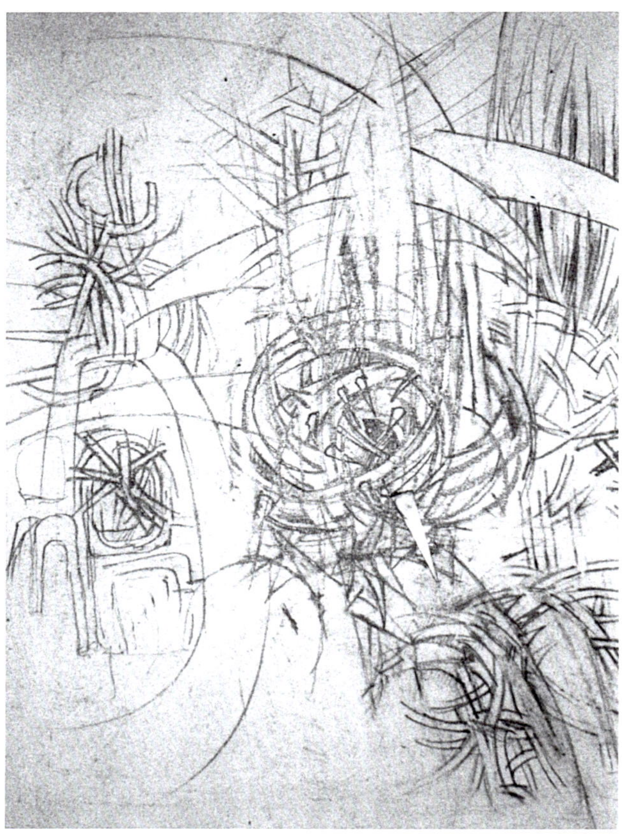

The Inner Plantation. Study. Pencil. Williams estate.

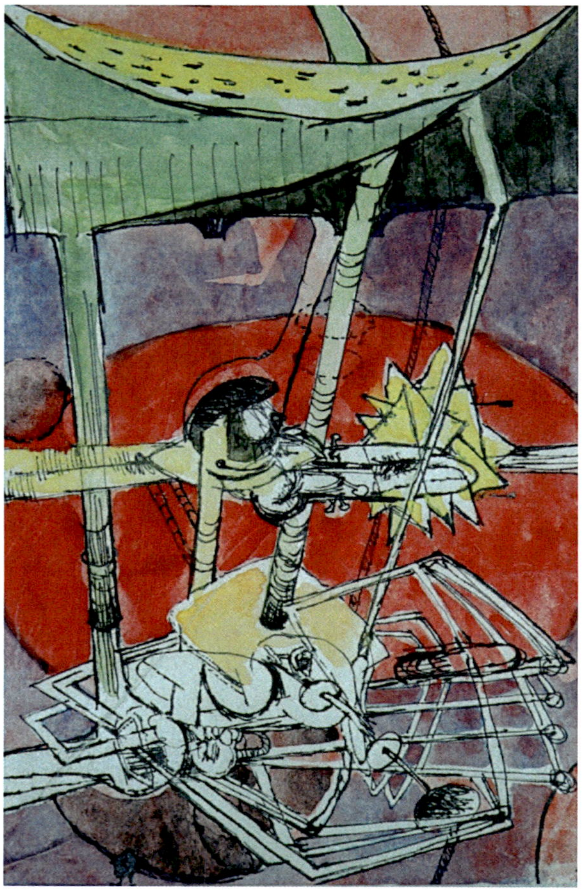

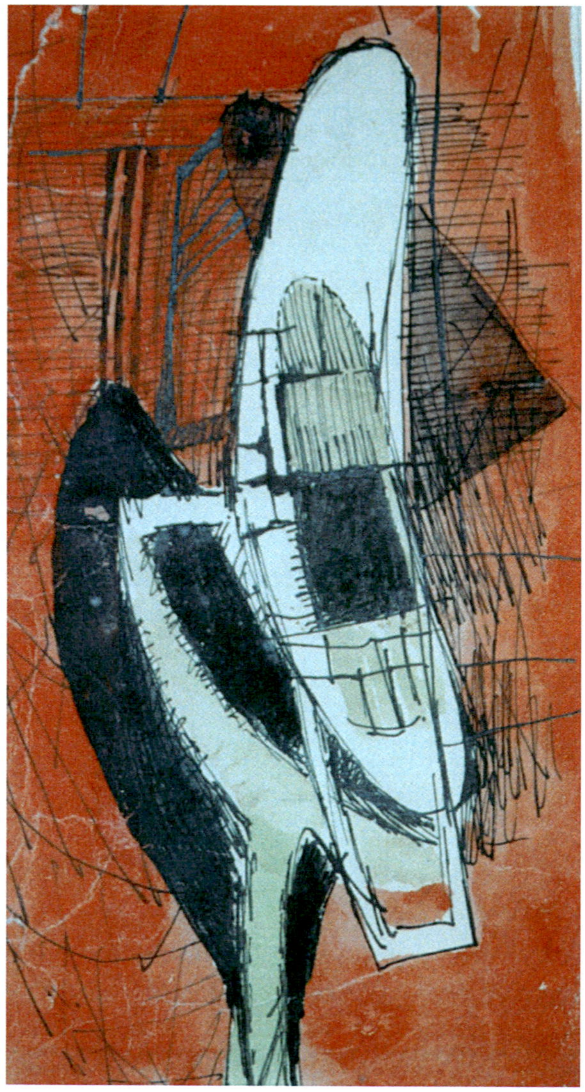

The Inner Plantation (1952).
Watercolour studies. Williams estate.

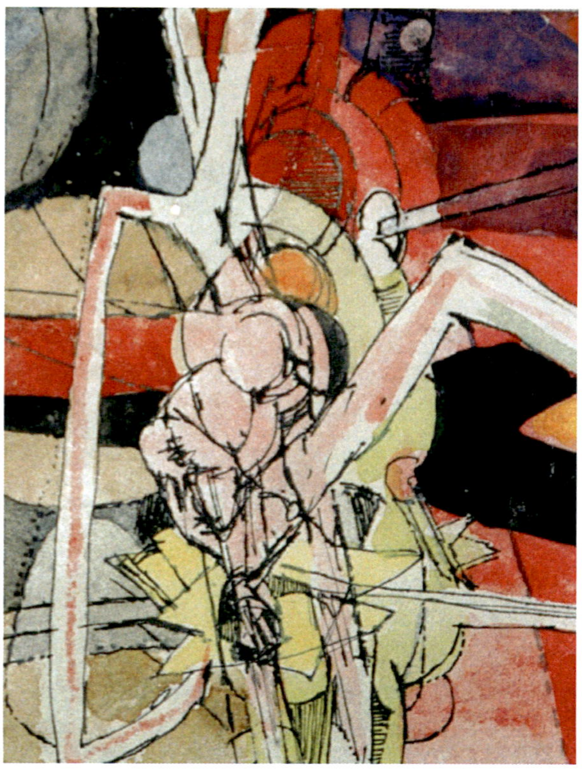

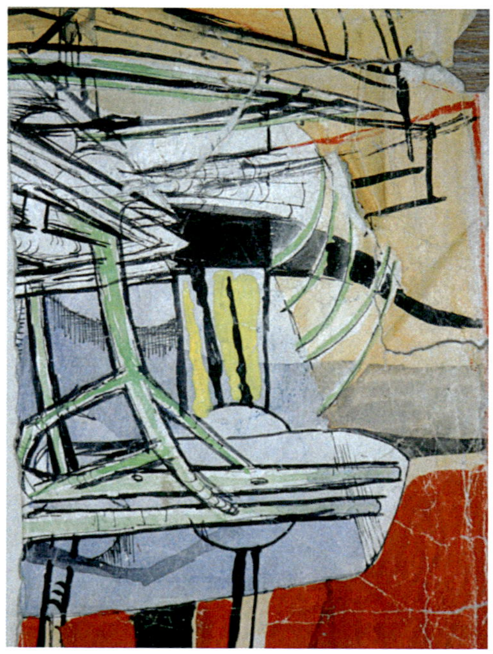

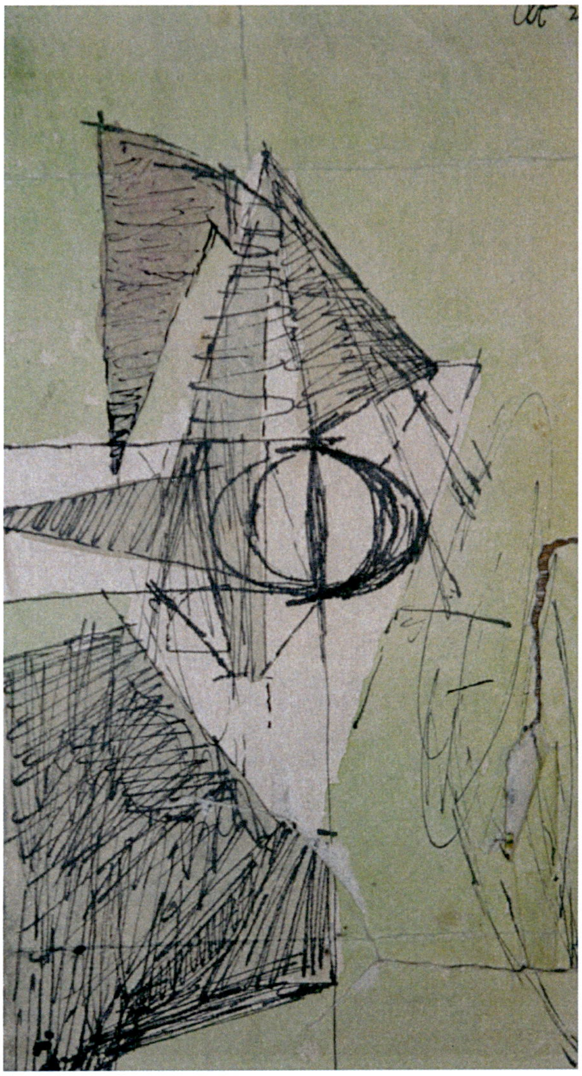

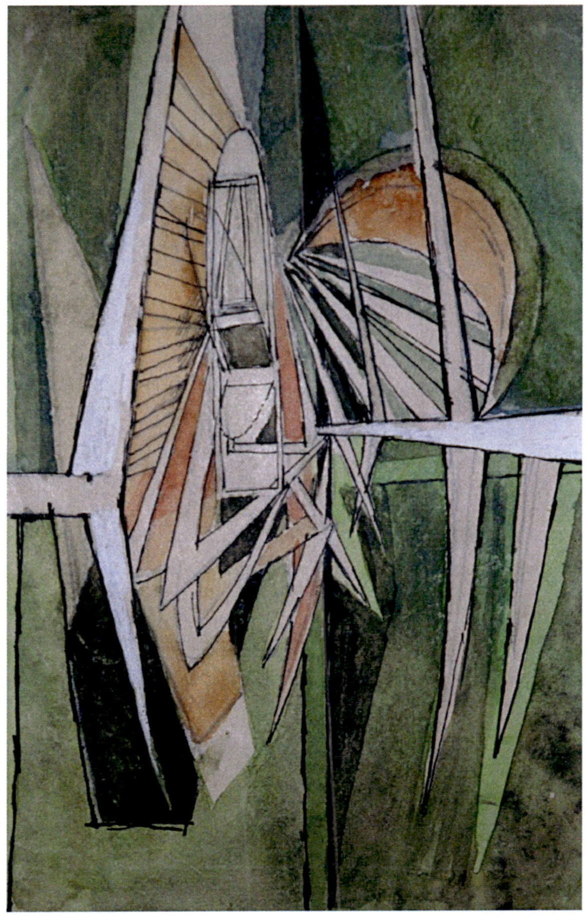

Colour, Weight, Sound (1952). Watercolour studies.
Williams estate.

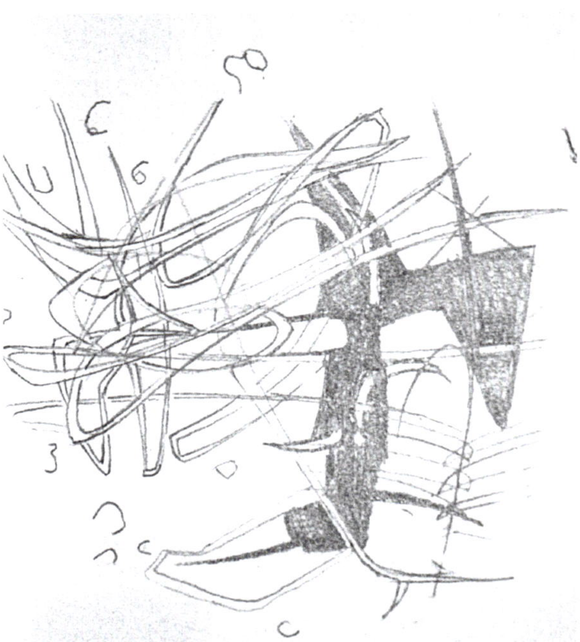

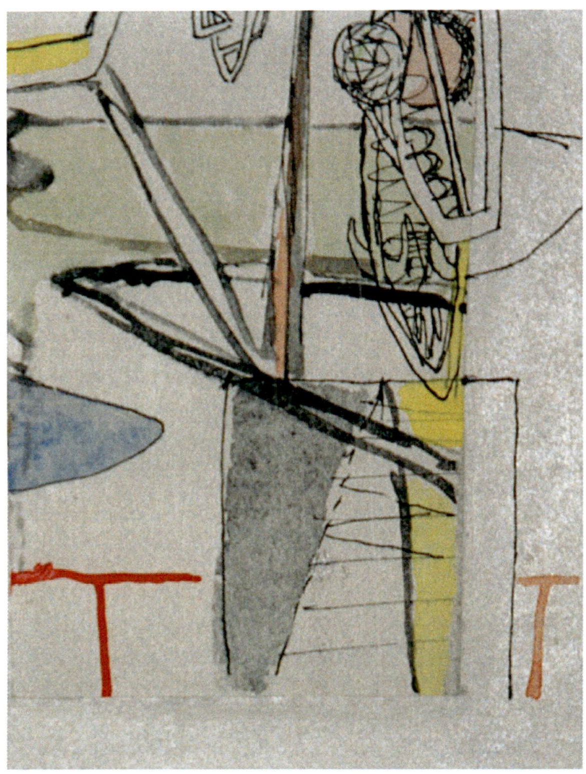

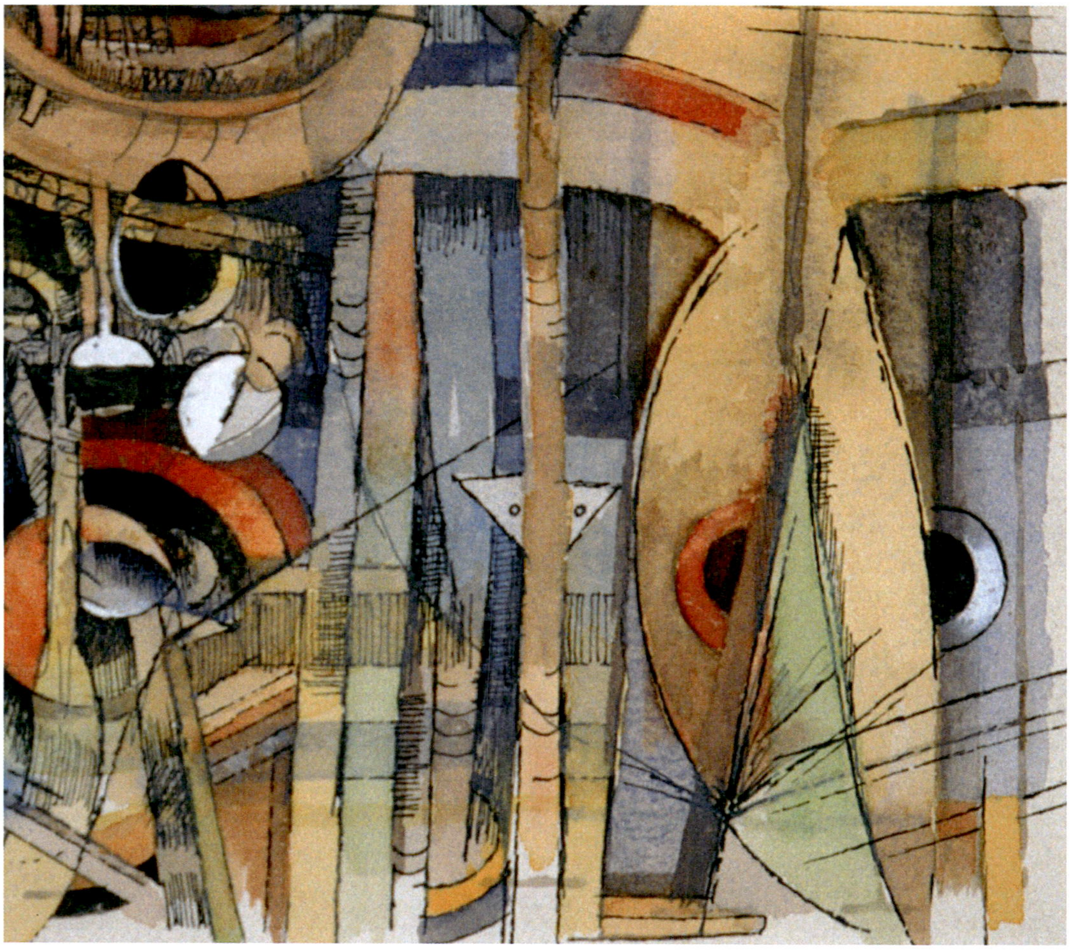

Colour, Weight, Sound (1952).
Pen, ink and watercolour study. Williams estate.

Matta exhibited at the ICA in 1951 and Williams uses a very direct visual quotation, seen in the preliminary studies for his large work *Colour, Weight, Sound* (1952).[11]

Williams' handwritten notes at this time also support the idea of the "restless course of experiment" in his search for new directions. As a tutor at a prestigious London art school he had an immediate grasp of his contemporary bearings. He was of the opinion that "the painters who have so far made the most serious experiments with colour have been non-representational. Robert Delaunay – 'Colour alone is both form and subject' – Morgan Russell, and Macdonald-Wright have been, in my view, the most successful of these. […] They succeeded in drawing a map of the territory of the medium – Colour."[12]

From this early period of experiment we can examine the folio works for *Picturesque Study of a Welsh Mountain* (1953) made during one of his regular visits to North Wales, the ancestral home of his wife Katie Alice. Works related to *Picturesque Study of a Welsh Mountain* comprise drawings and paintings that are part of a consecutively numbered group. Family trips to the mountains inspired these small vignettes of the spectacular Snowdonia landscape – mountain lakes and reflections; forested valleys; bracken and scree. His use of the term "picturesque" in the title implies the decorative and some of the effects are indeed decorative, particularly in the linear fringing and repetition. A preliminary drawing for these studies emphasises an analytical consideration of the curvilinear construction of the landscape. Multiple points of origin explore both visible mass and hidden mass by way of colours that could express how the material occupies the recursive. The creation is of simultaneous, dissociative viewpoints which allow that which is vast and monumental to be imparted on a jewel-like scale. In the paintings tone and colour are used in an abstracted manner with a play being made

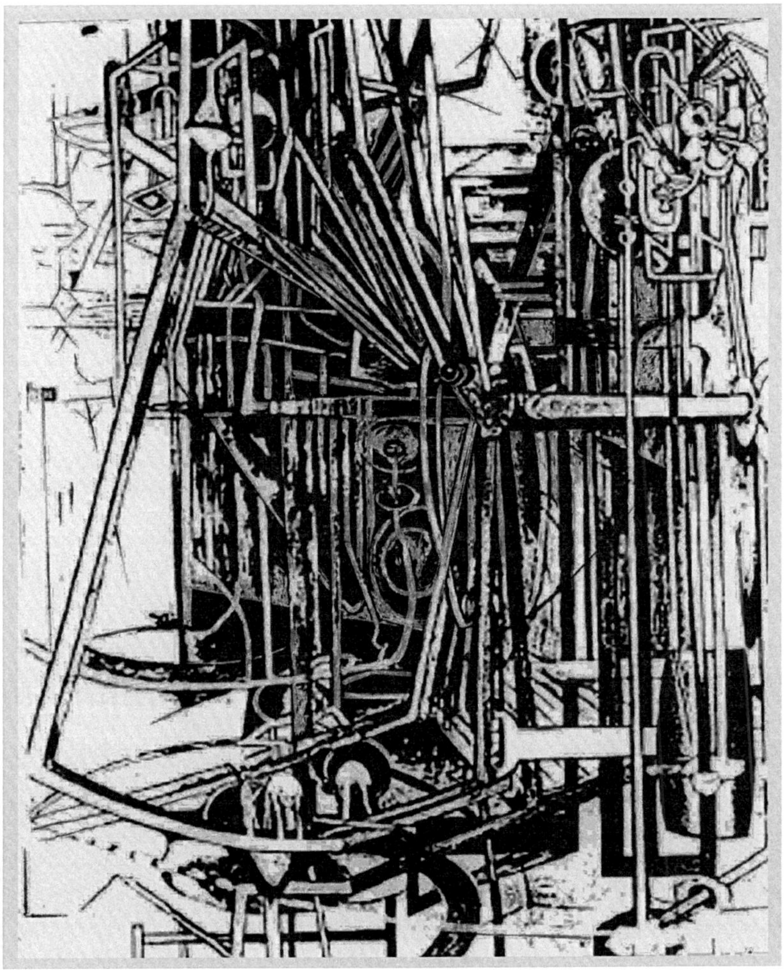

Colour, Weight, Sound (1952). Oil on canvas. 158×122 cms.
Retrieved image. Courtesy Gimpel Fils.

on the contrast of translucent and opaque paint and the contrast of its texturing. Such small folio works acknowledge an awareness of Mondrian's abstractions from landscape and demonstrate the range of investigation and consideration Williams was giving to major international developments in art practice and theory such as the constructivists, and De Stijl.

He exhibited again in Paris with Gimpel Fils in 1953, when the gallery participated in *Tendances de la Peinture et de la Sculpture: Britanniques Contemporaines* at the Galerie de France:

> De courageuses galeries, neuves, et osant prendre des risques, sont aujourd'hui les promoteurs du talent. [...] Denis Williams est noir, la pulsation fondamentale d'un monde industrialisé égale pour lui le malaise de la jungle, la crainte qu'inspire un masque d'initiation.[13]

Despite this continuing reference to his "jungle" credentials, a radical departure in his approach had occurred at this time. Alastair Grieve has recorded: "By 1953 Williams was producing mathematically-based paintings, reliefs and free-standing constructions."[14] We know that he became associated with the loose groupings of artists associated with abstract constructed art. He took part in the third Fitzroy Street Exhibition in May 1953, organised by Adrian Heath in his London studio. The group of exhibitors included Robert Adams, Terence Conran, Anthony Hill, Roger Hilton, Kenneth Martin, Ben Nicholson, Eduardo Paolozzi, Victor Pasmore, and William Scott. Adrian Heath had organised a series of such group displays of abstract work that were brought together in a highly designed manner, using the whole exhibition environment as an active architectural space. These displays included constructed art in three dimensions; painted reliefs; photomurals; prints; collage and drawing; printed textile; sculpture; mobiles and radical new furniture ideas alongside deliberately unframed

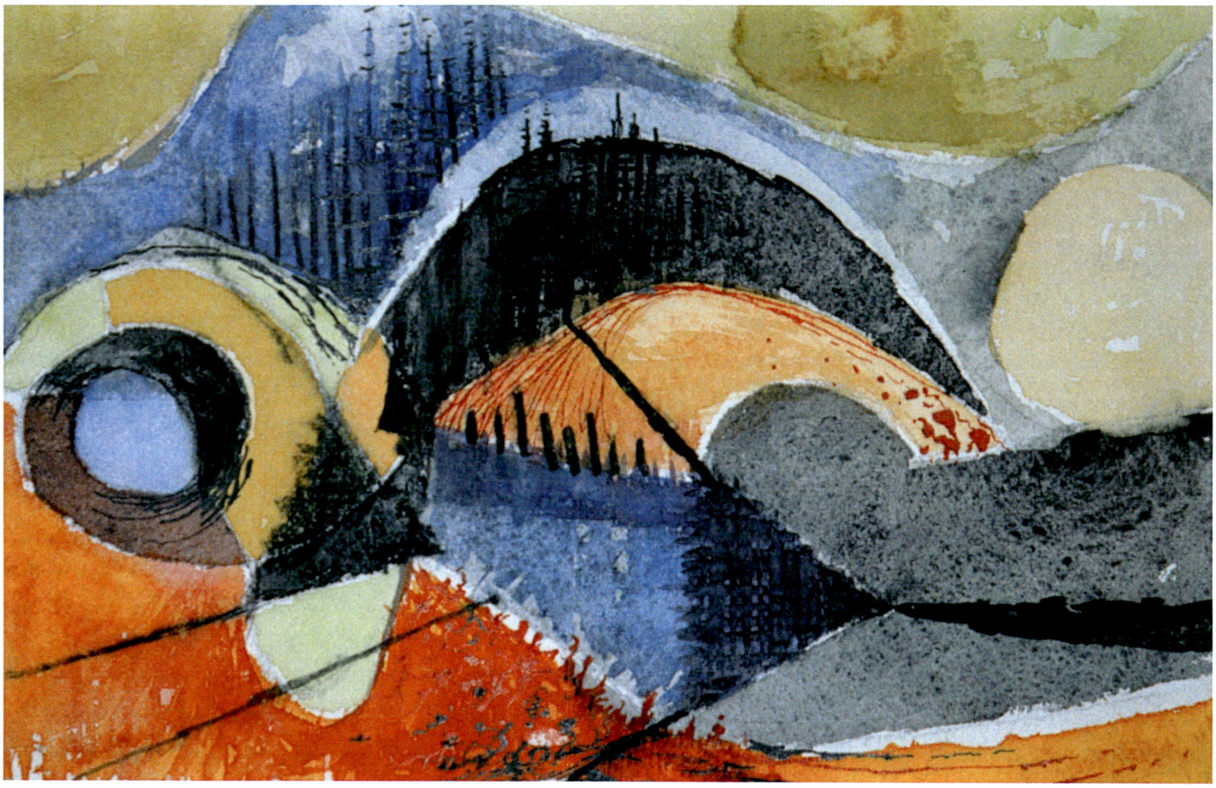

Picturesque Study of a Welsh Mountain 1 (1953). Watercolour. 20×15 cms. Williams estate.

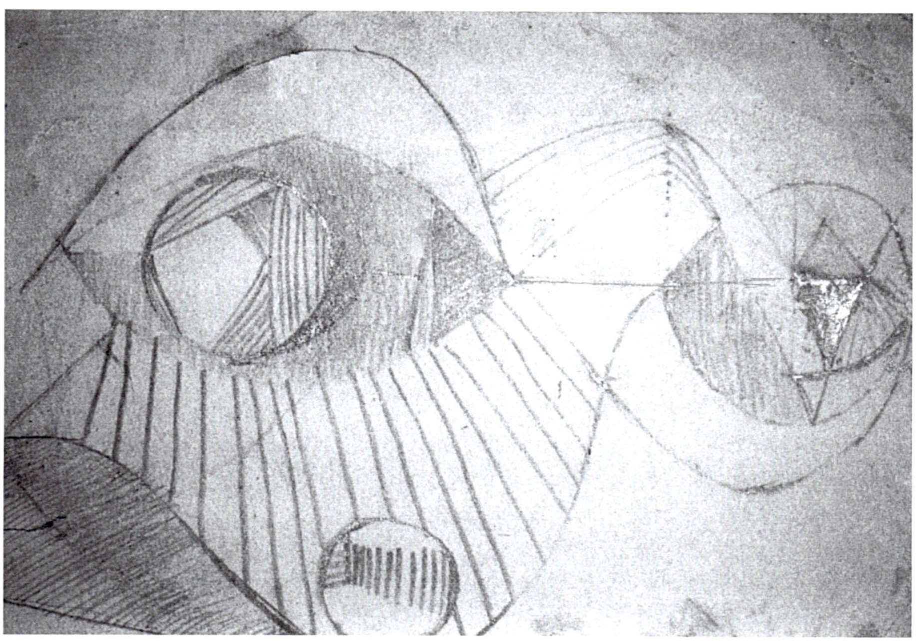

Picturesque Study of a Welsh Mountain 1 (1953). Preliminary drawing. Williams estate.

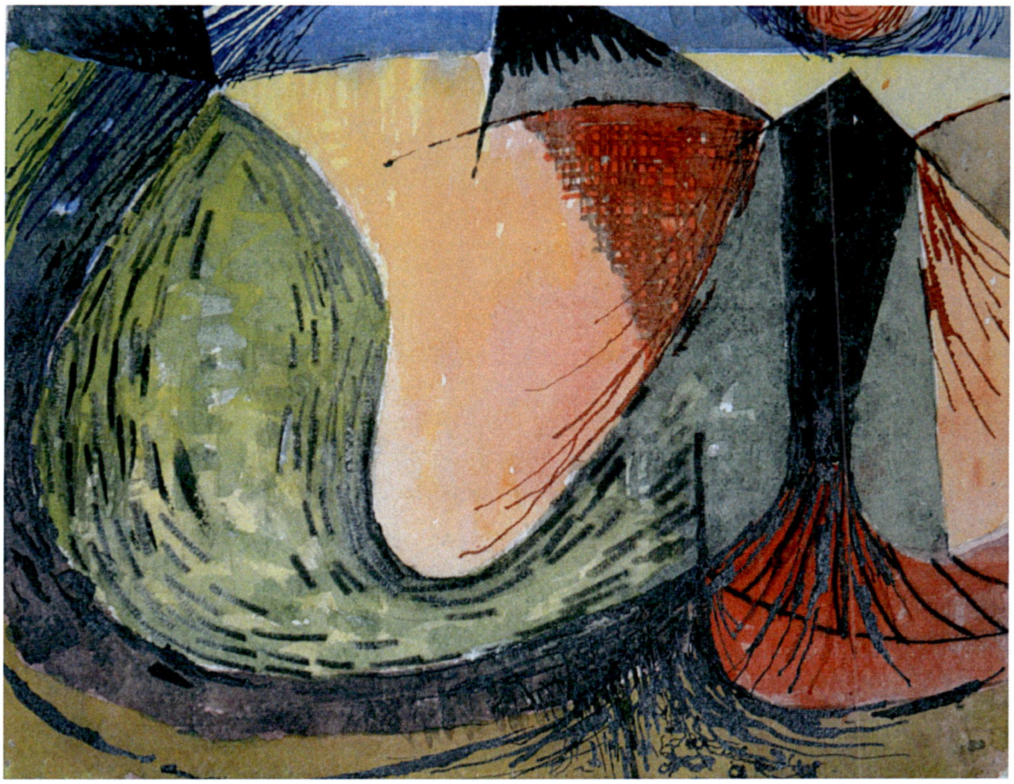

Picturesque Study of a Welsh Mountain 3 (1953). Watercolour. 20×17 cms. Williams estate.

paintings. There are surviving photographs that give a visual record of two constructed painted columns being exhibited by Williams – items 13 and 27 in the catalogue. This exhibition was described as the most ambitious of these radical shows given by the abstract artists' group exhibiting within the Pasmore circle: Pasmore had now emerged as one of the leading figures of the new abstract in post-war Britain.[15]

Chris Stephens recently noted: "In 1953 the painter Adrian Heath published his small book, *Abstract painting: Its Origins and Meaning,* which traced the development and provided commentaries on the main protagonists, including Mondrian and the Russian Kasimir Malevich."[16] He is of the opinion that in post-war Britain any direct contact with Mondrian's work outside of Amsterdam was unlikely and so it is quite possible that this association with Adrian Heath and Roger Hilton was the source of Williams' own interests in Mondrian in those early years before the Mondrian Retrospective exhibition at the Whitechapel Art Gallery in 1955.

In the summer of 1953 he took part in an exhibition entitled *Eleven British Painters: Recent Work* at the ICA Gallery, and the catalogue indicates that no "realist" works were exhibited. He was shown with Keith Vaughan, Harold Cohen, Victor Pasmore and William Turnbull. The two large works by Williams were titled *Painting* (1952),[17] and *Painting* (1953).[18] The absence of descriptive or literary titles is further indication of a rich, new direction. At the same time he was also included in the Gimpel Fils summer show: their *Collector's Choice* exhibition (1953).

This was an era of transition. The works of the major European abstract painters were known largely through published papers and reproductions in books circulated amongst colleagues and fellow artists, and their contents permeated their thinking. The history of Western art is punctuated by theoretical and experimental approaches to establish a universal system of proportion and harmony. We can bring to mind the Golden Section, the Fibonacci Series and Le Modulor. Paul Klee had been represented in major exhibitions between 1948 and 1950. His work emphasised a mathematical harmony in art, and the artists at the Central would have been familiar with his essay *On Modern Art,* published in 1948. The American constructionist Charles Biederman's *Letters on the New Art* appeared in 1951.[19] This

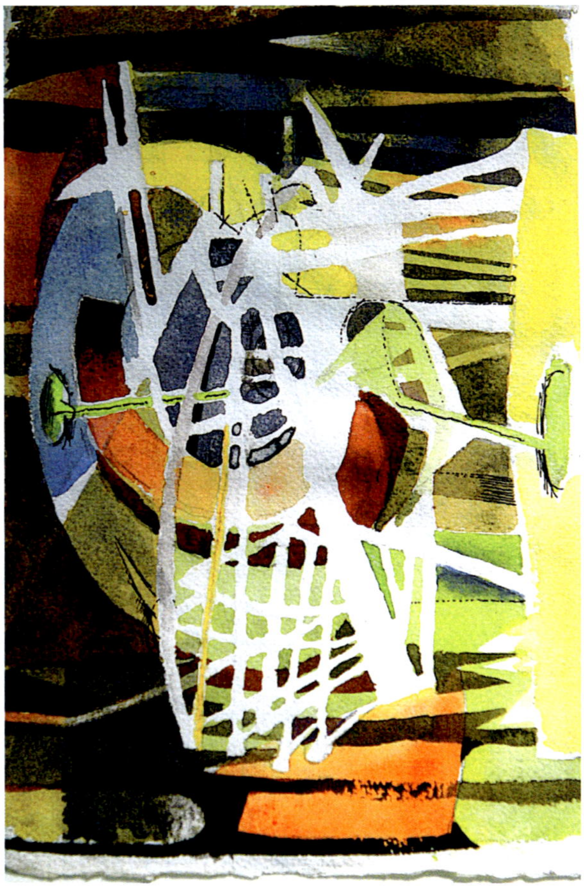

Composition V (1954). Watercolour. 25.5×16.5 cms.
By kind permission of Donald Locke.

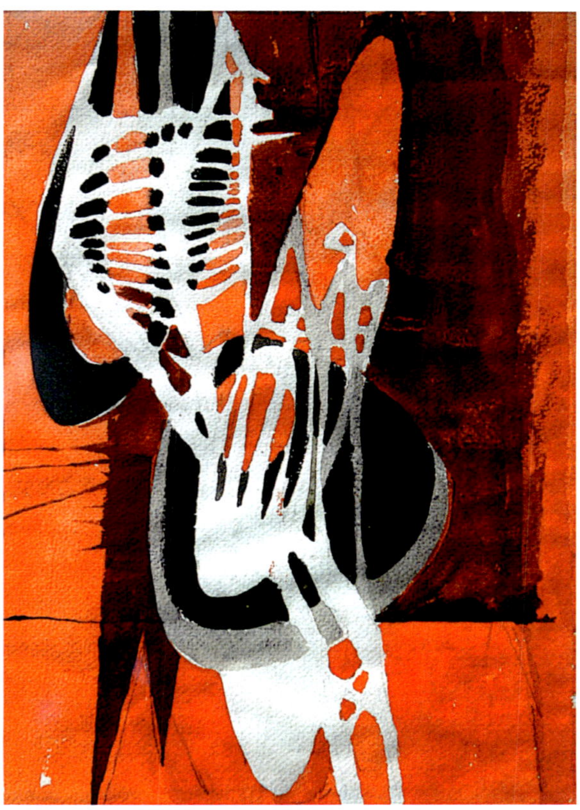

Composition I (1954). Watercolour. 30×20.3 cms.
By kind permission of Donald Locke.

Plane Compositions

1 Painting in five related rhythms oil on board, *Mar., 1954* 34" square

2 Painting in four related rhythms *oil on board, Mar., 1954* 30" square

3 Development of a regular octagon in primary colours, black and white. *Oil on board, Mar., 1954* 28" diameter

4 Vertical composition with the arc of a circle. *Oil on canvas, Feb., 1953* 53"×16"

5 Symmetric composition in primary colours, black and white. *Oil on canvas, Jan., 1953* 40"×48"

Reliefs

6 Composition in *n* parallel divisions of a rectangle. *Dec., 1953* 18"×24"

7 Composition in *n* parallel divisions of a rectangle. *Jan., 1954* 18"×24"

8 Composition in *n* parallel divisions of a rectangle. *Dec., 1953* 14"×32"

Constructions

9 Four-part composition of rectangles projected in space. *Perspex Feb., 1954*

10 Space construction in metal and perspex *Mar., 1954*

11 Plane construction in metal *Dec., 1953–Jan., 1954*

12 Construction in five related rhythms. *Mar., 1954*

13 Construction in five related rhythms (study) *Mar., 1954*

Drawings, Watercolours, etc.

Left: Two Watercolours from the Gimpel Fils Exhibition, April 1954.

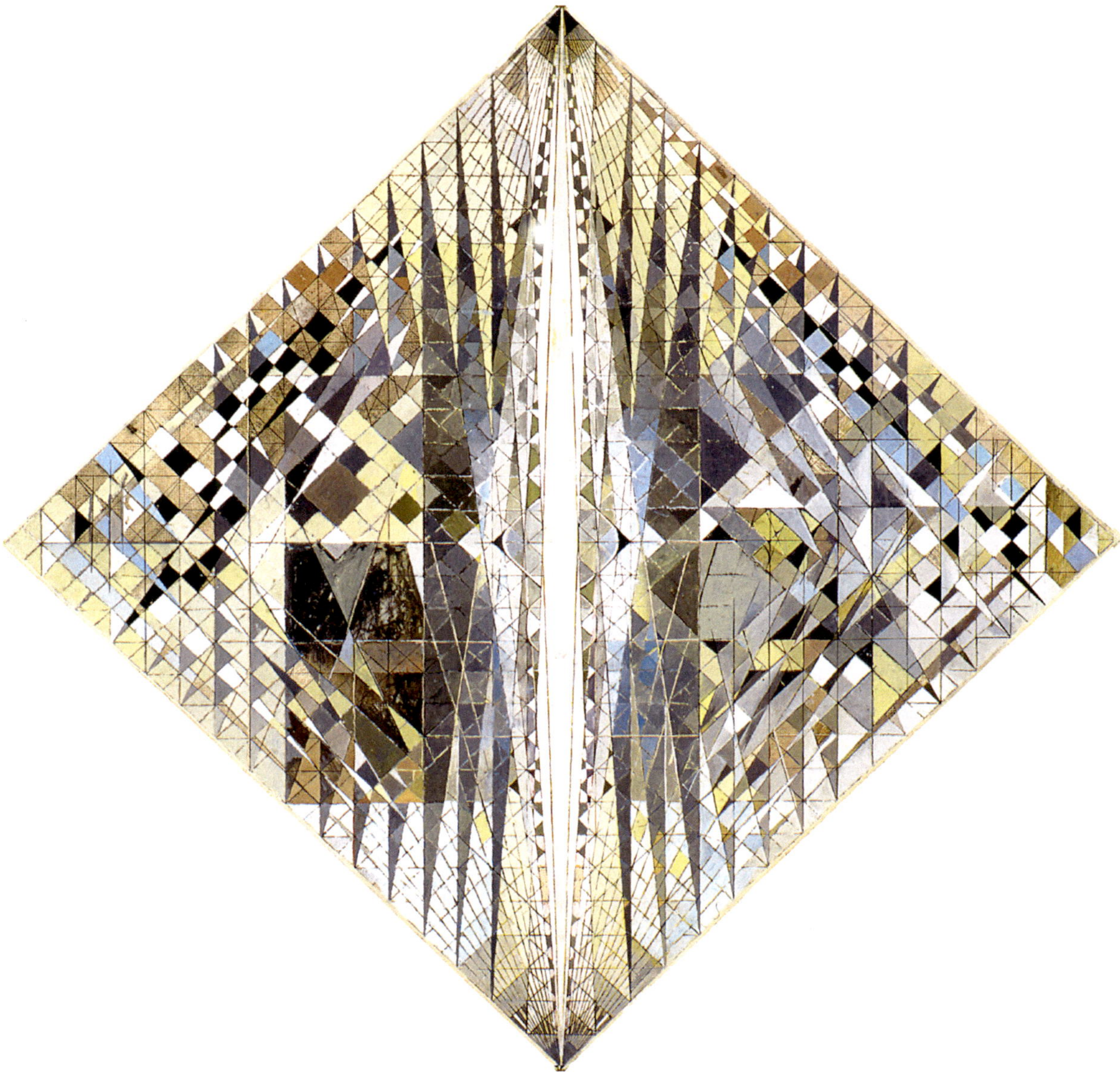

Painting in Six Related Rhythms (1954).
By kind permission of the Beaverbrook Art Gallery, Fredericton, New Brunswick.

publication emphasised the developmental line from Cézanne to the Cubists and to Mondrian's abstractions. Williams had become interested in the intellectual, analytical approach in the work of Mondrian (1872–1944) who had flattened the faceted planes of analytical Cubism and tied them to the two-dimensional surface of the canvas with his black lines.

His own work had started to explore rational, structural rectilinearities and mathematical geometries. But there were many experimental and theoretical ideas that promised new possibilities and directions for artists and new sources of inspiration within the language of the new abstract. Later he recalled: "I was painting these sort of reticulated little tiny pebbles of colour, and Wilson [Harris] said, it's like notes in a steel band."[20]

It is probably fair to suggest that it was the transition itself that was the important feature in acceptance of the new language of art and that this transition was more acutely experienced by those who were considering the move away from figurative art. To some extent this is true of Williams, though the most casual appraisal of his folio for the period reveals that throughout the research – and some was taken to a remarkable length – he actually never abandoned the image. Through this period of intensive investigation he continued to develop his approaches and it is evident that his work did not become exclusively abstract: for him, the new abstract provided a fresh framework of enquiry.

In April 1954 he had a two-man show with Roger Hilton at Gimpel Fils where he showed his *Plane Compositions*.[21] This was a singular opportunity, for, as Grieve points out: "Powerful figures of the art establishment [...] disliked constructed abstract art. Neither would London commercial galleries, with the notable exception of Gimpel Fils and Redfern, exhibit their work."[22] The extract from the catalogue reproduced above shows the range of Williams' works.

At the head of the catalogue Lewis wrote: "Denis Williams is 26, he is a Negro. He comes to us with canvases of such convincing power that this show will prove, I believe, to be the prelude to an exceptional career."

In July of that year Williams' work was included at Gimpel Fils in a group exhibition of recent paintings and sculptures called *Of Light and Colour*. One of his abstract constructions was simply titled *Mask*. Wilson Harris wrote:

> The artist worked with the utmost patience and skill in brass, cutting and saving his material, soldering parts together. The outcome was a space-work, an aloof and shining open spirit. It was curved and shaped like a mask: so unobtrusively, however, that an almost impassive quality obtained – a shining impassivity wherein the mask very slowly ingrains itself in the mind without compulsion or force as if withholding recognition until recognition is freely given.[23]

The function of the mask is to register the creative tension and encode the mystery of the transformative at the heart of many cultures; in this way it is able to preserve the potential ritual experience for future generations. Also contained in his mask reference is a kind of ironic reminder that the century-old appropriation of African art had expanded the horizons of Western art.

His *Painting in Six Related Rhythms* (1954) was one of the prize-winners in the *Young Artists' Exhibition* held at the New Burlington Galleries in 1955, and sponsored by *The Daily Express*.[24] The panel of judges included Herbert Read, Graham Sutherland and Anthony Blunt, and the work was acquired by the Beaverbrook Foundation.

His supporting notes and sketches are headed "The Infinite Implications of a Double Square", and refer directly to mathematical ideas governing dynamic rectangles and the seemingly infinite possibilities of division. Some of these notes are written on the back of booking sheets for classes in Life Drawing and Painting at the Central School of Arts and Crafts (Saint Martins). Alongside his preparatory sketches he has noted: "Each side of the rectangle can be seen as the radius of a circle of which one corner forms the centre. The implied movement is thus infinite. The boundaries are preserved but act as elements of construction, or turns in an internal movement articulating actual space. [...] The rectangle can be used as a source of energy radiating in two directions, vertically and laterally, to infinity. It is an area in movement, destroying its boundaries." *Painting in Six Related Rhythms* (1955) is signed on the back and its orientation is indicated. It is presented in the dramatic diamond format and, without prior knowledge of the intervening period of experiment by the artist, it represents a radical departure from the previously celebrated works of the *Human World* series.

The subject is based in the ideas expressed in the notes above, and was developed in three preparatory sketches. The content is a complex

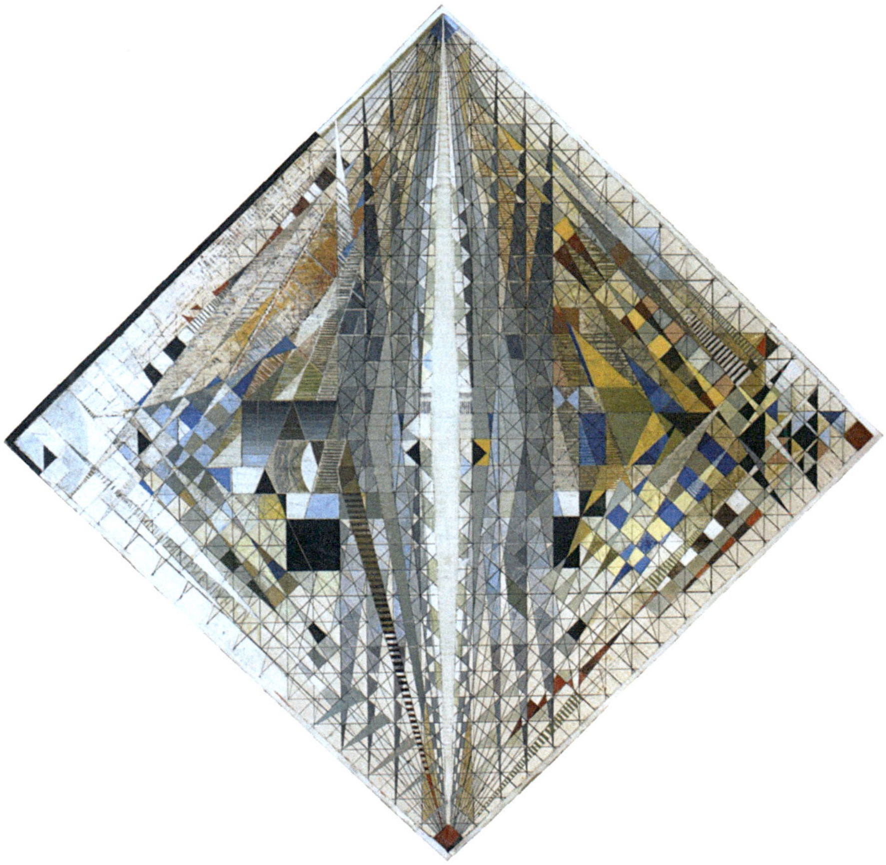

Painting in Six Related Rhythms (1955). Oil on wood panel. 79×79 cms. Collection E. Williams.

geometric play, or "rhythm" of the visual elements – line with line, line with shape, line with colour, line with tone; shape with colour, shape with tone, and so on. We can observe the rhythms and the play of the chromatic and achromatic gradations, or scale of graded tones. The musical metaphor extends and elaborates itself – the tension of the strings, the balanced harmonies. The reference to a musical scale that appears elsewhere in the handwritten notes supports an understanding of the work along these lines. Many abstract artists and colour theorists of the time believed that colour possessed sound equivalences, together with other musical allusions to notes, intervals, harmonies, and variations on a theme.

In *Painting in Six Related Rhythms* (1955) a grid is marked out on the pale gesso ground in near-accurate one-inch intervals using black pen-line. This grid is further elaborated in many directions creating a three-dimensional lattice resembling a transparent cubic form, balancing on a pinpoint. A vertical shaft of white elongates and emphasises the tension of this balance. Presenting the painting on an axis implies pivotal movement, just as time itself is measured by the earth turning on its axis – as Williams noted: "the implied movement is thus infinite." The artist has not developed the painting on a wholly systematic basis of mathematical proportion. Whilst a geometric control is supplied by the grid, the painting is spontaneous in its balance of relationships and in its use of colour. This plane painting is slowly and carefully constructed. In places, the underlying grid comes to the surface above the colours; in other areas it disappears or is masked; sometimes the grid is scratched back through the paint. The artist has used very fine brushwork in the line patterns and in the rendering of delicate suspended shapes. Other areas show a looser approach, but everything is orchestrated within the larger structure. He uses a wide range of techniques, creating a richness and subtlety that counters the severe geometry. Scumbling, sgraffito, fine brush hatching and overlays lead to soft textural effects and create painterly vignettes within the overall working. The brushwork deliberately remains a feature and is emphatically horizontal or diagonal, sometimes transparent, sometimes opaque. Thus, the surface of the painting – its two-dimensional reality – is complex.

The "rhythms" internal to the cubic lattice can be defined like the internal structure of a crystal or jewel, and this effect enhances the sparkle and luminous clarity. The artist used a restricted palette: Venetian red; cobalt blue; cadmium yellow; gold ochre; lamp black and zinc white. Sympathetic hues, warm and cool, blend in with the greys, and the tertiary browns and greens are yellow-rich. The Venetian red is calm. The weight of the colours is to the right of the painting and the neutrals dominate the elongation of the central shaft. The controlled use of colour expands the depth of field with the advancing yellows to the right of the axis, and receding grey-blues to the left. *Painting in Six Related Rhythms* (1955) is an example of the autonomous work of art that exists as an object in its own right. This is emphasised by its unframed format and its treatment of the concept of "edge" or boundary as indicated in Williams' notes. Chris Stephens has noted that: "The rôle of the edge would, like the relationship between figure and ground, become a leitmotif in debates about abstract painting during the 1950s."[25] A partial black line borders the left point of the diamond as if in a reference to Mondrian, otherwise the edge becomes the pure white of space.

In an enthusiastic account of the painting A. J. Seymour wrote:

> His *Painting in Six Related Rhythms* (1954) is a neo-abstract that goes past Mondrian with its timelessness and purity of inspiration, tied to no culture or creed, embarrassed by no sordid or distorted clichés.[26]

When Salvador Dalí visited the prize-winning exhibition, *Daily Express* columnist William Hickey remarked:

> The picture that made him enthusiastic was an abstract by Denis Williams. [...] He [Dalí] raised his stick to it with the grave dignity of a Spanish King giving an accolade. He moved into the middle of the room and then delivered a further judgement: "What I find strange here is the break in English tradition. There is no trace here of the Pre-Raphaelites".[27]

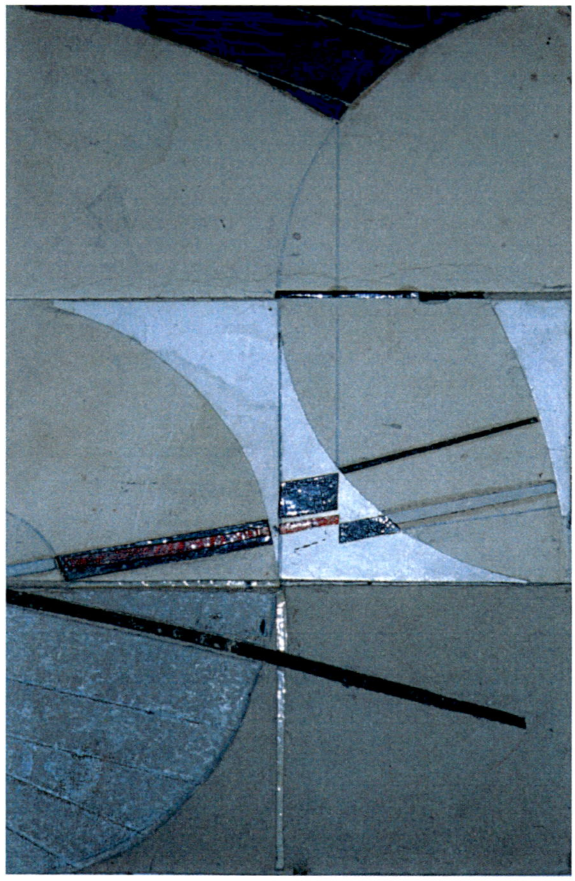

The Square Articulate (1955). Mixed media. 20×13 cms. Williams estate.

Williams' very public success as an artist meant that his aesthetic concerns, ideas, and dialogue with other artists and colleagues placed him within the inner circle of innovative artists in post-war London. There is a reference on one of his sketch sheets to John Ernest (1922–1994), the American artist whose own work explored visual equivalents of defined mathematical structures and progressions. Ernest had gone to London in 1951 and Williams was later to exhibit with him.

At this time he was also visiting tutor in drawing at The Slade, the establishment with the very highest reputation in the traditions of Fine Art, Drawing and Painting. His consummate academic skill in the traditions of anatomy and figure drawing continued alongside his experiments in abstract art. Despite the possibilities of his restless aesthetic trajectories this engagement saw him wrestling with dilemmas posed by art itself. He had to work with the tensions of teaching one tradition while his origins lay elsewhere, colliding with recent history and bound in challenging relationships.

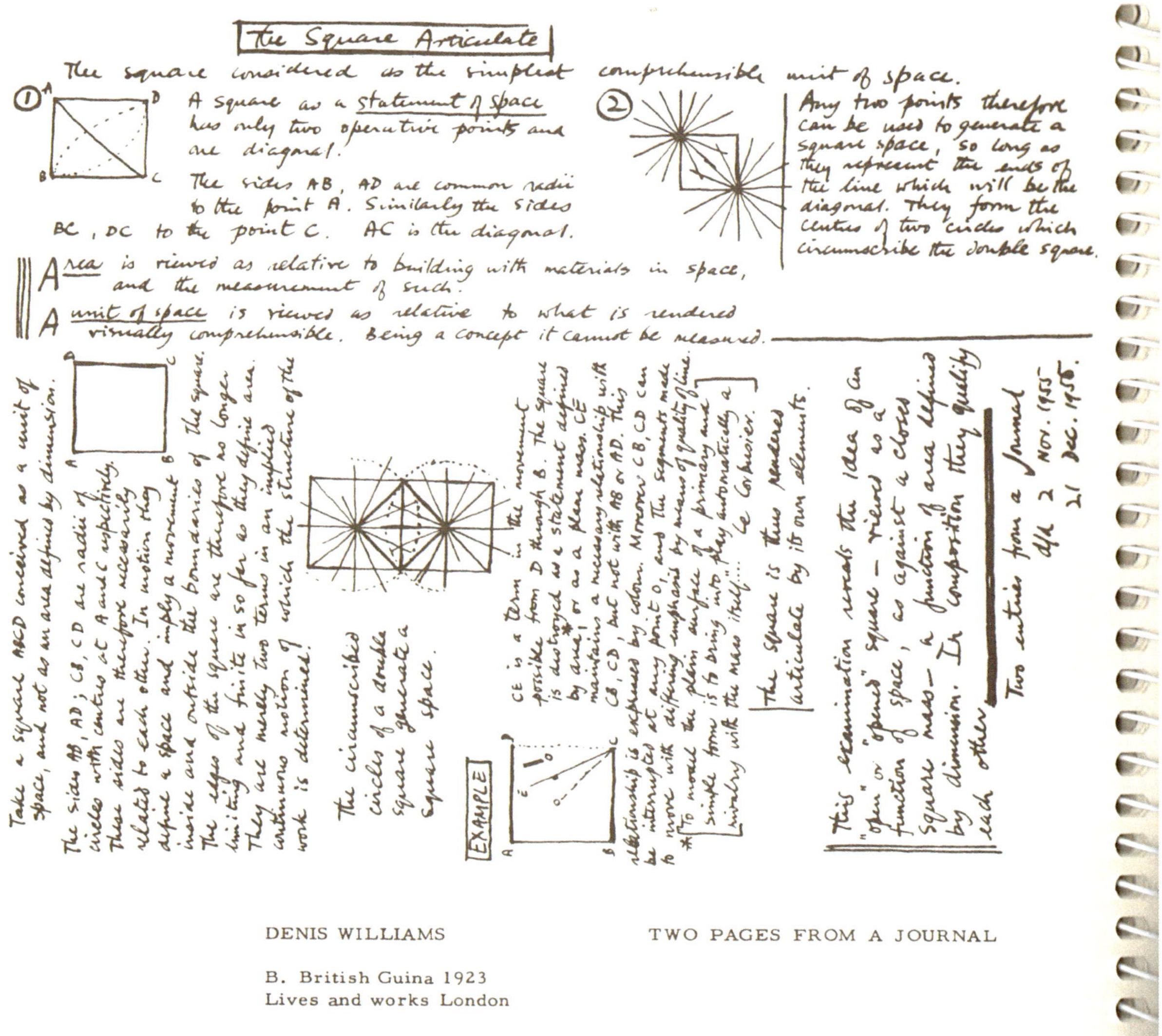

Two journal pages from the Exhibition Catalogue *This is Tomorrow* (1956).
By kind permission of the Whitechapel Gallery Archive, London.

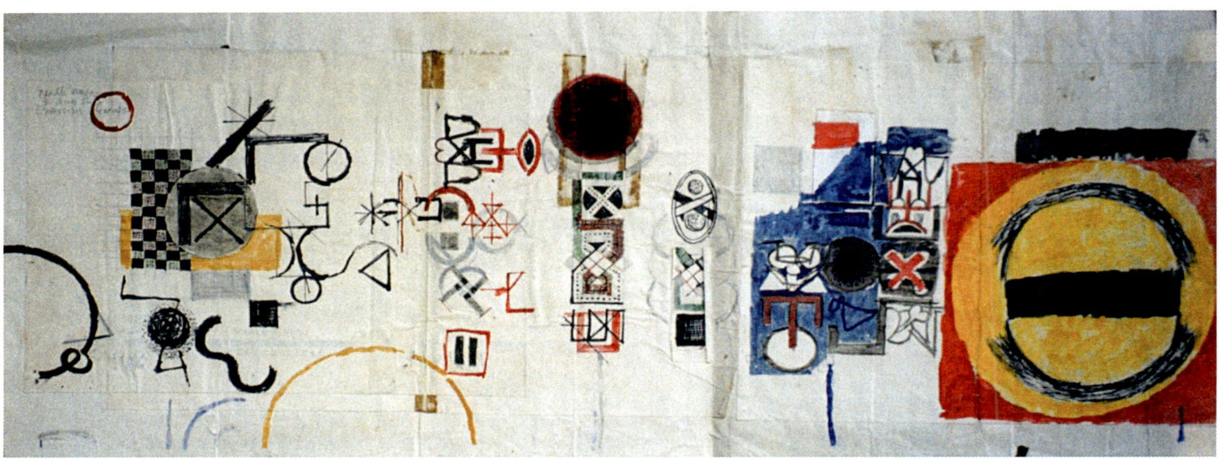

Groups (1954).Gouache and ink on paper.
65×20 cms. Williams estate.

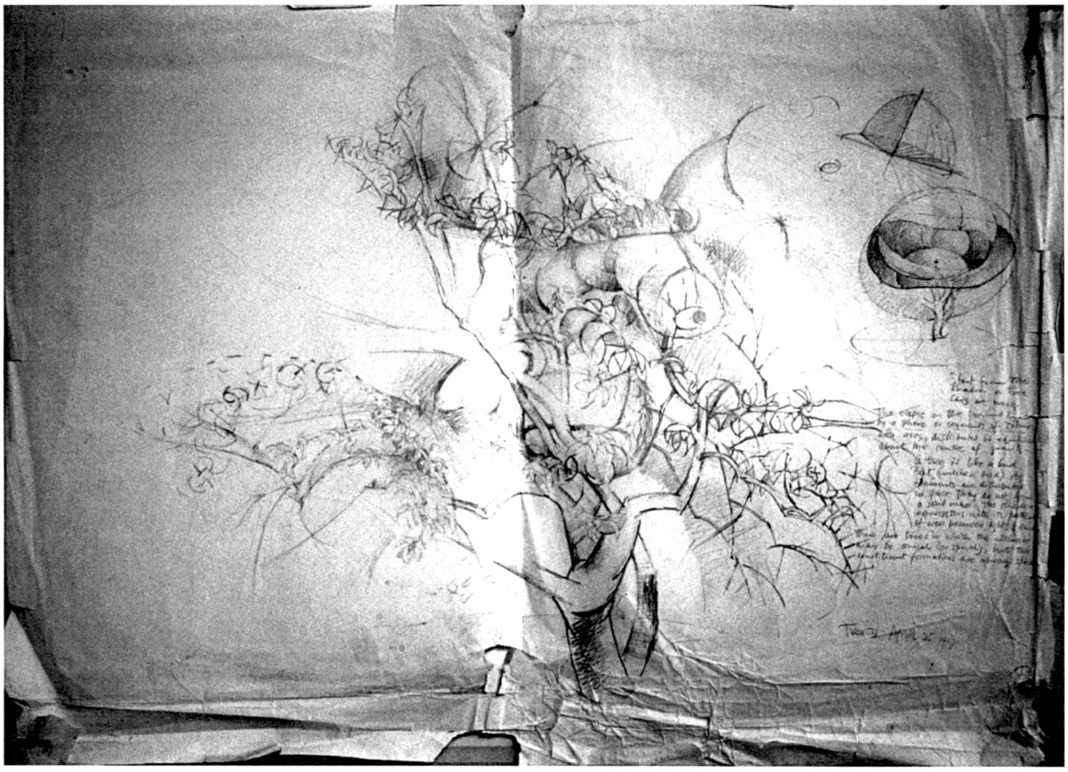

Tree V (1957). Sketch page. Pencil. Williams estate.

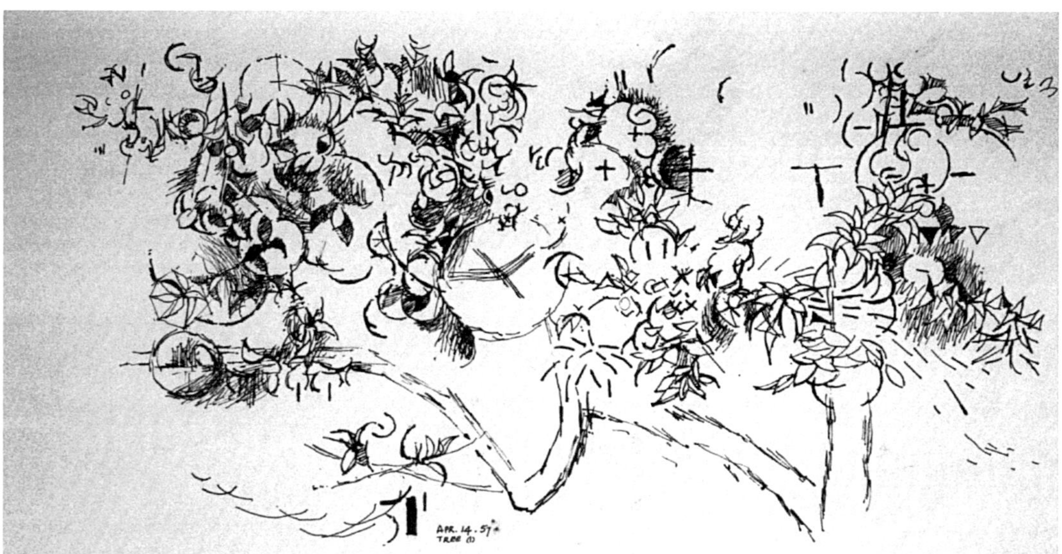

Tree (1957). Pen and ink on paper. 26×15 cms. Williams estate.

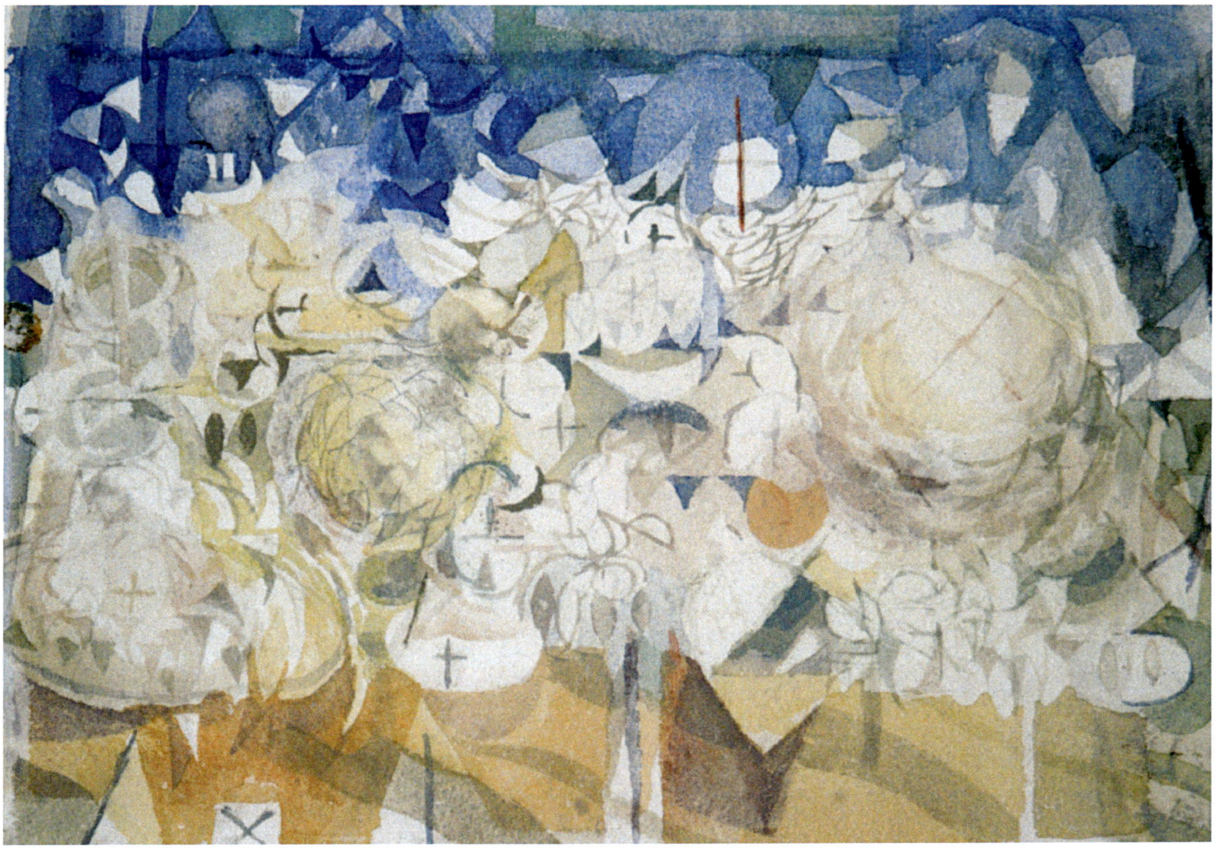

Tree 2 (1957). Watercolour. 23×16 cms. Williams estate.

He had become associated with the constructed abstract art group but it should be emphasised that the artists within this circle were only loosely linked through very diverse approaches and routes. Through his teaching rôle his interests became increasingly academic, theoretical and analytical. He described Roger Hilton as a "sharp kind of fellow" and his notes indicate that he was having a dialogue with him. It was in the nature of his motivation to engage fully with contemporary ideas. He certainly counted Hilton as a close associate at this time and, as we have seen, they exhibited together at Gimpel Fils in 1954.

The influences of non-European sources within the iconography of twentieth-century modernism are readily appreciated in the figurative legacy stretching back well beyond the Cubists. As a vital source these influences have been less immediately apparent in abstract art. This may well have been what Dalí recognised in Williams' painting. Where Wyndham Lewis compared Williams' highly successful, sustained use of the colour yellow to the effect of a tom-tom,[28] Harris references the West Indian steel band, and Williams also recalled his work being described as "Mau Mau Mondrian". This links with the emphasis on "rhythm" in the narratives of abstract art of the 1950s, and it is interesting to consider to what extent non-European "survival rhythms" are embedded in the subconscious personal iconography of Williams' abstract work. As Brathwaite was to put it: "The plantation does not contain all that is planted." In Williams' *Groups* (1954) and similar works[29] we can metaphorically bring together a number of abstracted elements which support this observation and suggest the reiteration of a subconscious iconography: a resounding repetition of motifs around the central composition; a roughly vertical symmetry; a primal punctuation of line; a balancing of massive three-dimensional form; parallel hatching; interlacing curves and the interlocking of planes.

Just as *Human World* arrived in British Guiana in 1956, Williams was taking part in the seminal group exhibition, *This is Tomorrow,* held at the Whitechapel Art Gallery in London. Two pages from his journal[30] were reproduced for the catalogue of this exhibition. These sketches and handwritten notes serve to illustrate the use of mathematical research and investigation as a source of ideas and they can be directly traced back to his 1954 exhibition. The "group" was a distinctive feature of the era with artists keen to share ideas, and *This is Tomorrow* saw a multi-disciplinary collaboration of artists, graphic designers and architects. Each group was charged with creating an exhibit that examined aspects of the contemporary environment. All work was to be newly generated for the exhibition space.

There was a fascinating ideological friction which became evident in the organising and presentation of the exhibition. As well as those who had their roots in the legacies of Bauhaus, the exhibition also show-cased artists whose radical non-figurative art derived from other important sources, most notably those interested in popular consumer culture. *This is Tomorrow* has been defined as the exhibition that launched Pop Art in Britain with the retrospective labelling and dating of the formation of "The Independent Group" and the consequent framing of the myth in history.[31] In his introduction to the exhibition catalogue, Lawrence Alloway wrote: "In *This is Tomorrow* the visitor is exposed to space effects, play with signs, a wide range of materials and structures, which, taken together, make of art and architecture a many channelled activity, as far from ideal standards as the street outside." Williams exhibited in Group 5 with John Ernest and Anthony Hill, both noted Constructivists, while Williams was described by Hill as an abstract painter. With the assistance of the architect Colin Glennie they constructed their section of the exhibition.

The three also jointly wrote the statement on constructed art as it appeared in the exhibition catalogue:

> *The Future*
> Constructed art is an independent art form and will be valued for its merits as art, and not because of some alliance with architecture. Like many other forms of art, it contains aspects of architecture in itself, but these have been heightened to a degree hitherto impossible.
>
> *The Issue*
> The evolution of mimetic art enlarged the ability of man to see nature. Non-mimetic constructed art will increase his ability to fashion and respond to the man-made world, the planned environment. It is an art that deals with carefully ordered visual stimuli, and in so doing, trains and conditions responses to these stimuli. [...] The challenge of the world today offers to both art and architecture the choice between phantasy, and the reality of a more precise aesthetic. A challenge to investigate the processes inside our skin and outside, that will determine the shape of our environment.[32]

What do we know of the installation of Group 5?

> Using screens faced with black and white vinyl sheet, Hill and his friends mounted a historically based, didactic display which included a "homage" to De Stijl and Constructivism alongside their own recent works. [...] Such a thorough investigation of Dutch and Russian abstract art was unusual at this date. [...] They showed photographs of important Dutch and Russian art and buildings, excerpts from pioneer texts such as *The Realist Manifesto* of 1920 and "translations" of paintings [...].[33]

They re-invoked the decade 1913–1923 and their ideas included exhibiting a Gabo and a Mondrian in their pavilion along with replicas and "translations" of some of the epoch-making artworks of that time. In the event, neither a Mondrian painting of 1933, lent by Mrs Nancy Roberts, nor the Gabo was shown as they were considered unstable. Williams is recorded as having exhibited a mathematical painting of a square composed entirely of smaller squares each of a different size. This seems likely to have been a further development from his *Plane Compositions*. "Like the work of Hill and Ernest," Grieve observes: "it would have reflected the work of the pioneer Dutch and Russian artists they so admired."[34] The three made versions in new materials of works by Malevich and Rodchenko, emphasising the links with their own contemporary ideas. Williams is also recorded as having made a "translation" of Rodchenko's *Black on Black* (1918).[35]

Summary statements of the rationale of the group exhibit were also included in the catalogue:

> *Painting Becomes Architecture*
> To be understood in the sense that prompted Marcel Duchamp to describe the constructions of Pevsner with the phrase, "a sort of chamber architecture".
>
> *Painting Becomes Construction*
> After Picasso and Braque pioneered the first constructions, the move to consummate the ensuing implications came from other painters and not sculptors.

> *The New Architecture and the New Art*
> "Never before in history had architecture been so influenced by painting [...] both De Stijl and Constructivism were to be assimilated by what was to become known as 'modern architecture'." (Philip C. Johnson, Mies Van Der Rohe, MMA 1947).
>
> *The New Has Just Begun*
> Constructed art, which began with New-Plasticism and Constructivism, is still at a very early stage. It is not, as the *status quo* holds it to be, merely a past phase wherein the idea of a logically pursued, non-mimetic art made its only possible contribution as an influence on architecture and design.

The author recalls two works that clearly belong to this period: small works in Royal format (20 ×25 inches), constructed in low-relief on shiny plastic or vinyl sheet. One had a shiny white base combining cut-outs and laminated pieces with small areas of thick texture; colourful but pale, with strong interest in the contrasting surfaces of the materials. The other had a glossy black base and was more dramatically colourful, also in relief and using thin pieces of wood laminate and bright red plastic shapes.

But it is clear from his notes from this period that Williams did not see himself committing to the universal aesthetic of abstract art. There are plans covering ideas for work indicating lines of enquiry exploring many different possibilities in his painting. He reiterates his intellectual engagement with the problem of creating a stereoscopic image of the human figure within the limitations set by the use of colour alone. As an artist he could not fail to return to the image, in fact he never left it. He stated: "My researches are not concerned with abstract or non-representational painting. [...] Nor am I interested in the completely abstract space-time experiments of some contemporary painters."[36]

The conflicts between abstraction and contemporary forms of realism that were a familiar feature of the era are clearly evident. We can see the continuing influence of an abstract analytical aesthetic being pursued in several studies of trees, studies of the nude and studies of figures from this period where the subject of verisimilitude is analytically deconstructed through a network of shapes and planes visible through vertical and horizontal axes and intersecting arcs. We may recall Mondrian's drawings and paintings of church façades and trees (1909–1914) in which the contemplation of verisimilitude is reduced to a geometrical, structural harmony.

> There are trees in which the ultimate form may be conical or spiral, but the constituent formations are always spherical. [...] Start from the shadow a tree casts at noon. The ellipse on the ground is cut by a sphere, or segments of spheres with axes distributed in equilibrium about the centre of gravity. [...] A tree is like a bud. But (unlike a bud) its elements are distributed in space. They do not form a solid mass. The shadow expresses this with its pattern of well balanced lights and darks.[37]

This aesthetic synthesis is linked with Williams' life-long interest in the human form and its underlying architecture. The figure, the nude and the self-portrait would remain formative, and studies in his folio reveal investigative approaches to realism alongside wholly abstract theoretical exercises.

Working within a framework of rational abstraction was a direction taken by many post-war artists. In such uncertain times it could be emotionally and politically neutral, concerned as it was with the lofty horizons of painting. For Williams it may have removed the immediacy of the complex issue of defining oneself. But estrangement from what Greaves refers to as "the support afforded by their own culture"[38] meant that the directions of Pop Art indicated in *This is Tomorrow* lay outwith his specific frame of reference. He stood aloof from the contemporary pop versions of modernism and the impact of mass culture, a culture that was not his own.

His drawings for *British Guiana: The Land of Six Peoples* by Michael Swan were completed at this time. These commissioned line illustrations represent the continuity of a thread of content that gave an opportunity to make some small reference to the memory of his own Guianese background. Derek Walcott called these drawings "incisive, skilful and trained."[39] He had also designed the book jackets for George Lamming's early novels, which are among the very first examples of book jackets designed by a West Indian for a West Indian.

It is possible to suggest then that both subject and style became an issue. Finding himself "practising an intrusive and historically recent art",[40] the reality of his position was now complex. It is clear from his notes that whether the idea was acceptable or not, his audience and critics were principally European. But it is also clear that he became cynical about the nature of his success. A few years later he reflects: "I should wish to abjure forever those white-hot spear points of ambition – London, Paris, New York – where reputations sizzle and glitter for a moment, sparking off new conflagrations which suffer the same fate, burning in these dying centres."[41]

He felt compelled to make a decision, and when he did his reasons were multifarious and self-aware in their complexity. Some were only crystallised retrospectively, but by the time of the second wave of post-war immigration to Britain – the mid-fifties to the mid-sixties – he had indeed decided to "get back to who he was."

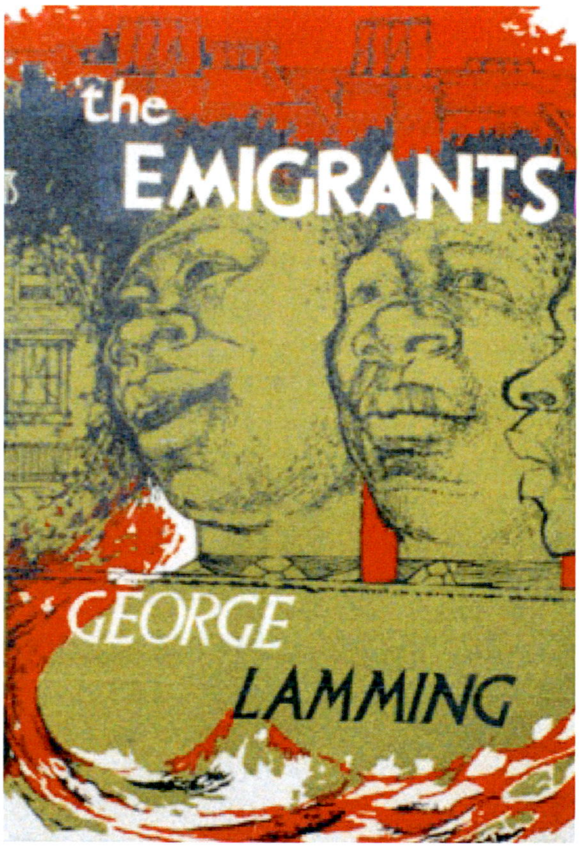

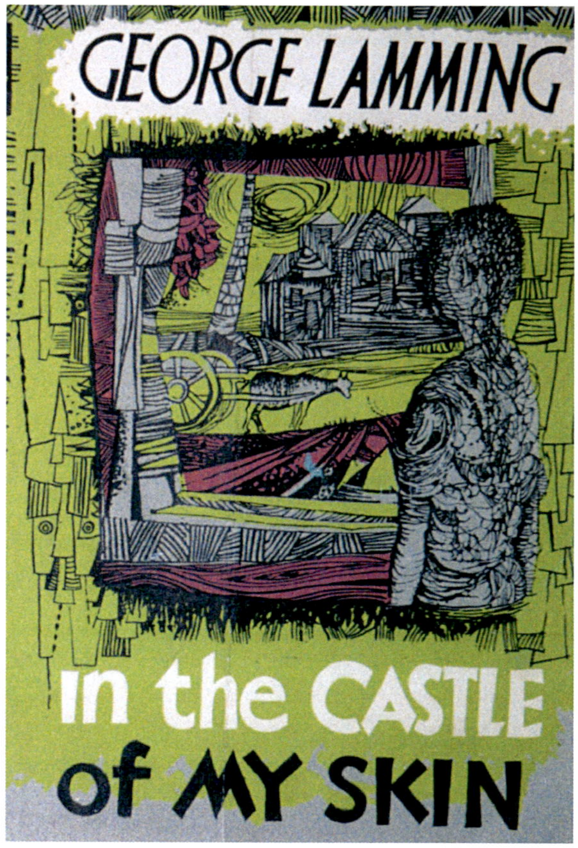

Jacket designs for George Lamming (1953 and 1954).

Pages 62–65: Commissioned illustrations for *British Guiana: The Land of Six Peoples* (London: HMSO, 1957), with the original captions.

NOTES TO CHAPTER 3

1 Denis Williams, *The Traditional Theme in African Art and Literature*. Lecture given at Makerere University, July 1966.
2 Alastair Grieve, *Constructed Abstract Art in England*. (Yale University Press, 2005), p. 37: "Pasmore's move from painting into construction had been one of the major influences on Anthony Hill, John Ernest and Denis Williams [...]."
3 "Exhibitions at the ICA", in *The Studio* (April, 1951).
4 William Fagg, "Science and Tribal Art", in *Nature* (Vol. 168, No. 4287, December 1951), pp. 1099–1100.
5 Wyndham Lewis, "The London Galleries", in *The Listener* (British Broadcasting Corporation, 14 July 1949), p. 68.
6 "Wifredo Lam at the ICA", in *New Statesman and Nation* (April 1952).
7 Penelope Curtis, *New Realities* (Tate Gallery: Liverpool, April 1992).
8 Charlotte Williams, interview with Denis Williams (1998).
9 Keith Vaughan, *Journal and Drawings 1939–1965* (London: 1966), p. 139.
10 André Breton, *Preliminaires sur Matta* (Exposé chez René Drouin, Paris, July 1947).
11 The original, oil on canvas, 157.5×122 cms., is currently untraced.
12 Stanton Macdonald-Wright (1890–1973) and Morgan Russell (1886–1953) renewed the colour theory of Synchromism after World War II.
13 Frank McEwen, catalogue notes.
14 Alastair Grieve, "Towards an Art of Environment: Exhibitions and Publications by a Group of Avant-Garde Abstract Artists in London 1951–55", in *The Burlington Magazine* (Vol. 132, No. 1062, November 1990), p. 777.
15 Alastair Grieve, *Constructed Abstract Art in England*, p. 222: "Pasmore showed his earliest relief at the first Fitzroy Street exhibition in March 1952."
16 Chris Stephens, *Roger Hilton* (London: Tate Publishing, 2006), p 25.
17 Oil, 157.5×122 cms. The medium, dimensions and date indicate that this was almost certainly *Colour, Weight, Sound* (1952). Untraced.
18 Oil, 134.5×40.5 cms. Later titled *Vertical Composition with arc of a circle* when it was exhibited at Gimpel Fils in 1954. Untraced.
19 See Alastair Grieve, "Charles Biederman and the English Constructionists 2: An Exchange of Theories about Abstract Art during the 1950s", in *The Burlington Magazine* (Vol. 126, No. 971, February 1984), pp. 67–77. [Special edition devoted to twentieth-century art].
20 Anne Walmsley, transcript of interview with Denis Williams (1993), p. 15.
21 *Recent Paintings by Roger Hilton; Recent Works by Denis Williams*.
22 Alastair Grieve, "Towards an Art of Environment...", pp. 773–781.
23 Wilson Harris, "Two Periods in the Work of a West Indian Artist", in *Kyk-over-al* (Vol. 6, No. 20, 1955), pp. 183–187.
24 Geoffrey Banks (*Departure for Cythera*) and Brian Kneale (*Pony in the Snow*) both won £750. Lucian Freud (*Hotel Room*) won £500. Denis Williams (*Painting in Six Related Rhythms*) and Henry (Heinz) Inlander (*Aneine Valley*) both won £250.
25 Chris Stephens, *Roger Hilton*, p. 27.
26 A. J. Seymour, *Art in Guyana* (Georgetown: National History and Arts Council, 1971).
27 William Hickey, "I Take Dalí to Look at the Art", in *The Daily Express* (London, 28 April 1955).
28 "A Negro Artist", in *The Listener* (British Broadcasting Corporation, 7 December 1950), p. 696.
29 Wall paintings in Chislehurst Caves, Kent (1954), *Reclining Nude* (1957), *Nude* (1957), *Circles and Arcs* (1958).
30 Dated November and December 1955 from *This is Tomorrow* exhibition catalogue designed by Edward Wright.
31 Alastair Grieve",'This is Tomorrow', A Remarkable Exhibition Born from Contention", in *The Burlington Magazine* (Vol. 136, No. 1093, April 1994), pp. 225–232: "It is also important to note that the idea for the exhibition was initiated by Pasmore's group of abstract artists and that they were the dominant contributors to it. The suggestion, in recent histories that *This is Tomorrow* was an "Independent Group" exhibition is a false one." See Alastair Grieve, *Constructed Abstract Art in England*, p. 256. He describes how Anne Massey has shown that the label "Independent Group" was first published in 1960 and received widespread currency only in 1966.
32 Hill, Ernest and Williams, notes in *This is Tomorrow* exhibition catalogue.
33 Alastair Grieve, *Constructed Abstract Art in England*, p. 37.
34 *Ibid*.
35 Recalled by John Ernest 28 December, 1990, quoted in Alastair Grieve, *Constructed Abstract Art in England*, p. 37.
36 Folio notes and papers. Williams estate.
37 From notes accompanying sketch page *Tree V*, 25 April 1957.
38 Stanley Greaves, "The Sustainable in Art", in *Sunday Stabroek* (Georgetown: 9 May 1999).
39 Walcott, Derek, "His is the Pivotal One about Race", in *Sunday Guardian*, (Trinidad, 1 December 1963), p. 23.
40 "The Cultural Heritage." (1976). Typescript, later published as "The Visual Arts in the Cultural Evolution of the People of Guyana", in *UNESCO Courier* (Vol. 1, No. 7, 1987), pp. 2–4.
41 With A. J. Seymour, "An Exchange of Letters", in *Kyk-over-al* (24 December 1958), pp. 93–99: p. 95.

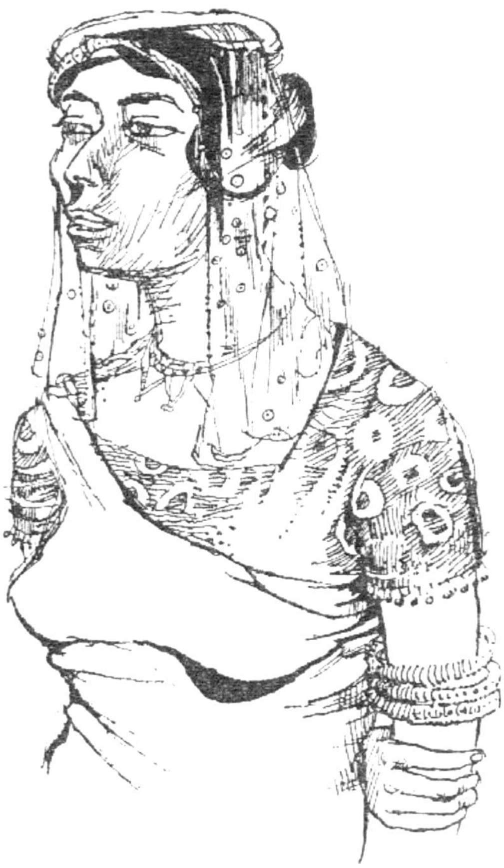

East Indian woman

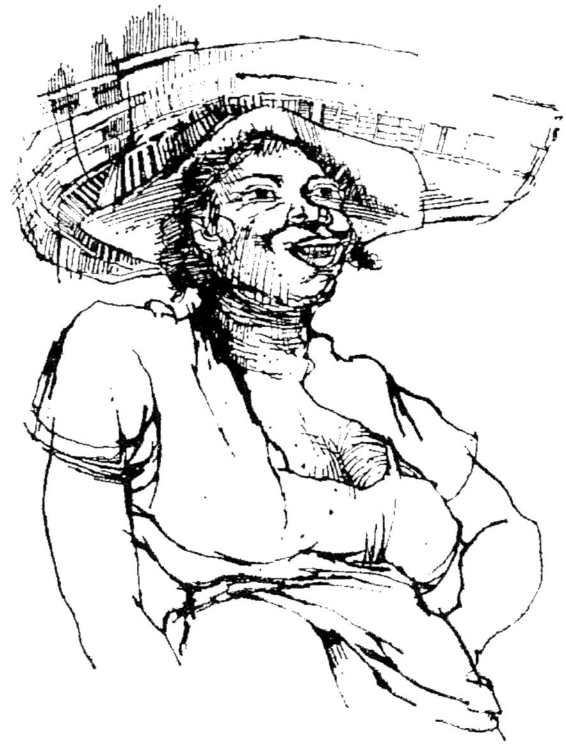

Negro fish-vendor

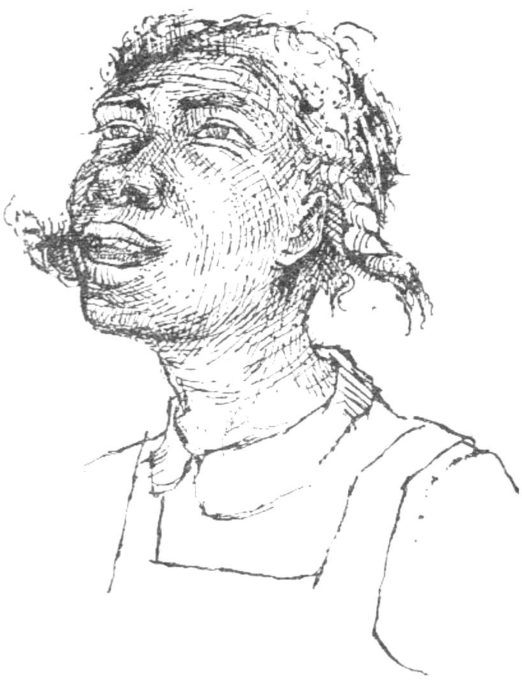

Negro schoolgirl

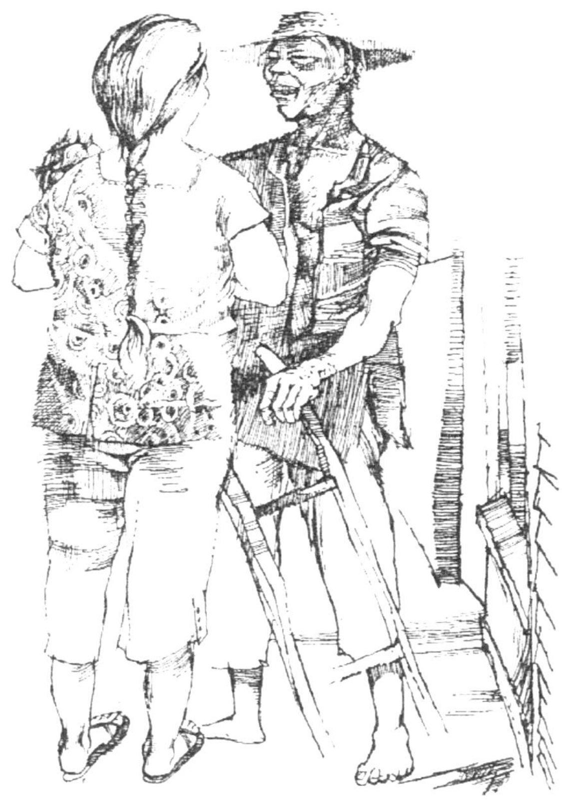

Chinese couple

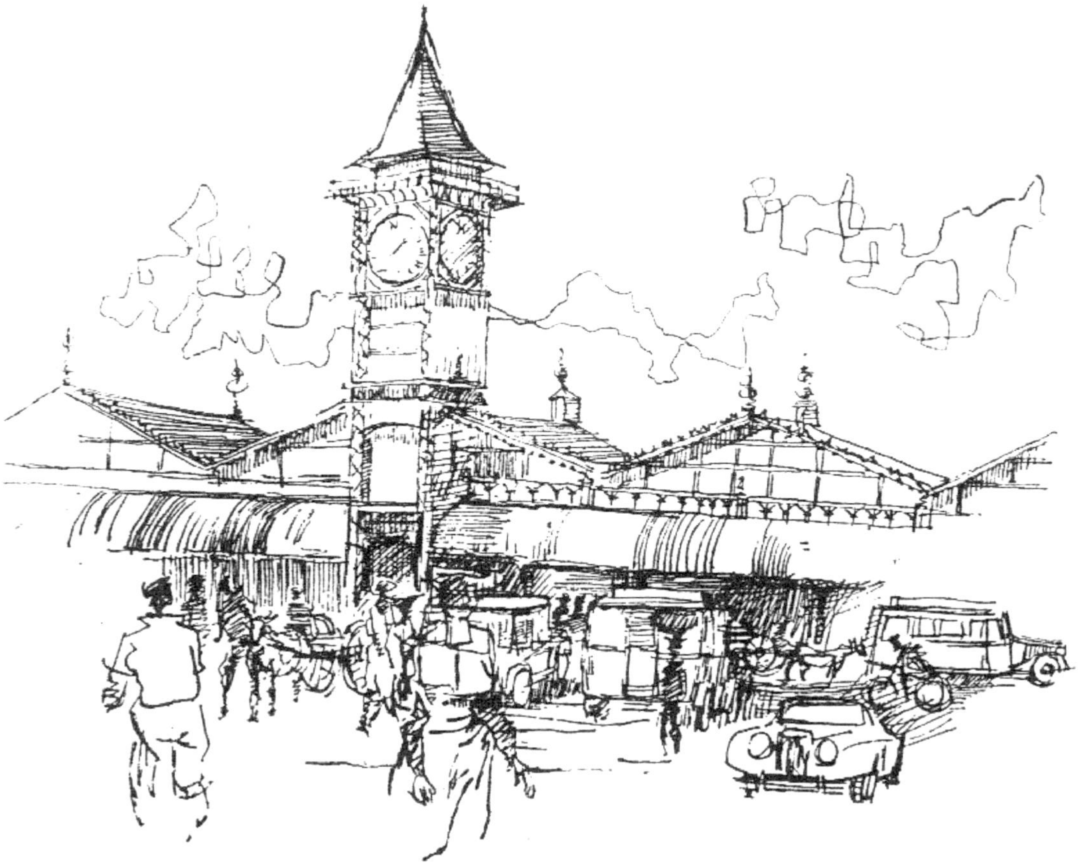

Stabroek Market (Georgetown)

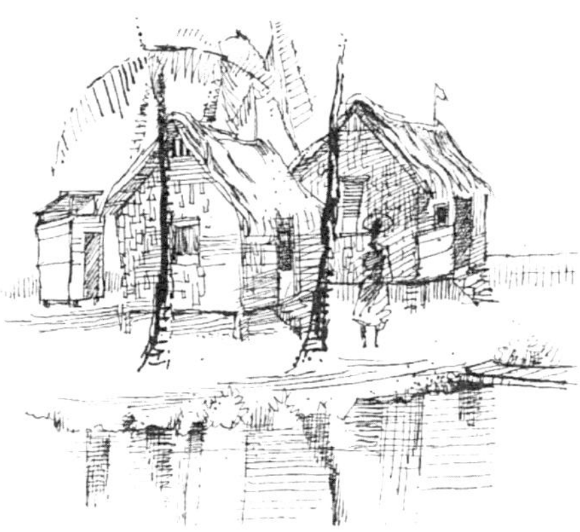

Thatched huts with "dry latrine"

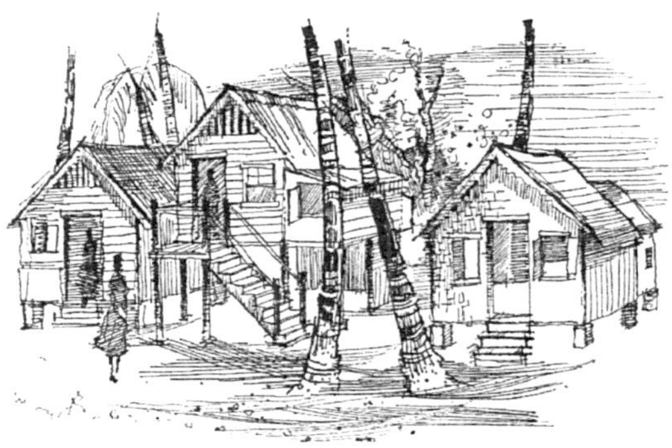

Village houses on stilts

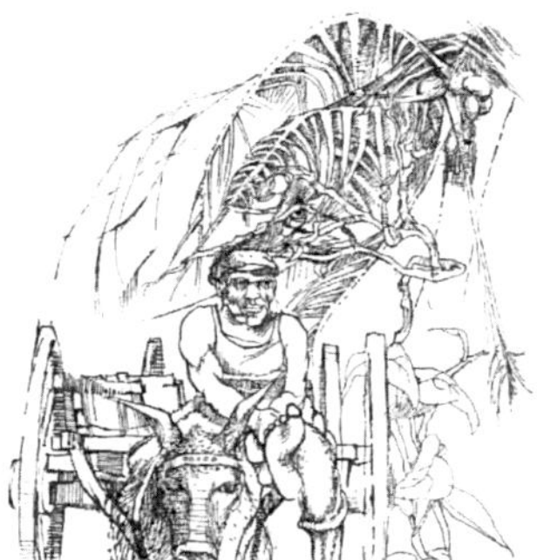

Donkey cart

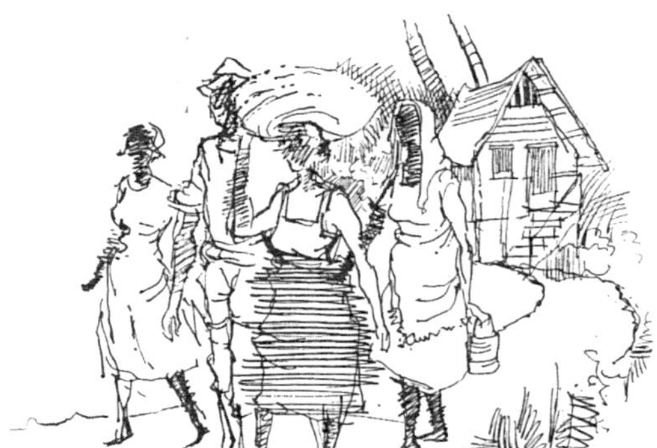

Workers on a red brick road

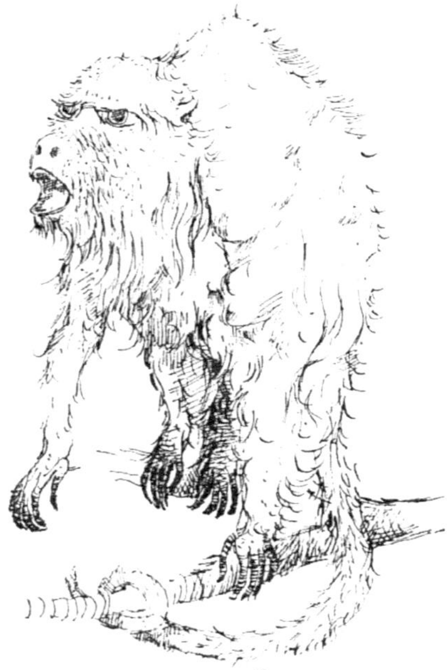

Red howler baboon

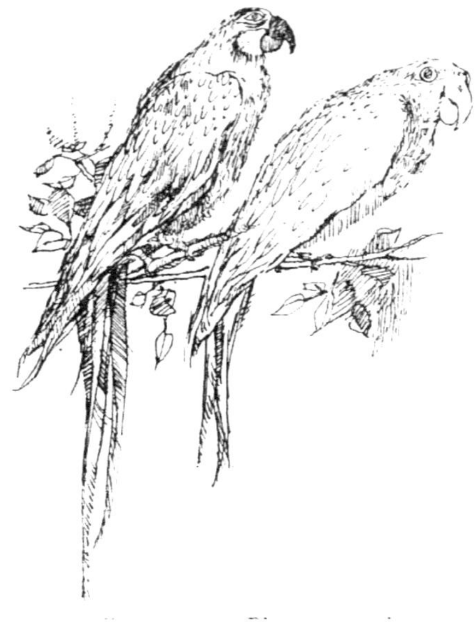

Blue and yellow macaw. Blue-crowned parrot

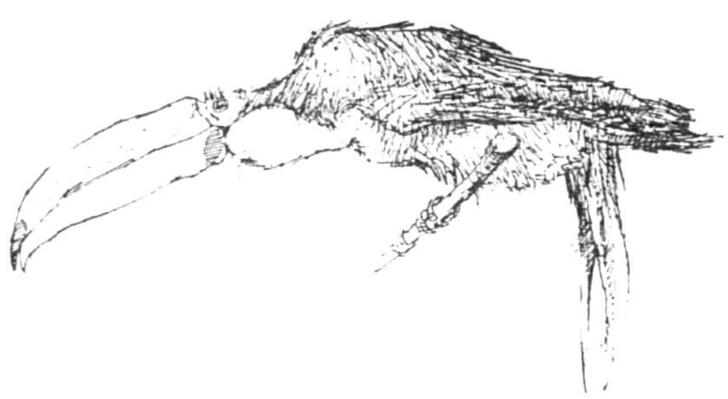

Toco Toucan

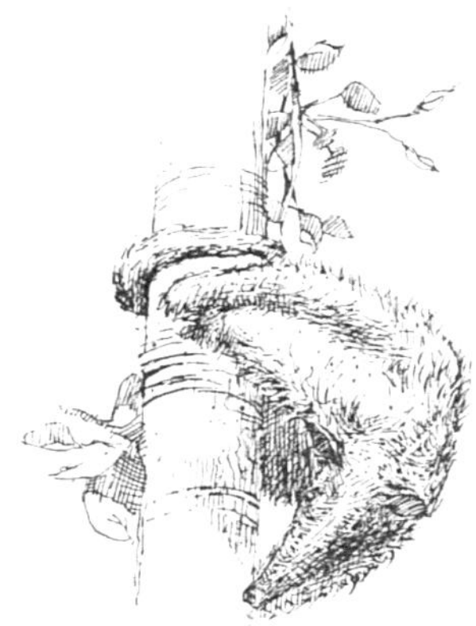

Tree Ant-eater

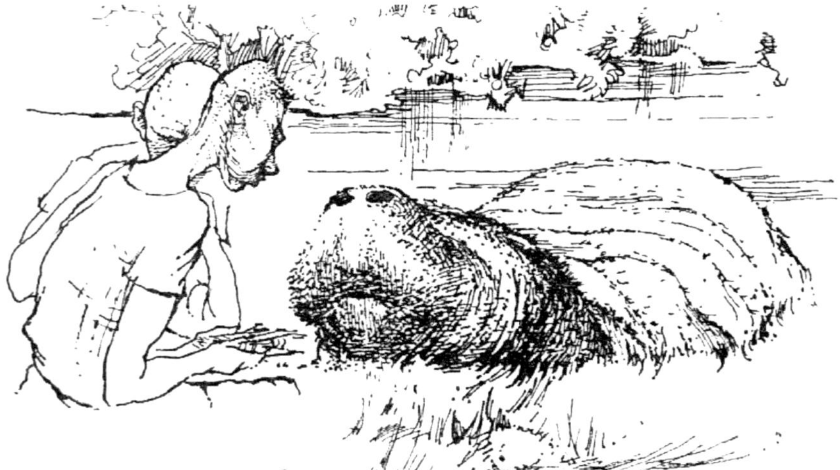

Feeding a manatee in the Botanic Gardens, Georgetown

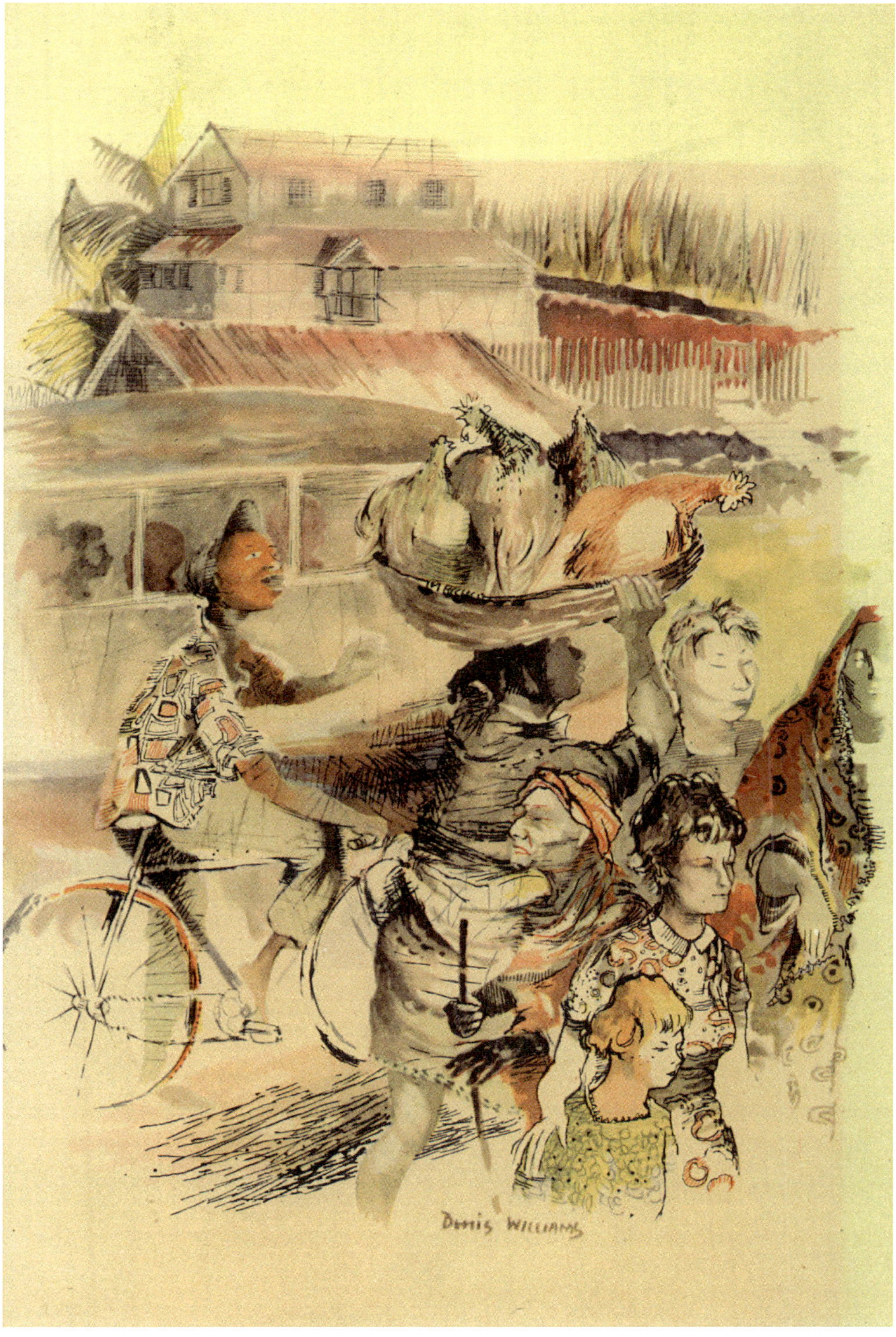

Jacket illustration for *British Guiana: The Land of Six Peoples* ((London: HMSO, 1957).

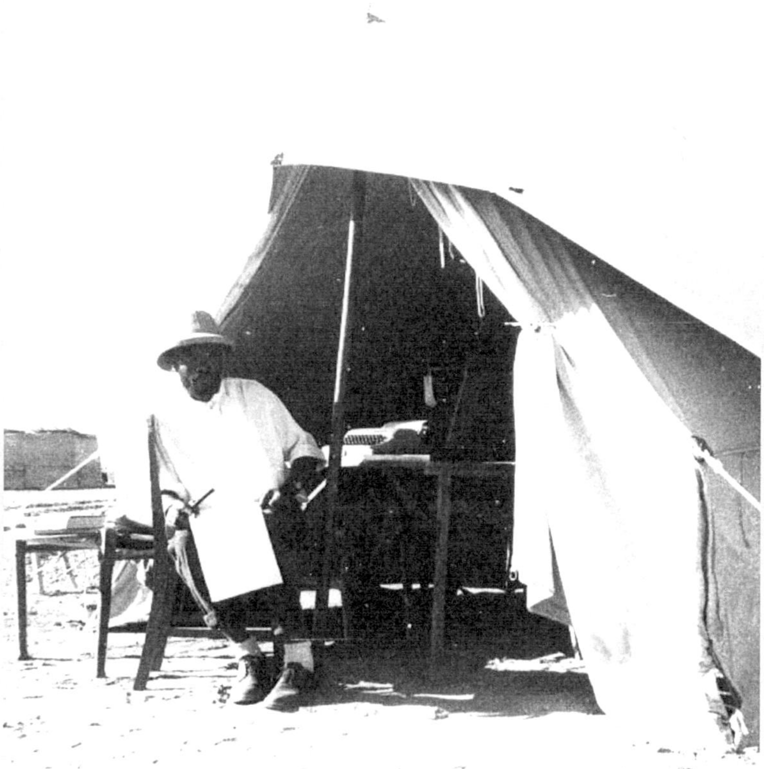

Field camp, northern Sudan (1958).

Chapter 4

A Triangular Dialogue

By the middle of the twentieth century, the calls for independence were resounding across Africa. Denis Williams left London in 1957 and made the voyage to Sudan. At that time the country was newly independent and undergoing Sudanisation by the government. This was against the background of the First Sudanese Civil War (1955–1972) which had been triggered by the fear that the new nation would see the southern, predominantly Christian people dominated by the Arab Muslims of the north.

He took up a post as lecturer in the Department of Fine and Applied Art at the Khartoum Technical Institute. At that time there were both male and female students. His work there included the teaching of drawing and painting in practical workshops and studios as well as lecturing in art history. He also held a remit as an archaeological draughtsman accompanying the last of the European-led expeditions to Meroë.[1] He supported and encouraged a gifted group of young artists in Khartoum, which he described as "a geographical and cultural cross-roads at the heart of the continent."[2] He came into contact with the work of young, talented Sudanese artists such as Mohammed Shibrain, also with a European training, and Ibrahim el Salahi, who had trained at The Slade and exhibited at Galerie Lambert in Paris. These artists were developing an Islamic aesthetic and Williams found much that was fascinating in their work; he observed that: "[...] the planar, frontal conception of the picture area is the idea which fuses the two visions, East and West, and causes them to merge in a common aesthetic."[3]

We can see in his surviving artworks like the *Portrait of Katie Alice* (1955) that he was applying the calm, simplified notation of an analytical approach to his portrayal of the human figure; this is supported in his use of a very restricted palette of tonal complementaries. Despite his radical change of location his artistic concerns show him still working towards a resolution in his painting – one which moves him forward, linking the subtle tonal hues and refined colour of his cerebral abstract work with the human dimension he had, publicly at least, appeared to abandon. We can characterise Williams as essentially a figurative artist who had explored the possibilities of the new abstract through his association with constructed abstract art. But it was of continuing relevance to the work that followed although he withdrew from any full-scale commitment to it.

He maintained contact with his BG friends in London, and from Khartoum he was in touch with A. J. Seymour, who presided over the pan-Caribbean periodical *Kyk-over-al* and who became Deputy Chairman of the National History and Arts Council of British Guiana. In an exchange of letters between Khartoum and Georgetown, he wrote:

> My painting is once more coming easy. Good and strong! Things are coming up in me here that I thought I'd lost forever, they're good. Yet this is not my environment. I enjoy an anonymity by which I can get more out of myself than I've ever known before [...] a great deal of writing and painting in the year I've been here. And much travel. This is welcome.[4]

One of the main features characterising any profile of exile is the need to communicate pride and validity in ancestral credentials. For West Indian migrants from the early twentieth century onwards, this brought into play issues surrounding personal identity in relation to an ancestral past that was considered to be lost or forsaken. In *The Pleasures of Exile* (1960) George Lamming articulated a far greater complexity compared with those migrants seeking their European ancestry:

> The West Indian Negro who sets out on a similar journey to Africa is less secure. His relation to that continent is more personal and more problematic. It is more personal because the conditions of his life today, his status as a man, are a clear indication of the reasons which led to the departure of his ancestors from that continent. [...] His relation to Africa is more problematic because he has not [...] been introduced to it through history. He knows it through rumour and myth which is made sinister by a foreign tutelage, and he becomes, through the gradual conditioning of his education,

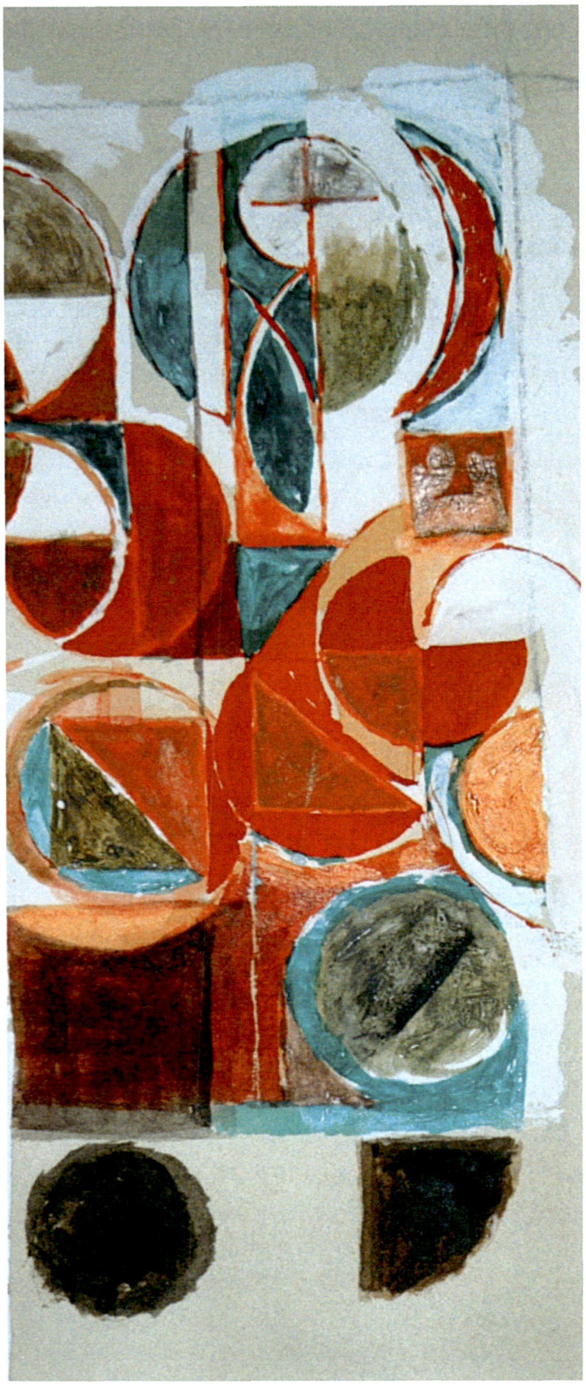

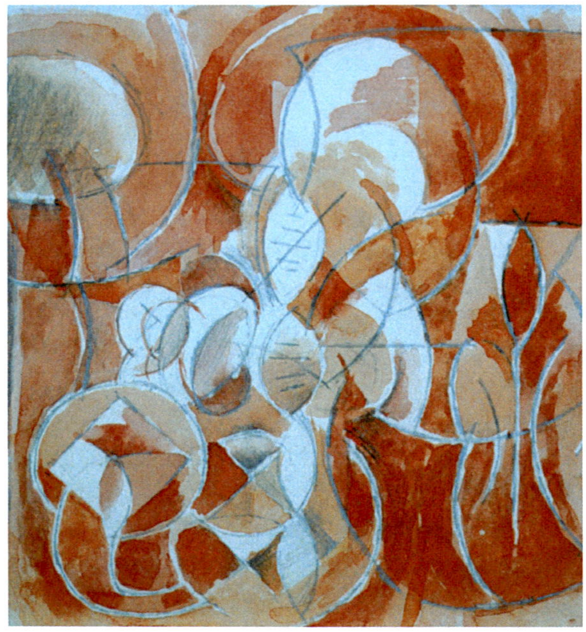

Drawings and studies (1958)

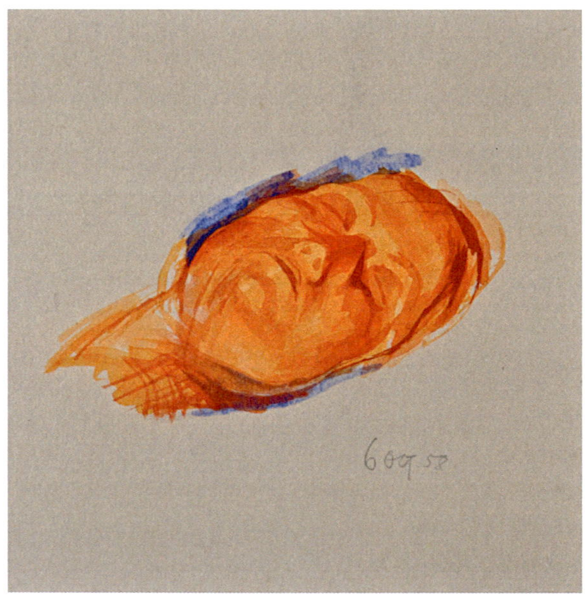

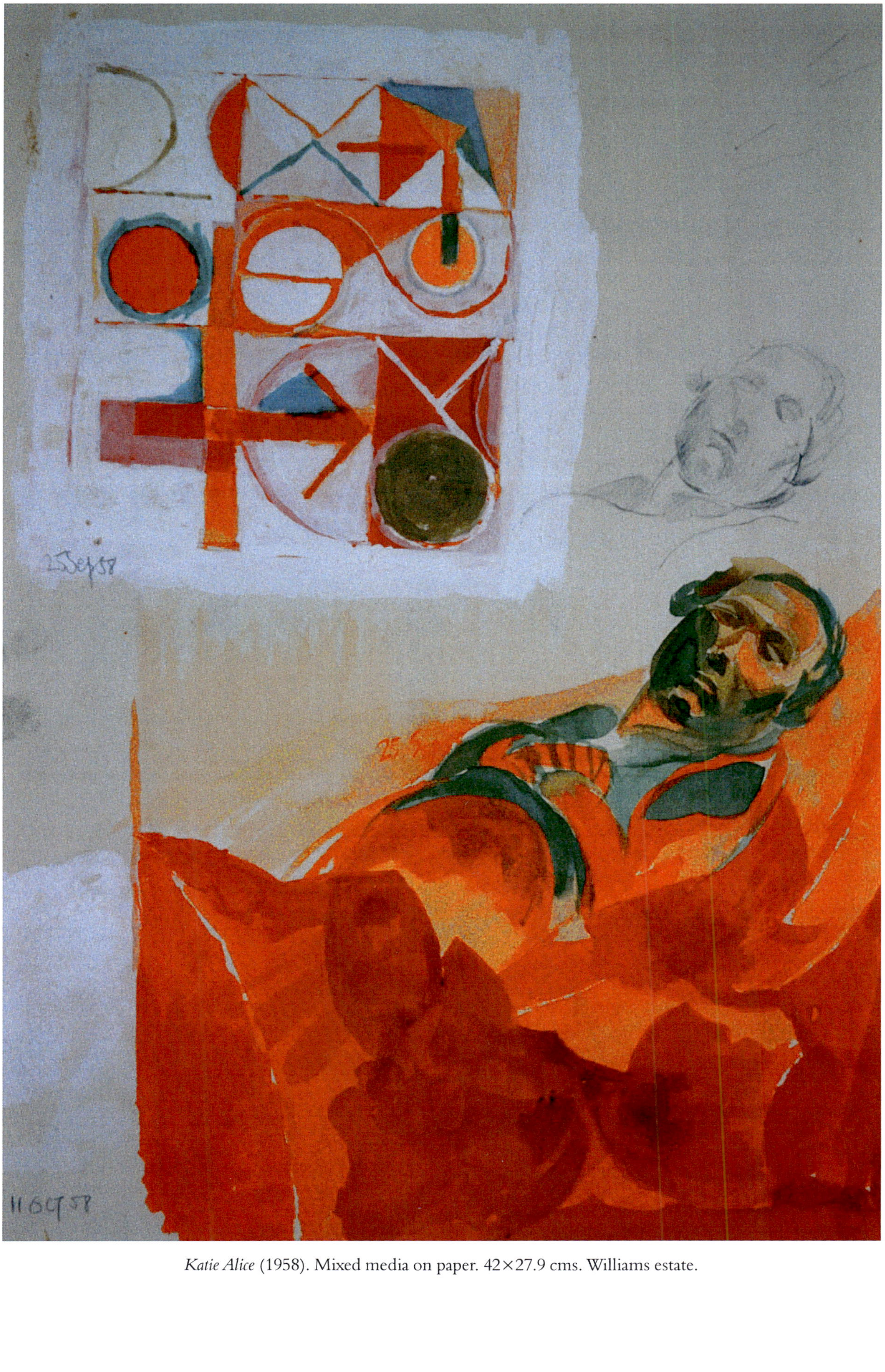

Katie Alice (1958). Mixed media on paper. 42×27.9 cms. Williams estate.

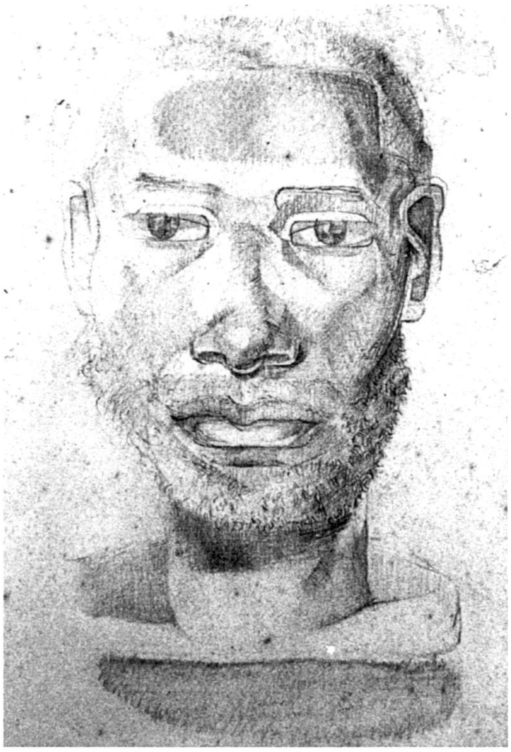

Self-portrait (1958). Pencil. 26×19 cms. Collection E. Williams.

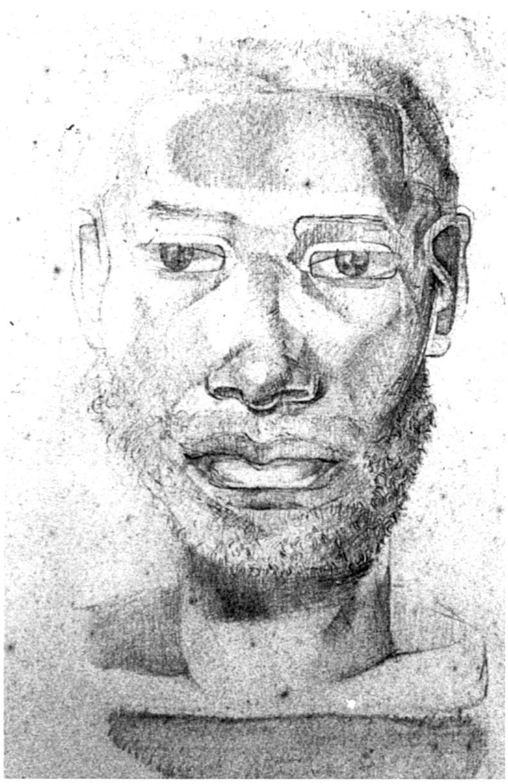

Self-portrait–Symmetry (1958). Pencil. 33×22 cms. Collection E. Williams.

> identified with fear: fear of that continent as a world beyond human intervention. Part product of that world, and living still under the shadow of its past disfigurement, he appears reluctant to acknowledge his share of the legacy which is part of his heritage.[5]

Like every West Indian intellectual of the era, Williams was familiar with the work of the West Indian poet Aimé Césaire; with his reclamation and use of *nègre* as a positive rather than a pejorative term and with his rejection of assimilation as any kind of valid direction for "the Negro". *La Négritude* in its turn had been influenced by the African-American Harlem Renaissance of the 1920s through writers and poets claiming ownership of the black experience. Likewise we know Williams was familiar with Senegal's philosopher-president Léopold Senghor's influential theory of culture and with Frantz Fanon's uncompromising theory of revolution. It was Fanon who saw violence as an essential part of any anti-colonial struggle. Fanon ridiculed the notion of a "peaceful handover" of the former colonial countries and reserved his most withering contempt for the post-independence westernised nationalist bourgeoisie. And it was a reading of Fanon that was at the heart of Black Power politics for several decades. Some were cynical of the more naive assumptions of the new black consciousness. Kenneth Ramchand observed:

> All these literary manifestations share certain features: a celebration of Africa as a cultural matrix; a favourable interpretation of the African past; a pride in Blackness; a contrast between a harmonious way of life and a decadent White civilization lost in materialism; and a joyful proclamation of the sensuous and integrated African or Negro personality.[6]

But the social and political theories of culture which underlined West Indian, African-American and certain African ideologies seem to have been a necessary and integral part of the intellectual discourse of the Western-educated black élites in the process of claiming and framing their own cultural identities in the 1950s and 1960s – whatever route they had taken from Africa.

Self-portrait (1958) is a metaphorical statement that makes obvious reference to the African mask as if to emphasise the uncompromising pursuit of the theme of identity at the heart of Williams' progression. It shifts his ancestral past into a new

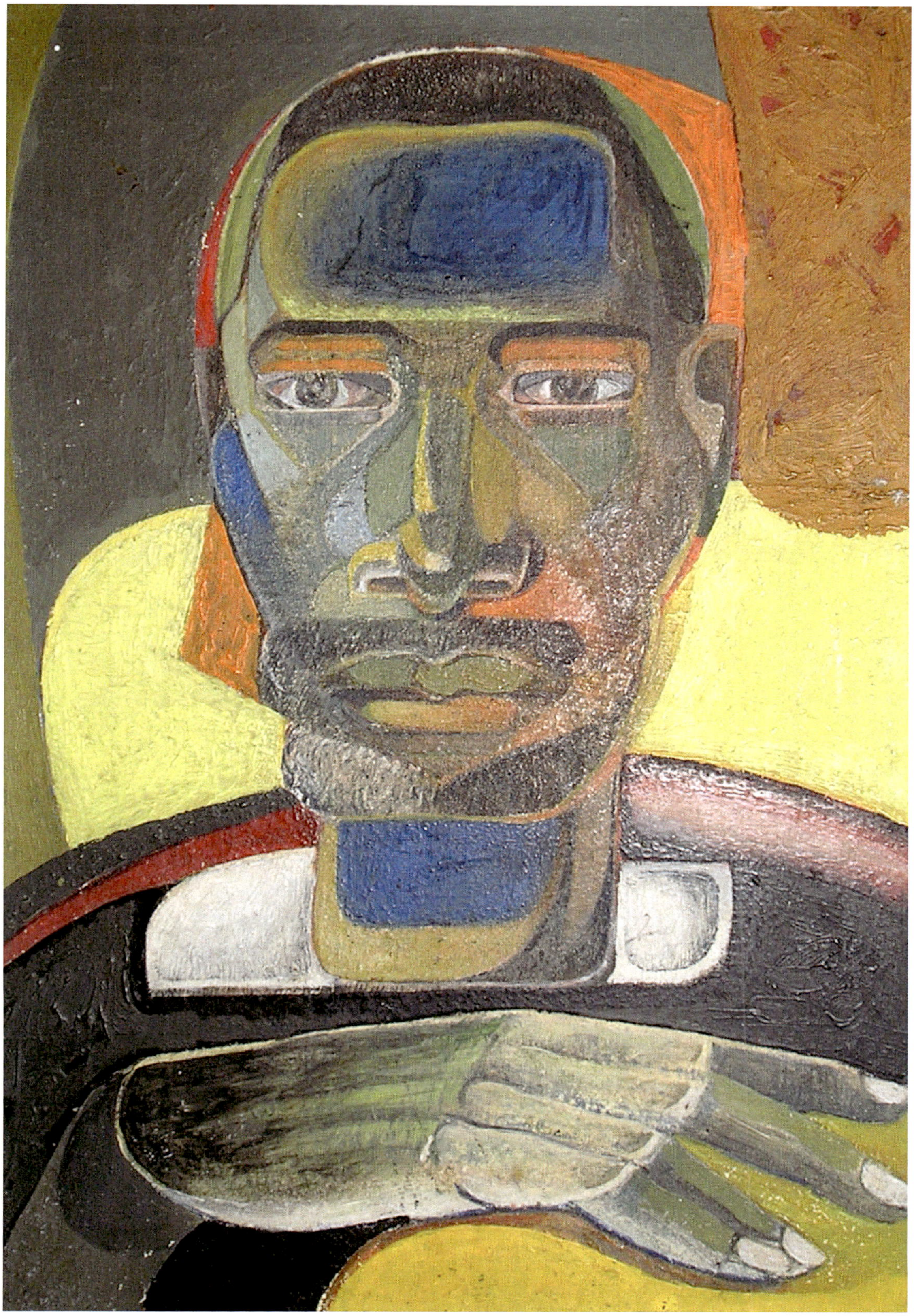

Self-portrait (1958). Tempera on board. 33×21 cms. Collection C. Williams.
Photograph by Arlington Weithers.

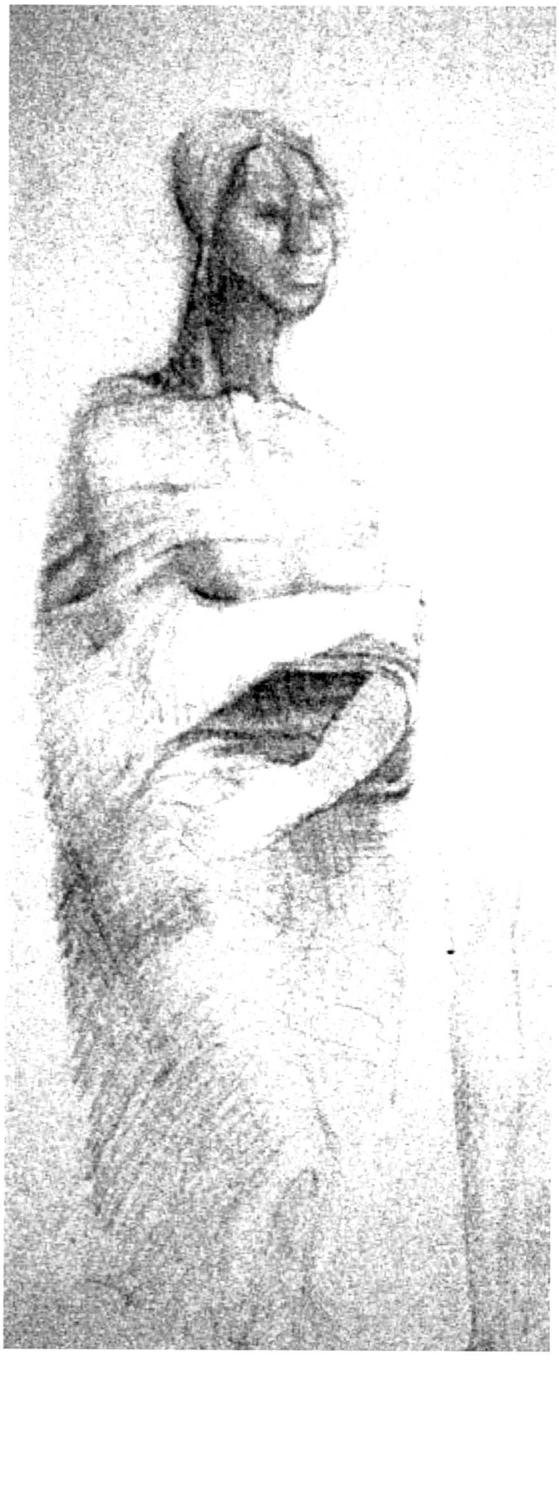

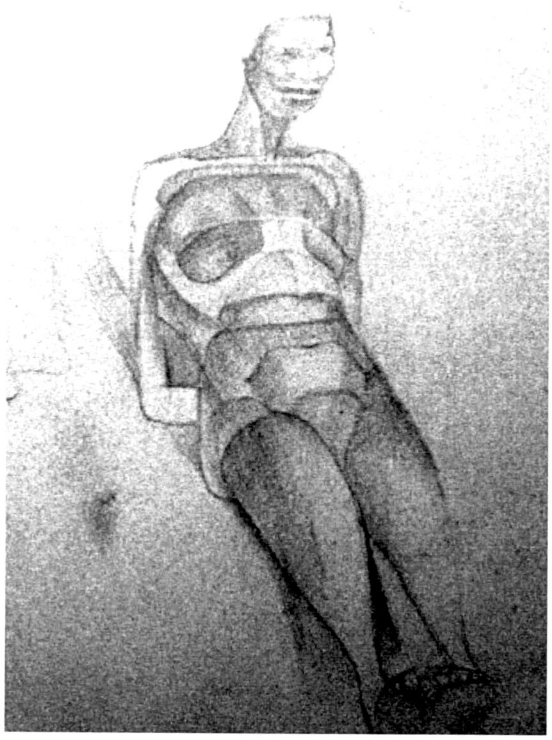

Figure studies (1958). Sudan. Pencil.

Opposite: *Katie Alice* (1958). Pencil.

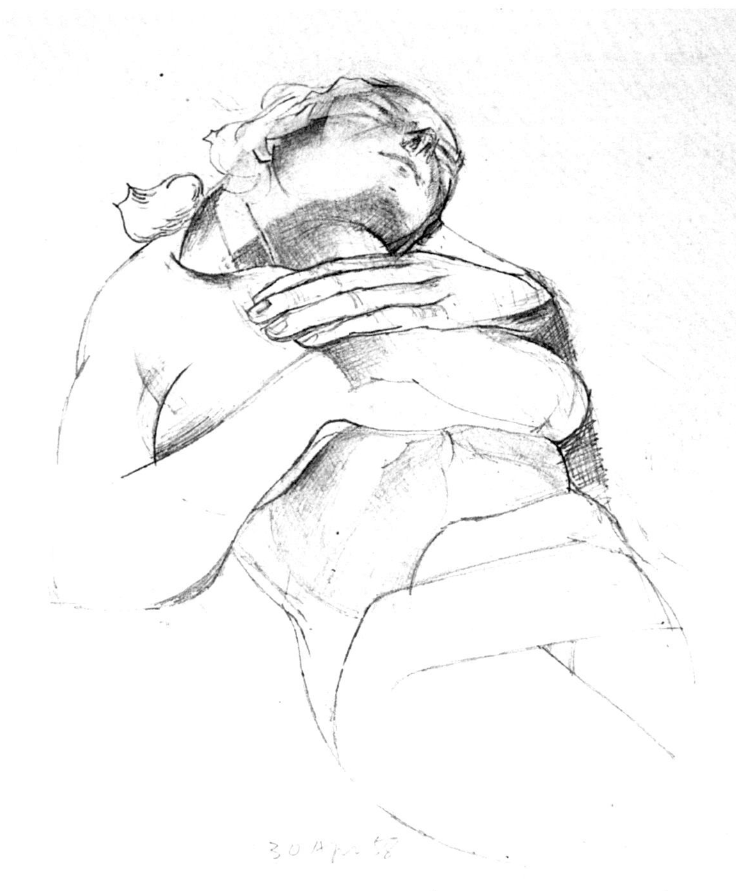

configuration with his present. It evokes the ancestor in its iconography but it also voices the self-questioning unease of his present. It attempts to accommodate the communal cult stereotype of the ancestor with his acquired Western intellectual affirmation of the artist as individual. It is within the creative matrix that internalised anxieties can be explored and this portrait bears the aura of such a function. The portrait communicates the symbolism of the head as the spiritual receptacle of thought; as the repository of memory, and as a symbolic link with an antique culture.

Self-portrait–Symmetry, a drawing dated August 1958, is one of two preliminary studies for the work. It shows the portrait head in a highly constructed composition of its constituent parts, which emphasises the vigour of three-dimensional form. Other elements have been closely worked from a study of abstracted surface texture. The drawings do not rely on the acquired formalism of sphere-cylinder-cone reduction but build on years of careful scrutiny and probing draughtsmanship, a hallmark of his approach. The obvious symmetry in the preliminary studies is extended into the final painting where the controlled balance of the desert-chroma of Sudan – the golden-yellows and ochres and subdued shadow-greens – show a palette that is refined and elegant. The use of a contrasting cool, atmospheric blue for the forehead is striking and draws the eye to the surface reality which claims Williams' attention. The material texture of the paint appears to employ the actual substance of the desert sand of Africa, particularly in the grainy working of the beard, as if to give a heightened sense of actuality, and providing a link between material and spiritual, past and present.

In the portrait the artist has exploited a bold, frontal concept of presentation. The pose is immediately sculptural in its curvilinear geometry referencing an African context and the magical function of the head. It is a statement that suggests that the artist is in possession of a potent legacy and the head is the seat of its creativity, with the hand of the artist the symbolic instrument of that gift. The painting has been developed as a series of independent relationships of rich tactile colour and texture. The shapes exist in an ambiguous non-illusionistic dimension of space. In this approach the artist finds a resolution between the figurative and the abstract which was at the heart of his aesthetic search, combining aspects of the expressive and gestural with the stillness of his neo-abstract experiments. This approach signals the future direction of his art and the development of what might be called his mature style.

If *Self-portrait* (1958) communicates the possibility of renewal through the inner reconstruction of origins and identity in Africa, it is the impact of the external location suggested in *Moulid el-Nabi*[7] that communicates the artist's awareness that he is witness to the continuity of a culture to which he has no access. As he wrote in his *Africa Journal* (1959–1967): "I acknowledge it as one of the revolutions of my awareness to have lived in such homogeneous societies of the Old World where the idioms of culture are reflected in every detail of language, of thought, of custom and in the very architecture of the individual mind."

Moulid conveys something of the artist's response to the environment of Sudan: the powerful visual-shock impact this new location had on the artist. It depicts a devotional dance performed by men at the Zikir of the crescent moon. We see the symbolic richness of the sacred Koran, a glimpse of the exquisite decoration of the interior of a mosque, the crescent-moon symbol and the calligraphic styling he described as "an endless development and refinement of the linear, lyrical form of the Arabesque."[8] In this work he acknowledges the continuity of the footprints of human existence and the trace of past events, matter and memory.

This painting also uniquely provides us with a concrete reference to the seamless approach that links Williams' painting, his creative writing in *Other Leopards* and his early engagement with archaeology. It demonstrates the systematic, synthesising methodology that came to characterise his output. He appreciated the historic canon of ornamental space, expressed through the calligraphic Arabesque in Islamic art, describing it as "a space not of the concrete world, not environmental, but timeless as it were, in a continual present."[9]

The artist registers this concept of space creating a highly charged atmosphere within an architectural setting. An Islamic ogee archway resting on intricately decorative pillars supports a screen colourfully worked in motifs of crescents, stars, circles, dots, banners, flags and twinkling lights "where ornament is in fact its own environment".[10] The ogee frames the central space where the body of men move as one in their worship-dance, accompanied by a drummer. This colourful decorative framework contrasts with "a mass of white gone grey at its limits."[11] The

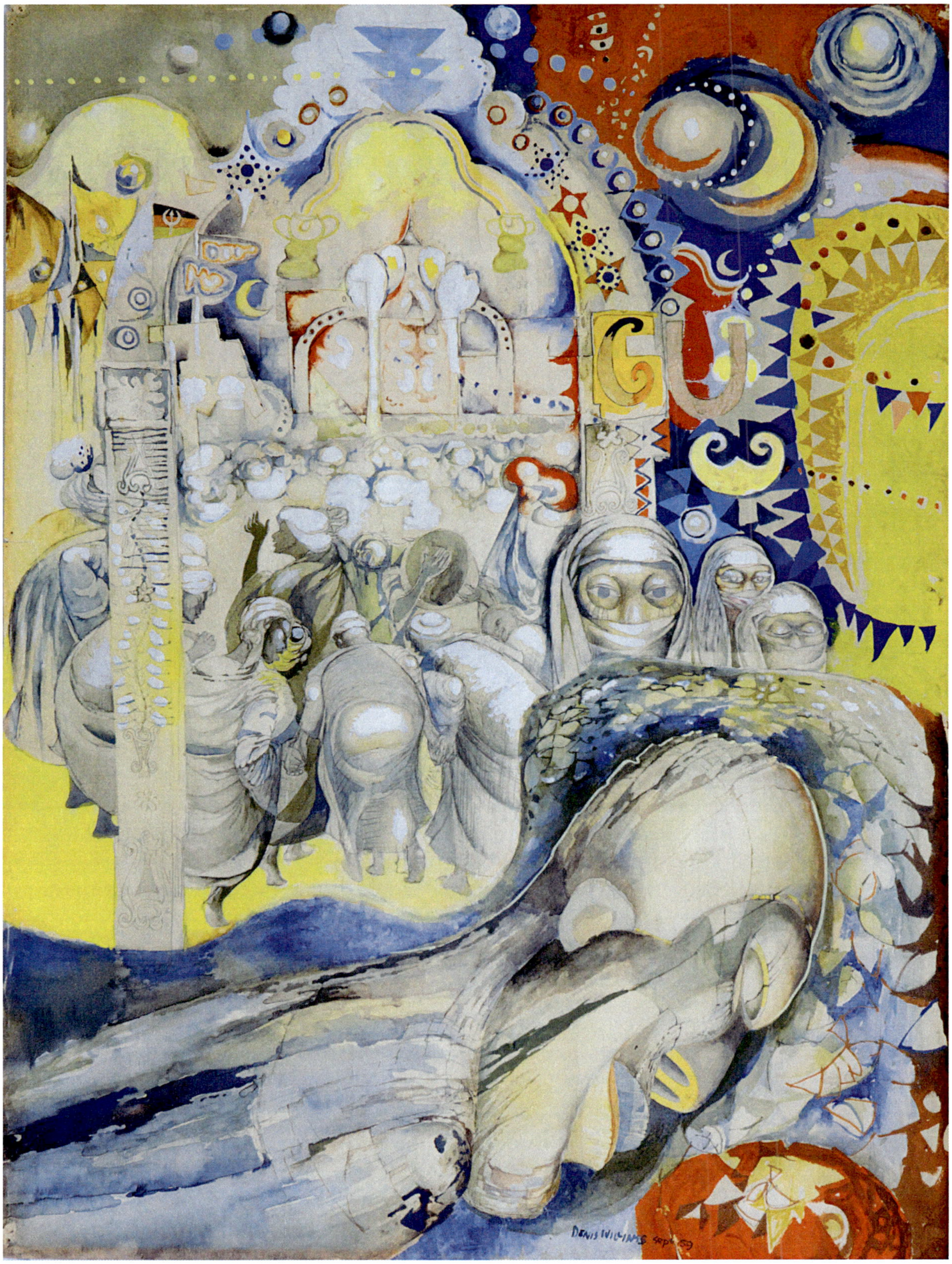

Moulid el-Nabi (1959). Mixed media on paper. 76.2×56 cms. Collection E. Williams. Photograph by Arlington Weithers.

colours of the desert are evoked in the range of whites, the dust-greys and the pale ochres. More complex arches and screens create the ambiguous, abstract, interior space above the dance and this middle area is cut and pasted using techniques seen in earlier works on paper. Floating pale forms, puffs and glows, hover and ascend – first opaque, then transparent and finally invisible.

The arrangement of the host of female figures to the right of the composition is stylistically reminiscent of *Human World* as they face outwards and move away; they are separated by the screen from the devotions of the men. The artist observes at a distance but the eyes of the women engage directly with the viewer.

The sculptural form of a recumbent holy figure dominates the foreground, isolated in an ethereal, flowing blue contour. This form is painted in modelled overlays of thin broken washes of blues, greens and greys, and rests in a powerful, bowed attitude. It resembles crumbling, aged, weathered stone and we are reminded of Williams' description of Amanishakete, the Queen of Time, in *Other Leopards*:

> She towered before me in the ancient blackened stone. There were all manner of lines incised and dreadfully alive. She was the lines. She had eaten into the stone the way that grey matter etches itself into the interior of the skull, the way a vine eats into stone and leaves itself behind long after it has died.[12]

Throughout the painting the artist uses the contrast of subdued tonal watercolour transparency with striking opaque primary colour. Line drawing with tonal cross-hatching is an integral part of the work. Lines are hard-edged or broken: sometimes high-definition, sometimes vague suggestion. Deliberately unpainted areas allow an airiness to anchor the eye where the drawing might indicate further elaboration. The paint is layered from transparent to opaque to insistent flat colour. These delicate layers of paint readily suggest a metaphor of time: mirroring its shadows, layers and instants. Layers of time reflect his immersion in archaeology, which is itself predicated on paralysis and suspension in time. To the artist, time itself can be observed and deconstructed. In a painting, time past, present and future can lapse; interval, instant and rhythm can be suspended; meaning is where interpretations lie thickest. Chronological time disintegrates; the trails, the traces, the fragments, the layers and the repetitions – all of these are elements that help to build up the complex metaphor of time in this work.

While in Africa Williams conducted a triangular dialogue. He maintained contact with colleagues in Britain and as part of his regular visits to family in North Wales he would typically stop off in London to visit the British Museum and Dillons book shop. All his life, wherever he was, he continued his practice each evening of listening to the BBC World Service. He had contact with a tiny West Indian community in Khartoum and he continued an exchange with A. J. Seymour in British Guiana. "I've written no one at home for such a long time. But all my growth and effort is of course pointed in the direction of my eventual return – my 'recall' as you so gratifyingly put it."[13]

Seymour replied:

> You like the word "recall" which I used to describe your coming back home. I don't belong to Africa now. As a transplanted bloom of many generations grafting with mingled bloods in my veins, I want to help build the greatness of my country, to cross the racial barriers which would and might separate me from my neighbours in BG. To go back to the Continent of my origin is natural but impossible.[14]

So far as the development of his painting was concerned, the reality was that over any extended period he found it very difficult to paint in Sudan. Although fascinated by it, he found no natural empathy with the Islamic culture. Because he clearly found the desert landscape conditions blindingly hot and disorientating he had begun to write. Typically he would go to sleep in the early evening and wake at 2 a.m. to write through to daylight to avoid the heat, dust and glare. In letters to his daughters he wrote:

> [...] when I wake up it's much cooler, so I do a bit of painting in the garden. There are very many beautiful things to paint in this country [...] all kinds of lovely birds (like Tu-Tu and Po-Po) and wonderful flowers and lots of strange trees and many nice fruits to eat! When I'm finished painting the moon and stars come out [...] and it's so very lovely. [...] I really can't do much more in this heat. You may have forgotten what it is like here during the summer, but really one feels continually on the brink of madness.[15]

The Williams estate holds dated drawings, sketches and studies which show that, although small, his output of artwork was maintained throughout the Sudan period while he was engaged with the writing of *Other Leopards*.

The enigma of the Meroë civilisation and the identity of Amanishakete, Queen of Time, remained unresolved. Layers of paralysed archaeological time contribute to a sustained metaphor for Williams. He kept a journal of notes and drawings that accompanied him on the expeditions to Meroë. He possessed a consummate skill in drawing and where photography was unreliable his methods were predicated on a studied draughtsmanship. The art of Denis Williams was central to his approach. It enhanced the close attention to detail which is a distinctive feature of all his archaeological studies. These skills even metamorphosed across disciplines to characterise the prose of his novels and short stories.[16]

From 1959 onwards Williams began making extensive tours of East and Central Africa – Northern Rhodesia, Kenya, Uganda, Tanganyika and Zanzibar – in pursuit of "the Negro mind and personality". The process of the quest provides the imaginative, intellectual and creative material and the shifting time framework present in *Other Leopards*. He wrote: "The accepted idea of Negro Personality, dominated as it is by the image of the American Negro and to a lesser degree by the West African, is very wrong."[17]

Louis James wrote:

> *Other Leopards* (1963) made a major contribution to the Caribbean literature of the 1960s. In the years of widening political independence for the region, West Indian writers were seeking an identity, trapped as many saw it, between the intellectual hegemony of Europe and the ancestral culture of Africa. Williams, writing out of his own experience, created in his protagonist Froad an archetype of this dilemma."[18]

Derek Walcott immediately recognised the importance of the novel:

> It is the most complex and brilliant book I have read on this theme. Even if he chooses not to write another novel, he has written our pivotal book about race.[19]

Kenneth Ramchand noted:

> The power of Williams' novel is the power to suggest in concrete terms the menace and comfort of discovering origins. [...] By the end of *Other Leopards* the need either for roots or for spiritual transcendence has been concretely established, but the central character has achieved neither.[20]

In 1962 Williams moved from Sudan and journeyed to Nigeria. It had gained its independence from Great Britain in 1960 and was governed by an unbalanced coalition of ethnic parties. He took up a post as lecturer in the School of African Studies at the University of Ife, then still housed at Ibadan. The Meroë archaeological excavations form an intellectual link through the historical movement of ideas along the Sahara corridor from the deserts of Sudan to equatorial Africa and this link parallels his personal movement and location at the time. *Other Leopards* was published in 1963, but he returned briefly to Khartoum in February 1964 to conduct research at the museum and to go back into the desert. The move to sub-Saharan Africa marks the second phase of the Africa period and had greater impact for Williams as a concretely lived experience.

The author O. R. Dathorne[21] was a close personal friend, and he makes it clear that, beyond those who made brief visits, Williams was one of the very few West Indians who gained any substantial first-hand experience of living in Africa. West Indian concepts of Africa – either from the Anglophone Caribbean or from London – were largely acquired vicariously and often based on unsubstantiated assumptions. The psychological urge towards Africanism was tied to a retention of cultural survivals in language, folklore and lifestyles, and the need to claim a heritage, as Dathorne put it, combining "a mixture of fertile wish and barren memory."[22]

In 1962 Williams had attended the first African Writers' Conference at the University of Makerere in Uganda. This was to become the regular venue for conferences on developments in emerging definitions of black identity in African literature. One delegate wrote:

> The Conference itself marked the final climax of the attack on the Négritude school of Léopold Senghor and Aimé Césaire. For some time now African writers of English expression like Ezekiel Mphahlele, Wole Soyinka and Christopher Okigbo, have treated this kind of literature which expresses sterile concepts such as "négritude" or the "African personality" with utmost derision.[23]

Later, Andrew Salkey was to recall a social gathering with the Jagans in Georgetown in 1970 during which the subject of black identity was being discussed. Dathorne was present and he made pointed reference to "African antipathy":

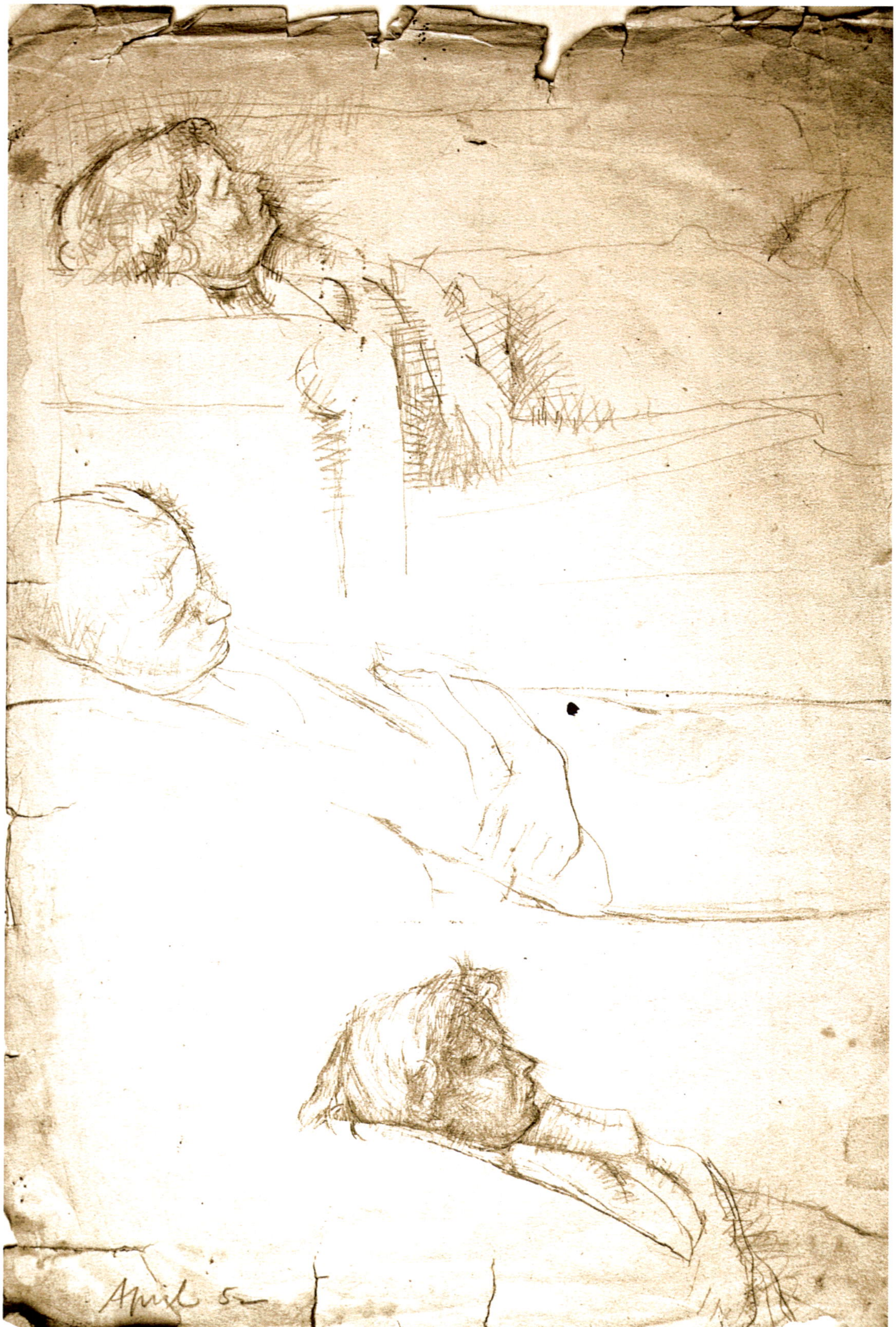

Katie Alice. Pencil studies (1952).

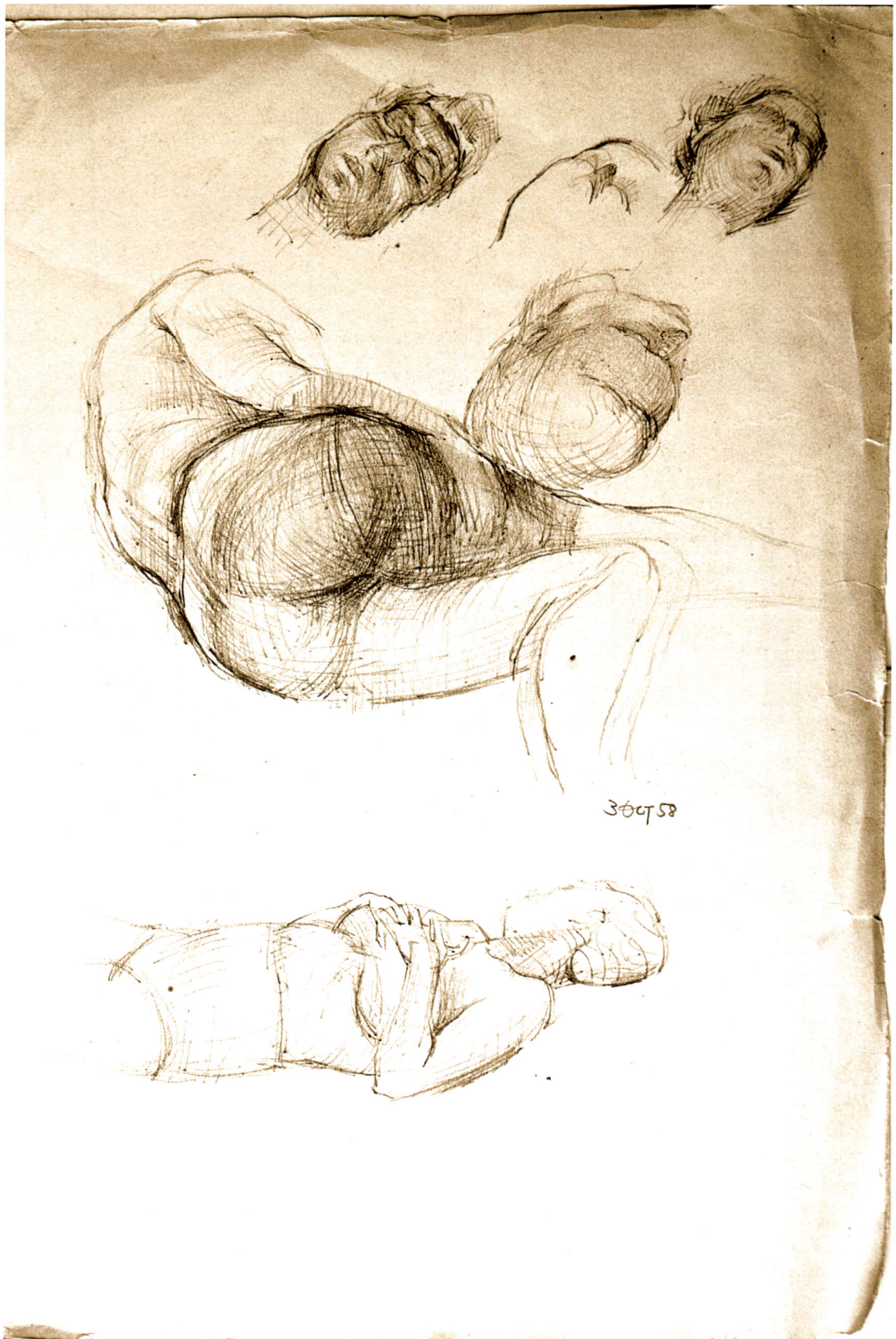

Katie Alice. Pencil studies (1958).

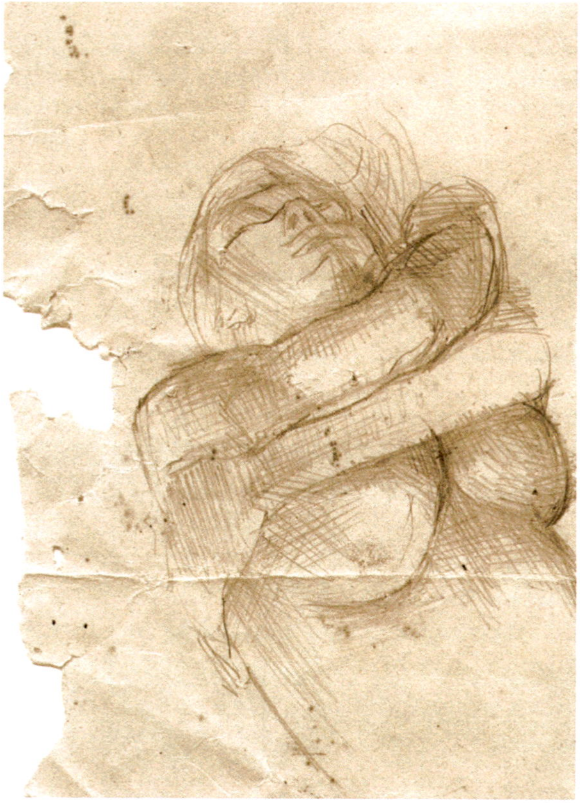

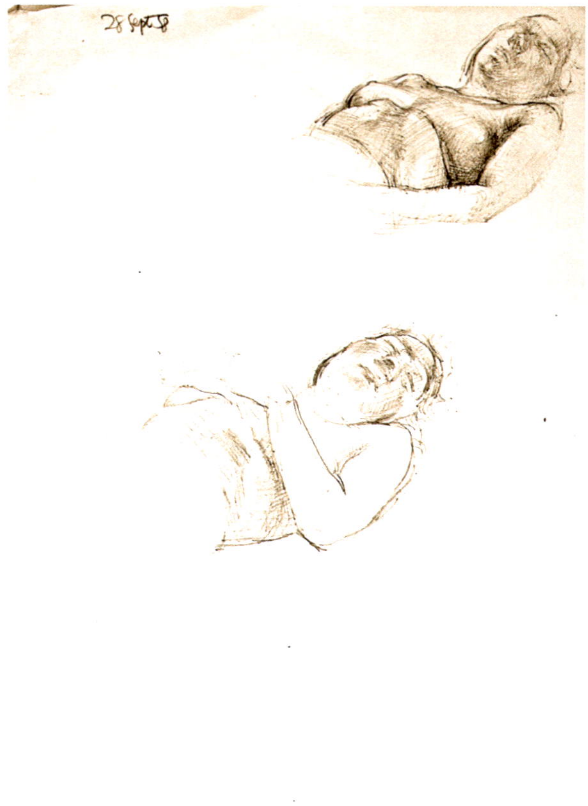

This page: *Katie Alice* (1958). Pencil.

Opposite: *Katie Alice* (1963). Blue biro.

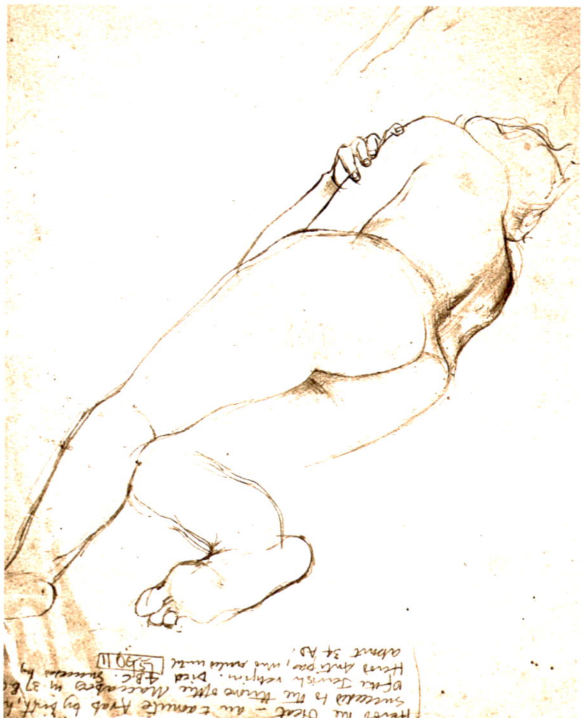

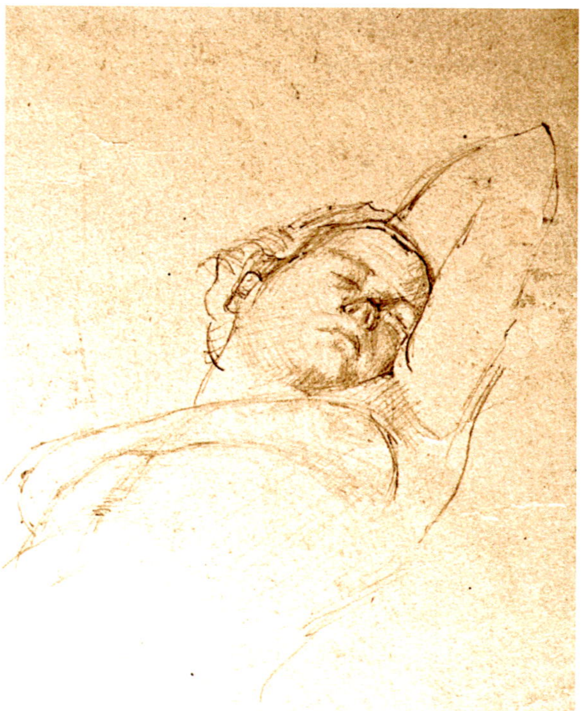

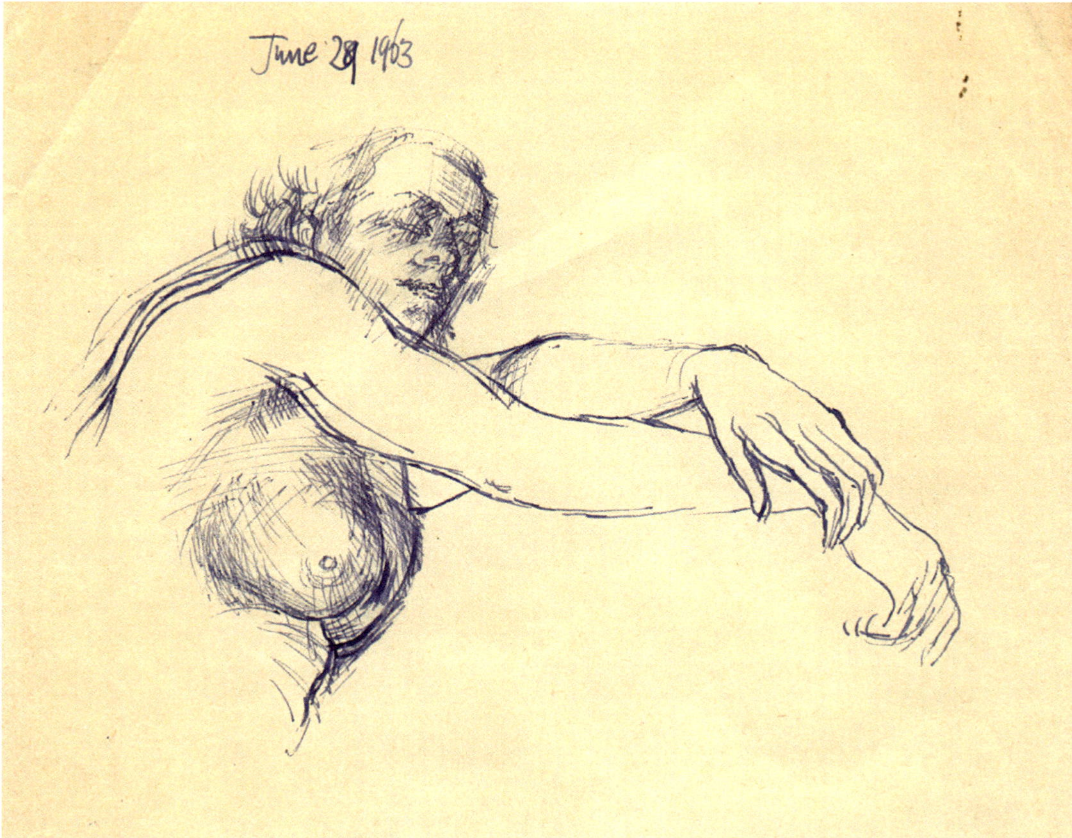
June 29 1963

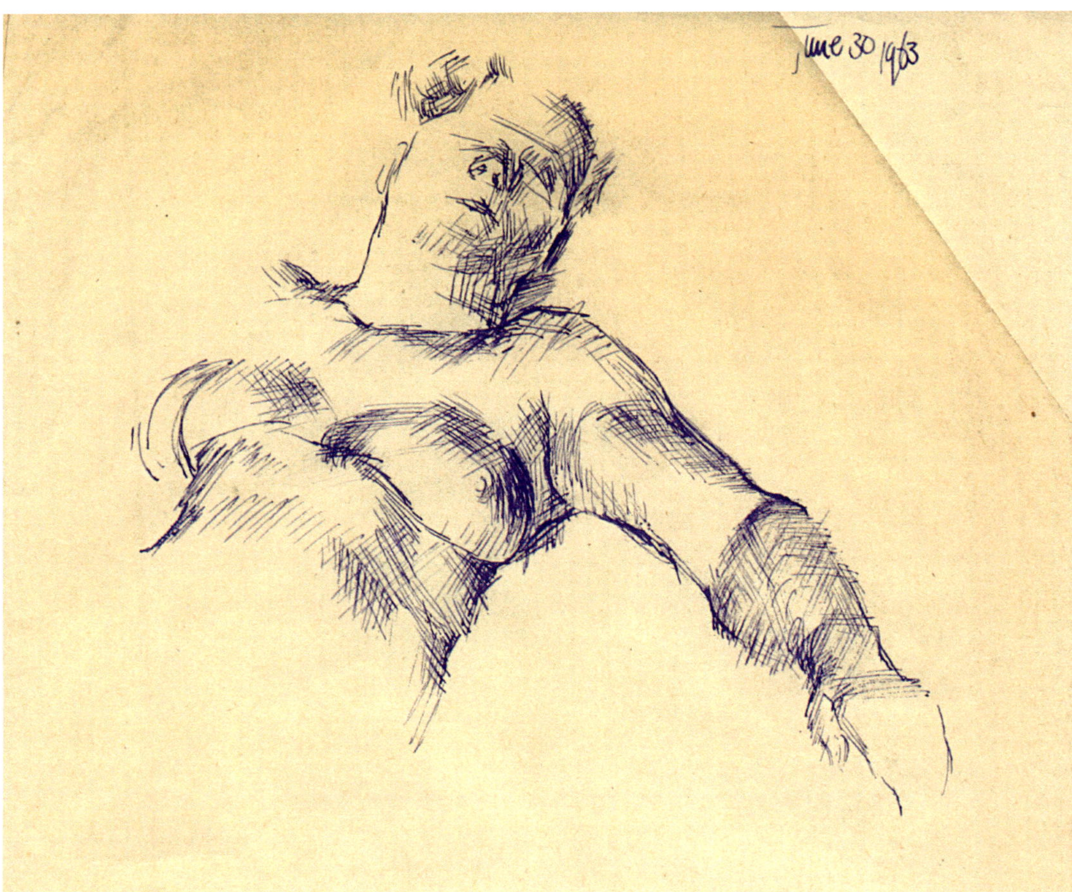
June 30 1963

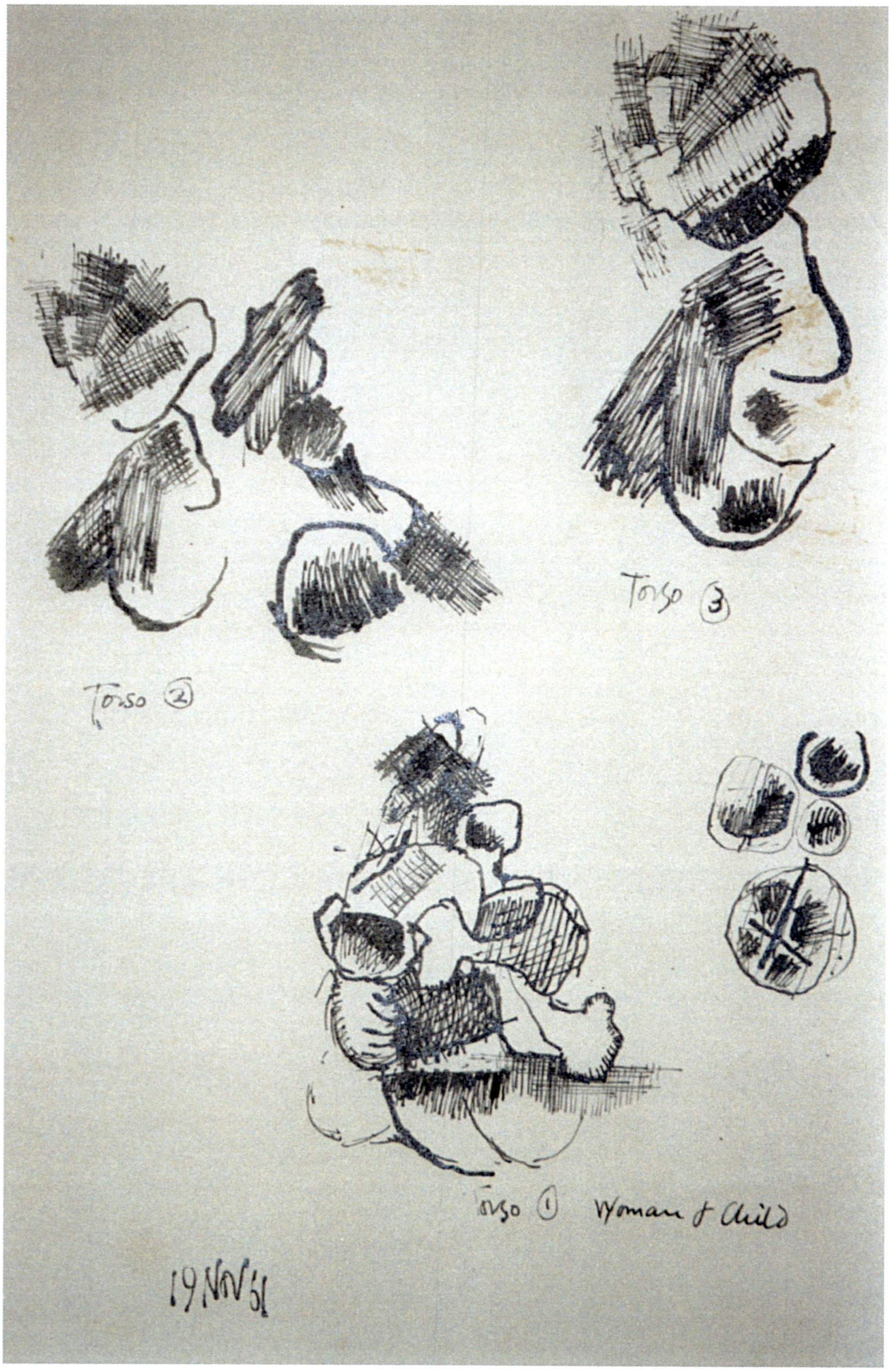

Woman and Child (1961). Pen and ink. 29.7×21 cms. Williams estate.

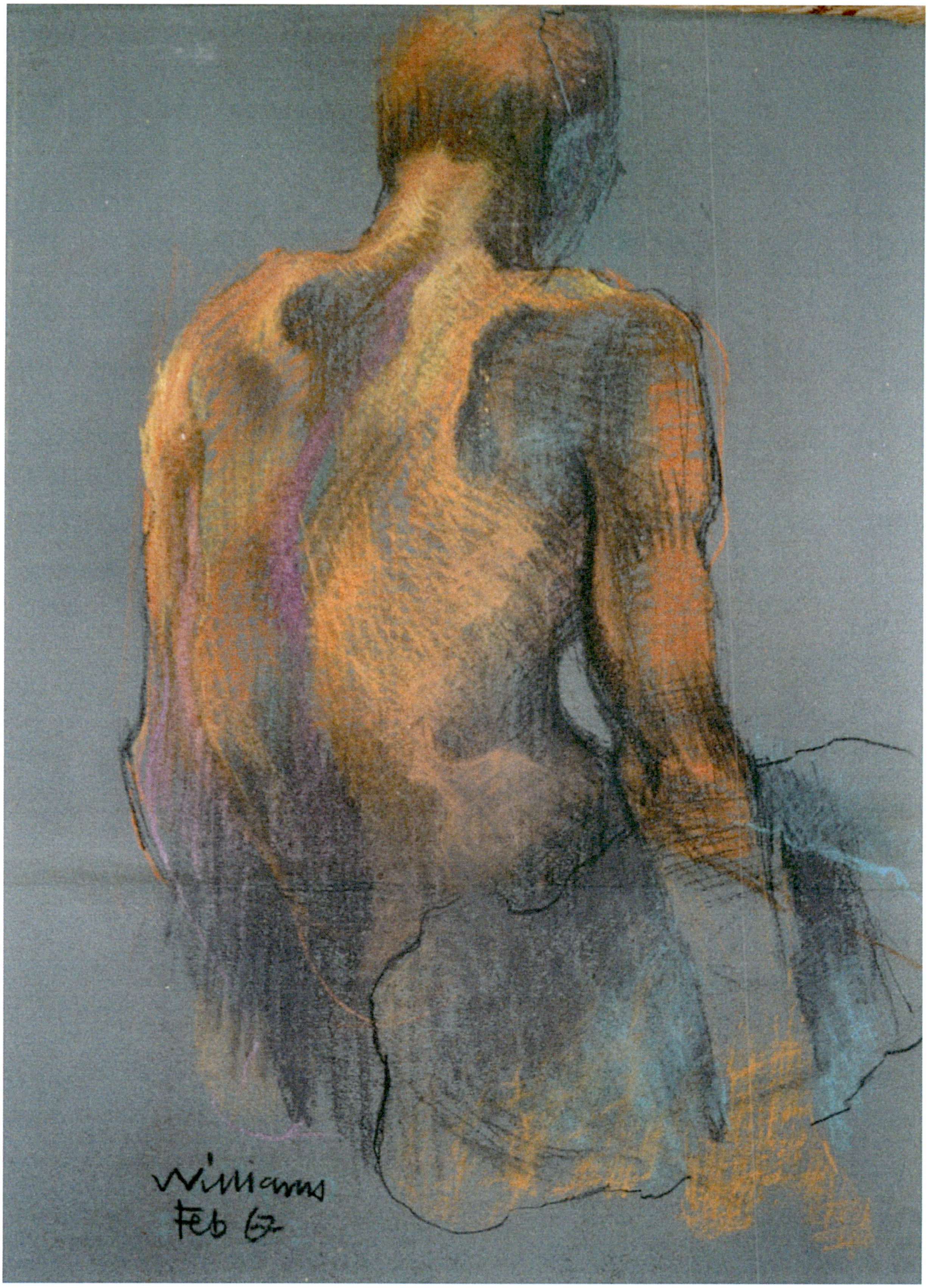

Seated Figure (1962). Chalk pastel. 45×30 cms. Williams estate.

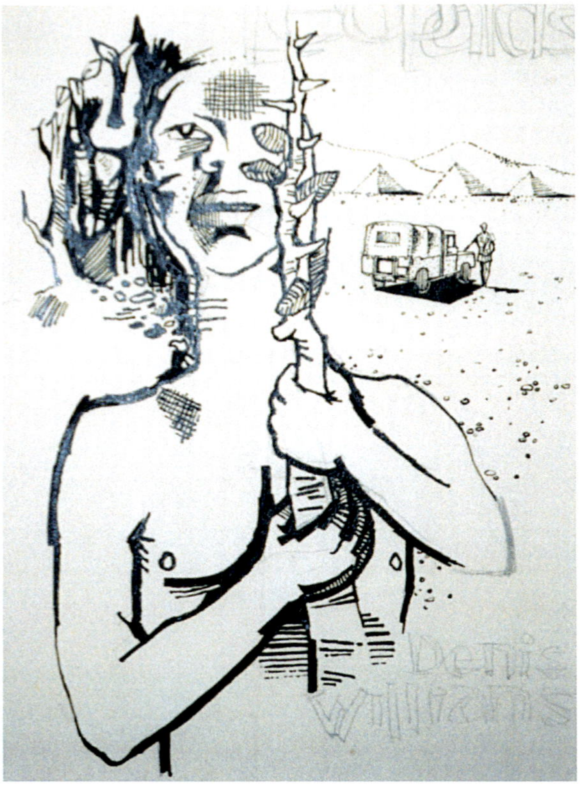

Jacket ideas for *Other Leopards* (1961–1962). Williams estate.

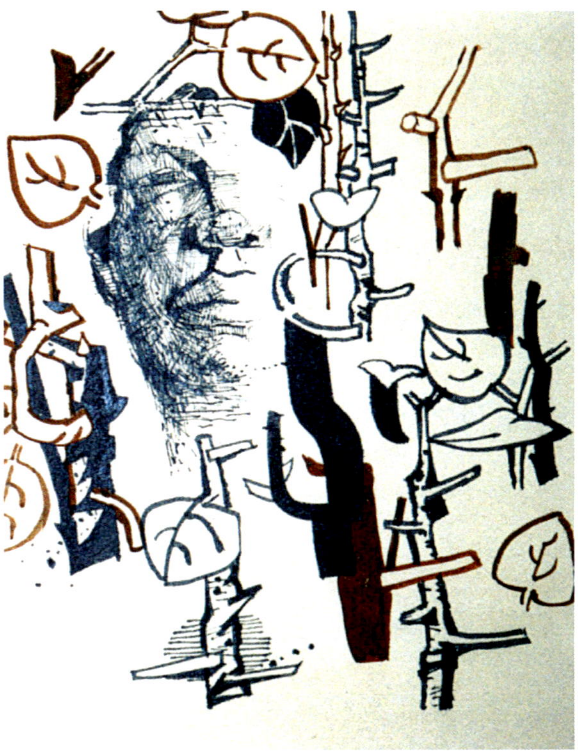

> Africa is Africa, eh, and it's not asking for any links to be forged with you lot, this side. Don't force them. Remember that in your Black Power euphoria. You have some very, very reluctant brothers on that continent.[24]

In terms of the continuing triangular dialogue, a tendentiously critical piece by Rita Hinden entitled "A Letter on British Guiana" was published in Nigeria in *Transition*. She wrote:

> In 1950, the British Guiana Constitution Commission (of which I was a member) was sent out to draw up a constitution. [...] Dr Jagan visited Europe and came to see me; I had then my first grave doubts as to how things would work out. Dr Jagan had been behind the Iron Curtain, and was immensely impressed by East Germany and Czechoslovakia. [...] He then went home to win the first democratic election. As soon as he was in office, he commenced on his course of subverting the constitution and twisting it to totalitarian ends. The country was in turmoil, the government called for help, and in 1953 British warships were on their way to British Guiana and the constitution was suspended. [...] The fierce resistance of the Guianese workers of African descent – who built up the free trade union movement – of clerks, professional, commercial and middle classes generally, springs from the fear that the country is to be handed over to communism [...] it fills them with horror.[25]

In contrast, a Central Office of Information document of a similar era gives a milder picture of the process of radical political change underway in British Guiana:

> By the post-World War II era the Caribbean plantation economies were in a run-down state and ill equipped to face an uncertain future. Preferential tariffs for colonial produce had been removed and vulnerability to increased competition of European sugar beet had dealt further blows to the sugar industry. [...] The formation of political parties occurred later in Guyana than in some of the islands of the British Caribbean. The elections of 1947 were the first since 1935 owing to war-time conditions and several new parties came into being. One of the parties which contested this election was the Political Affairs Committee, a group founded in 1946 by Dr Cheddi Jagan who had returned in 1943 to BG from the US. Dr Jagan and his American wife both took an active interest in politics and interpreted the situation in BG in terms of Marxist principles, although their actions when in office did not adhere to the traditional communist pattern. Dr Jagan was returned in the 1947 election and in 1950 formed the People's Progressive Party (PPP) which soon became the leading political organisation in British Guiana.[26]

Williams later recalled:

> Cheddi Jagan was unquestionably the founder of the movement to overthrow the British. Its heroes were also Martin Carter, Eusi Kwayana and Rory Westmaas. In 1946 Cheddi Jagan was forming the first political cells; they met in different persons' homes. When he saw my earliest paintings, Cheddi Jagan said "this is not socialist art" and there we parted company. Forbes Burnham returned to Guyana in 1949 and joined the group.[27]

Despite the information reaching Williams of a continuing unstable political climate, British Guiana at that time could still boast a continuous progression of art from the nascent British Guiana Arts and Crafts Society to the Guianese Art Group and the Working People's Art Class. The art critic, patron and broadcaster Basil Hinds suggests: "Guiana's geography and a paternal colonialism had been physical and psychic disadvantages up till 1953. Thereafter an awakening seems to have been materialised and artistic adjustments achieved in terms of universal means of expression."[28] Hinds refers directly to the work of Stanley Greaves, Michael Leila, Donald Locke, Patrick Barrington, Aubrey Williams and Philip Moore.

But for Guianese artists in general the barriers facing them were significant. There was the lack of status and a constant philistinism to confront. There was a general absence of a supportive climate and clear continuity of patronage in which an artist might flourish. There was an unconfident art criticism due to insularity and lack of exposure. There were limited opportunities in which ideas, concepts and convictions could be challenged. These were all factors that typically led to an uneven quality amongst the many and to the perceived élitism of a favoured few. This was the community to which Williams knew he would eventually return and writing to Seymour from Khartoum he confided "[…] more and more the idea of personal success, as opposed to communal growth, has less and less appeal for me."[29]

The work he carried out during the second phase of his Africa period – a close study of West African antique art forms – later led to the publication of *Icon and Image*.[30] His researches were wide-ranging and he combined his findings in a wholly unique perspective. From within the iron- and bronze-working societies he entered the Ju-ju world of arcane West African cults, ceremonies and shrines: the world of Sàngó and the Ogboni. On his reconnaissance visits and surveys he met with

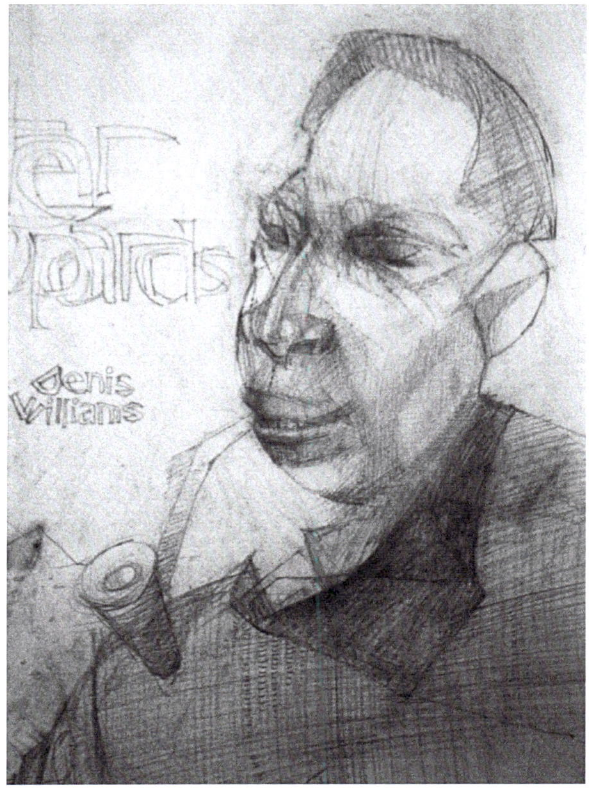

Jacket ideas for *Other Leopards* (1961–1962). Williams estate.

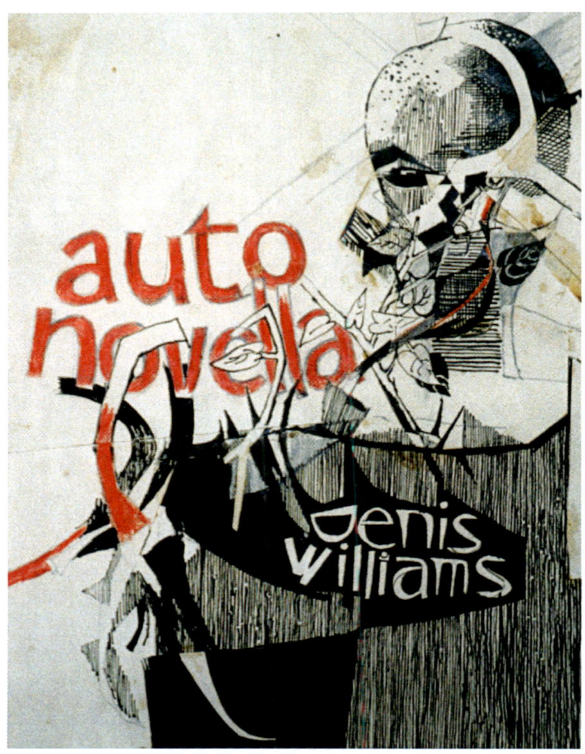

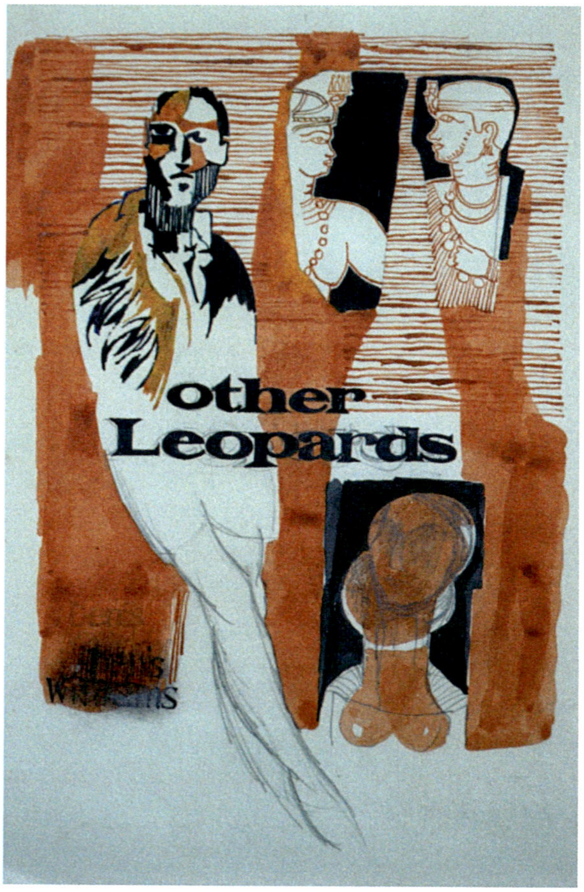

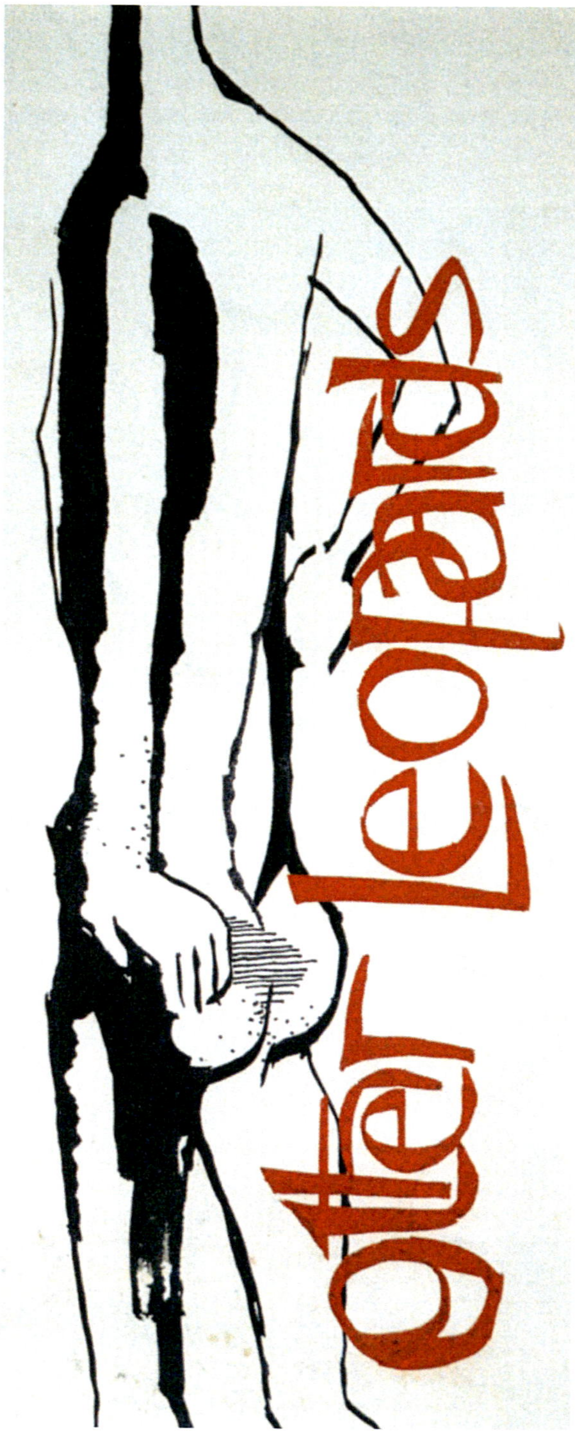

Jacket ideas for *Other Leopards* (1961–1962).
Williams estate.

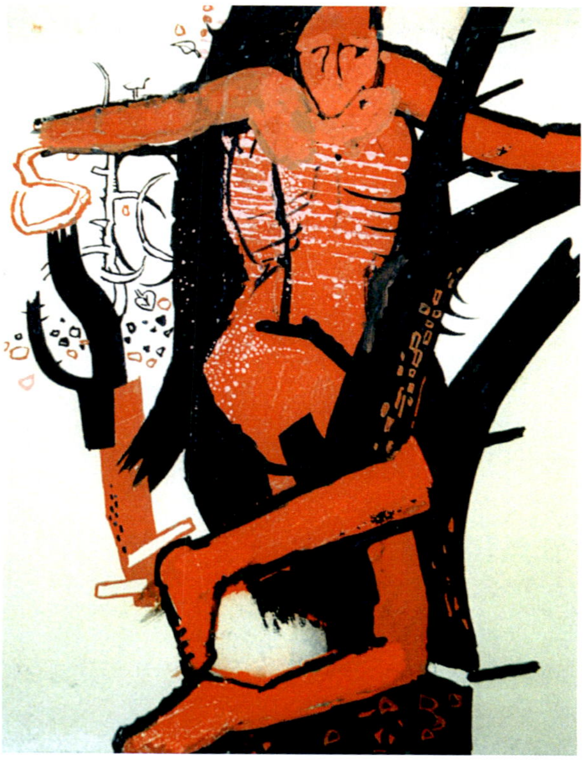

chiefs and kings and lived and worked alongside blacksmiths to gain intimate knowledge of their hands-on practice. Although he spoke no African language, he found this "no great handicap in the field in view of the articulateness of the language of practical demonstration."[31] His daughter Charlotte describes these excursions:

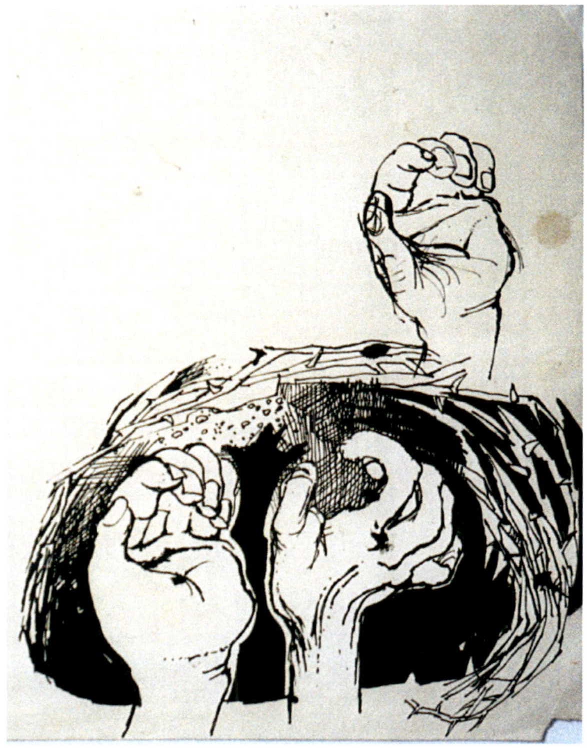

Jacket ideas for *Other Leopards* (1961–1962). Williams estate.

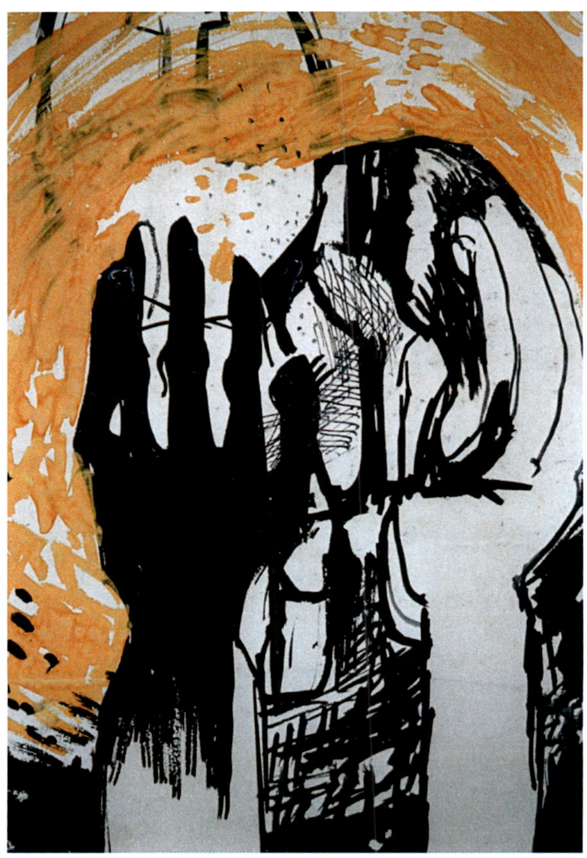

> During the Africa days, I would go with Dad on field trips; days and days of excavating, tagging, numbering, cataloguing and documenting evidence for his lifetime work on African art. We were digging out relics in the ancient provinces of Ife and Benin, Ogbomosho, Oshogbo, Abeokuta; in search of the sacred figures of these old communities. Dad was studying the technique of the blacksmiths and trying also to make sense of the images they produced and the meanings they held. Those were wonderful days. It could take hours of travel in the Landrover across difficult terrain to reach a village were Dad was working. Sometimes we would travel in a convoy with other anthropologists and archaeologists like Ulli Beier and his wife Georgina and Robin Horton. The welcome we received was always magical. There would be food and there might be dancing. There would be demonstrations of the smelting process or a group of budding village archaeologists – young and old men alike – would lead us to a prime excavation site. Other times it was just a matter of examining artifacts and listening to the stories that went with them. We visited shrines where ancient effigies had stood undisturbed for generations. Sometimes the icons were so sacred that Dad had to be satisfied with drawing them from a distance. He would sketch them into his journal as they stared silently back at him from their primeval worlds.
>
> There's an African proverb that goes: "A thing is always itself and more than itself." It means that even inanimate objects have a life within them. That's the African way of thinking, the African physics of matter. These effigies were objects but at the same time much more than mere objects. They were symbols of worlds of meaning; sacred representations of ways of life long gone. They held within them tales of war and combat, tales of love, of fertility and prosperity and more. The craftsmen were the inspired artisans of the villages who were able to interpret stereotypes; templates which had been handed down to them through generations and generations in their reproduction of the icons.
>
> We watched the blacksmiths work their magic and they in turn marvelled at mine. I showed them the magic of ice and they gasped in amazement. Grown men who had never seen ice, never mind touched and tasted it. "Eh eh," they said. "Eh eh" when they stared at the green eyes in my box of marbles. "Eh eh" at the picture box camera they

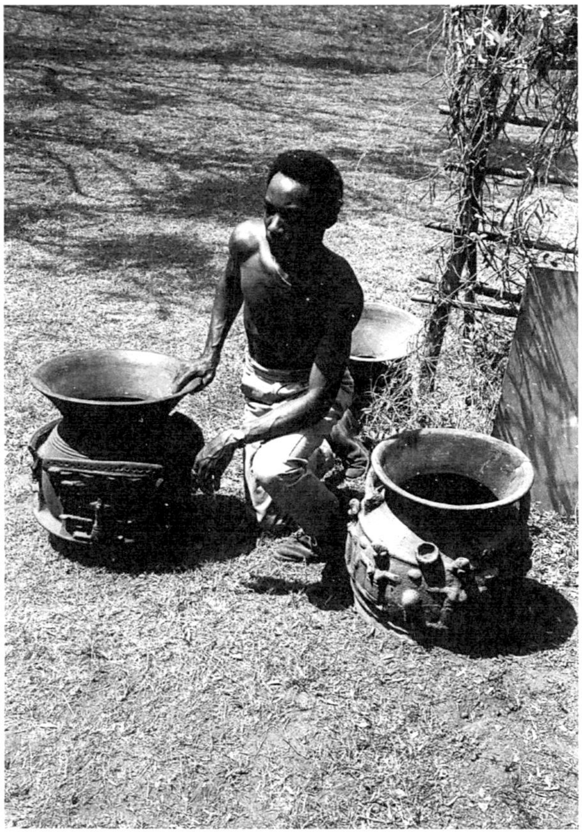

Examining ritual cult objects in Nigeria.

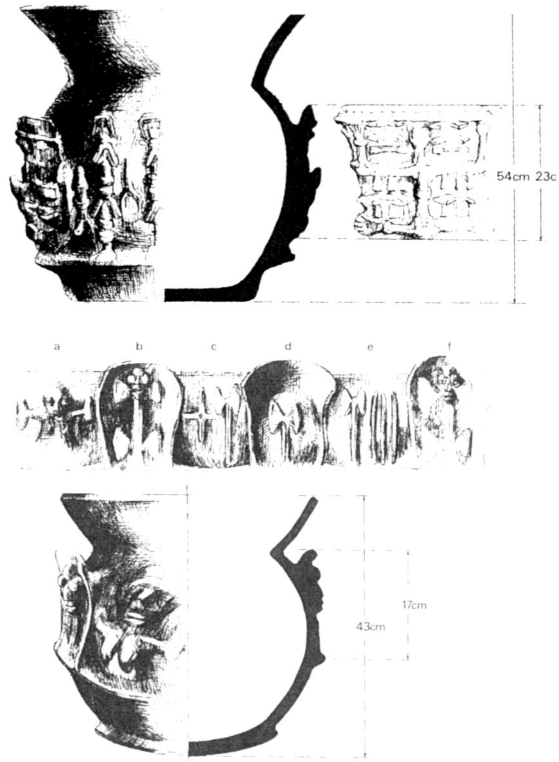

Sketch pages from field journal.

> mistook for a gun. So each trip I would try and take some wonders from other worlds to share with them and they humoured me.[32]

During such excursions Williams made extensive purchases of antiquities on behalf of the University of Ife (Obafemi Awolowo University) – then housed at the Ibadan campus – and the School of African and Asian Studies at the University of Lagos. For both of these institutions he founded museum collections of African art. He had the support of Vice Chancellor Saburi Biobaku, who was amongst those Nigerians who secured the foundations of Yoruba historiography, and to whom *Icon and Image* is dedicated.

We can learn much of his position in relation to a non-European aesthetic from *Icon and Image*. The briefest examination of the literary references in *Icon and Image* reveals that it was the opinions of establishment art historians and essayists of his European encounters that Williams has cited and challenged throughout – such figures as Fry, Berger, Gombrich and Panofsky. But it is the forensic eye of the artist that remains at the core of this work. From the outset it questions the usefulness of applying the critical terminology of European art scholarship to the aesthetics of African art; it examines the appropriateness of the conceptual apparatus in conventional use. He challenges the validity of the ethnographical gaze on Africa and the purely deductive, scientific appraisal of its archaeological artifacts and products of material culture. As he wrote: "Form in plastic art is an aspect of thought whose expression is not verbal and not rational."[33] A sketch of Katie Alice sleeping, dated 1 July 1963, is illuminating. The notes below, written at the right-hand side of the sketch, show that his mind is sifting over his African art studies while he is in the act of drawing:

> The student in a European School of Art who has learned to treat Nature by the cube, the cylinder and the cone; or who glibly describes at the morning coffee break the "planes" by which he has been rendering the model, has already digested more of what African sculpture has to say than the scientists, exclusively concerned with meaning and function, will ever understand. For Visual Art ought to be discussed, predominantly at any rate, in visual terms.

For Williams, it followed that form and function could not be strictly divided. This

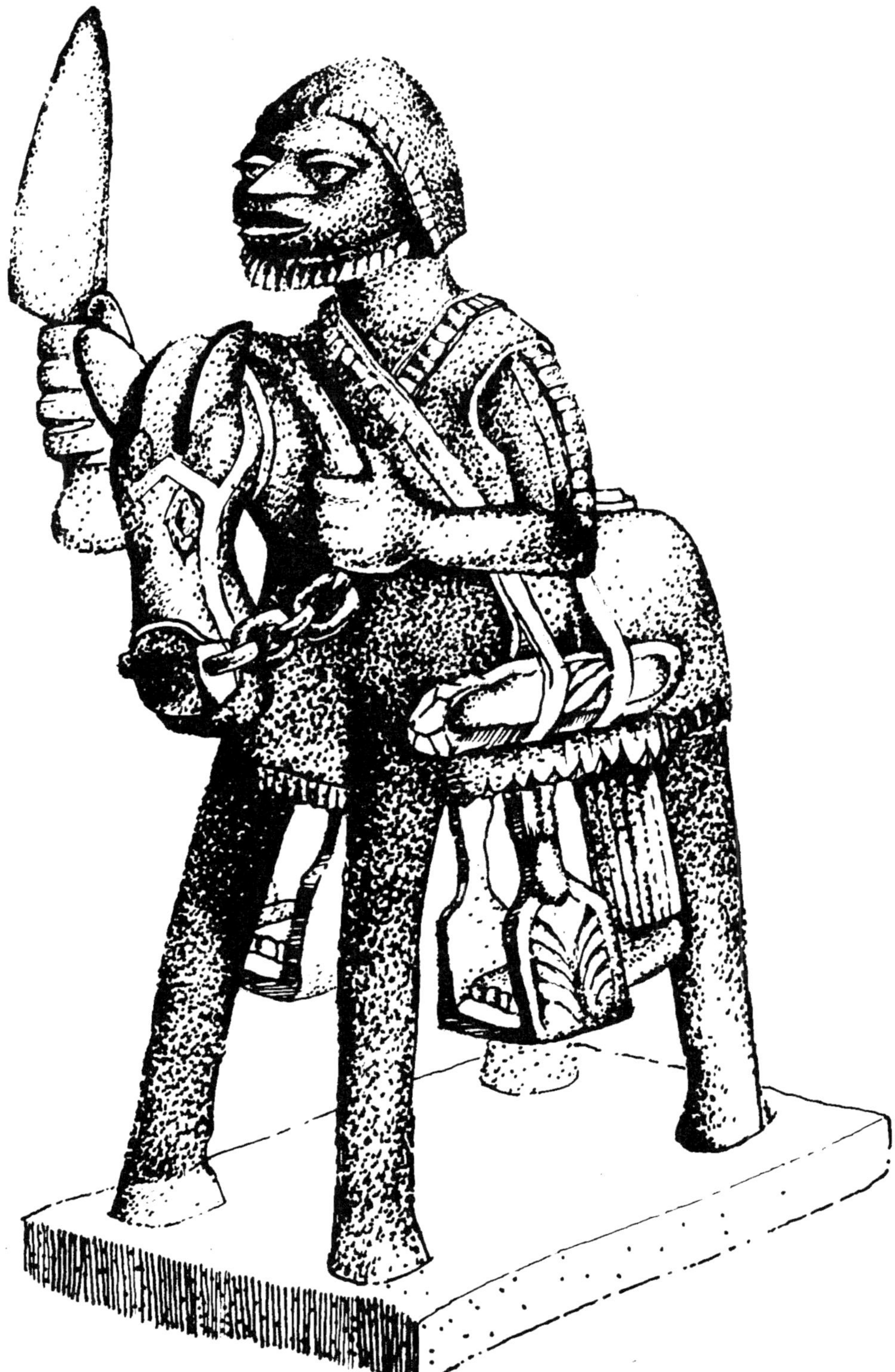

Illustration prepared for *Icon and Image*. Pen and ink.

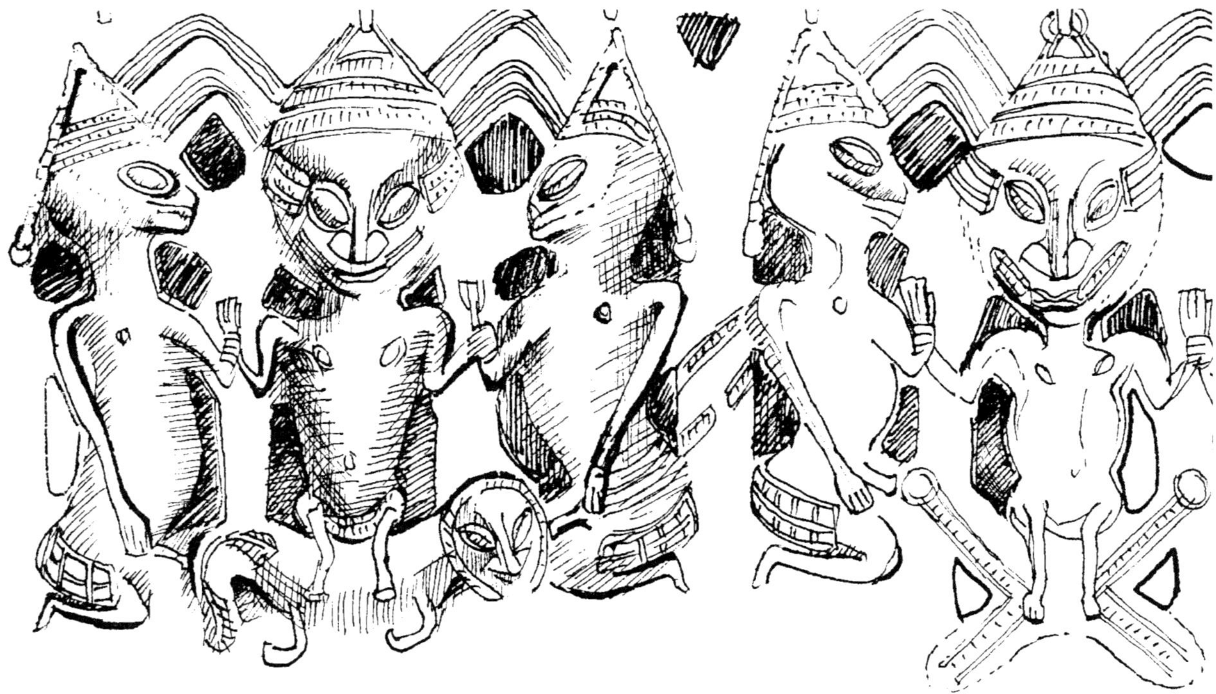

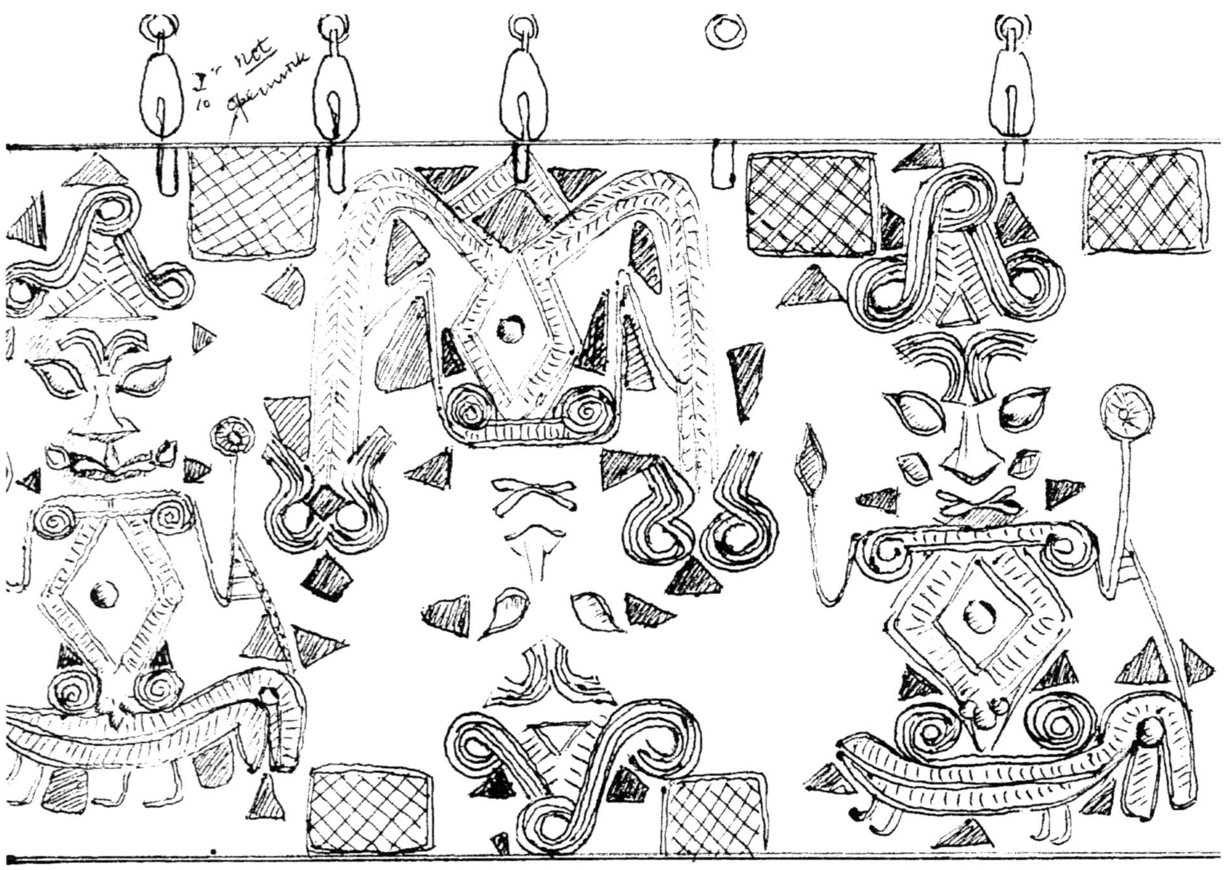

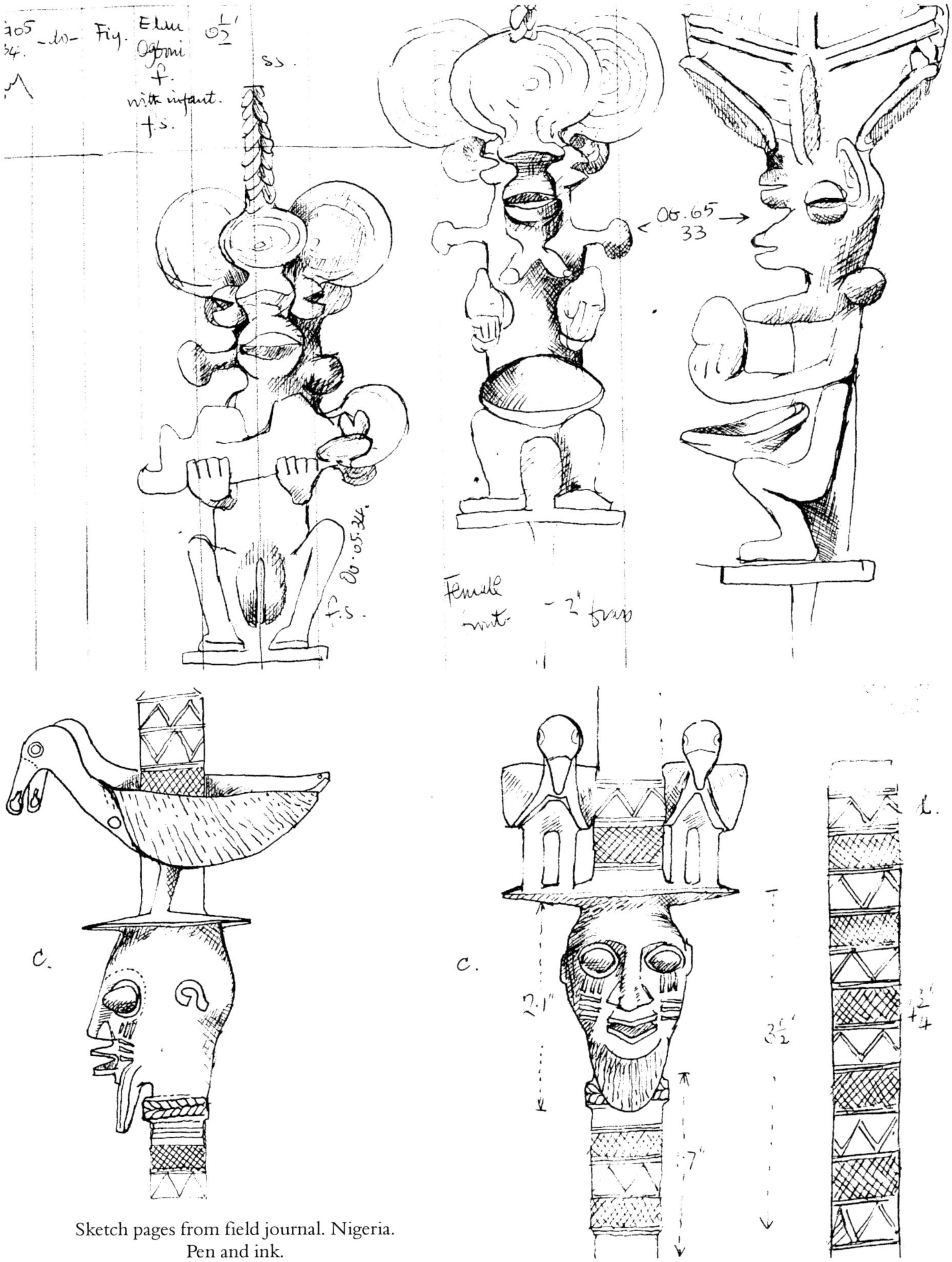

Sketch pages from field journal. Nigeria.
Pen and ink.

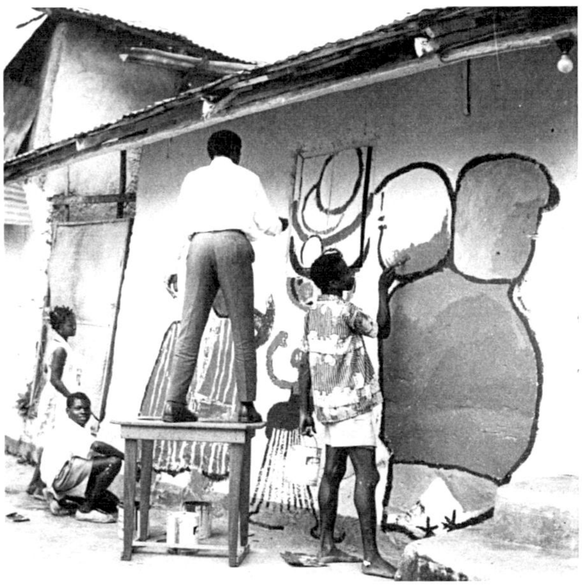

At the Mbari Art Workshop, Oshogbo (1963).

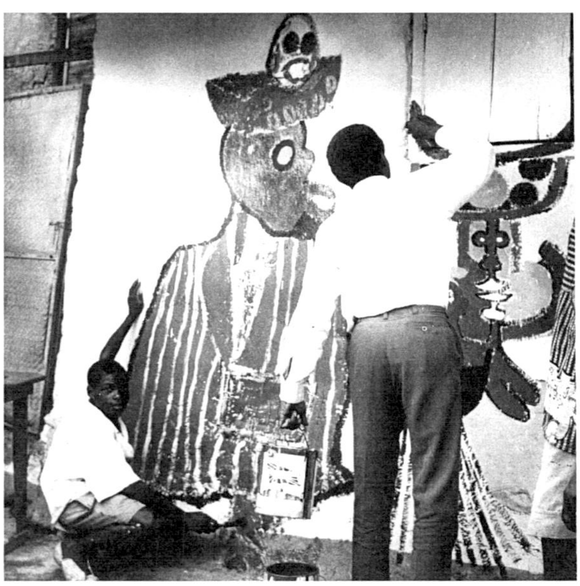

aesthetic approach to his research material, supported by his established authority as an artist practitioner, together with his command of art history and art theory determined his appraisal and interpretation of his material. He was fearless in the face of received evidence and his findings in *Icon and Image* were provocative in some quarters of academia.

Intense artistic activity supports this enormous creative study; its sustained, systematic thought and reflection is rooted in his advanced aesthetic judgement. He made over two hundred pen-and-ink drawings and sketches, many of which required hours of painstaking spot-density and cross-hatching. Practitioners alone will appreciate the extent of this task. What better way to appreciate the aesthetic qualities and to understand the meaning of form than through drawing? This ability to "see" his material as an artist-practitioner lies at the heart of his approach: the ability to channel his creative instincts in synthesising his evidence.

In Nigeria artistic life was greatly enriched through association with the German writer and critic Ulli Beier[34] and the Mbari experiments.[35.] In the Ibo culture Mbari is enshrined in a chosen building that acts as a focal point for the artistic and spiritual needs of a community in its attempts to make sense of the myths of the past and to represent present and future aspirations. Ulli Beier founded the Mbari Mbayo writers' and artists' club at Ibadan in 1961. Williams became one of the committee members together with Christopher Okigbo, Georgina Beier, Wole Soyinka, Chinua Achebe, Ezekiel Mphalele and Amos Tutuola, working among a wave of second-generation Nigerian novelists writing in English. Referring to the Mbari experiments Williams explains: "The idea of introducing African traditional artists to a systemised course of training [...] was first attempted some twenty years ago in the Caribbean island of Haiti [by] a young American painter, de Witt Peters [...] the principal characteristic of which was the obvious survival of the traditional plastic impulse in spite of detribalisation and the uprooting of cultures."[36] This examination of the relative orientations of these groups to the past – to the concept of the ancestor – became a continuing question as to the nature of the impulse, heritage, or memory that survived the transatlantic voyage.

The first Mbari workshop was conducted at Ibadan in 1961 and targeted art teachers from all over Nigeria. In 1962 the first Oshogbo Art

Workshop was conducted by Julian Beinart and Williams. This was additionally open to passers-by who were curious enough to drift in. In 1963 Williams conducted a second Oshogbo Art Workshop joined this time by Jacob Lawrence, a leading artist of the Harlem Renaissance, who later painted *Street to Mbari* (1964). Oshogbo art was to become something of an African cultural revolution: a collective of painters with little or no academic training or connection with Western art schools out of which came artists Rufus Ogundele, Jimoh Buraimoh, and Twins Seven Seven. These were "boys off the road" who had dropped by and that Williams had taught. He was thus in the vanguard of those promoting contemporary African visual and literary arts.

Williams became an associate editor of the Arts magazine *Transition*, contributing alongside artists and writers from several other African countries. In 1963 he designed and illustrated a book of plays by Wole Soyinka.[37] He also designed and illustrated a collection of poetry for the imprisoned African poet Dennis Brutus,[38] who was banned from teaching, writing or publishing in his native South Africa. These works were both produced by Mbari Publications. He was editor of *Odu* (1964) and *Lagos Notes and Records* (1967) and there was now a synthesising cross-fertilisation of art, archaeology and literature in his life.

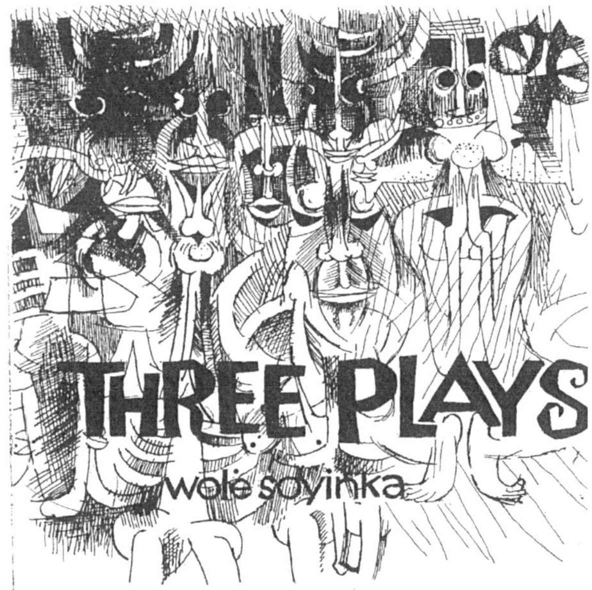

Jacket designs for Mbari Publications (1963).

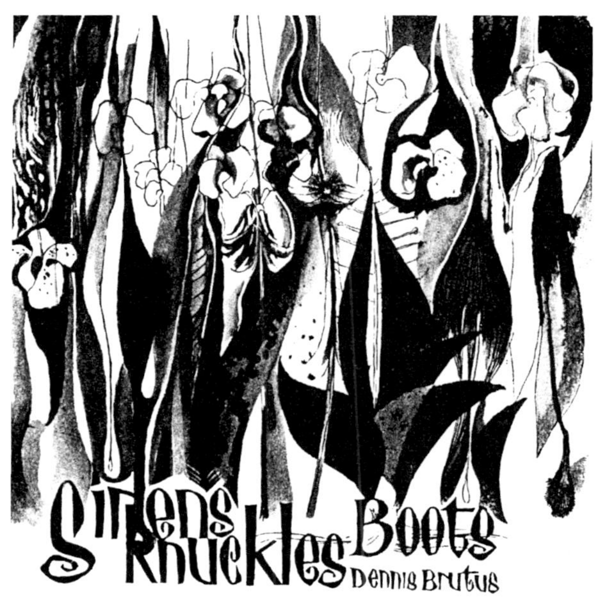

But at street level Williams was regularly mistaken for and pointed out as an Igbo from the secessionist south-eastern region. The ethnic, cultural and religious tensions between the various peoples came to the surface in Nigeria during the dubious electoral circumstances of 1965. From 1966 onwards there followed several military coups and counter-coups in the increasingly tense atmosphere that led up to the violent repression of the Igbos in the Nigerian Civil War. The country was unsafe for him.

On the eve of Guianese independence he was still in Nigeria but had moved to the capital, now working at the School of African and Asian Studies at the University of Lagos. His association continued with Makerere where in 1966 he was appointed external examiner and visiting Professor of African Art and Literature. At the summer conference that year he gave a paper entitled *The Traditional Theme in African Art and Literature*.

Black polemics, which had infused the international struggle in the Third World, had often contributed to emotive constructs of reality, sometimes degenerating into a racialism as intolerant and arrogant as any other. More extreme positions were challenged and rejected. Meanwhile in Great Britain in the mid-1960s, West Indian creative and intellectual polemics became loosely formalised and focused in The Caribbean Artists Movement (CAM),[39] its implicit ideology exploring the idea of a West Indian identity: a Caribbean aesthetic.

Williams was amongst the outstanding figures of his generation who were invited by Forbes Burnham to attend the Independence celebrations in Georgetown in May 1966. Many of the cohort from his London days were there, including artists and writers like Wilson Harris, Jan Carew, George Lamming, Aubrey Williams and O. R. Dathorne, together with many others associated with CAM. The prospect of independence in 1966 rekindled Williams' London dreams of forging a nation: there was a job to be done. He had never seen himself as a permanent exile. He had never seen himself becoming a British-based black artist or an African returnee. Rather he saw himself as part of a privileged intellectual circle who bore the responsibility to take a lead in shaping the future of the newly emerging, independent nation of Guyana. The wider group had included Burnham and Shridath ("Sonny") Ramphal as well as all the leading intellectuals and writers of that generation who were expected to return to their country. He recalled:

> In 1966 the glory of owning your own country, your own flag, was the most profound thing that happened in my life. I said at that same banquet in Burnham's house, "You fellas, do you realise that from today you have no excuse for holding another man's passport?" This was not well received. Not at all. It led to a roaring row and we were almost thrown out of the place. [...] For me there was no "but anything [...]" and I made up my mind that as soon as I got back to Africa I would apply for my Guyanese passport. This idea was not at all agreed or well received. Perhaps they felt too much personal investment elsewhere. It was the personal context of each man rather than an ideology that provided their rationale.[40]

With independence came a heightened awareness of the question of Guyana's own cultural identity – both independent and in relation to that of the wider Caribbean. Williams had been early to recognise the formidable issues arising from Guyana's complex historical past. In Africa he had composed a long letter to Harold Drayton, an academic who was to become one of the founders of the University of Guyana.[41] In it he set out his vision of the central rôle of art in creating any sense of a national identity for an emergent nation. As he saw it, moving forward as a nation would mean laying the foundations of the institutions that would enable the dissemination of knowledge and the development of a culture that would offer all its peoples validation within an acceptable context. His extended triangular dialogue had emphatically culminated in the decision and acceptance that his true home could only be the newly independent Guyana. By 1967 he had obtained his passport and had returned to Georgetown. He had crossed the Atlantic, as so many generations of his ancestors had been compelled to do, and returned of his own free will to his new nation as one of its foremost intellectuals.

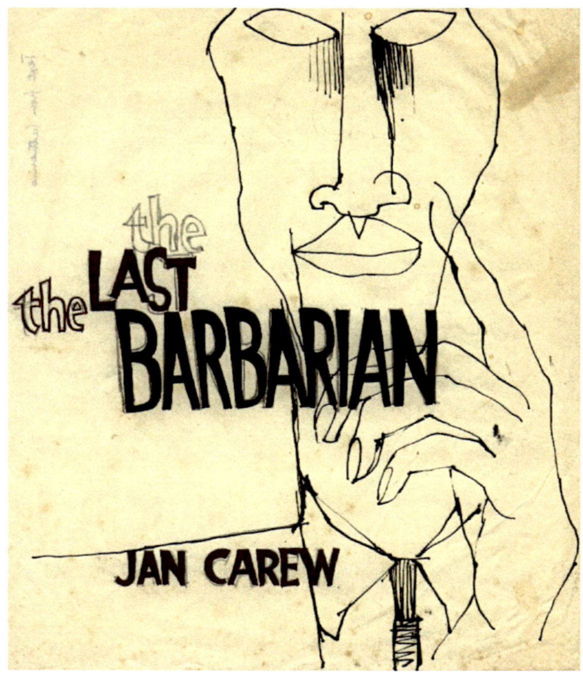

Jacket idea for Jan Carew. Williams estate.

NOTES TO CHAPTER 4

1 In the deserts of Northern Sudan lie the remains of the Napatan and Meroitic cultures, the latter perhaps the very earliest of Iron Age societies on the continent.
2 *A Plastic Calligraphy.* Williams' exhibition notes for *Arabic Calligraphy* by Ahmed Mohammed Shibrain.
3 *Ibid.* Brought to exhibition at Mbari in Ibadan, 25 January 1963.
4 Denis Williams and A. J. Seymour, "An Exchange of Letters", reproduced in *Kyk-over-al* (24 December 1958), pp. 93–99: p. 94.
5 George Lamming, *The Pleasures of Exile* (1960) quoted in Kenneth Ramchand, *The West Indian Novel and its Background* (London: Faber & Faber, 1970), p. 133.
6 Kenneth Ramchand, *The West Indian Novel and its Background*, p. 133.
7 *Moulid el-Nabi*=The Birthday of the Prophet.
8 Denis Williams, *A Plastic Calligraphy*.
9 *Ibid.*
10 Williams first uses this phrase in *A Plastic Calligraphy* and it would seem to reflect a reading of Faure.
11 Denis Williams, *Other Leopards* (London: Hutchinson, 1963), p. 23.
12 *Ibid.*, p. 154. He also uses this image in *The Sperm of God*, an "extract from an experimental work in progress."
13 "An Exchange of Letters", p. 95.
14 *Ibid.*, p. 98.
15 These letters date between 1957 and 1967.
16 See Andrew Lindsay, "Preparing the Palette: The Artist in Words", in C. & E. Williams (eds), *Denis Williams: A Life in Works. New and Collected Essays* (Cross/Cultures; Amsterdam & New York: Rodopi, 2010), pp. 125–141.
17 "An Exchange of Letters", p. 94.
18 Louis James, in *The Dictionary of Literary Biography* edited by Bernth Lindfors and Reinhard Sander (Detroit, London: Bruccoli Clark Layman, 1992), p. 117 and pp. 313–316.
19 Derek Walcott, "His is the Pivotal One about Race" (*Sunday Guardian*, Trinidad, 1 December 1963), p. 23.
20 Kenneth Ramchand, *The West Indian Novel and its Background*, p. 162.
21 He was born in Georgetown, and taught in Africa between 1959 and 1963. He was the author of a novel of African return, *The Scholar-Man* (London: Cassell, 1964).
22 O. R. Dathorne, *The Black Mind: A History of African Literature* (Minneapolis: University of Minnesota Press, 1974), p. 438.
23 Obiajunwa Wali, "The Dead End of African Literature?" in *Transition* (Vol. 3, No. 10, 1963), pp. 13–15.
24 Andrew Salkey, *Georgetown Journal: A Caribbean Writer's Journey from London via Port of Spain to Georgetown, Guyana, 1970* (Trinidad, Port of Spain: New Beacon Books, 1972), p. 256.
25 Rita Hinden, "Simple Slogans and Good Intentions: A Letter on British Guiana", in *Transition* (Vol. 3, No. 10, 1963), pp. 35–36.
26 *Guyana* (London: Central Office of Information, February 1966).
27 Dictated statement to Albert Rodrigues (1998).
28 Basil Hinds, "'New Art' in British Guiana", in *Kyk-over-al* (Vol. 9, No. 27, December 1960), pp. 113–118.
29 "An Exchange of Letters", p. 95.
30 Denis Williams, *Icon and Image* (New York University Press, 1974).
31 Denis Williams, *Icon and Image*, p. 325.
32 See Charlotte Williams, *Sugar and Slate*, pp. 89–90.
33 Denis Williams, *Icon and Image*, p. 4.
34 Williams wrote a review of Ulli Beier's *African Mud Sculpture* (1963) in the journal *Ibadan* (No. 17, University of Ibadan, November 1963), pp. 31–32.
35 For more on Mbari, see Frank Willett, *African Art* (London: Thames and Hudson, 2002). In particular, chapter 7: p. 242.
36 Denis Williams, "Second Experimental Art School, 27 April to 4 May 1963", in *Ibadan* (No. 17, November 1963), pp. 22–26.
37 *Jero*, *The Strong Breed* (Nigeria, Ibadan: Mbari Publications, 1963).
38 Dennis Brutus, *Sirens, Knuckles, Boots* (Nigeria, Ibadan: Mbari Publications, 1963). The University of Ibadan offered him the Mbari poetry prize, but he turned it down because it was only open to black poets.
39 For a thorough account, see Anne Walmsley, *The Caribbean Artists Movement 1966–1972: A Literary & Cultural History* (London and Port of Spain: New Beacon Books, 1992).
40 Charlotte Williams, interview with Denis Williams (1998).
41 A draft of this letter, dated 22 July 1966, appears in his *Africa Journal*, which he kept between 1959 and 1967. (Williams estate).

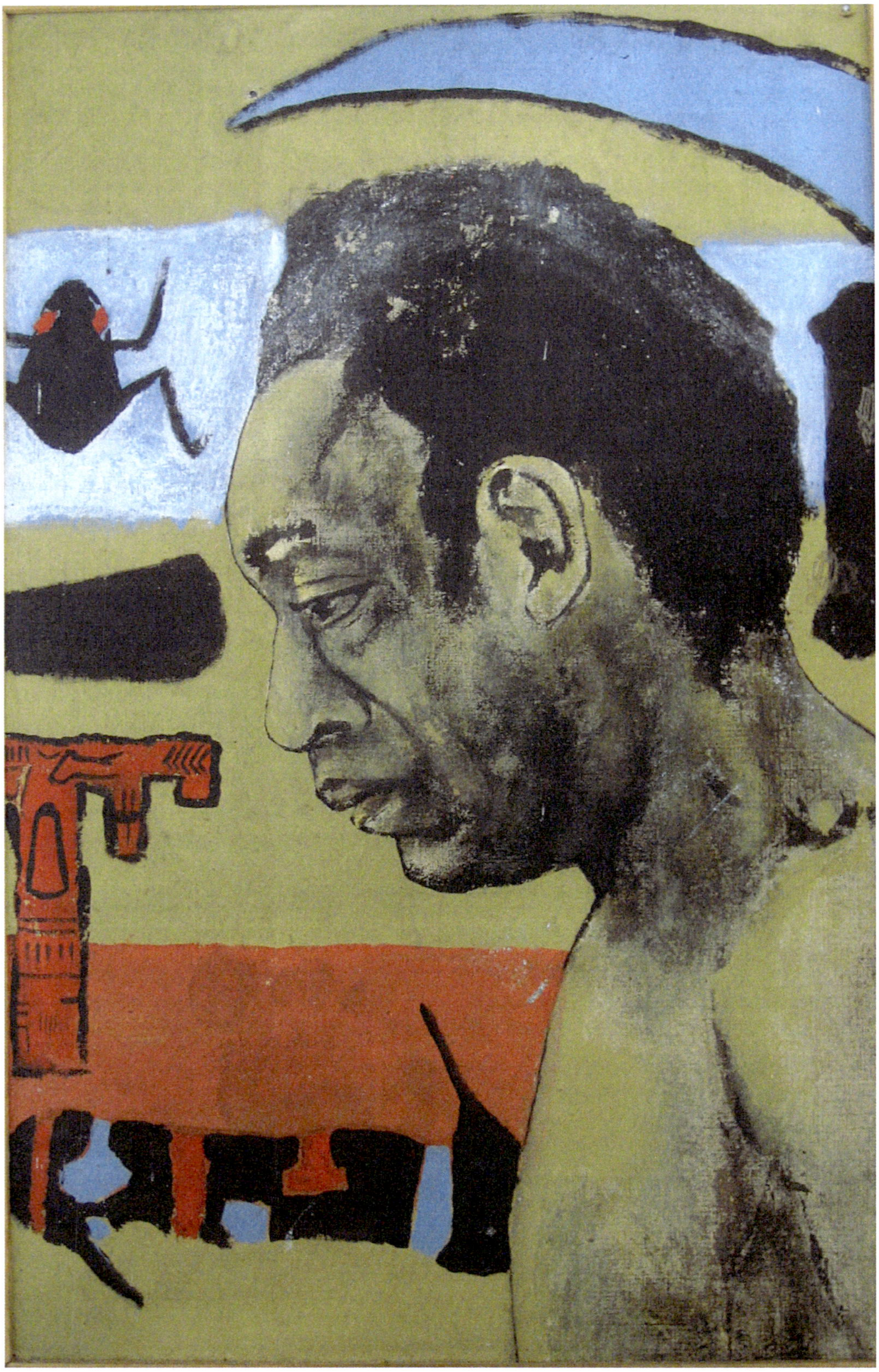

Denis Williams by Aubrey Williams (1970). Oil on canvas. 61×38 cms.
By kind permission of Ras Camo Williams.
Photograph by Andrew Lindsay.

Chapter 5

Majestas

IN *OTHER LEOPARDS*, the central protagonist expresses a desire to go "[...] back to the swamps and forest and vaguely felt darkness of my South American home."[1] Williams returned to the interior of Guyana, to a forest glade on the edge of the tree line beyond the Mazaruni landing at Issano, two days' jouney from Georgetown – a magnificent rainforest setting. It was also to be the setting of *Majestas*, the painting he regarded as his best work. In common with the majority of his compatriots he knew little about the interior of his country and its history and this was part of his reason for settling in the Upper Mazaruni. We can detect something of his awe in response to life in the rainforest in the subtext of his biographical publication *Giglioli in Guyana*, which was written at Issano.[2] The text of this work is much more than a record of Giglioli's scientific achievements. It is suffused with Williams' knowledge and understanding of Giglioli's artistic heritage in the Italian Renaissance. The generous appreciation of Giglioli's sculpture, produced during his internment in British Guiana between 1940 and 1942, shows sensitivity towards the man he later described as "unquestionably one of the greatest men who have ever dwelled in this country."[3] It gives an indication of the care that Williams was prepared to devote to the art of others.

Pencil drawings of Giglioli – now in the National Collection – were made in Georgetown, at the home of a family friend:

> I got to know a fellow called Arthur Goodland, a top Bookers Director. He was a man interested in Archaeology and a man who had been in Guyana a long time and lived there as a resident. He had a big house on Main Street and spent a lot of time sculpting. He would invite us to come from Issano and spend the summer in town with him.[4]

It was Goodland who gave Williams a copy of Evans and Meggers' *Archaeological Investigations in British Guiana* (1960), which contributed to the in-depth study of the ancient material he had begun to uncover in the hinterlands.

Relative to its overall size, the area of land routinely populated and cultivated in Guyana amounts to a narrow strip on an Atlantic coastline that stretches some 270 miles. The continuing costs of importing consumer goods and raw materials to sustain its population and the need for a greater self-sufficiency and a less dependent economy had led to politically-driven ambitions for opening up the hinterland. Forbes Burnham's National Service Programme was to become part of one such plan. It was in this spirit that Williams himself became something of a pioneer in taking up the challenge of developing the interior. At Issano he cleared land and built a homestead, where he planted peanuts and grew tomatoes on a commercial basis.

He described the Issano years (1967–1973) as idyllic. That life must have invoked the memory of the subsistence plantation maroon who had fled to the hinterland to escape slavery. They were productive and rewarding years on many levels and provided a thinking and breathing space. This period represented a kind of El Dorado moment for the artist. Sporadic funding[5] provided a modest living and fellow artists and art students visited, stayed and studied with him. For example, in 1970 when Guyana became a Co-operative Republic, Aubrey Williams painted the five Timehri murals[6] and spent ten days at Issano where he painted his portrait of Denis Williams, "my old friend and mentor."[7]

If there were exuberant post-independence aspirations at home in Guyana then there were equally optimistic ambitions being sought overseas. In the work of those artists who became permanent aesthetic exiles, like Aubrey Williams and Frank Bowling or contemporary Guyanese-born artists like Arlington Weithers and Carl E. Hazlewood, their ambitions would be long sustained by the inner reservoir of their heritage. They could evoke their vaguely remembered South American hinterland and fall back on its spectacular imaginative and visual resources. Working within an abstract expressionist style means figuration can be suppressed and the plastic qualities of paint and surface can dominate the visual experience. Subject matter is subsumed in a suggestion, becoming a mere hint in an imaginative visualisation. This approach can be very attractive for a painter seeking an international platform, as it readily frees the artist to engage in an internal dialogue in the quest for content whilst casting off the burden of compulsion towards what might otherwise be confining subjective issues.

Williams acknowledged the issues raised for the New World artist of his own era by the paradoxes of the colonial condition when he wrote: "Unlike the West Indian 'migrants with manuscripts' of the fifties and sixties, the West Indian painter in the metropolis creates problems for himself by adopting the paradigms that result from an evolutionary agenda outside of his history and impossible for him to share."[8]

Richard Powell expands this thesis:

> Beyond an aesthetic affinity for abstraction, some [...] artists saw their move to abstraction as a personal and professional step toward artistic integration: a step that symbolised their willingness to subordinate blackness – and all that was associated with it – and to place themselves and their work in a larger, wider and, ultimately, whiter art world that provided more opportunities to exhibit, sell, and enter into artistic dialogue with others.[9]

But neither did Guyana seem to need these artists at this time. Williams noted the paradox for the post-colonial generation of artists that lay in "[...] a society producing what it is proud to call 'world' artists, or artists of 'international acclaim', or 'well-known' or 'celebrated' artists, whilst remaining in whole ignorant of who or what is doing the acclaiming, and even indeed of what is being acclaimed."[10]

> [We thought that] the Caribbean Artists Movement would soon become redundant – as all the Caribbean countries now had their independence and the leading lights had gone back home with this revolutionary feeling that there is a job to do, we have a country to mould. [...] But by and large this feeling petered out because those who were at home did not share this revolutionary spirit. The movement around the Caribbean at this time was political not artistic. It was politics that had provided the cutting edge mentality back home, and therefore there was no real need for us.[11]

The "island of Guiana" is bounded by the courses of the Amazon and Orinoco rivers and their bridging stream the Casiquiare Canal. The Precambrian Guiana Shield forms the nucleus of the territory which is all but separated and isolated from the South American mainland by its surface geography.[12] It is remote and peripheral. This may well account for the early if sporadic interest Guyanese took in pursuing the idea of a pan-Caribbean artistic community. Guyana differs from the other countries of the Caribbean as it occupies a far greater land area. It is the only English-speaking country on the South American continent, and it differs from other countries of the Caribbean (other than Trinidad and Suriname) in the greater diversity and balance of its racial make-up, with consequent tensions. The very particular context of Guyana meant that there were inherent difficulties for any ideology specifically seeking to rehabilitate the African self-image when that was connected to the issue of state power.

Williams readily contrasts a homogeneous Old World with the "peculiar consciousness"[13] of the polyglot New World. He saw miscegenation as the kingpin of the Caribbean psyche, the symbol of the process of cultural catalysis. He believed that "Its resolution in literature and art will certainly distinguish our work in the Caribbean, will give it originality and resonance, for no other people of the New World are faced with this problem to the degree in which we know it."[14]

At that time, most other countries of the Caribbean were identified as "black" but by their nature the high-profile black consciousness movements of the era had not been racially inclusive. Since the Montego Bay Conference of 1947, the idea of a West Indian Federation had long been mooted:

> The period involved an important but unsuccessful attempt to form a federation of the 13 English-speaking Caribbean islands. The Federation of the West Indies was created out of two impulses. On the British side was the impatience with dealing with so many small principalities and powers across the many islands of the archipelago. On the Caribbean side was the view, largely restricted to the intelligentsia of the middle class, that the Caribbean islands would be stronger and have a more meaningful voice in the world if they combined.[15]

A. J. Seymour had commented:

> Of course there was great interest in British Guiana in the idea of Federation. The BG Union of Cultural Clubs considered the question of British Guiana joining the Federation to be a matter of some importance and discussions took place within the framework of the Union's programmes.[16]

As a Civil Servant, however, Seymour had been forbidden to take part in any public debate on Federation.

Writing in *Venture* in 1949, an anonymous correspondent described how the idea of federation had "received the support in principle of all of them [the West Indian colonies] except British Guiana."[17] In Georgetown, rejection of the Federation arose, ironically, from concern over a loss of identity. It was feared that "in any Federation of the West Indies the Africans would form a vast majority and the East Indians would suffer a consequent decline in power and influence."[18] The idea failed to gain ground at that time.

High expectations had built up through the 1950s with the urgency of the post-war campaigns for independence. Boundless realms of possibility seemed within reach, but were typically never attained due to disastrous human failings, denials and evasions of responsibility.

> The first general election under the new constitution (known as the Waddington Constitution, 1953) was held in April 1953 and resulted in the People's Progressive Party, led by Dr Cheddi Jagan with Mr Forbes Burnham as deputy leader, winning 18 of the 24 elected seats in the House of Assembly. In October 1953 the British Government decided that circumstances in the colony made it necessary to suspend this advanced constitution.[19]

The ensuing commission of enquiry[20] found that there was a communist influence within the PPP that was, in their view, a barrier to constitutional progress. The "invasion" of 1953 and the suspension of the constitution saw the fragile nationalist movement undermined. This resulted in heightened suspicion and distrust and a growing institutionalisation of ethnic polarisation. The period leading up to independence in British Guiana was characterised by political rivalry, frustrated ambition, grievance, resentment and hostility. This led to social tension, demonstrations, strike action, civil disturbances and, most seriously, politically and ethnically motivated killings, rioting, looting and disorder.

It was the hope of many that independence would bring social cohesion and the common purpose necessary to develop an egalitarian society. But like many other newly independent countries, Guyana suffered the all-too-familiar rites of passage, not least from its legacy of authoritarian control. Guyana has demonstrated that it remains challenged to combine political and economic growth with an inclusive social vision. The inability to do so creates trauma in the psycho-social dynamics of the country, and this has hampered progress in defining national identity.

It was in the Mazaruni that Williams wrote his contribution to the Mittelholzer Lectures in which he began to exercise his ideas on the particular difficulties that cultural nationalism would face in Guyana. In 1969 he delivered this series of Lectures in Georgetown.[21] The four published Lectures are a closely argued summation of his position on the subject of cultural identity, raising issues which he believed had currency throughout the Caribbean.

In his foreword to the publication A. J. Seymour emphasised:

> Mr Williams is one of the few West Indians who have retraced the Middle Passage and lived in Africa and so is in a position to speak with authority on the cultural origins of an important segment of Guyanese society.[22]

The Lectures set out his long view of the imperatives governing adaptation in an alien environment. His thesis examines the relationship of the creative artist to the uniquely polyglot, multi-ethnic society of Guyana. He suggests that the continuing filialistic relationships to the various homogeneous cultures of the Old World are socially divisive. He signals his view of the creative potential made possible through the dynamic process of catalysis as peoples and cultures collide. He saw the future of Guyana developing as "a complex plurality in continual process of achieving a complex singularity – a singularity which is always itself open to change."[23] This context provides the creative artist with new ground where the obvious and prosaic facts of life "might come to be invested with a quality of miracle."[24] In these papers he presents a theory of cultural progression he sees as being of explicit national and regional relevance for any society which is divided along interfaces created by its several relationships to a racial ancestor.

As part of the Republic celebrations of 1970 Forbes Burnham had called for a Caribbean Writers' and Artists' Convention. But as Anne Walmsley has pointed out "[...] the sense of continuity between the 1966 conference and the 1970 convention was stronger within Guyana itself than in its visitors."[25]

> Particular attention was being paid to Guyana calling its artists and writers home because of this issue

> of identity – the question "Who are we?" Burnham held a conference in his home and asked us the open question "Gentlemen, what do you want?" – from the discussion that followed Carifesta was born. The idea of bringing together the artists and literature of the whole Caribbean together.[26]

The Caribbean Festival of the Arts (CARIFESTA) was conceived in a revolutionary climate of idealism following the establishment of the new Republic in 1970. Throughout the Caribbean, political leaders were becoming increasingly conscious of the pivotal rôle culture could play in uniting its peoples in the process of national development. Carifesta was therefore a signal event and Guyana was its first host nation. It was intended to provide an example of pan-Caribbean cooperation and unity and an international platform for that unity, both spiritually and culturally. The Guyanese stalwarts of the art world at that time, the Pilgrims, the Dolphins, Fernandes, Seymour and many of the overseas Guyanese associated with CAM, were closely involved with Carifesta in 1972. Burnham was publicly critical of those who did not return as active participants:

> [...] Prime Minister Burnham expressed his "disgust and disappointment with those writers, artists and others of the region who like to distinguish themselves by their contributions outside of the Caribbean."[27]

It has been suggested that it was in fact Williams who conceived the idea of Carifesta. Though this remains undocumented, it is clear that he saw Carifesta as a positive attempt to examine cultural identity outwith what might narrowly be interpreted as a political agenda. Its ideal of working towards a vision of a larger grouping was a symbolic marker, demonstrating his conviction that the Caribbean had at least the potential to be more than a fractured island chain adrift in tropical seas. For Williams, Carifesta formalised the debate in the ongoing process of regional self-definition, including the possibility for greater regional cohesion. These are issues which remain a challenge to governments, artists and intellectuals.

The first publication to emerge from Carifesta contains the papers presented at the very first Carifesta Symposia. They were published in a special edition of *Kaie*, the official organ of the National History and Arts Council of Guyana. Williams made a seminal contribution to the legacy of that first Carifesta in his conference symposium address – "Art and Society".[28]

His thesis argues that, in the Caribbean, artistic activity did not prefigure social change – indeed the reverse – and that, as a consequence, the surge of creative activity that characterised the immediate post-colonial period was unlikely to be maintained without further policical stimulus. There were specific reasons for this, one being that the intrusive art forms of the imperial period were the only ones to hand for the artist, since the traditional forms had been devalued or erased. He suggests that this may explain the apparent decline from the "heroic" decade in art between the fifties and sixties in the Caribbean. "There being no historical or cultural warrant for the practice of these art forms among these ex-subject peoples, they can be expected, after Independence, only to run down."[29] Williams believed these observations might also provide a key to appraising the evolution of the visual arts in the wider Caribbean.

Expressionova may have exemplified his points. It was founded in Georgetown by a small group of radical writers, painters and poets of the early seventies, including Terence Roberts who wrote their manifesto, Keith Khan, Janice Lowe and N. D. Williams. Critical of the general profile and lack of provision for the arts, they published their ideas and action plans towards creating a national artistic idiom. Williams recognised this initiative as a first – the first such formal grouping in Guyana that could really articulate itself as a movement, in the metropolitan sense of setting out its aims in a manifesto.[30] There is no evidence that he questioned its labelling as an appropriation from the western art model. Rather, the evidence of his attitude here is one of recognition for the group's attempt to negotiate a parallel Caribbean model. *Expressionova* held an exhibition in 1974 but received little popular attention. Indeed, its demise suggested that it was politics and not art that created the dynamic, and many artists, including most of the *Expressionova* group, were to migrate.

In "Art and Society" Williams argues that the practice of extrinsic forms of art in an "unknown foreign language" represents a "culture of culture, and not a culture of people," with a resulting diminishing social significance as the deculturation process proceeds. In his view, the close of the colonial period was accompanied by the emergence in art of exaggerated ancestral references – of folk forms and tribal forms – which he saw as withdrawal symptoms, as a retreat to the past, "[...] they are the forms of refuge; they are not the forms of challenge, they are the forms of complacency."[31] For him, it was a direction which had litle relevance to a contemporary living culture. Change occurs more slowly in art and literature than in politics, and he was left to question whether there was any revolutionary function for the Third World artist to serve.

In 1973 practical imperatives brought him back to Georgetown permanently and this was the year in which he was awarded the Golden Arrow of Achievement (AA) by the Government of Guyana. In Georgetown he circulated amongst a group of steadfast patricians and a small intelligentsia – a dedicated, supportive group of people drawn from a range of backgrounds with varied interests and experiences in the fields of the arts and culture – a fragile yet steadfast local élite.

Within the context of art, Guyana displays all its unresolved problems and he was well aware of the potential rôle of the artist in opening up the space in which multiple narratives could emerge. We can access his views in relation to the world of art through his writings, his letters and his publications. But it is also the case that he constantly refers to painting for his personal clarification, validation and catharsis. The process of painting thus became an outward manifestation of his intellectual stance. Art is a means of expressing universal meaning and enduring truths, and the areas of consciousness he explored often defied verbal expression.

There are significant examples of such intellectual conflict and tension that are recorded in his notebooks, which remain invaluable in understanding the intention of his work. Throughout his life, wrestling with such contentions provided the catalyst for creativity. He had noted:

> Guyanese women don't believe themselves supported by their men: they regard them as shallow, vain, irresponsible, ignorant; without centre or direction. The male is merely a provider with no abiding attachment to home or family; he can't set an example or gain their respect. Morally impotent, futile in action, therefore inherently incapable of creativeness or of facing challenge. She feels alone, frustrated, unprotected; and she feels psychically unwanted, that though content with her as a servant to all his wishes, the male tends to look elsewhere – to members of other races – whenever he needs true companionship or moral and intellectual stimulation. She seems among the unhappiest and most unrealised of women notwithstanding her increasing material well-being and the undemanding quality of life in this society.
>
> One woman, a member of the Guyanese social élite enjoying a standard of living comparable with any anywhere, told me she thinks the Guyanese Negro, for all our political emancipation and power, has proven impotent historically and incapable of holding his own in what's expected of him today; generation after generation have passed without mark or effect and now it's too late: we won't be able to stand up, we're already crumpling. "It is your duty, you're obliged, as a writer, to show us what's happened. So we'll know how we're dying. It's too late to try for anything else, you can't help us, you're too late too!"[32]

Pauline (1973–1974) is a three-quarters seated portrait showing the family housekeeper with a large bowl on her lap, possibly in the act of preparing food. She is depicted as a striking black woman asserting her identity with a massive New World "Afro" hairstyle. Seen as such, *Pauline* is a work that allows a fragmentary glimpse into the psychic life of an ordinary woman – a poor, black Guyanese working mother and provider. In psycho-historical terms, through the generations, the plight of the powerful black female at the centre of the New World experience has been debased by the accusations of collusion with the oppressor that have been directed at her. She reminds the black male that he has no power and remains impotent in the control of his own destiny. For many black men the *Pauline* archetype represents that which needs to be left behind. This was not the case for Williams who was brought up in an environment where there was a strong presence of African Guyanese women at the forefront of the practice and development of art, organising painting groups and conducting teaching.

Pauline is a painting in which the artist reminds us of the validity of the subject's African heritage and of the strong personal female dignity that transcends the menial rôle she has always been required to perform. The artist has used a close-cropped compositional device that frames part of a larger space and offers an intimate immediacy of presence. The academic modulations of the draughtsman in pursuit of a faithful likeness are seen in the powerful tonal solidity of form of the head itself. However, this gives way in the torso area where the artist has chosen an expressive, abstracted approach. This allows the eye to engage

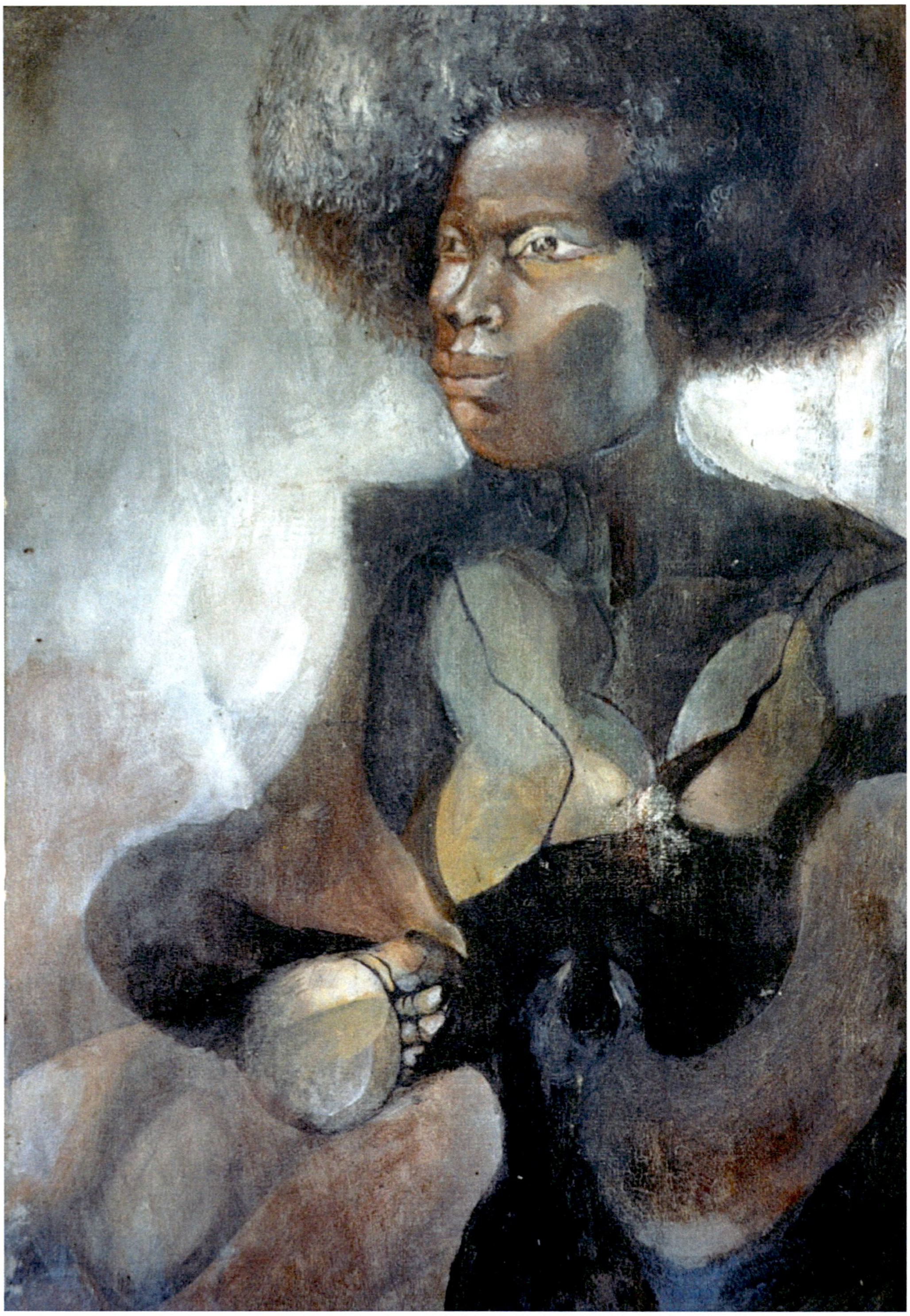

Pauline (1973–1974). Tempera on canvas on ply. 60×60 cms. Williams estate.

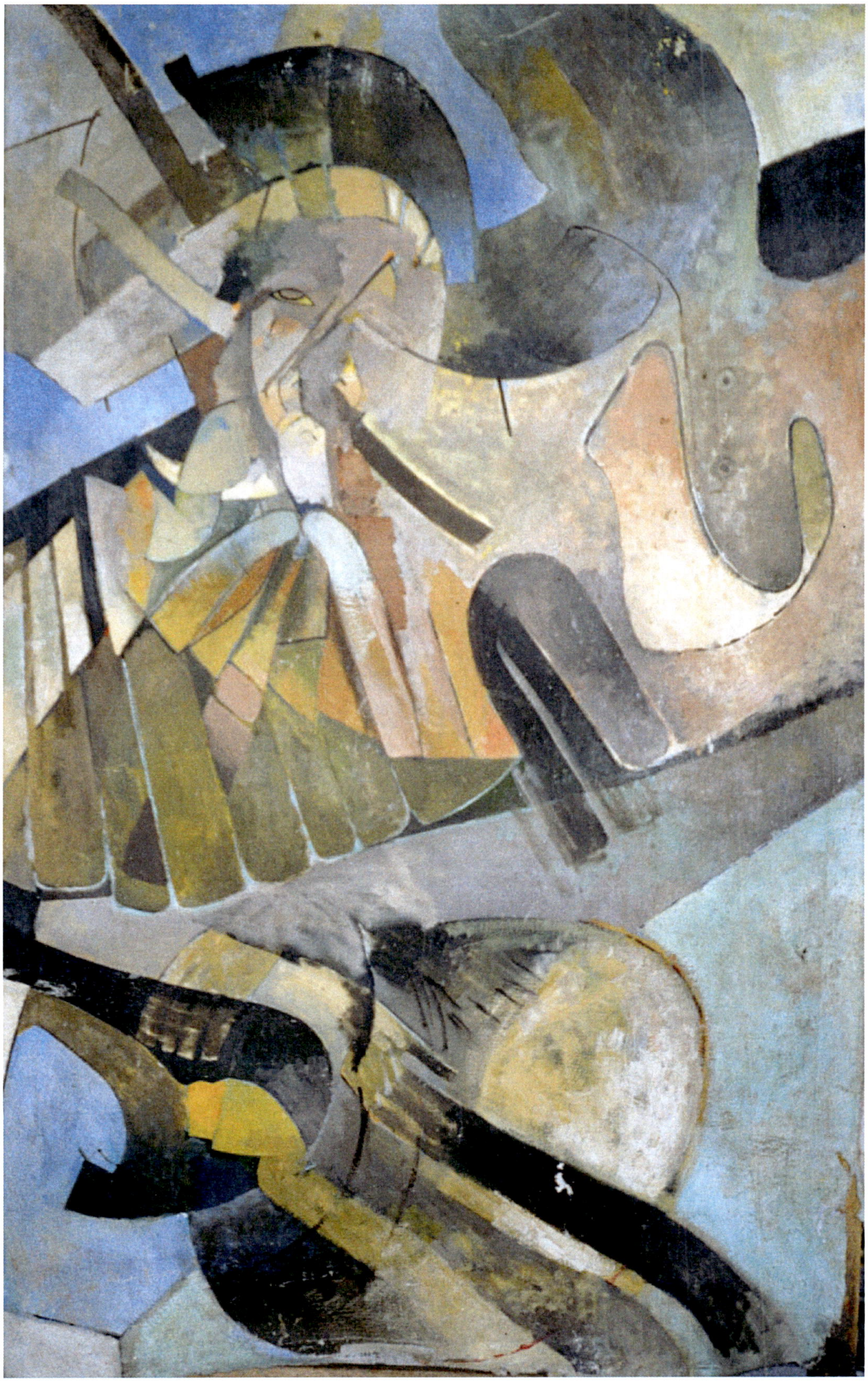

Pauline (1973–1974). Unfinished. Tempera on canvas. 115×75 cms. Williams estate.

with new forms arising from the shadow at the cheekbone and moving down the torso where an expressive configuration contrasts with the faraway stillness contained in Pauline's expression.

This is clearly a portrait painted from life and there are few such dignified portraits amongst the black cultural representations in the history of art, reflecting in part the issues surrounding the marginalisation and general invisibility of black women. The erasure of her self-image and the consequent near-dysfunctional self-hatred have resulted in a socially repressive beauty regime for many black women involving skin lightening and hair straightening using hot irons and chemical relaxers. Hair as a political symbol is a part of the reality of identity within the community of the African diaspora where, in the late 1960s and early- to mid-1970s, the New World "Afro" indicated a partial revolution of the black female self-image. It is interesting to note that those natural hairstyles of the 1970s often seemed to connote a strength and emerging self-confidence that others found intimidating. Sympathetic representations of such black women in a normalised non-exotic context are unusual, and the frank, candid representation of a black woman by a black man is exceedingly rare. There is agreement in the transaction of sitter and artist that is uncompromising: the portrait is a tribute to Pauline, and to African Guyanese women in general.

Pauline – the unfinished development – highlights many relevant aspects of Williams' approach as an artist and indicates what might be drawn from the conjunction of subject and style at this point. We can see in the *Pauline* development many of the elements that later become part of the repertoire of *Majestas*. Firstly we are reminded that the catalyst for and the intention of the work is inspired by an internal intellectual tension. But then the image comes to embody a profound, non-verbal statement. The figure is isolated and realised in an ambiguous space without edge. There has been a dramatic enlargement in format as if to suggest a move to make the subject more dominating and powerful. We can still discern the massive "Afro", the hand and bowl, and the palette of colour remains familiar. The contours of shapes and the tonal modelling of three-dimensional forms have been released and associated as dynamics of the composition rather than tied to the subject. The fundamental visual elements are abstracted. The pattern of independently worked shapes exists within different layers of a luminous, softly-textured space. The strong chiaroscuro pattern of light and reflection bounce back from their different levels in a repetition of rhythmic movements.

His painting clearly helped him to reflect on the New World context of an independent Guyana. Miscegenation, which he described as the first reality of Guyanese being – "this tangle of ancestry" – would have to be addressed if the arts were to achieve "autonomy and authority". "As a premise to any further creative work in art or literature," he wrote, "I have been obliged to give this problem rather prolonged thought. The results have often seemed as paralysing to me as they might seem confusing or even confused to you." [33]

This was the year in which he began the huge canvas he called *Majestas*, which was commissioned by Canon John Dorman as the centrepiece of a proposed triptych for the Anglican church of St Francis de Sales Church at Kamarang. At the time of writing it is in the care of Castellani House, where the author viewed it in 2009.[34]

Williams uses *Majestas* to define his vision and we have a first hand record of the artist's clear intentions behind this vast work:

> I say slavery has been traumatic for the New World Negro as a whole, not only Guyanese or Caribbean Negroes. The life-course has been cut, some inviolable law broken. In such a situation, I can't say whether there's hope, or whether we're dead. All nature works by law, and we're products of nature just as plants are and you can't interfere with the law plants work by. They die. Perhaps we're dead. But to know this would, at least, be a triumph over death. It is the business of the artist to know this. I feel that only in the midst of this death – if it is – can you deal with it. No use being tempted to run to Europe or America, you cannot deal with our particular death that way, only find ways of becoming blind to it. That way death has truly dealt with you. [...] Then I can't sleep for thinking about this thing. I get up to write these notes and come across another note I wrote for the *Majestas*: "It is hoped that the theme of the work, 'The Resurrection', realises something of the mystery of the sovereign human spirit in its limitless capacities, in its apprehension of the eternal and in its infinite powers of self-renewal. In all these senses 'The Resurrection' might appear to be of some special relevance at this period in the history of our country." So perhaps we've died in order to live differently? – without father, mother or home?[35]

For Williams it is the probing of this deep anxiety at the heart of the New World experience which is the significant narrative. The creative possibility of real transformation was directly linked to the presence of culturally diverse influences. In a spirit of affirmation the artist signals the spiritual resurrection he believes possible out of the sense of degradation at the death of the ancestor, a plight he saw as "the distinguishing characteristic of all New World societies." He brings into focus the redemption possible from such a point of view:

> As the revolution is inevitable, so the forms of the new self-image in art are inevitable. For the artists of Guyana, the quest for identity is the most revolutionary possibility that exists [...] The problem of identity is strictly the problem of déraciné and decultured immigrants, the crucial need is for a self-image which is true and therefore liberating.[36]

The optimistic symbolism of the resurrection of the fractured self-image is a Caribbean theme which resonates. For example, in his introductory paper at the 1972 Carifesta Symposium A. J. Seymour had described political independence as empty unless artists come out from under the "domination of the Euro-centred traditions and assess the new and gathering strength of the values of the Afro-centred past, no longer recessive and welling up from the deeps into the dignity of contemporary life." He had called on the need for "resurrection of the image of the African slave, but invested with a power and dignity not known before."[37] And Stanley Greaves has made the point that the task facing Caribbean artists was to define "the fundamentals of a Caribbean experience that cuts through or transcends the history of colonialism."[38]

There are three supporting studies for *Majestas*. One is a damaged fragment, but it is worth recording as it suggests a composition based on the idea of a vaulted, branching vortex through which a central image emerges. It is interesting to emphasise here the resonance of the "inner plantation". The linear directional interlaced dynamics of plant forms creates a grid reminiscent of earlier work and its rhythm sets up a flicker that suggests a symbolic spiritual light penetrating the dark forest canopy: the light that is sublime, transcendent and transforming. We know that Williams always challenged the riot of exotic colour that many claimed to characterise the rainforest, memorably describing it in the Aubrey

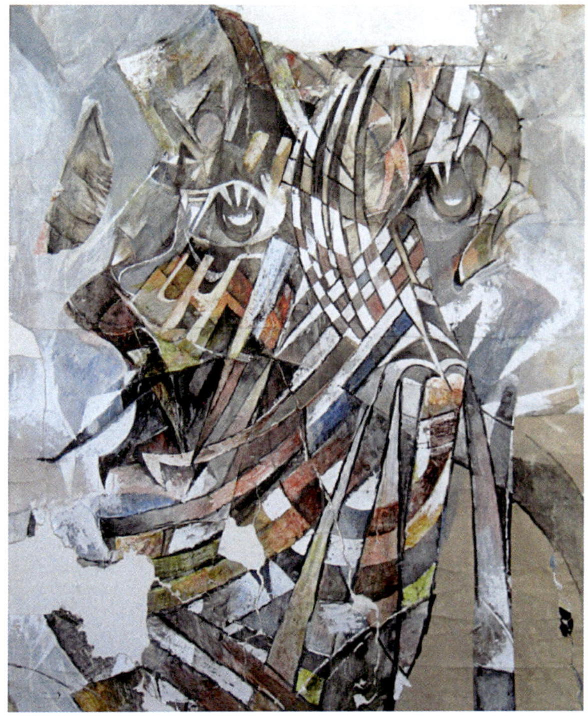

Majestas (1972). Preliminary study. Fragment. Mixed media on paper. 55×75 cms. Williams estate.

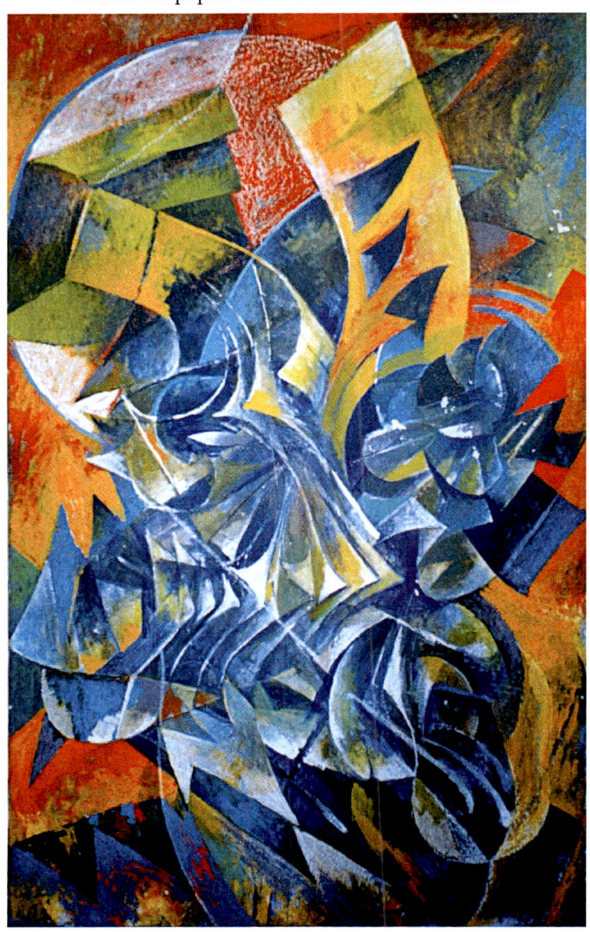

Majestas (1972). Study. Tempera and oil on canvas. 114×76 cms. Williams estate.

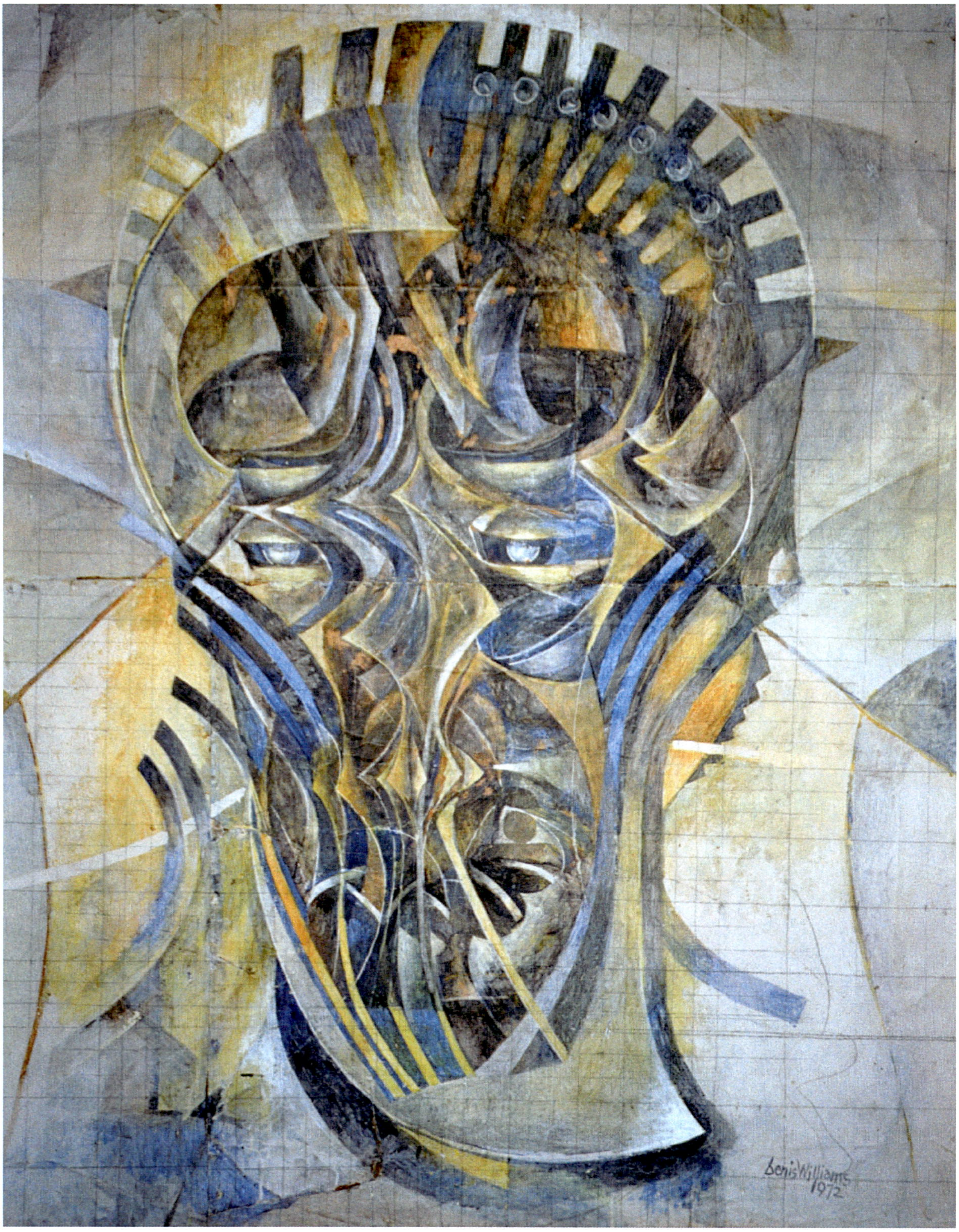

Majestas (1972). Study. Tempera on paper on board. 130×130 cms. Williams estate.

Williams monograph as black "giving way to green, grudgingly." He continues: "Living the past many years in its dense and dank environment, the virtual absence of colour in the forest was as absolute to me as had been my experience of the Sudan's Bayuda desert."[39] When the author visited Issano in 1973, Williams was working on a huge canvas stretched directly on to the wall of his logie; it was so big that the lower section rested in folds on the floor. The artist was highly animated as he worked. He spoke about using the leaf motif to paint the forest; how the leaves flickered and turned dark and light; how you could not use viridian; the forest was not viridian; that nobody had painted the forest: its mystery, haunting echo, its silence, the rain, its age.

A second study reveals the idea for the central *Majestas* image; it fills the space and is constantly elusive, veiled by repeated translucent shapes. In this study the underpainting is bright and primary, but it is evident from the direction of the overworking that the resolution is towards a muted tonality. Many of Williams' most powerful works are evidently autobiographical. *Majestas* is not a self-portrait but a portrait of the process of reconstructing the self. The painting is metaphorically exploring the space in which new identities can be conceived and nurtured.

The viewer is unable to determine the attitude or contour of the head: it seems to pivot. We are reminded of the function of the artist as an observer, the omnipotent eye adjusting its lens, independently of time. We are reminded of the complex of techniques employed to create an image with shifting points of view. The challenge of creating a stereoscopic image recurs for the artist as one that centres on the very nature of perception.

Contemporary with Williams this process of subtle and multiform orientations is described by Brathwaite "in terms of a dialectic of development taking place within a seamless guise or continuum of space and time; a model which allows for blood flow, fluctuations, the half-look, the look both/several ways; which allows for and contains the ambiguous, and rounds the sharp edges off the dichotomy."[40]

The third study is closest to the final concept. The paper-on-board support is marked off in a familiar grid-rhythm. The overall effect symbolically suggests the pursuit of an autonomous identity backwards through archaeological time. The excavation peels away at time, revealing layer upon layer with each shift. The painting fixes time in each layering of paint and each shift in tonal colour, as if revealing our origins by degrees. It is as if the artist is attempting to scale and map his subject. This study for the head of the composition is constructed in overlapping areas of colour: pale, ethereal blues are combined with earthy yellow ochre. At the outer edges the shapes are expansive and almost transparent; as they move to the centre to construct the head they fracture and become meshed in a complex layering of forms, transparent planes, delicate lines, and graded tones of colour. Much of the technical approach can be seen to be carried over to the final painting.

Majestas was painted at Issano and consecrated at St George's Cathedral, Georgetown. St Francis de Sales Church, Kamarang, was specifically designed to include the housing of the tryptich which was to be displayed on the central East wall above the Sanctuary and lit from above by transparent roof panels. In a letter, Canon Dorman reveals how the triptych might have been completed:

> Before it was exhibited at Umana Yana, Denis and I had met several times to discuss the subjects for the two side wings and he had done some sketches to assess how he would treat it if one side were to be the Crucifixion and the other the Resurrection: but these were inevitably uncertain as they had to be done without reference to the *Majestas* central panel. Later he suggested that as he had been doing some studies of Hominids for an archaeological purpose, something of that nature could be created on the side-wings. We raised our thinking in accordance with that suggestion and tried to envisage the two long narrow panels as a vision of the ascent of mankind and perhaps of other earlier living creatures reaching their culmination in Jesus, God and Man in heavenly majesty. After that we heard nothing and it became very difficult to keep communication open on the subject.[41]

Majestas is vast and expansive. Elfrieda Bissember described it as "overpowering",[42] and, in 1996, on the occasion of the twenty-first anniversary exhibition of the Burrowes School of Art, she wrote:

> [...] The *Majestas* reminded one of the technical brilliance of Denis Williams the artist. Very evident was his expert draughtsmanship and the boldness of his intellectual vision as a painter, in his conceptionalization of the Christ in Majesty, executed as a towering monumental figure (some 16'/4.8 m high in tempera on canvas) in faceted, semi-figurative, semi-abstract form which only reinforced the power of the image.[43]

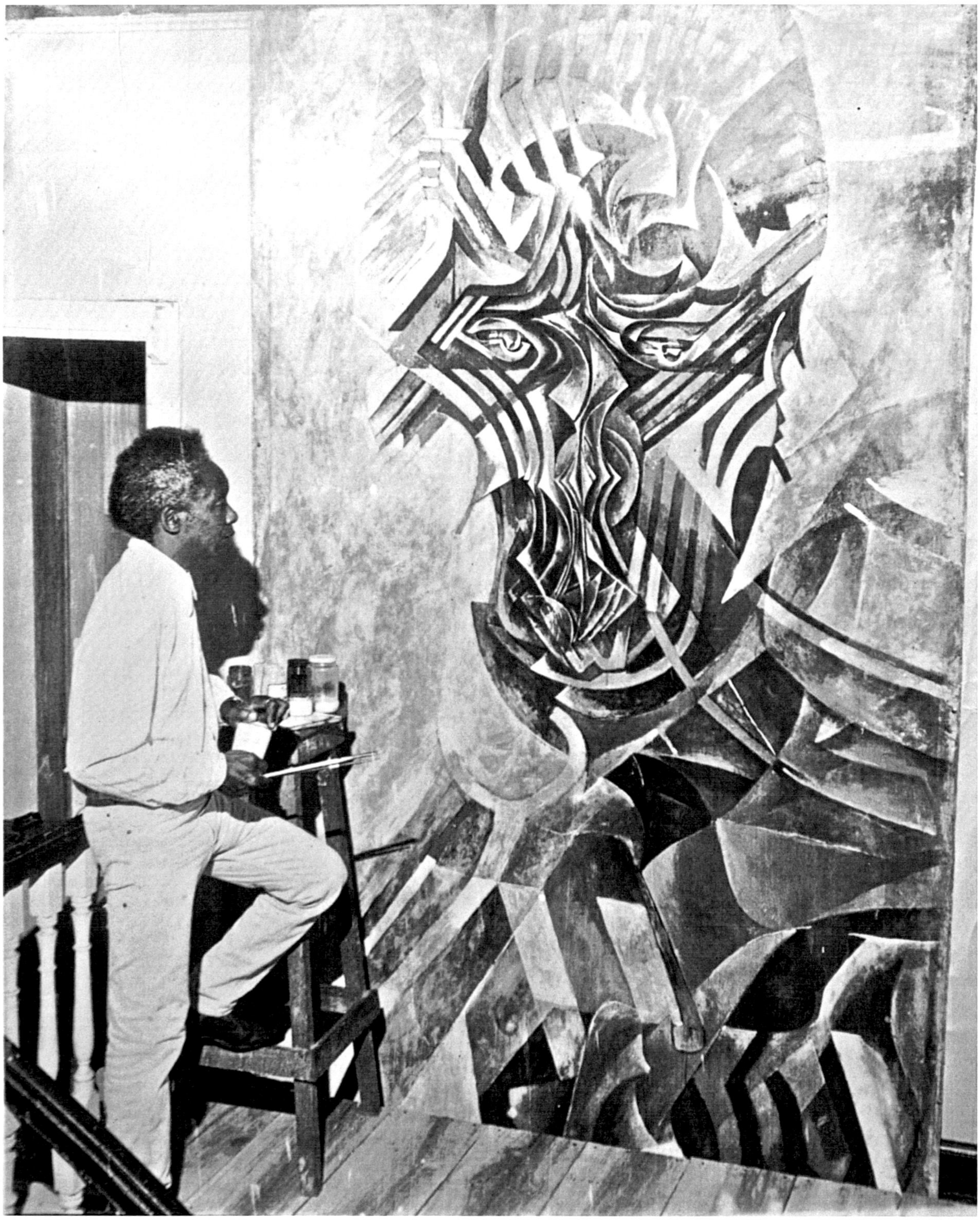

At work on *Majestas* (1973–1974). Tempera and oil on canvas. 465×170 cms. National Collection.

The artist himself conceived it as a towering, dominating image presiding in an ambiguous location in space, visible throughout the church through the flickering natural lights. This aspect is emphasised in the composition where the criss-cross lights and shadows radiate upwards from the head and down through the robes like fragments of bright sunlight breaking through the forest canopy.

The image is radical in conception unlike any prayer-book godhead but rather a personification charged with the majesty of the primal rainforest of the Guiana Shield; it is meant to evoke the sublime and most elemental forces of nature. Unexpectedly, it is spiritual but not religious.

The central image encodes the potential of "multiform orientations". It is tantalising and elusive. It is as if the artist is reconstructing the conscious, cognitive self within the landscape of his creative imagination prior to resurrection. The composition and identification of the central image is ultimately determined by the viewer from the combined mass of overlapping areas. The pursuit of an autonomous identity is conjured through this symbolic shifting of our perspective. With each tonal play our perspective is reconfigured by degrees. There is neither pessimism nor despair; the artist does not give way. The psychological weight of the inherent and accidental futility of life is never indulged. Williams believed that "It is possible, in fact open and necessary to man, to conquer the futile."[44]

Majestas is a reckoning, a manifesto: the product of a grand imagination. It emerges from a combined distillation of preceding works and can be seen as a summary of Williams' artistic and philosophical position in relation to New World realities. It provides a metaphor of the ability of the human spirit to transcend personal annihilation, to refashion itself in a new relationship, to undergo "a catalysis where the obvious is transcended by a re-interpretation of the present – creating new ground in thought and art."[45] His position points to the "uncanny-potency of art" in defining new possibilities in allowing the transformation necessary for growth and renewal. It is a culmination of his personal journey and dialogue on the situation of the "New World Negro". Williams believed that the artist had a duty to engage in the cultural debate; that it was the rôle of the artist to inhabit this domain, for culture is the platform where the battle for identity takes place.

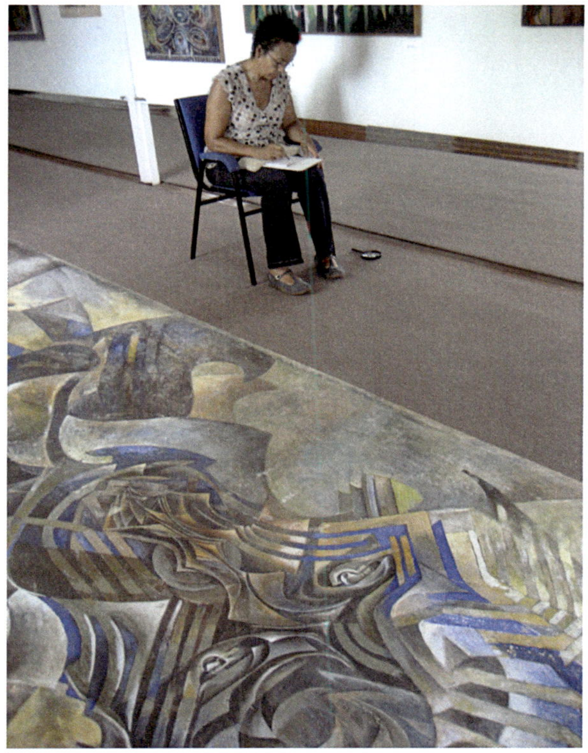

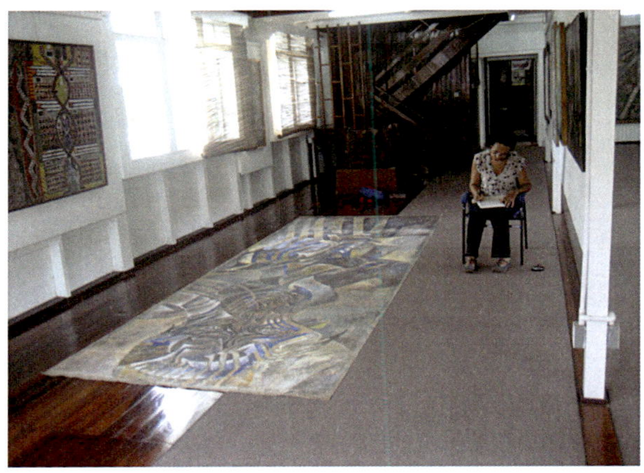

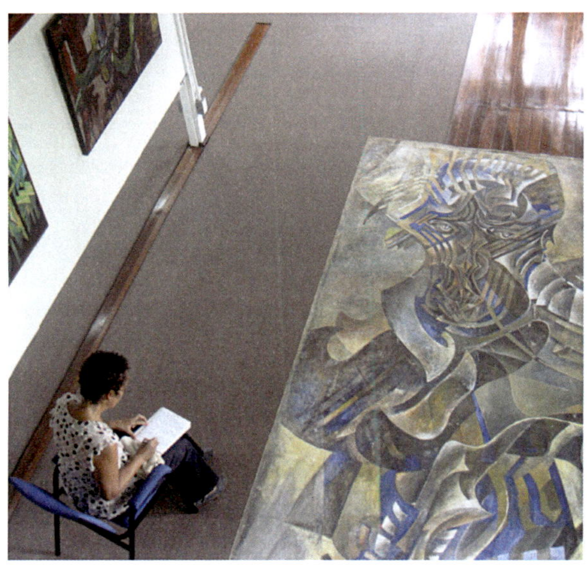

Right: the author with *Majestas* at Castellani House. Photographs by Andrew Lindsay.

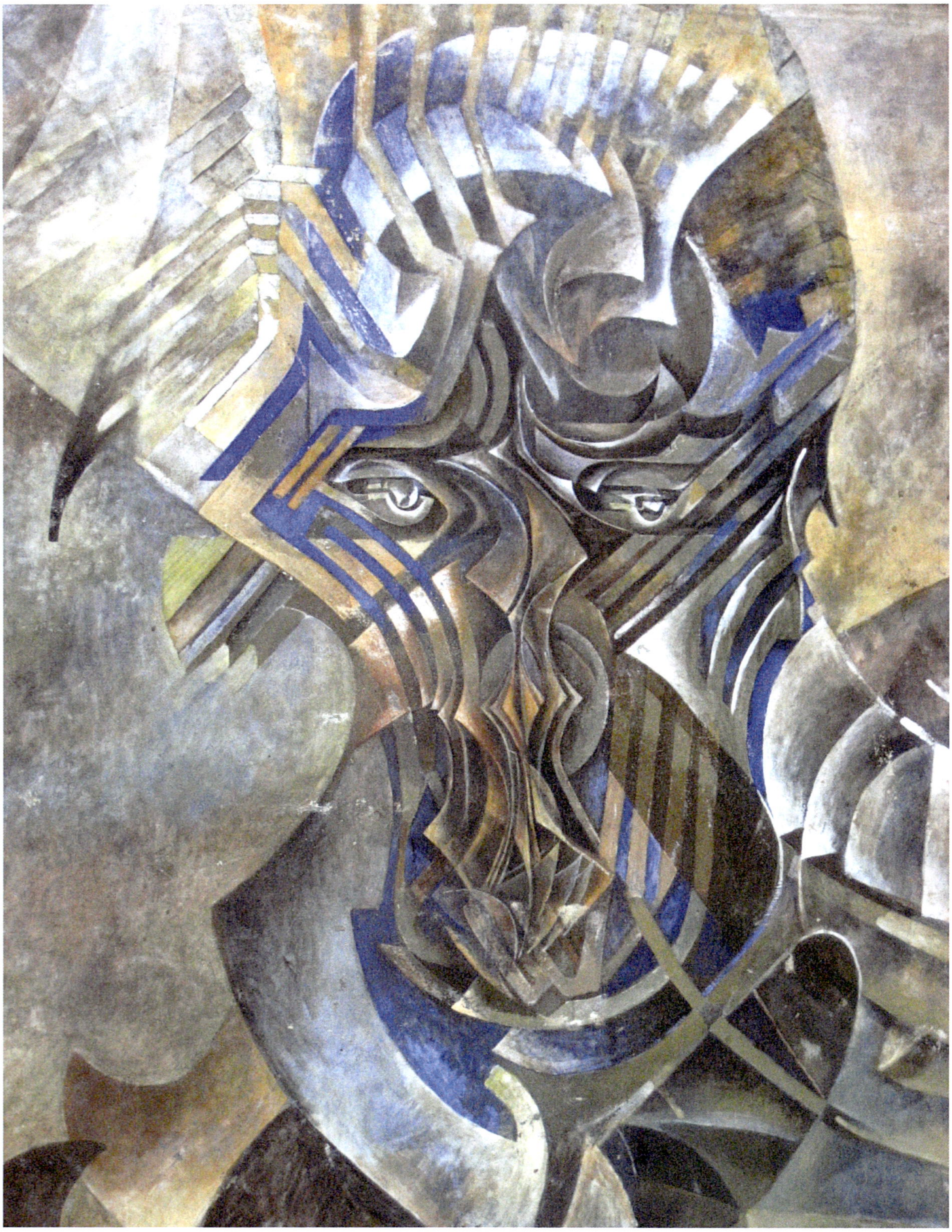

Majestas (detail).
Photograph by Andrew Lindsay.

NOTES TO CHAPTER 5

1 Denis Williams, *Other Leopards*, *ed. cit.*, p. 20.
2 Denis Williams, *Giglioli in Guyana (1922-1972)* (Georgetown: The National History and Arts Council, 1973). Dr George Giglioli was an Italian malariologist who did much to eradicate the disease in the coastal regions of British Guiana. He was interned for just over two years during World War II.
3 Denis Williams, "Giglioli and the Redemption of Guyana", in *Sunday Chronicle* (26 January 1975), p. 6.
4 Charlotte Williams (1998).
5 In 1970 he was awarded the Walter Roth Bursary for Anthropological and Archaeological Research, and, in 1973, a Smithsonian research grant for archaeological investigations on the Mazaruni River.
6 These are within Cheddi Jagan International Airport. In 2007 they were partially obscured during the process of constructing a new roof.
7 Quoted in Anne Walmsley, "Chronology", in Andrew Dempsey, Gilane Tawadros & Maridowa Williams (eds), *Aubrey Williams* (London: inIVA, 1998), pp. 65–90: p. 83.
8 Denis Williams, "Aubrey Williams in Guyana". Monograph in the above publication, pp. 36–45, p. 44.
9 Richard J. Powell, *Black Art and Culture in the 20th Century* (London: Thames & Hudson, 1997), p. 102.
10 Denis Williams, "Art and Society", in *The Literary Vision of Carifesta '72: The Role of the Artist in Third World Society*, *Kaie* (11, August 1973), p. 106.
11 Charlotte Williams (1998).
12 See the Introduction to *Prehistoric Guiana* (2003).
13 Denis Williams, "The Complex Womb", in *Image and Idea in the Arts of Guyana: The Edgar Mittelholzer Memorial Lectures*, Second Series (Georgetown: Ministry of Information, National History & Arts Council, January 1969), p. 15.
14 *Loc. cit.*
15 Michael Manley, *Jamaica: Struggle in the Periphery* (London: Third World Media Limited, 1982), p. 22.
16 A. J. Seymour, *Thirty Years a Civil Servant*. Typescript. (Georgetown, 1982), pp. 76–77.
17 "Caribbean Development", (by "A West Indian Correspondent") in *Venture* (Vol. 1. No. 10, November 1949), p. 5.
18 Michael Swan, *British Guiana: The Land of Six Peoples*, p. 147.
19 *Guyana* (Central Office of Information, London, February 1966).
20 Colonial Office: *Report of the British Guiana Constitutional Commission*, 1954 (The Robertson Report).
21 Denis Williams, *Image and Idea in the Arts of Guyana: The Edgar Mittelholzer Memorial Lectures*, 1969.
22 *Ibid.*, A. J. Seymour, foreword.
23 *Ibid.*, "The Complex Womb".
24 *Ibid.*, "Image and Idea in the Arts of Guyana".
25 Anne Walmsley, *The Caribbean Artists Movement 1966-1972: A Literary & Cultural History* (London and Port of Spain: New Beacon Books, 1992), p. 212.
26 Charlotte Williams (1998).
27 Rickey Singh, "Artists told: Think as Caribbean Nation", in *Guyana Graphic* (8 September 1972), p. 3.
28 Published as "Art and Society", in *The Literary Vision of Carifesta '72: The Role of the Artist in Third World Society*, *Kaie* (No. 11, August 1973), pp. 100–115.
29 *Ibid.*, p. 104.
30 Denis Williams, "Guyana", in Jane Turner (ed.), *The Dictionary of Art* (34 volumes) (London: Macmillan, 1996): Vol. 13: pp. 873–78: p. 877.
31 "Art and Society", p. 110.
32 Note dated 1973. Williams estate.
33 Denis Williams, "The Complex Womb".
34 In 1998 Williams expressed the hope that it would soon be brought to Georgetown for restoration. Canon Dorman's *Majestas* file was made available to the author by kind permission of Ms Bissember who also arranged a private viewing of the painting.
35 Private papers dated 6 January 1973. Williams estate.
36 "Contemporary Art in Guyana". Text of catalogue for the exhibition *Republic of Guyana: Contemporary Art* as part of Carifesta '76 in Jamaica (Georgetown: Bovell's Printery, 1976), pp. 1–5: p. 3.
37 *Kaie* (No. 11, August 1973).
38 Quoted in Rupert Roopnaraine, *The Primacy of the Eye: The Art of Stanley Greaves* (Leeds: Peepal Tree Press, 2005), p. 130.
39 "Aubrey Williams in Guyana", (London: inIVA, 1998), pp. 36–45: p. 39.
40 "Caribbean Man in Space and Time", in Hearne, John (ed.) *Carifesta Forum: An Anthology of 20 Caribbean Voices* (Jamaica: Institute of Jamaica, 1976), pp. 199–208.
41 Letter to Elfrieda Bissember, January 1998. The reference is to the 21st anniversary exhibition of the Burrowes School of Art in Georgetown in 1996.
42 "Burrowes School retrospective", in *Guyana Review* (July 1996), pp. 38–39.
43 Letter to Peter Dorman, 22 July 2002.
44 *Africa Journal*, p. 311. Written at Makerere, dated 23 July 1966.
45 Denis Williams, "The Complex Womb".

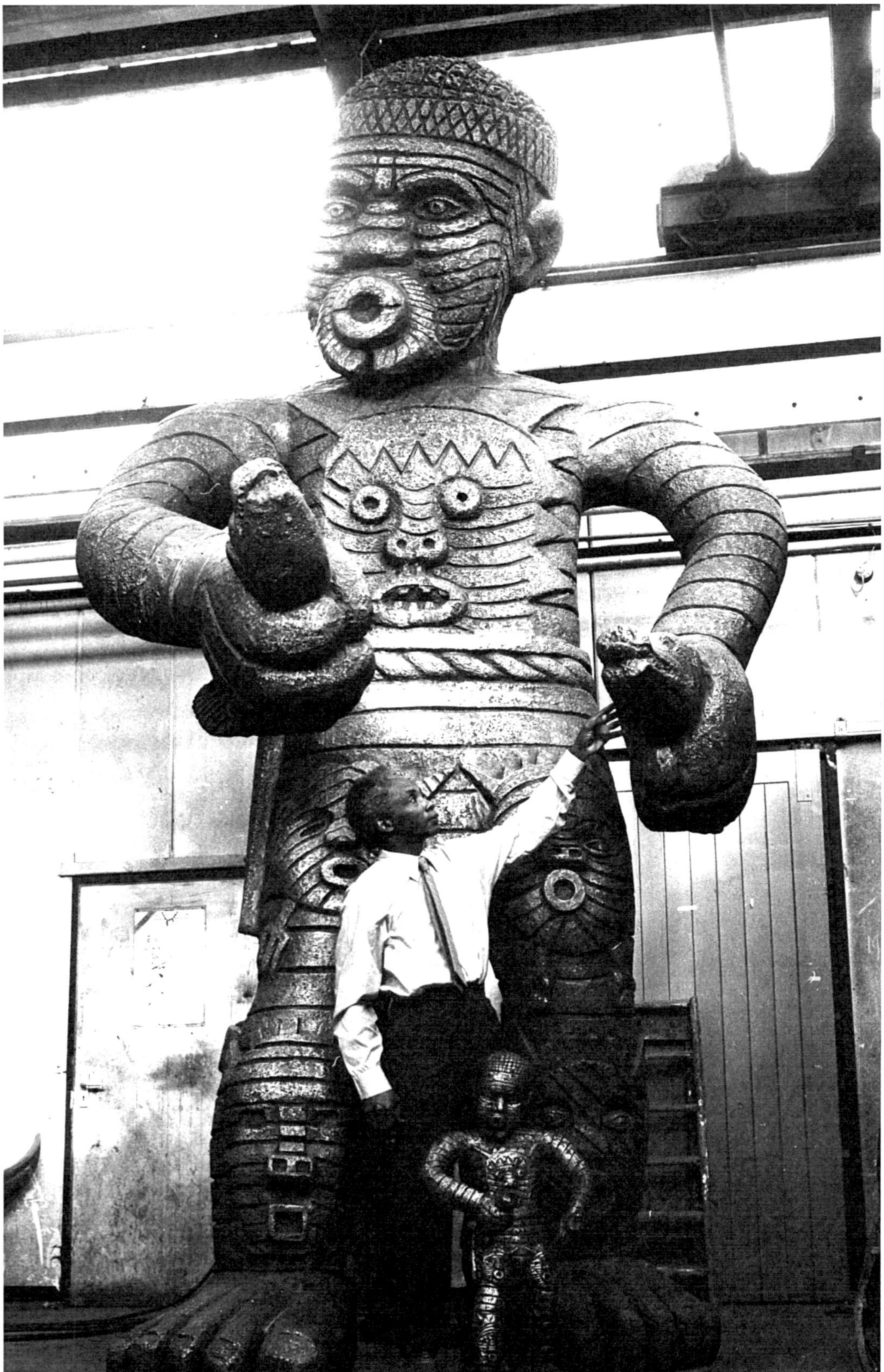

At the Morris Singer foundry in Basingstoke
with the 1763 Monument, designed by Philip Moore.
(By permission of *The Times* / NI Syndication).

Chapter 6

Memorabilia

THE POLITICISATION OF CULTURE was occurring throughout the Caribbean as the new nationalist politicians came to recognise the advantages of exploiting the arts. Following his return to Georgetown from the interior, Williams was appointed as Director of Art for the new Republic. In his view, the history of the West Indies with its short historical context, its multi-ethnic heritages and its mixed European legacy, created circumstances that were central to the urgent question of national identity. He believed that "the transformation of a multi-racial colony of dispossessed immigrants into a dynamic modern state entails thoroughly rebuilding the national self-image."[1]

He believed that people must begin their journey to nationhood from a secure position of self-worth and shared values and that art and culture must acknowledge aspects of the common experience of the people and eventually come to reflect the reality of their lives. But in Guyana there was no cohesive, integrating culture, not even in its music, and no obvious, popular visual arts culture. This absence of a unifying cultural revolution of the collective mind at the grass roots level ensured that racial and religious chauvinism and dogma persisted as forces obstructing meaningful notions of progress. Whilst this was not an unusual predicament, Guyana was unique in the Caribbean in its peculiar ethnic mix existing alongside autochthonous peoples with a continuous relationship to their past. Whereas the original populations of the islands of the Caribbean Sea had been effectively eradicated by the Spanish, in Guyana the system of administration had allowed the Amerindian peoples a relative liberty in both their territory and their beliefs, and in addition their mainland location meant they had been less easily contained and controlled.

For Williams, it was this very specific diverse makeup of Guyana that brought him to focus on the practical need to establish the context of life in the region; to record its history, its customs and language. His lofty long-term aim was to establish and build a framework of national identity within the wider context of the South American continent.

He became an active figure as Chairman of the Board of the National Trust of Guyana, charged by the cultural revolution to accelerate the process of defining and safeguarding the cultural property of the nation, simultaneously preserving and conferring a value on all that was Guyanese. He was instrumental in the preservation of Fort Kyk-over-al and Fort Zeelandia and the move to declare the Fort Nassau area a National Monument.[2] He worked to protect archaeological sites and caves like those at Aishalton[3] and the country's national cemeteries and burial sites. He drew the government's attention to the illegal trading and plundering of Guyana's objects of material culture and warned against allowing *ad hoc* permits to conduct marine archaeology in Guyanese territorial waters. On the nationalisation of Bookers holdings in Guyana in 1976, he saw to it that their museum assets were transferred to the National Trust.[4] He supported research projects into the religious sites and places of worship of Hindus and Muslims,[5] and research into Amerindian visual and material culture.[6]

He was also a member of the Central Housing and Planning Authority from where he assured a focus on protecting the traditional vernacular architecture of the cultural heritage against unauthorised developments. There was a lack of finance available to preserve plantation buildings and because of the association with slavery many people were not interested in the distinctive wooden architecture of their heritage. For Williams this represented a missing transition: people needed to recognise a shared cultural history and the prominent part the skill their ancestors had employed in – literally – building the heritage that makes a nation.

In Guyana, following much delay, the new National Cultural Centre, begun in 1972, was nearing completion. It was anticipated as being a venue for cultural expressions at home but also, significantly, with those countries with which it had close links, thus mobilising the cultural and artistic potential of the country. An open competition was eventually held for a large mural for the foyer. The panel of five judges included Dr Frank Williams, who had been instrumental in procuring *Human World* for the National Collection. Denis Williams submitted a study, now called *Memorabilia I*, and was commissioned to carry out the work.

In the Declaration of Sophia (1974)[7] President Forbes Burnham had identified his idiosyncratic cooperative socialism as the way forward. He set out in idealistic terms a plan to address the issues of racial conflict and what he referred to as the needs of the "little man". On the occasion of the Guyana Festival of the Arts (Guyfesta) 1975, which was organised around the theme "My Community, My Nation" Burnham insisted:

> Cultural expressions must be encouraged. There cannot be a real political and/or economic revolution, nor can the Guyana man or the Guyana way of life be identified, unless there is a cultural revolution. The cultural revolution is not cultural chauvinism, but just an expression of what we know, what we are familiar with, what we have experienced, regardless of the origin. It represents the will of the people to express their own way of life.[8]

For Williams it stimulated thoughts on the purpose of public art in a revolutionary phase of society. He saw his public position as creative, and neither political nor wholly administrative. His writing demonstrates a commitment of social responsibility within the climate of this revolutionary phase in Guyana but he clearly sought to avoid the more obvious route of cultural propaganda.

As Barrington Braithwaite recently noted:

> The persons that held the official offices that interacted with artists and artistes were not politicians but were themselves Masters in their specific artistic disciplines [...] Politics played second fiddle [...] and Forbes Burnham left them alone; the arts had strong personalities that contributed significantly to the period of decolonisation.[9]

Stanley Greaves explained that:

> The notion of [Williams] working in a post-colonial context did not enter my mind at all. I felt he was working through rather than for the Government because he was the originator of practical policies for art. [...] I was somewhat sceptical of the polemics of the day as regards the legacies of colonialism and the conceptualising of post-colonial strategies.[10]

However it is clear from numerous cross-references to published material by Williams that he made a significant contribution to the official document entitled *Cultural Policy in Guyana*:[11]

> For the artists of Guyana, the revelation of a national identity is the most revolutionary possibility that exists. The [...] work of art in revolutionary Guyana must amplify the interpretation of the words "meaning" and "truth" in areas that yield the new self-image as the pearl of all artistic enquiry [...].[12]

Cultural nation-building had produced mural art in Mexico and Williams realised its pedagogical value and popular appeal. He had executed a large-scale mosaic mural in Nigeria and when he attended a conference in Mexico in 1975 he was able to study works by *Los Tres Grandes*: Rivera, Orozco and Siqueiros. It is likely that he visited Rivera's murals in the National Palace and his writing demonstrates his familiarity with the Siqueiros manifesto. Williams too had raised the issue of an art the population could understand in terms other than European.

The content of his large study *Memorabilia I* (1974–1976) explores a symbolic interpretation of the concept of revolution as a heroic battle presaging profound historical change. It adopts an allegorical approach to content that dramatically embodies the global revolt against any assumption of inequality. The artist conveys the universal struggle as one of the overthrow and displacement of a great mechanistic system of oppression. He uses a combination of figures together with features of the man-made environment and presents them exploiting an abstracted, fractured style of composition. Against a skyline of the built environment we see split images of figures, smashed tiles, displaced brickwork and crumbling edifices. Areas representing the bright light of day and the dark silhouettes of night are patterned throughout the composition in a great turning and unbalancing effect. Images are literally turned on their head and the overall effect is of an epic battle. Visually the composition divides in three. The central image embodies a complex articulation of power, momentum and destruction that combines human and mask forms with European-style metal body armour, horse and machine: we see a fallen saddle, a displaced helmet. Heavy-limbed, truncated legs crush through shattered terracotta; we can trace the path of a muscular arm swinging back mechanically before a strike. Nuts and bolts are falling loose and mighty dark cogs and wheels are set to topple. All symbolically weigh down on a fragile humanity in the destructive path of revolution. The imagery to the left and to the right of centre concentrates on the human emotional content. On the faces of three of the figures picked out of the crowd to the left we see expressions of fear and anguish. But the mass is mobilised. With clenched fists, beating of breasts, screaming and mayhem, the mob moves as one, and all is crushed underfoot. Williams wrote:

> As subject colonials, we had long been familiar with riot and revolution as forms of mass protest; but these primitive forms of confrontation not infrequently leave power even more firmly entrenched than before, more unassailable, more repressive. [...] Ours is characteristically the era of moral demonstration, of the defeat of the oppressor not by violence necessarily less than his own, but by assault on the tissue of his very beliefs. [13]

This initial large study was shown as part of the exhibition *Colonial Art to Revolutionary Art 1966–1976* which Williams curated. It focuses on quite different content and on an entirely different stylistic approach from the final version as it exists today. Although *Memorabilia I* is effective as a concept and composition, we know that he rejected this initial idea for the National Cultural Centre mural. There has to be a contradiction of élitism in any concept of transcendentalism and he remained keenly conscious of the question of the appropriateness of the alien and the esoteric in his art. He was not claiming a position as a hero-artist of the republic and he was also clearly rejecting the idea of the celebration of the mythology of violent revolution. "The contemporary Guyanese artist therefore has no need of iconoclasm [...] his concern is not to destroy tradition but to create it. And here the question of national identity arises."[14] In Guyana he knew that art did not hold central stage as a key cultural manifestation of revolution as it had done, for example, in Mexico. The exclusiveness of the restrictive colonial system meant that there was no widely understood existing cultural form for a Mexican-style revolutionary art to symbolically overthrow.

> Guyana has never known an art of the bourgeoisie – the socialist revolution does not therefore have that problem to deal with. [...] it will be necessary to replace the forms, the idioms of a colonial art; necessary to replace the ideology of an art based on those aesthetic preferences of the colonial system which necessarily devalued creative expression amongst its subject peoples. This, in a word, boils down to a problem of identity. [15]

There is no doubt that he set himself a punishing personal agenda in the context of cultural nation-building. This is clear from his *Africa Journal* in which he had early signalled his own "grand design". It is also clear from his letter to Harold Drayton in 1966 in which he indicated the need to take the long view in the development of a society beyond its immediate struggle for survival: a reality that all ex-colonies had to face. He regarded it as self-evident that any future for Guyana was dependent on a thorough understanding of its own past. He believed that it was essential to equip the nation with knowledge of all its inhabitants in order that they might co-exist. In the Drayton letter he had described his long-term plan. He anticipated the creation of "The Roth Museum of American and Caribbean Antiquities", and "The Guyana Academy" which would encompass "The Burrowes School of Fine Art" and "The Pilgrim School of Music". For him these were the models of the cultural institutions that would facilitate the dissemination of knowledge and the development of an inclusive ethos. His view placed the creative imagination at the centre of any debate exploring the future possibilities of nationhood. The letter continues: "I see a University Museum as a research unit focusing (and publishing) the work of Anthropologist, Ethnologist and Art Historian." He noted the necessity for a study of the sociology of the peoples of Guyana; the sociology of slavery and Indian immigration, and the need for linguistics in order to study Amerindian and non-European languages. In his view the academic priority in all disciplines was aimed at establishing a unified consciousness in defining the emerging national imagination. Artistic criteria determined this view of the cultural map of the future of Guyana in a social vision predicated on broadening the cultural experience of the nation. This remained his visionary artistic and intellectual approach despite the prevailing economic and social difficulties.

Many of the newly independent countries of the Caribbean symbolically marked the black experience of resistance to slavery when establishing their public monuments. Resistance had been an ever-present fact of life on the plantations of the New World. Each nation's

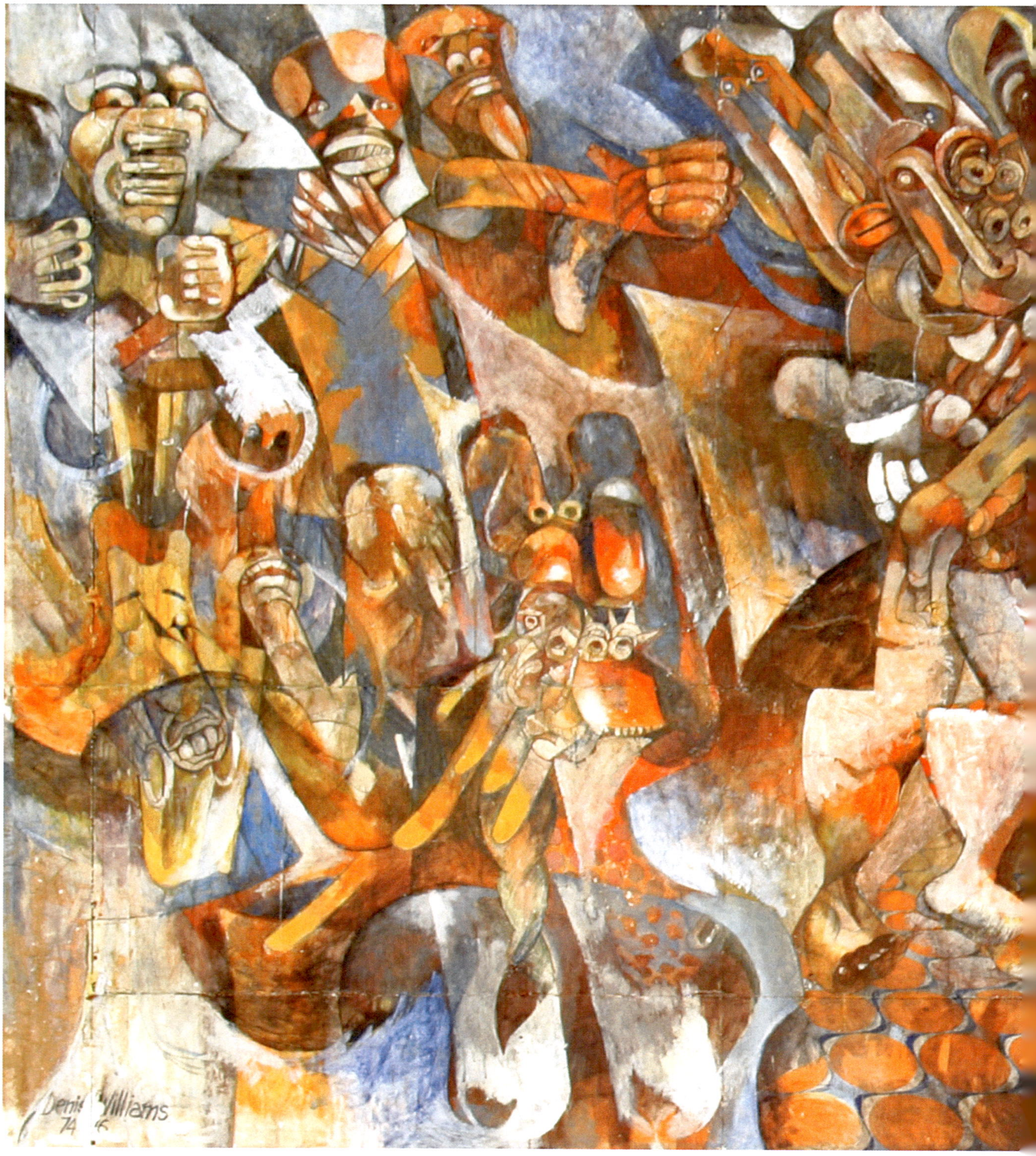

Memorabilia I (1974). Tempera on paper on board. 230×137 cms.
National Collection. Photograph by Ohene Koama.

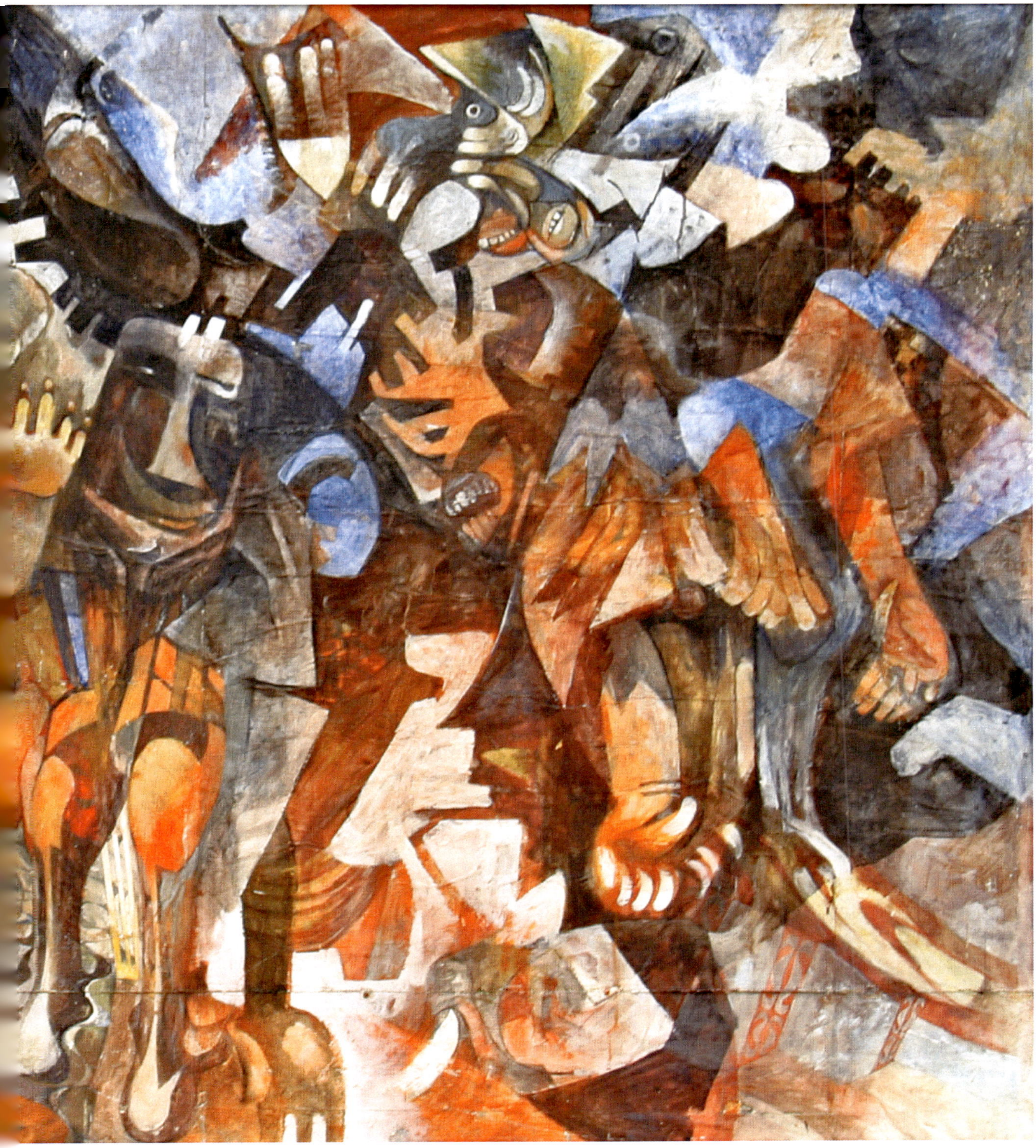

recognition of this historical, systematic rejection of the excessive psychological degradation of enslavement was central to any concept of self-worth.

The Berbice Slave Revolt (1763–1764) takes a special place amongst other major Caribbean slave revolts as one that was organised along military lines, and the one in Guyana that came closest to success. But throughout the country there was continuous black resistance particularly through desertion from Essequibo and Demerara plantations. This had led to the formation of bush communities in the hinterlands. It was Cuffy (Kofi), the "Governor of the Negroes of Berbice", who was singled out in the historical unfolding of events, and who would be elevated as a heroic symbol in the national consciousness of Guyana's people of African heritage.

Williams initiated and co-ordinated the first home-grown, large-scale public art monument in Guyana.[16] It sought to validate all that was implied in the struggle for freedom from slavery in a monument to commemorate the 1763 revolution. The artist Philip Moore was repatriated to Guyana from the United States to undertake this work. His fifteen-foot bronze statue, weighing two and a quarter tonnes, was cast for Guyana at Britain's famous Morris Singer foundry in Basingstoke where the work was overseen by Williams in his position as Director of Art for The National History and Arts Council of Guyana. The original maquette that Moore had sculpted in wood was also cast in bronze and later formed a central exhibit in Guyana's exhibition at the Jamaica Institute during Carifesta 1976. The completed monument was unveiled in Guyana by President Burnham to mark the tenth anniversary of independence in 1976. It is mounted on a concrete plinth designed by the architect Albert Rodrigues and dominates the Square of the Revolution in Georgetown.

In an article to mark the unveiling ceremony Williams wrote:

> This image goes beyond merely illustrating revolution in being itself a revolution of vision. Philip Moore's spectators need equally a revolution of vision in themselves in order to understand this work. When we look back at this monument we will see that it is truly historical not only in symbolising 1763, but also in being the watershed that offered a new image of ourselves and so a milestone in the cultural revolution which freed us from self-doubt and self-contempt implanted in our peoples during the nineteenth century. Philip Moore's image of an eighteenth-century African ought to revitalise our thinking on the corporate image of all our peoples, and this we have to do without reference to definitions of ourselves which were formed in alien cultures.[17]

Of the adverse comments from some quarters which greeted the unveiling of the monument he noted:

> The history of art is rich in controversy of this sort. Great works of art survive, however. Controversy never does. That which survives is the unassailable and absolute truth about a people. It is what most folks proudly call tradition – the thing they fight and die for.[18]

Carifesta '76 was held in Jamaica. The overall theme of the festival was "Self-Reliance Through Creativity". Williams was among four writers from Guyana who were taking part in the Symposia on the state of the arts in the Caribbean alongside Martin Carter, A. J. Seymour and Mahadai Das. *Carifesta Forum: An Anthology of 20 Caribbean Voices* set the tone for the festival as a collection of works concerning the "[...] relationship and response to one of the world's most confused cultural battlefields."[19] Williams curated *Contemporary Art in Guyana* as part of Carifesta '76 in which he exhibited *Majestas*. His detailed exhibition notes for this exhibition provide an enduring reference for what he was to label the "Guyana School".

The Enmore Martyrs Memorial (1977) was designed by Williams and erected by Zenith Industrial Construction Cooperative Society.[20] It is situated on the road to the Enmore Sugar estates and it was constructed to commemorate the five sugar cane workers martyred during a protest over working conditions.[21] Little is known of the circumstances of its commission or design. It appears to be an unresolved work, perhaps awaiting additional consideration or funding. It is an unlikely, contemporary architectural structure formed in cast white cement. It rises some twenty-five feet from a six-foot base plinth. There are five fluted standing columns, each bearing a cast bronze symbol reminiscent of a cutlass, designed by Cletus Henriques. The monument is symbolic of the resistance against a system of labour universally regarded as unjust. The Enmore Martyrs incident is one that Williams revisited in the subject matter of *Memorabilia II*.

He was instrumental in establishing the Burrowes School of Art in 1975, and was its first

Principal.[22] It was one of the five departments of the Institute of Creative Arts. However when he was interviewed about the BSA some twenty years later[23] it is clear that in retrospect he viewed his original concept – to "promote the highest professionalism in the practice of art through institutionalised training"[24] – as only partially valid and he conceded that the approaches and practices that he introduced, based on western models of academic and artistic discipline, were at odds with the profile of the many BSA students. Stanley Greaves records that Williams was engaged in an ongoing debate about the terms of reference of the project.[25]

> Because of the traditional proletarian basis of the visual arts in Guyana, aptitude and enthusiasm need be the only prerequisites in recruitment for training and not necessarily the attainment of irrelevant academic skills. The creative pursuit of art is acknowledged to be an academic discipline in its own right.[26]

A contradiction would seem to have arisen for Williams in pursuing an open access policy – perhaps guided by his experience of the Mbari projects in Nigeria – while at the same time seeking to teach disciplines like anatomy and perspective in a bid to raise standards. It is certain that a degree of ideological conflict was present amongst the staff of BSA. In several of his critical writings he refers to the disdain from certain quarters for any art that was not wholly "intuitive". Henwood Adrian had been responsible for coining the contemptuous expression "Book Art", meaning European-derived.[27]

Williams had noted: "Reaction to the internationalising process, when it came, was not uniform. Among certain artists it took the form of qualified acceptance whilst, among others, rejection was total."[28] These securely anchored views lay at the heart of the ground to be negotiated. There was the perceived danger of wholesale appropriation of received ideas and a deep suspicion of the intellectual in art. He attempted to steer a course towards raising standards and towards widening and improving technical ability. His objective he summarised thus:

> Our young people are extremely good image makers, but they have no control over those images. They can not manipulate these images, because they don't have the technical control. What we want to do is to bring the two together.[29]

The issues facing BSA – the ideological schisms; lack of funding; the absence of public support and an uncertain destiny – demonstrate something of the contradictions and conflicting views that the circumstances of reconstruction exposed. How to deliver a New World status and destiny out of Old World forms and institutions? How to move from the exclusive models of Empire to an egalitarian inclusiveness?

His contribution to the development of the cultural profile of his country extended to his ability to write with critical insight on the practice of art. He did not consider himself to be an art critic but was prepared to build on the foundations laid by others like A. J. Seymour who had consciously developed a healthy art criticism in the country. His specific contribution was in his ability to place the work of individual painters and sculptors in a wide contextual setting that recognised and placed a value on the emergence of a Guyanese aesthetic:

> In addition to its aesthetic content [...] we should expect a work of revolutionary art in Guyana to extend our notion of "meaning" in areas that yield the new self-image as the pearl of all artistic enquiry. [...] this constitutes an extension of our traditional understanding of the relationship between "meaning" and "form". [...] Vision is paramount.[30]

He was capable of revisiting and revising his own opinions: for example, the view that Caribbean expression was necessarily a province of European expression and its norms of idiom, judgement and criticism, and its intellectual conventions were unavoidably dependent on it. "In the light of my thinking on the nature of our present since returning home, this is an opinion which I would now retract."[31]

He recognised Philip Moore as a pioneer of the "Guyana School" with the emergence of a host of home-grown artists for whom the forms of European-American art had become increasingly less important. In recognising the "Guyana School" he separated and delineated his own position alongside others schooled in the metropolitan centres, including Donald Locke, Stanley Greaves, Aubrey Williams and Frank Bowling:

> [...] we belong to that generation of the bridge. Shostakovich and all that for Aubrey Williams, and Mondrian for me and such things, it was a necessary bridge. [...] the painters produced within that bridge experience, could only be like Bowling and

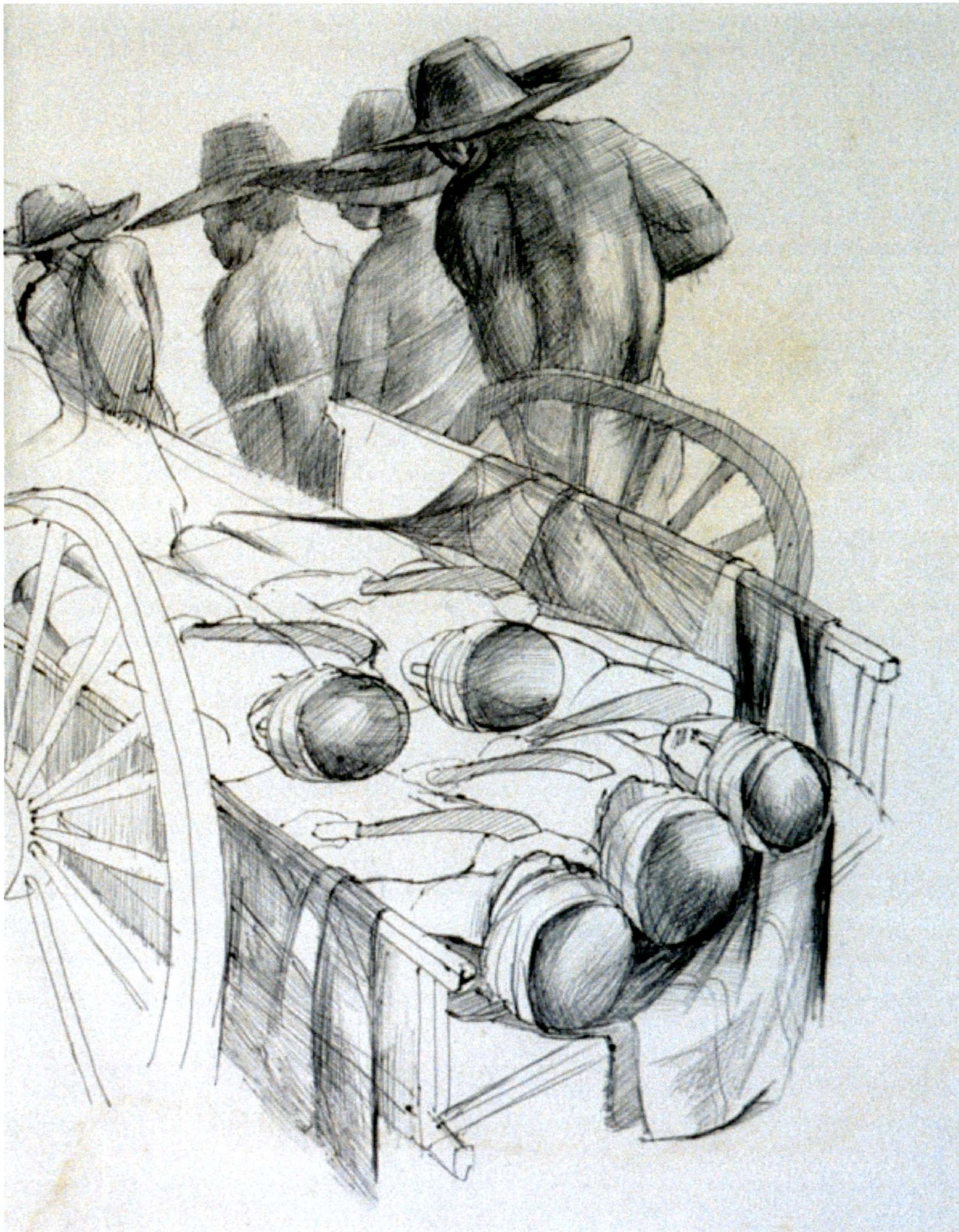

Memorabilia II. Preliminary drawing for the Enmore martyrs. Biro. 59.4×42 cms. Inscribed "Minister's pictures, Matthews archives".

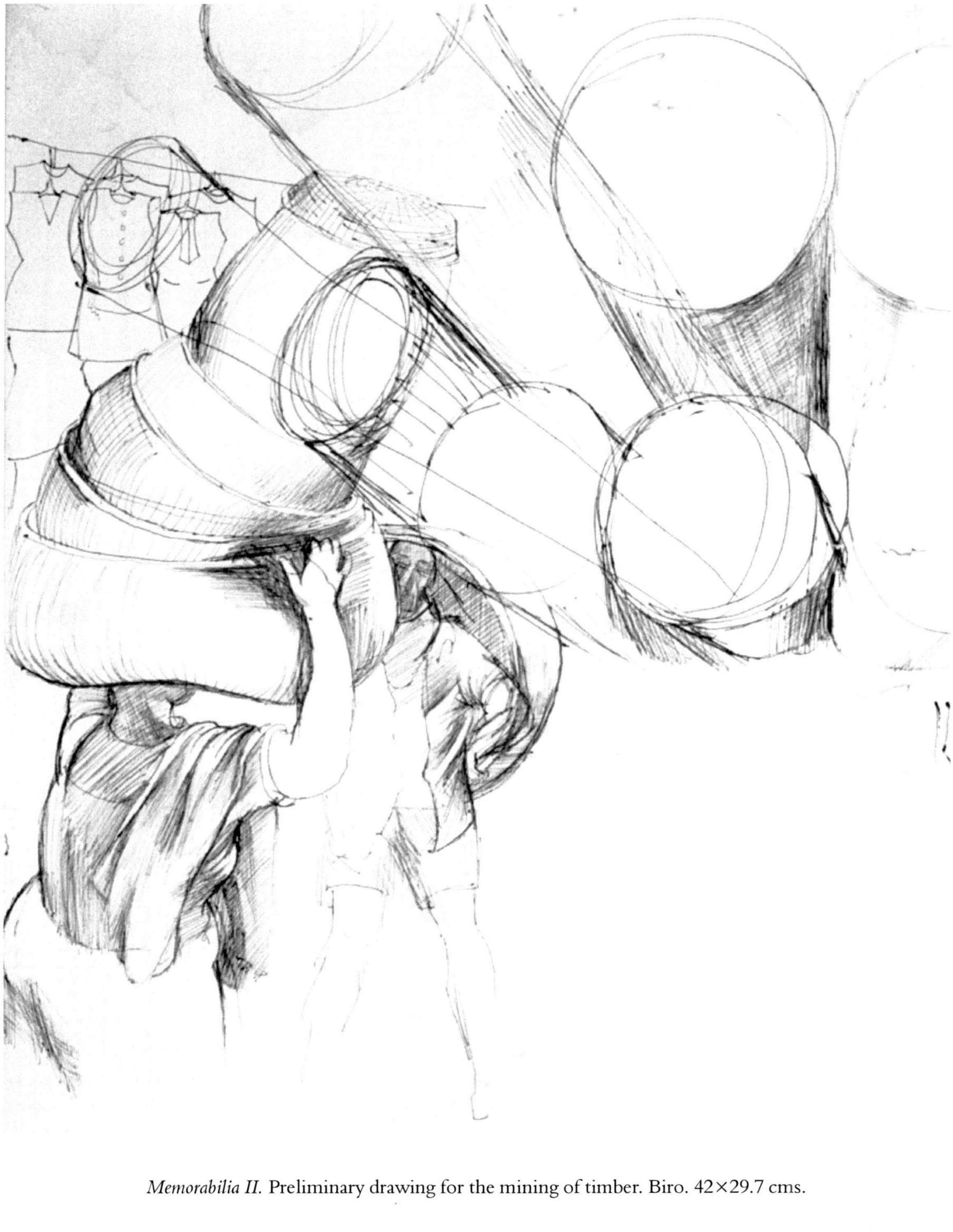

Memorabilia II. Preliminary drawing for the mining of timber. Biro. 42×29.7 cms.

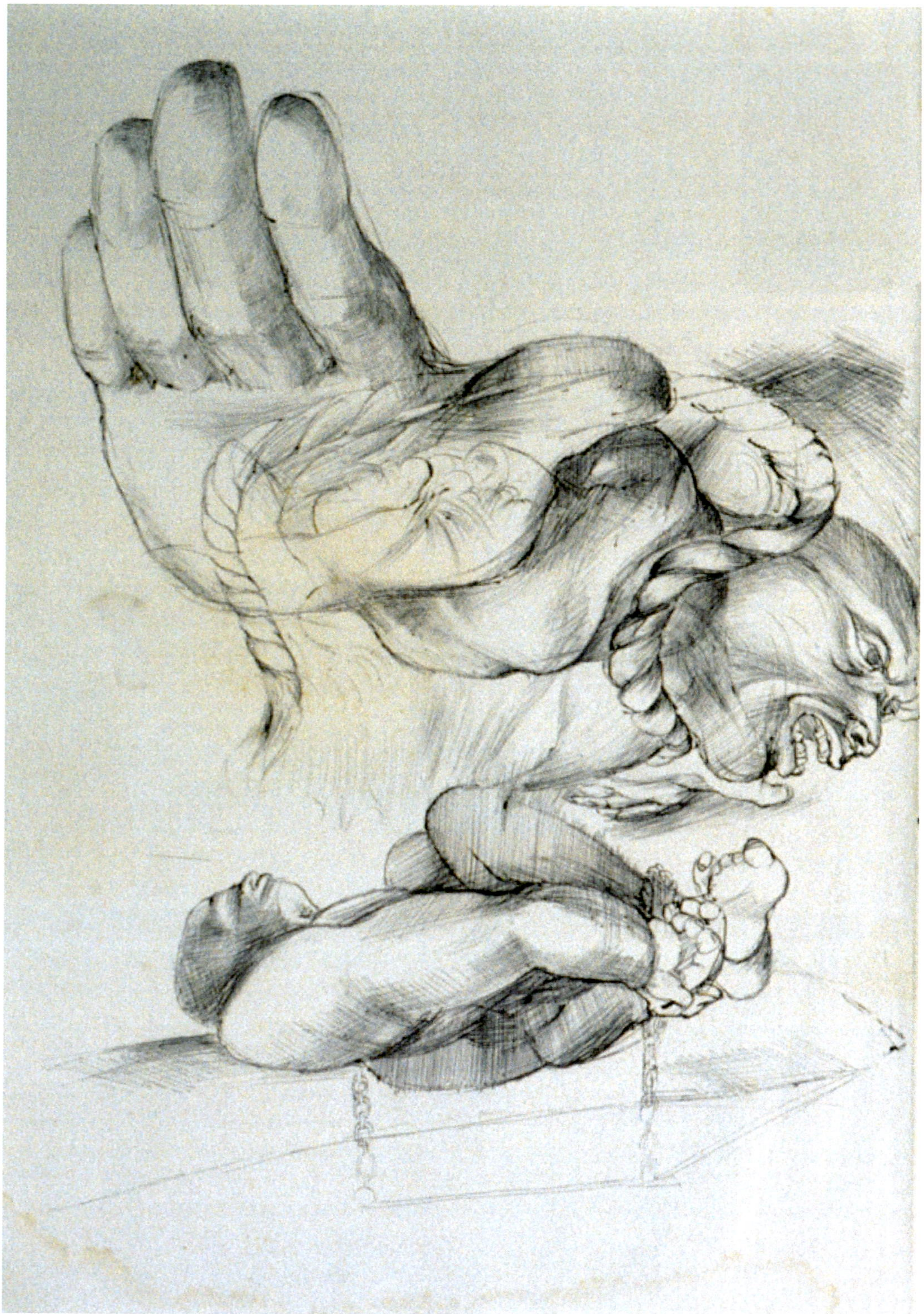

Memorabilia II. Preliminary drawing of bound figures. Biro. 42×29.7 cms.

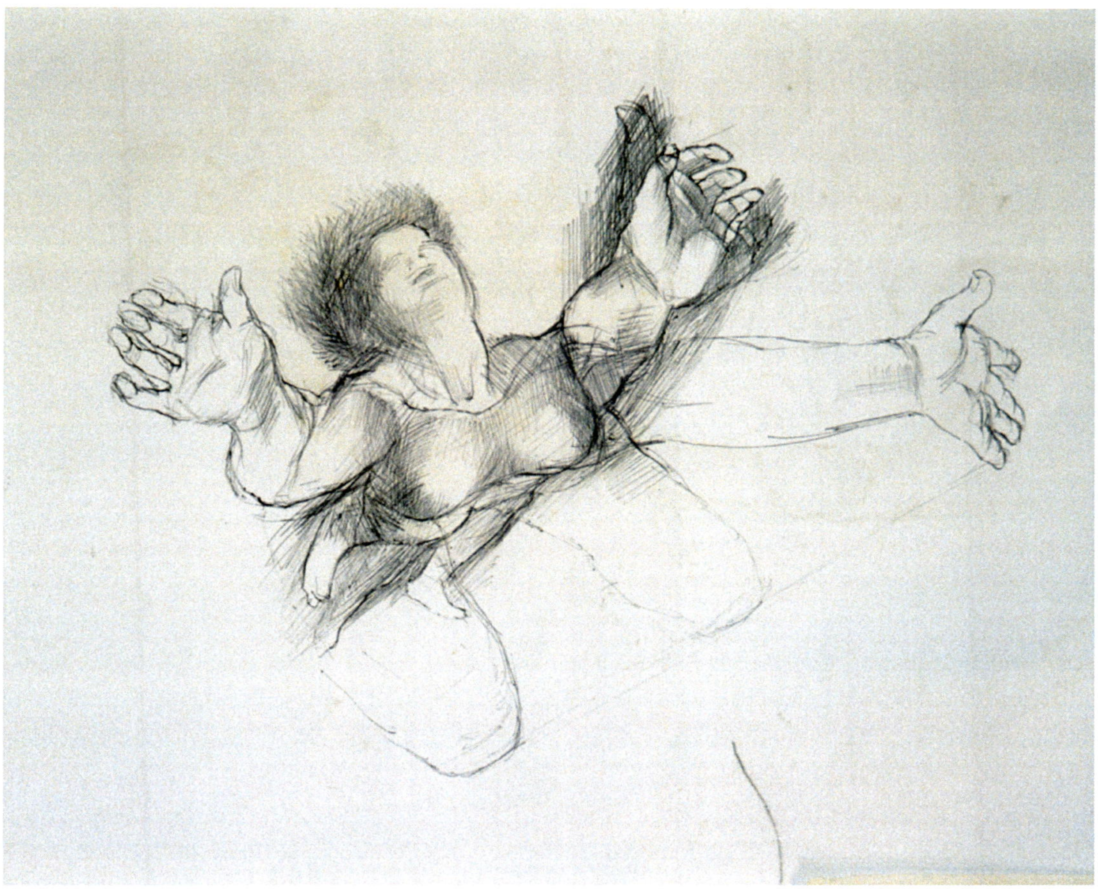

Memorabilia II. Preliminary drawing of kneeling figure. Biro. 42×29.7 cms.

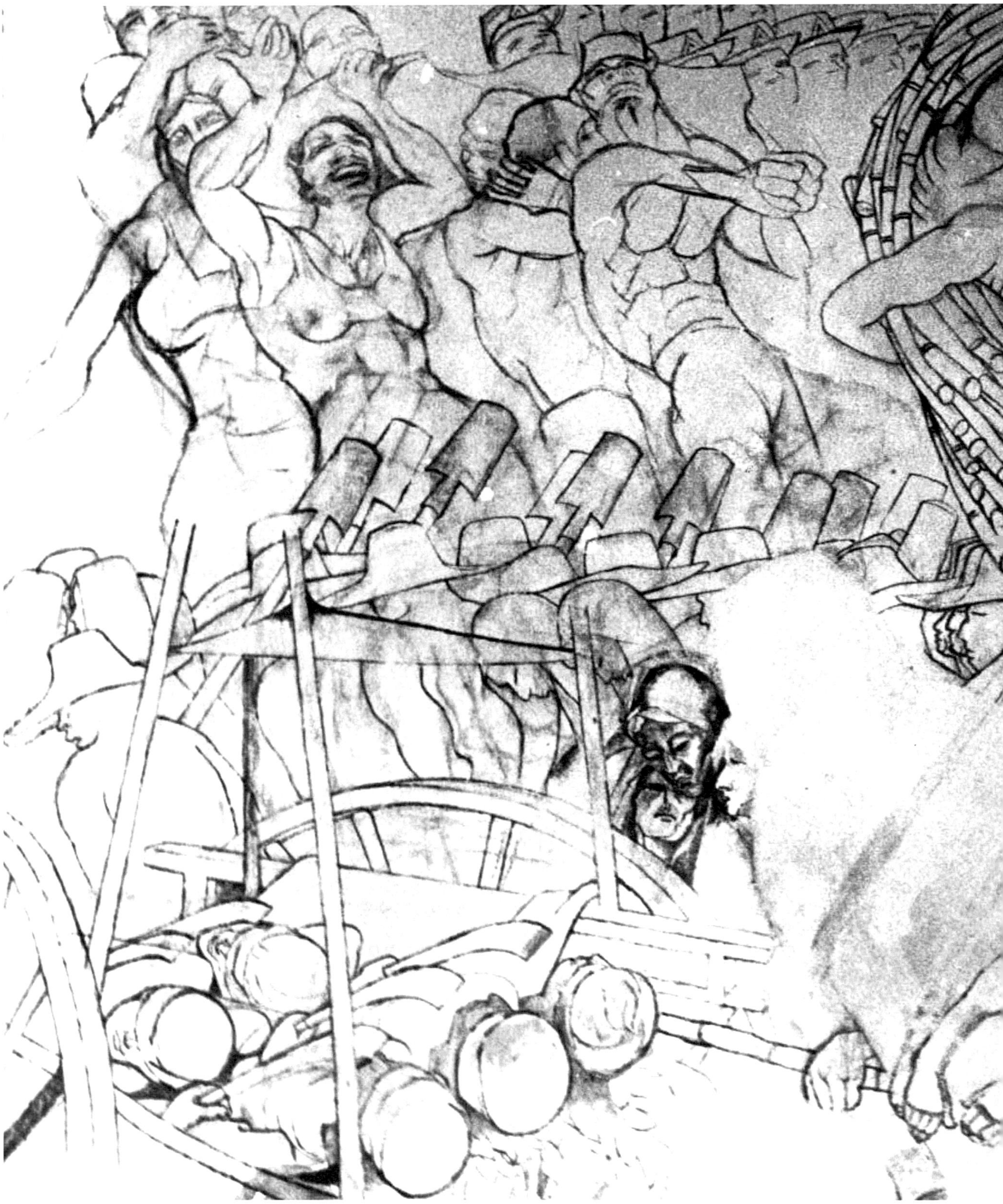

Memorabilia II (1975). Charcoal cartoon *in situ*.
National Cultural Centre, Georgetown.

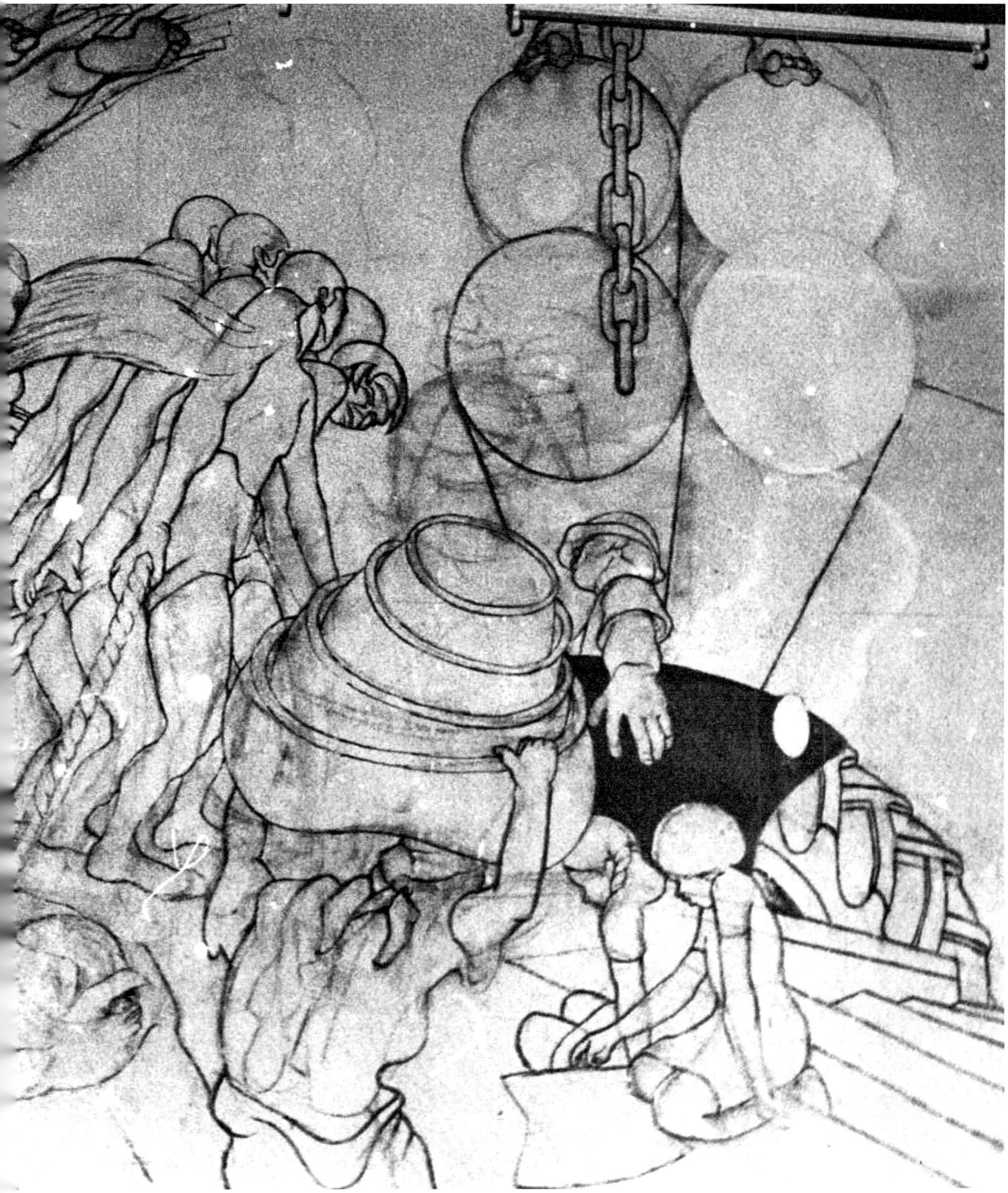

> myself and so on, but beyond that. [...] That era is over, the end of the bridge era. The end of that bridge era now that the black man has taken his own decisions you've got a different matrix. Yes, and our artists were the prophets of the bridging, your Aubrey Williams and so on. But today, you're not going to get any black artist wanting to paint no Shostakovich, no it's not going to happen.[32]

There is a sense of progression contained in the subtext of these references which perhaps brings one closest to an understanding of how he saw his contribution as an artist. This is supported in his own presentation of the development of the visual arts in Guyana in the formal entry published in the Macmillan *Dictionary of Art*.[33] He observed:

> By the sixties, a third generation of Guyanese artists had emerged [...] and founded their vision entirely on Guyanese national awareness [...] the extreme fertility of invention is without doubt to be credited to a universal indifference to metropolitan art forms, and this may in turn be due to a total absence of a prevailing metropolitan market, Guyana not being a tourist oriented country. [...] The two most dominant features of this most recent period are the sudden maturity of sculpture and the emergence of the Amerindian artist in the continuing creolising of Guyanese culture. The latter is the most reassuring factor in assessing the validity and direction of a culture in which five percent of the population are Amerindians who have populated this land for at least the past 7000 years.[34]

> When we began to talk about the Guyana School, it was not meant to be an ethnic definition, it was meant to be a nationalist definition [...] but it has got a powerful ethnic component. As it happens they were all Creole boys, and that is part of the definition. The roots are really deep. What is happening in the art of these young sculptors and painters is something that happened out of their experience on this soil.[35]

Williams advanced the theory that the artists of the "Guyana School", its painters and particularly sculptors, shared a common origin in the lineage that lead back to the rural Village Movement.[36] He believed that many of these country villages became the repository of the roots of memory of the attenuated African cultures, somewhat in the same manner that saw significant survivals among the "Bush Negroes" of Suriname, where Ndjuka and Saramaca carvings indicate a legacy of Ashanti sculpture from the eighteenth century. "The work of sculpture represented the place where the undifferentiated spirit could be localised and addressed; the Kalabari of the Niger delta called it the 'forehead' of the spirit: the place where the spirit is confronted."[37]

In *A Given Dream*, Williams reflects that:

> Philip Moore's bronze 1763 has got the same technical proportions of the Dogun [African sculpture]. Head to figure, one fourth; that is a standard in African carving. Philip Moore has never heard of such a thing. If I tell him [...] he wouldn't want to hear, he wouldn't be concerned. Technologically some things survive; frontality in the work. That 1763 Monument, you have to stand in front of it. When you go around the other side you're at the back. The front of it is the man's address to his audience, which is again a dominant trait. The concept of frontality has survived in his work from his African ancestry. So to that degree Philip Moore is a Caribbean adaptation of a great African tradition. He paints his wood – the man is operating as a sculptor and a painter in one piece of work! [38]

Elsewhere he observes:

> The Village Movement can be seen in retrospect to have been more seminal to Black survival in this area of the New World than even the economic viability that it espoused. Concurrently the "bound yard" was serving a similar function in forging and guaranteeing the survival of the East Indian Creole identity under conditions of extreme economic deprivation.[39]

He took great personal delight in these local manifestations in art as truly Guyanese milestones of progress. To him they celebrated a fertile visual power that sprang from a cultural reservoir that had long been sequestered in the rural areas. "[...] and particularly sculpture, particularly the confidence we have in sculpture is unparalleled anywhere in the Caribbean."[40]

With reference to Amerindian artists, he had also coined the label "St Cuthbert's School". The intention of its use was to group and elevate the community of artists based in the work of the Amerindian painter George Simon, and sculptors Ossie Hussein and Telford Taylor. Their work is rooted in a very specific Guyanese experience, not found elsewhere in the Caribbean. African Guyanese dominance in the visual arts was at that time unchallenged, and it was Williams' stewardship of the Burrowes School of Art that gave the encouragement to Amerindian and Indian participation that was directly responsible for the flowering of Lokono and Carib artists as well as young Indian painters. As Errol Brewster noted in an appreciation: "Indeed, there aren't many artists who have not come under his influence."[41] In terms of developments in cultural expression, Williams himself described this now passing era as "a brilliant chapter in this country's post-colonial history."[42]

He saw such expressions as an intrinsic vision of Guyana. Within the consciousness of this emergent artist he signalled that "New Guyana Man" had symbolically come to terms with the dichotomy of the past and present; he emerges unfazed by western artistic canons and their audiences. "Their concern with identity, with jettisoning the Greco-Roman assumptions of the colonial aesthetic in favour of a more personal and profound search for spiritual anchorage is the hallmark of the "Guyana School."[43] He believed this art to be improvised from an immanent local perspective in which the artist had now established a unique platform of private communication, conception and approach; an inhered vision of Guyana accessing and referencing a local aesthetic characterised by ingenuity, improvisation and optimism.

His labelling of the "Guyana School" was transmitted through his exhibition catalogues for national consumption; through the many pan-Caribbean touring exhibitions he curated; through platforms provided by development agencies and through his publications. Specifically we find his label used in *Cultural Policy in Guyana*. So, what was the intention behind his labelling? To some extent it balances out the focus on the European imprimatur with a sense of counter-response, though he does not confront the fact that the categorisations he introduced themselves implied exclusions and inclusions, by giving agency both to the nationalist "Guyana School" and the specifically local "St Cuthbert's School". The easy appropriation of the canonical label "school" can be seen to suggest additional rather than alternative categories. It suggests an attempt to mediate an acceptable position beyond the European imprimatur. Equally, they are labels that imply a mindset seeking to negotiate a dignity of its own. They may also imply a belief that such labels were required at that time in order to enter the global story.

His mural, *Memorabilia II* (1975–1976), occupies the western wall of the foyer of the National Cultural Centre in Georgetown. It provides an opportunity to examine his stance in relation to the prevailing political climate as the development of his ideas for this important work is well documented:

> So important is this quest [national identity] that it seems likely to add an extra criterion to the art criticism of the Revolution: Does a given work contribute or not to expanding our awareness of the environment and of ourselves [...] this criterion may even take precedence over questions of a purely aesthetic nature.[44]

The artistic approach and impact of the spatial organisation would seem to owe much to that Mexican trip. The content is symbolic and didactic; the subject matter is figurative and the aim is idealistic and social. He held a faith and commitment to his people that led him to search beyond the vicissitudes of his present to a future he always believed possible. He always took the long view. The concept of rapid revolutionary transformation of society could only be a dream: "What essential thing is revealed when aspirations and anticipated possibilities have been cancelled out?" he wrote. "What direction for the shattered revolutionary spirit?"[45]

For the National Cultural Centre mural he chose an artistic approach and resolution that neatly side-stepped and ultimately survived the prevailing political environment. The future that he foresaw depended on knowledge and appreciation of the past. It required one to think outside the boundaries of race in order to frame the experience of self and nation. In a note he describes the intention behind the project:

> The themes of *Memorabilia II* are taken from various events in the recent history of Guyana. At bottom left the martyrdom of the five sugar workers from Enmore Estate, on June 16, 1948. The martyrs are portrayed lying in state on a donkey cart, with their cutlasses held in their left hands across their chests. A procession of distraught relatives and village mourners with down-turned spades forms the cortege. Above this section of the mural there is a group of swirling masquerade band images bearing the flag of Guyana. This represents the attainment of independence on May 26, 1966. Occupying the central position of the mural is the statue of Sir James Carmichael Smyth, the Governor who presided over "the grand design" of Apprenticeship following upon Emancipation in 1834. The statue is portrayed bound in ropes and being removed from its position of honour, by the "New Guyana Man". The dancing female figure

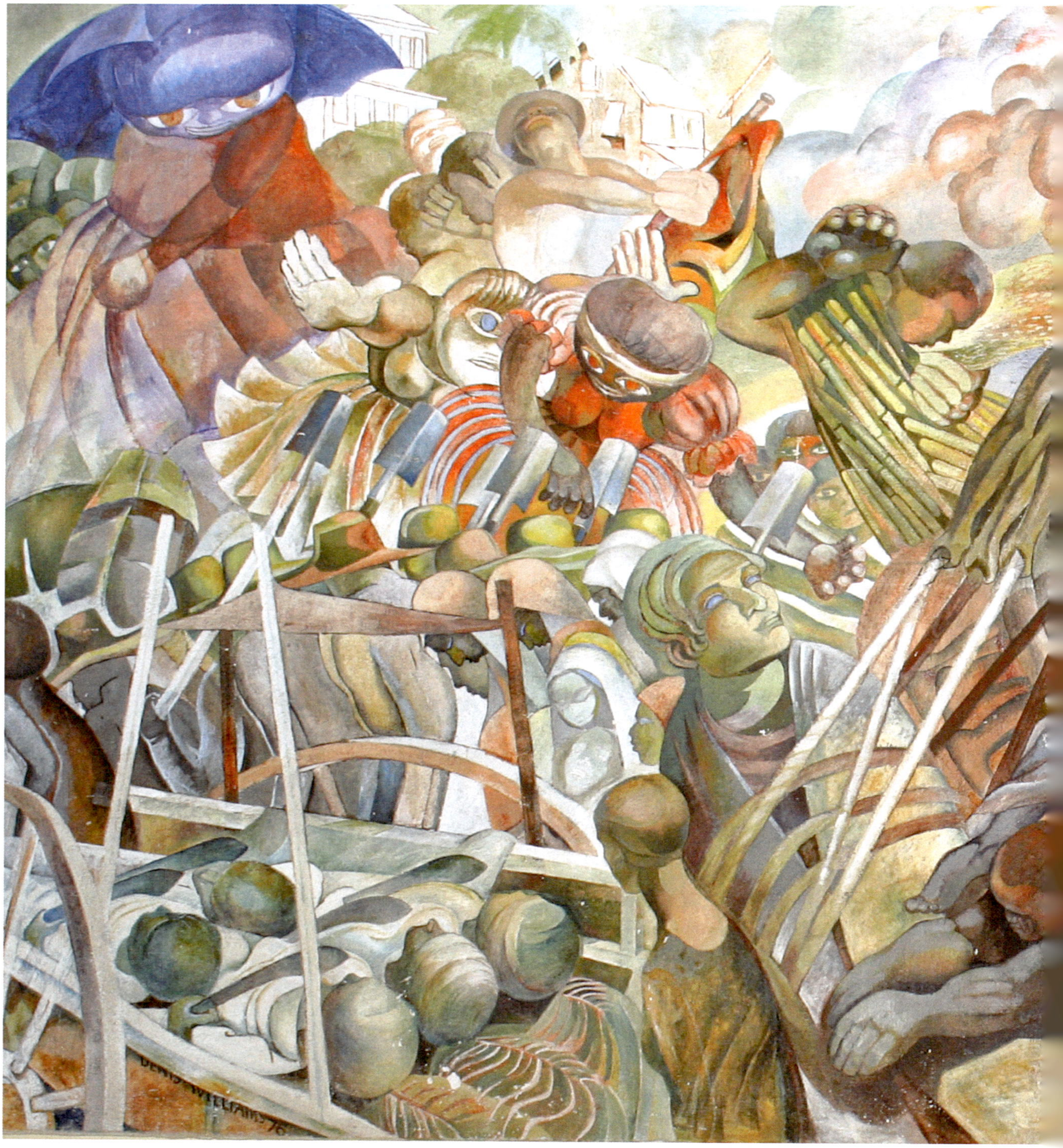

Memorabilia II (1976). Mural. National Cultural Centre, Georgetown. Photograph by Ohene Koama.

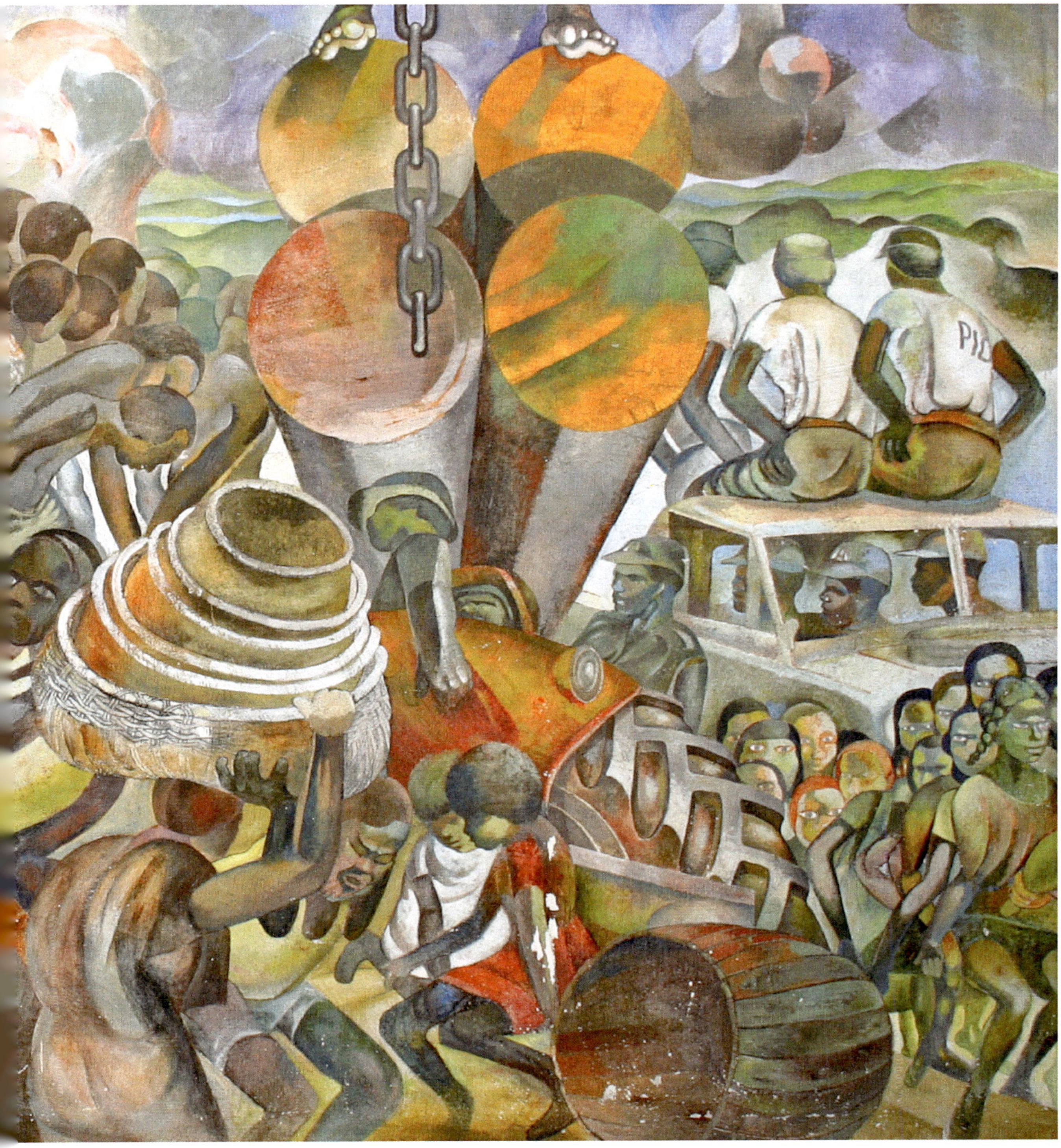

> immediately above this group represents the Spirit of Agriculture bearing gifts of sugar-cane and rice. To the right of this, scenes depicting the winning of timber in the Guyana hinterland are portrayed, while below this two figures under a load of baskets mark the importance of our craft industries. At far right of the mural young pioneers of the Guyana National Service are associated with a group of school children led by a girl carrying cochineal leaf – a symbol of healing. Thus, a sequence which commences at one end of the picture on a theme of martyrdom and sorrow, ends on the other on a note of life and hope.[46]

In a consciously graphic style, *Memorabilia II* depicts his view of the possibility of an optimistic journey from oppression to transcendence. It provides a compelling record of his theoretical speculation and of the energetic rôle the artist played in developing a vision for his country. It is a symbolic cultural marker that seeks an elevated position for all its peoples, free of the redundant definitions of the past. This positive possibility for the future, viewed in the context of increasing globalisation, was re-examined by the author in the Mittelholzer Lecture Series in 2009.[47]

Early in 1977 the Second World Black and African Festival of Arts and Culture (FESTAC) saw Williams back in Lagos, Nigeria.[48] The aim of the festival was to provide a forum in which to celebrate the cultural and spiritual flow of black peoples from the original source of Africa. Williams attended FESTAC in the company of Frank Pilgrim and Shirley Field-Ridley along with many others from Guyana. Among artists whose work was used to represent their homeland in the Guyana National Art Exhibition was Donald Locke who also exhibited in "The Work of Artists from the UK and Ireland" under the banner of "British-based black artists."[49] In an era of post-black-consciousness there was a repositioning: a revising and redefining of the varied identities and issues for the artists of the African diaspora. In art there was still the uncomfortable awareness in both thought and practice of the continuing pervasive pull of the psychic harness of the colonial masters, particularly with reference to terms of reception and patronage.

People like Denis Williams were now in a position to survey the arena from an autonomous platform. Art as a pathway towards self-realisation saw many artists embark on the process of conscious deconstruction of an entire sensibility. Many artists were subsequently drawn towards examining concrete themes of black subjectivity. Others pursued a vision of abstract concepts. All were in fierce pursuit of a valid cultural pedigree.

Williams' own agenda at this time focused on the need to secure the cognate areas allied to sustaining art activity in his own country. One such area had to be a national collection. The purchase of *Human World* by popular subscription in 1956 had highlighted the issue of organised patronage in the visual arts as a function of the modern state. The National History and Culture Council had a National Art Purchasing Committee – NAPC – for the long-established vision of a national art collection. The Council of the Arts of the late 1950s and the History and Culture Council of the early 1960s had been brought under the aegis of the National History and Arts Council in 1965.[50] It had inherited a legacy of various holdings amounting to over two hundred paintings and over forty pieces of sculpture. Under the reorganised institution, he had made systematic purchases on behalf of the state to advance Guyana's long-established national collection. He proposed the creation of a Board of Trustees to oversee the management of the nation's artworks; he then addressed the urgent question of suitable facilities to house and curate them. By the mid-seventies, Guyanese architect Albert Rodrigues had been commissioned to design a suitable building to house a national collection, and provide the joint facilities of display, conservation and training in art. But by the late seventies the project had to be abandoned as the national economy faltered. As Director of Art, he had supported the inaugural exhibition by The Creative Arts Association held in the former residence of President Burnham. After the elections of 1992 it was renamed Castellani House and became home to the National Collection in 1993.

Where the state was unable to assume responsibility in the long term for the patronage of the visual arts the question of the security of its very existence was challenged. Within the complex of interrelated perspectives the former colonial sponsors now had to be accommodated as benevolent patrons in a relationship of refashioned paternalism. In addition there was the continuing development of a small middle-class Caribbean-American audience and collectors.

The influence of Caribbean migration was making itself evident in metropolitan art particularly where its numbers were beginning to shape the character of sections of US society.

Guyana had produced artists who could take their place on an international stage – Denis Williams, Aubrey Williams, Frank Bowling, Donald Locke, Philip Moore – and there was a talented younger generation ready to claim its own place. However Williams regretted that many gifted artists were unable to take up the responsibility for forging the destiny of their own nation through their creative work.

He had initiated the process of inviting artists to tender for Guyana's large public artworks, and this led in 1986 to the successful commissioning of the two bronze high-reliefs by the artist and sculptor Ivor Thom for the mausoleum of President Burnham. The bronze memorial to the slave martyr Damon (1988) at Anna Regina in Essequibo is also by Ivor Thom, and George Simon recalls the energetic encouragement Williams gave Thom as the clay model was being prepared at the Burrowes School of Art.[51] Stanley Greaves has also noted that Williams had wanted to see the establishment of "a prestigious prize for the visual arts."[52]

In 1983 he held three posts simultaneously – Chairman of the National Trust of Guyana; Director of the National History and Arts Council[53] and Director of the Walter Roth Museum.[54] In 1985 he founded The Museum of African Art and Ethnology, now the African Heritage Museum, to which Dr Bertie Nicholson generously dedicated his home. Williams had previously founded extensive museum collections of African Art in Nigeria and was able to evaluate the Nicholson collection and advise on its purchase for the nation. This allowed first-hand access to a display of products of African material culture including sculpture, carving, casting and fabrication.

What made him care? The urgency and empowerment born of hope for his new country gave him the inspiration and energy to pursue his vision. It was a big vision and one we know he worked towards for the rest of his life. We can be certain of this when, during an interview with Spencer Richards in June 1997 he reiterated his theory of art and culture as being central to the social underpinning that would allow the nation a sound framework for supporting cultural diplomacy in the deliberations of state. His aim was to secure the foundations of the Guyanese nation through achieving a three-dimensional grasp of the history and standing of all its peoples. And he clearly saw his archaeological work and museum work as extensions of that aim. There was a need to give expression to what the country had been through over the centuries:

> [...] and when I say "Museum of Pre-Colonial Civilizations: Americas" so that you know something about Brazil and Peru, Maya and all that – Americas. The other museum that I have, "Pre-Colonial civilization: Africa". And the third museum – I've got a building in mind – "Pre-Colonial Civilization: Orient": such a museum for us would mean redemption![55]

Guyana faced problems that were in many respects unique in the Caribbean and which combined to produce an atmosphere of continuing instability. There were changing dynamics within the country which exacerbated the haemorrhage of talented individuals with their expertise and patronage. The radical anti-colonial socialism of Jagan and Burnham, compounded by Guyana's physical isolation, meant that the country was unlikely to be on the popular and lucrative Caribbean tourist map. Indeed, the very concept of tourism had implications that were at odds with prevailing political ideologies. Therefore the culture arising from regular exposure to international consumers, which brought with it a wider audience of art patrons and buyers, did not extend itself to Guyana. Political insecurities also saw large sections of the business and commercial classes, and the moneyed classes, withdrawing their interests. The collapse of the urban middle class during the latter stages of the Burnham era brought an end to a whole range of the externally projected values and aspirations that had been actively promoted through an inherited culture of social manners and a European culture of aesthetic élitism in music, theatre, dance and art. For many this demise was not unwelcome. Some have remarked on the irony that the ensuing vacuum was not seized upon more urgently as a great opportunity for a new order to promulgate its own "grass roots" ideology. Instead, the forces that began changing Guyanese society are creating a socially surreal cultural admixture, predicated upon external values and fed by Bollywood, predatory American evangelism, populist but dated commercial TV shows and counterfeit consumer products.

The *Self-portrait* (1986) is the last known portrait by Williams, showing the artist aged sixty-three. In it, the narrative of the adventurous spirit is heavily loaded. It seems to combine the gravitas of wide experience with the flame of curiosity about that which it has not yet succeed in knowing. In this small, striking work he portrays himself with a frank, enquiring gaze, the eyes alert and watchful. The face is set in a serious expression and he makes a feature of the distinctive upward hairstyle of his later years. This self-portrait stands alone but is linked in format to a series of nine roundels made between 1986 and 1988 as part of the *Human Evolution* exhibit for the Walter Roth Museum. The roundels appear to have been made on small pieces of scrap canvas from the large central work of the permanent exhibit and are a reminder of the severe financial constraints prevailing in Guyana.

The portrait composition within a roundel shows a remarkable use of limited space. The image is treated as a series of interlocking and overlapping shapes each independently worked. It has focus and points of fixation. The arabesques suggest an environment without representing it: perhaps it is a forest reference with the collar of his shirt characteristically turned up to protect his neck from mosquitoes whilst excavating in the field in the interior. Each shape articulates tonal colour, structure, form and character. For example, taking the bold vermilion shape of the forehead, it simultaneously conveys many qualities of character in articulating the brow, furrow, hairline, attitude, and expression. Similarly, the upward curl of the collar, its colour, texture, a certain transparency and its shadow, are all contained in one abstracted shape in the foreground. The painting has a richness of colour in the balancing of intense blues with warm ochre and vermilion, into a chromatic harmony of opposites. The warm neutrals at either side of the head support and balance the flourish of the bright flames that make up the hair while clear black shadow-shapes are used in a dynamic play to emphasise the complex composition. White light is projected from behind while a golden light falls from the front and this lends luminosity to the colour. His use of colour and the roundel format have an intimacy which references familiar aspects of the miniature genre. It is a point of reference that suitably reminds us of the interplay of associations and homages within the visual arts.

His work in design and illustration culminated in *Human Evolution* (1988). It is a dramatic piece that is recorded as a Denis Williams artwork as it is signed and dated. It was designed for the Walter Roth Museum, forming the centrepiece of a museum display. Its concept as an artwork is supported in the evidence of the surviving preparatory pencil drawing (1988) which, despite its damaged condition, remains a clear example of his prowess as a draughtsman. It combines the function of communication with imagination and vision as it evokes the memory of our ancestors. In addition two of the roundels, *Homo sapiens – Archaic* and *Homo sapiens – Neanderthal* are also both signed and dated works of 1988. The other seven roundels are much more functional to the exhibit, and are unsigned. It is worth remembering that in a letter about *Majestas*, Canon Dorman noted that Williams "had been doing some studies of Hominids for an archaeological purpose, [and that] something of that nature could be created on the side-wings. We raised our thinking in accordance with that suggestion and tried to envisage the two long narrow panels as a vision of the ascent of mankind."[56]

As far as is known, he did not paint again. Many have speculated on the reason for this, suggesting perhaps that he had reached an impasse: after all, he had been part of the bridge experience that had effectively done its job. In a letter to the author in the UK, dated April 1992, he wrote:

> A friend in the U.S. sent me this book[57] December last, and I enjoyed it very much. I hope you do too, though it will probably mean much less to you by virtue of having similar fare in your newspapers every Sunday, at least. Also there are the paintings, which of course I never see, though, strange to say, I never miss.

The unfolding political environment in Guyana and the continuing absence of a shared vision were disheartening and in 1989 he had written: "I think one needs a strong positive reason for enduring such an environment though of course there's patriotism for some of us."[58] The simple reason why there were no more paintings is most probably that he had little time. This was confirmed in his last interview in 1998, when he said adamantly: "I am a painter, I think and see as a painter all the time. I always feel I am coming back to it when I get the time. It's just 'on the shelf' waiting, and it is my real self."[59] As the Chronology indicates, he became increasingly devoted to archaeology and the preparation of his final text: *Prehistoric Guiana* (2003). The fundamental importance, belief and direction of his work in the field of archaeology fed his intellect and his ambitions for his country: this was work that simply had to be done. Despite the importance of the Guianas to

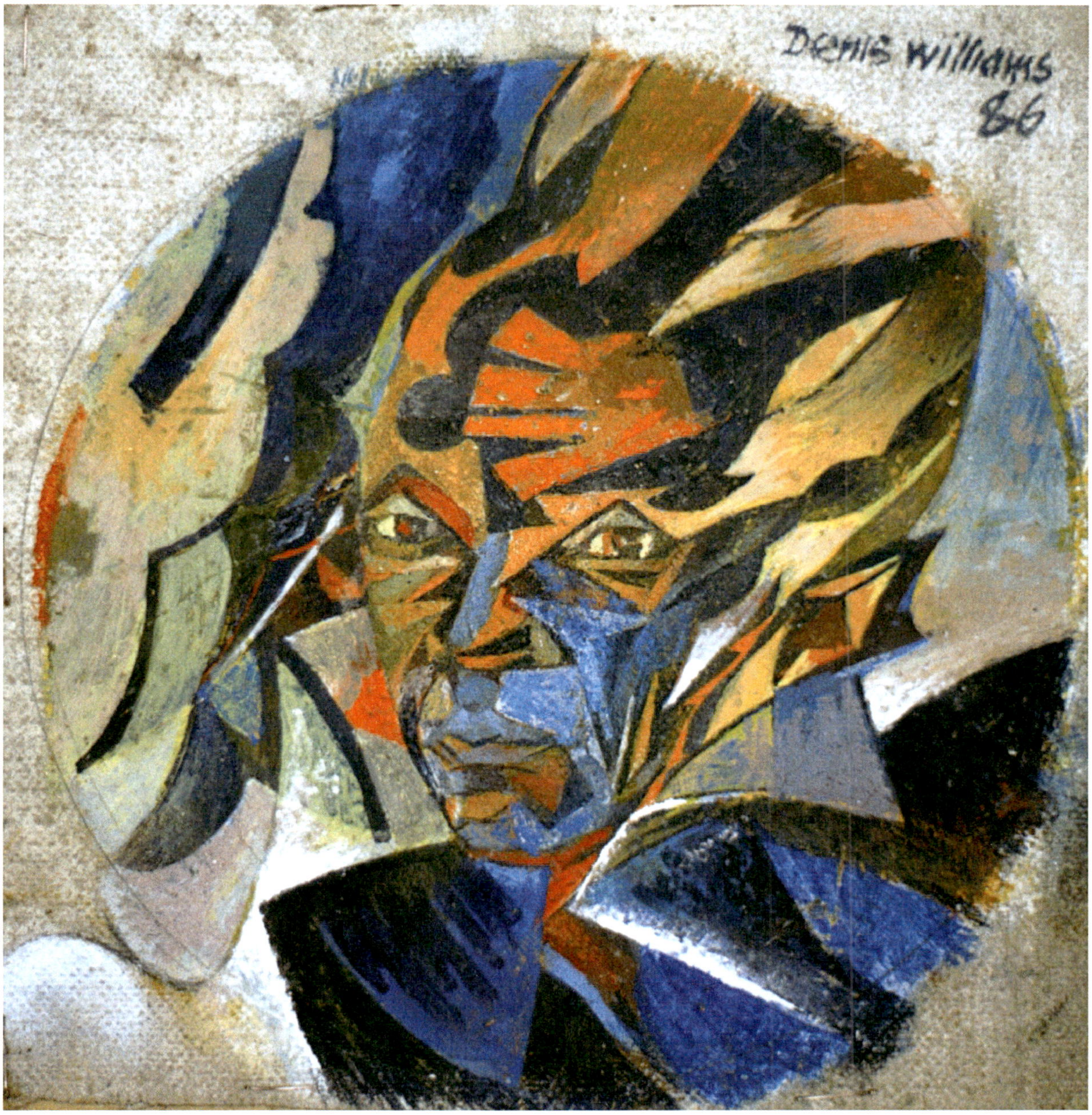

Self-portrait (1986). Tempera on canvas. 21×21 cms. Collection E. Williams.

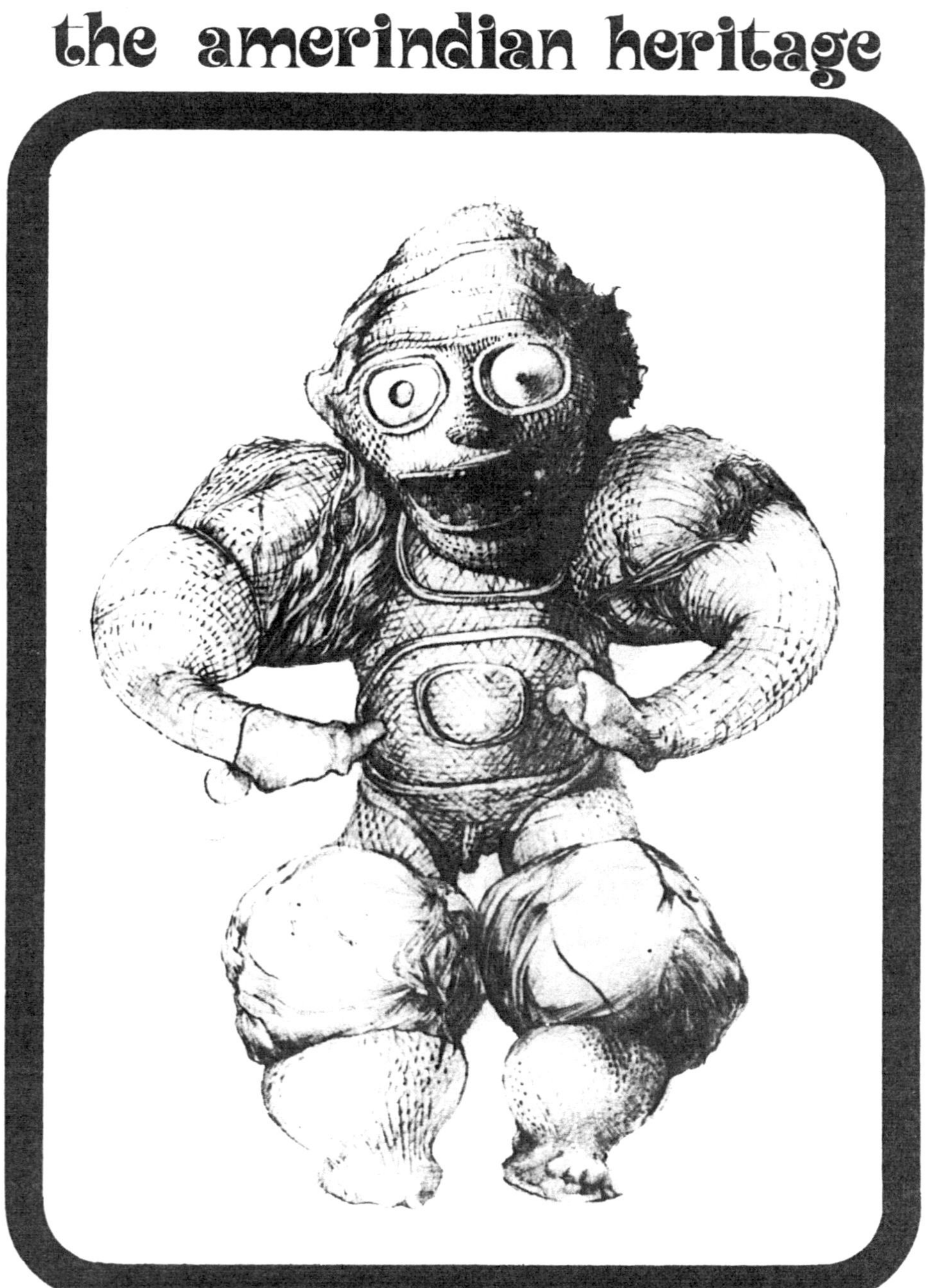

Jacket illustration for a mobile audio-visual display prepared for UNESCO by the Walter Roth Museum (1984).

the pre-history of South America, archaeological investigations had been rare, sporadic and conducted by foreigners. In his ground-breaking works on the prehistory of Guyana he was able to visualise and shape abstract theories that remain provocative and challenging. In 1989 he was awarded the Cacique Crown of Honour (CCH).

He saw that art and politics were both inevitably linked to any construct of a cohesive modern state and there is a continuity of vision that places his archaeological ground-works in an equal relationship. As George Mentore has pointed out:

> In a world where archaeology has been directly appropriated by politics so much seems to be at stake for modern nation states across the globe in having to maintain that most difficult evidence of their existence – their history. The past is not self-evident and is thus constantly contested. When history takes hold of it, the agenda of nation-states can make itself very obvious.[60]

The subtext of *Prehistoric Guiana* suggests the theoretical possibility of a positive future for all the peoples of Guyana, predicated on the imprint buried in the soils of the forests of the Guiana Shield. It is a theory that addresses the demise at the heart of the cultural schism which he had elucidated earlier in the 1969 Mittelholzer Lectures:

> Collectively we are a people without a myth, without the unified consciousness of the indwelling of a common ancestor, without any charter whatsoever for a destiny.[61]

His vision went beyond the idealised romance of rainforest allusions present in the creative imaginations of many West Indian writers and artists of the twentieth century as a means of replenishing the ancestral void. His theories were based on first-hand experience of living with the Akawaio, Karinya, Arawak and other peoples over some thirty years. *Prehistoric Guiana* points to the potential for a great flexibility and diversity in approaches to living, celebrated in the positive human qualities he identified as contributing to the success of Guyana's autochthonous peoples – cooperative endeavour, egalitarian attitudes, communal pride and self-sufficiency. His hope for the future of his people lay in acceptance by all Guyanese of a filialistic relationship to this common South American heritage.

Denis Williams' initiatives and theories as an artist are all the more remarkable when considered against the background of a society under constant stress. He did not lament the trials of his personal journey. On Sunday 21 June 1998, aware that he did not have long to live, Williams called in Albert Rodrigues, a prominent Guyanese architect, and dictated a long statement in which he outlined his vision for Guyana in the twenty-first century. The conversation turned to the subject of *Majestas*, of which Williams said: "Please remember, that is the best painting I have ever done."

He addressed issues many others were to ignore. He had a vision of his duty as an artist to bring light to the dark recesses of the fractured Caribbean psyche. He faced up to the dilemma of migration that aggravated the poverty of cultural life in Guyana. For him there was no choice, no alternative.

He posed broadly provocative questions on the nature of a Caribbean identity and whether art could act as a vehicle for an implicit national and regional identity. He pioneered critical theories and identified distinctive continuities that still inform critical debate on the evolution, characteristics and definition of New World identities. He examined the rôle of the artist in the development of a public understanding of nationhood. He drew upon his unique position and experience in narrating and reviewing local developments and placing his critical evaluation within a wider context of historical reflection. His native Guyana was and remains a microcosm: an intimate stage on which are played out many of the familiar paradoxes significant to national cultural debates within the global context.

Denis Williams' art was ultimately one of affirmation that reflected high points in his philosophical speculation. It was to art that he turned at times of intellectual turmoil in the face of overwhelming realities. For him the creative process offered the real engagement from which grew the possibility of real transformation. He saw the future in the twenty-first century as one that would eventually dismantle the institutions that had suppressed others. At the end of his life he welcomed the approach of the new century as he anticipated it as being "a century of disrespect" in which the imperial powers would shrink back in ways that could not have been imagined.

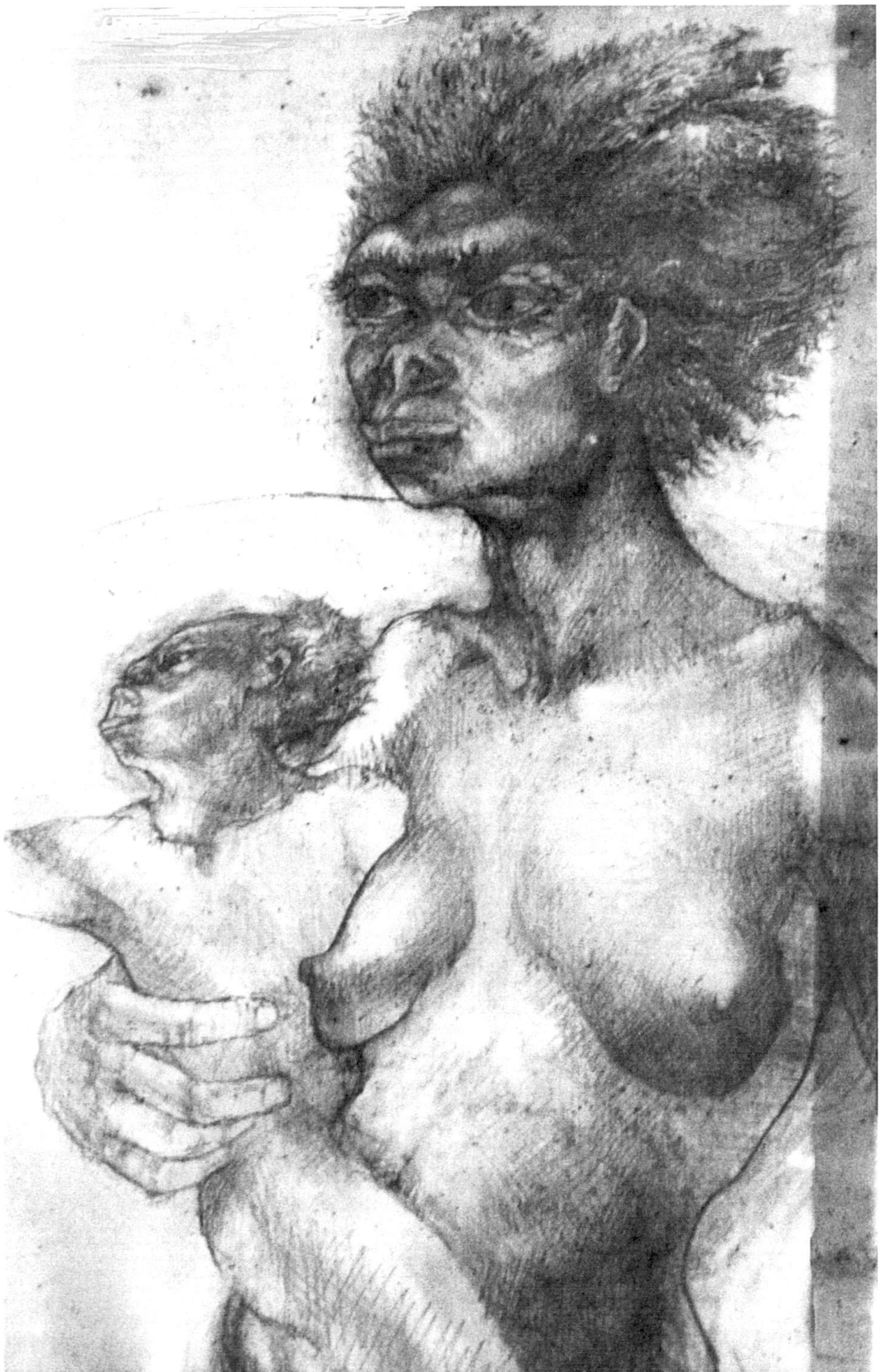

Human Evolution (1988). Preliminary study. Detail. Pencil. 46×57 cms.
By kind permission of Ras Camo Williams.

Opposite: *Human Evolution* (1988). Detail. Tempera on canvas. 180×120 cms.
Photographs by Andrew Lindsay.

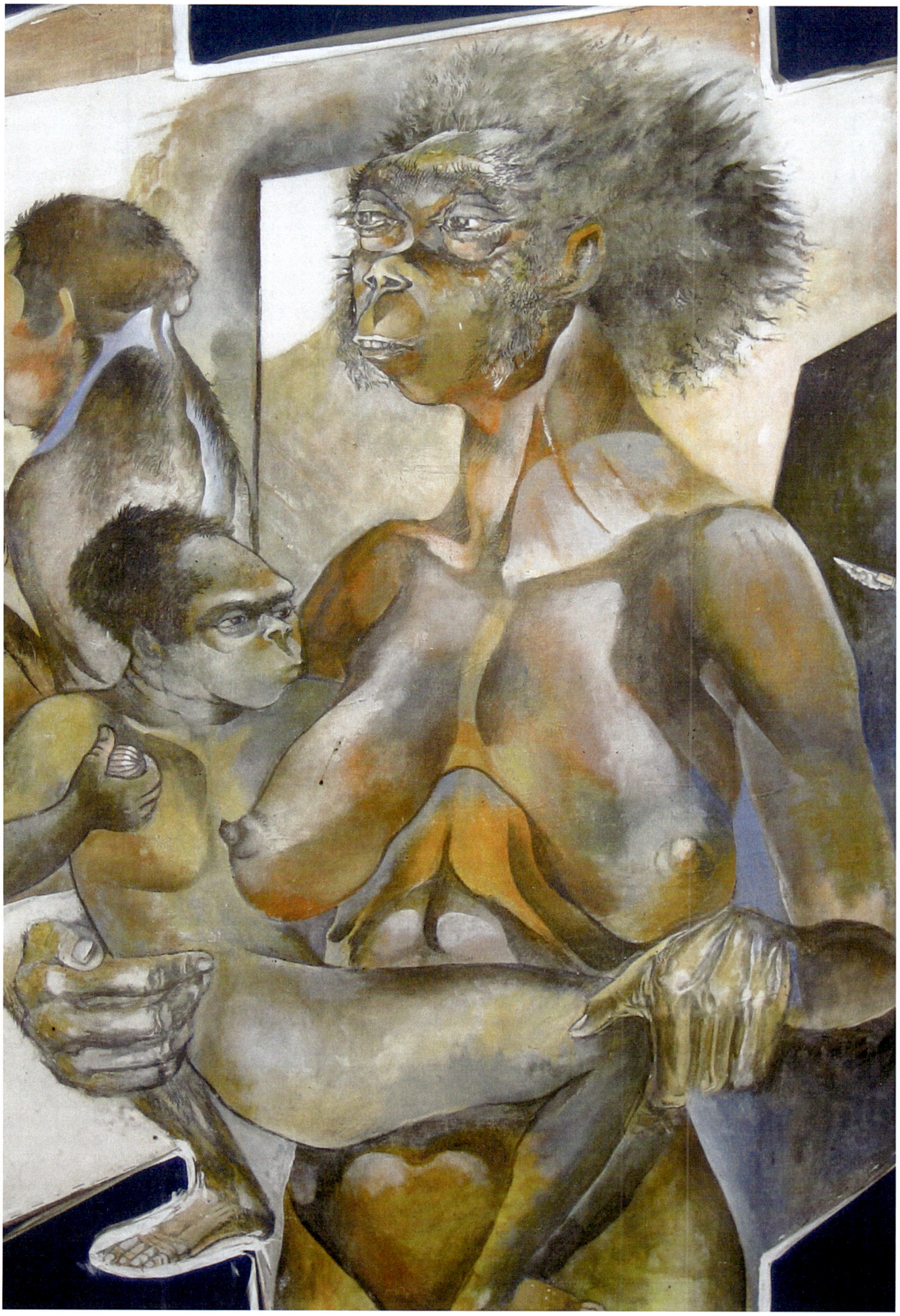

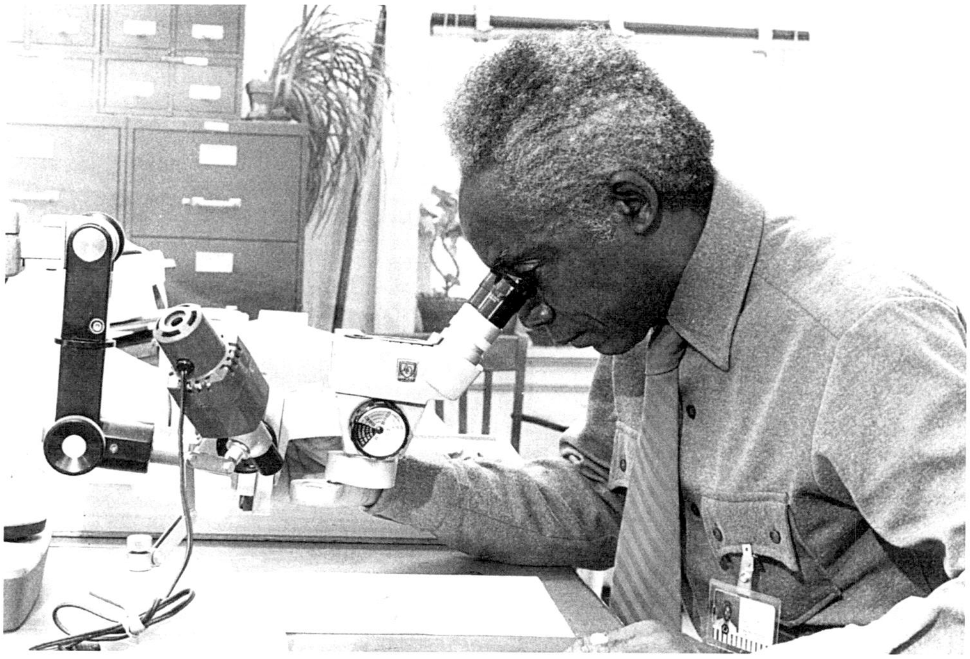

At his desk at the Smithsonian Institution

NOTES TO CHAPTER 6

1 "Colonial Art to Revolutionary Art, 1966–1976". Exhibition catalogue (1976).
2 Minutes of the National Trust of Guyana, 23 March 1976 and 17 August 1977.
3 *Ibid.*, 26 October 1978.
4 *Ibid.*, 29 April 1976.
5 The Minutes of the National Trust in December 1979 show that Williams had actively supported the research work of Karna Bahadur Singh in these areas.
6 For example, Faye Case's researches into Akawaio basketry traditions (1975–1977).
7 Address given at a Special Party Congress to mark the 10th Anniversary of the PNC in Government.
8 Cited in A. J. Seymour, *Cultural Policy in Guyana* (UNESCO, Paris: Imprimerie des Presses Universitaires de France, 1977), p. 17.
9 Barrington Braithwaite, "The Arts in the 90s", in *Sunday Stabroek, Guyana Review* (Vol. 15, Issue No. 185, May 2008), pp. 5, 7.
10 Stanley Greaves, "Meeting Denis: A Mind Engaged", in C. & E. Williams (eds.), *Denis Williams: A Life in Works. New and Collected Essays*. (Cross/Cultures; Amsterdam & New York: Rodopi, 2010), pp. 169–185.
11 Part of a UNESCO series, prepared by A. J. Seymour and published as *Cultural Policy in Guyana*.
12 *Op. cit.*, 39–40.
13 Denis Williams, *Giglioli in Guyana (1922–1972)* (Georgetown: National History and Arts Council, 1973), p. 48.
14 "Colonial Art to Revolutionary Art, 1966–1976". Exhibition catalogue (Georgetown, 1976).
15 Denis Williams, "Contemporary Art in Guyana". Text of catalogue for the exhibition *Republic of Guyana: Contemporary Art* as part of Carifesta '76 in Jamaica (Georgetown: Bovell's Printery, 1976), pp. 1–5: p. 2.
16 Minutes of the National Trust of Guyana, 24 July 1975.
17 Denis Williams, "What image of ourselves?" in *Review of the 1763 Monument*. Published by Castellani House, Georgetown, in May 1976.
18 Denis Williams, "1763, Carl Blackman and all that..." in *Kaie* (No. 14, July 1976), pp. 52–55.
19 John Hearne, Introduction to *Carifesta Forum: An Anthology of 20 Caribbean Voices* (Jamaica: Institute of Jamaica, 1976), p. viii.
20 Minutes of National Trust of Guyana, October 1975.
21 Pooran, Lallabaghee, Harri, Rambarran and Surujballi. They were members of a group of workers on strike as part of a protest over wages and a new working practice called "cut and load" that had been introduced by the British. They were shot by colonial police.
22 The idea of a school of art was not a new one. H. Kirke, Vice President of the Royal Agricultural Commercial Society (RACS), is reported as having given "notice of a motion with reference to a School of Art in connection with the Society" as early as January 1886. (*Timehri*, Vol. 5, p. 134).
23 Errol R. Brewster, "'A Given Dream' – Dr Denis Williams CCH in his own words". Transcript of a series of interviews. Dated 14 July 1998. Intended as the basis of a television documentary, *If Dream there is ...* [See Bibliography].
24 Cited in A. J. Seymour, *Cultural Policy in Guyana*, p. 39.
25 Stanley Greaves, "Meeting Denis: A Mind Engaged".
26 Cited in A. J. Seymour, *Cultural Policy in Guyana*, p. 39.
27 Quoted in Denis Williams, "Achievements and

Potentialities in the Guyanese Plastic Arts". Text for Exhibition Catalogue accompanying items from the National Collection of Guyana exhibited in Caracas, Venezuela, in March 1987, p. 14.

28 *Ibid.*, p. 25.

29 Errol R. Brewster (1998).

30 Denis Williams, "Contemporary Art in Guyana", p. 4.

31 Denis Williams, "Image and Idea in the Arts of Guyana", collected in *Image and Idea in the Arts of Guyana: The Edgar Mittelholzer Memorial Lectures*, Second Series (Georgetown: Ministry of Information, National History & Arts Council, January 1969), p. 36.

32 Interview with Spencer Richards (1997), p. 12. [Transcript. Williams estate].

33 "Guyana", in Jane Turner (ed.), *The Dictionary of Art*, in 34 volumes (London: Macmillan, 1996): Vol. 13, pp. 873–78.

34 Denis Williams, "The Visual Arts in the Cultural Evolution of the People of Guyana", in The Caribbean Supplement to the English Language Edition of the UNESCO Courier (1, 7, 1987), p. 4.

35 Errol R. Brewster (1998).

36 This followed the full emancipation of the slaves in 1838, when groups of individuals began to purchase the declining plantation lands.

37 Denis Williams, "Identity in Guyanese Plastic Art", in *Carifesta Forum: An Anthology of 20 Caribbean Voices* (1976), p. 179.

38 Errol R. Brewster (1998).

39 Denis Williams, "The Sculpture of John Clowes". Exhibition catalogue (Georgetown: Department of Culture, April 1995).

40 Spencer Richards (1997), p. 5.

41 Errol Brewster, "Denis Williams 1923-'98: An Appreciation", in *Caribarts*, July 2004.

42 Denis Williams, "The Sculpture of John Clowes". (1995).

43 Denis Williams, "Contemporary Art in Guyana", p. 2.

44 Denis Williams, "Colonial Art to Revolutionary Art, 1966–1976".

45 Personal papers. Williams estate.

46 Notes on *Memorabilia II* in the First Performance Souvenir Programme for the National Cultural Centre (Georgetown: Guyana Printers Ltd., May 1976), pp. 14–15. Judges of the competition were: Rosemary Ramdehol – musician; Cicely Godette – Managing Director, Design and Graphics; Dr Frank Williams; Salim Bastany – architect, and Norris Mitchell – architect.

47 Evelyn A. Williams, "Art, Blood and Heritage". *The Edgar Mittelholzer Memorial Lectures*, Thirteenth Series (Georgetown: Walter Roth Museum of Anthropology, Ministry of Culture, Youth and Sport, 2009).

48 Guyana Participation at *Second World Black & African Festival of Arts and Culture*: Lagos, Nigeria, January 15–February 12, 1977 (Georgetown: National History & Arts Council, Ministry of Information & Culture, 1977).

49 Andrew Dempsey, Gilane Tawadros and Maridowa Williams (eds), *Aubrey Williams* (London: inIVA, 1998), p. 89.

50 The NHAC assumed responsibility for a growing number of government-owned works of art. Quarterly reports were published and housed at the Ministry of Culture, Youth and Sport in Georgetown.

51 The maquette is currently housed at the Museum of African Heritage.

52 Stanley Greaves, "Meeting Denis . . ."

53 Founded in 1963 to extend and democratise Guyanese cultural forms and to develop a sense of historical awareness.

54 Having founded the Museum in 1974 Williams had secured the present building in Main Street, Georgetown in 1979. It occupies a position next to State House in the heart of the capital city of Guyana.

55 Spencer Richards (1997).

56 Letter to Elfrieda Bissember, January 1998. Canon Dorman died later that year.

57 Robert Hughes, *Nothing If Not Critical: Selected essays on Art and Artists* (New York: Alfred A. Knopf, 1991).

58 Letter to Isabel Adonis, 13 March 1989.

59 Charlotte Williams (1998).

60 Personal communication from Dr Mentore.

61 "The Complex Womb", in Image and Idea in the Arts of Guyana: *The Edgar Mittelholzer Memorial Lectures*, 1969), p. 17.

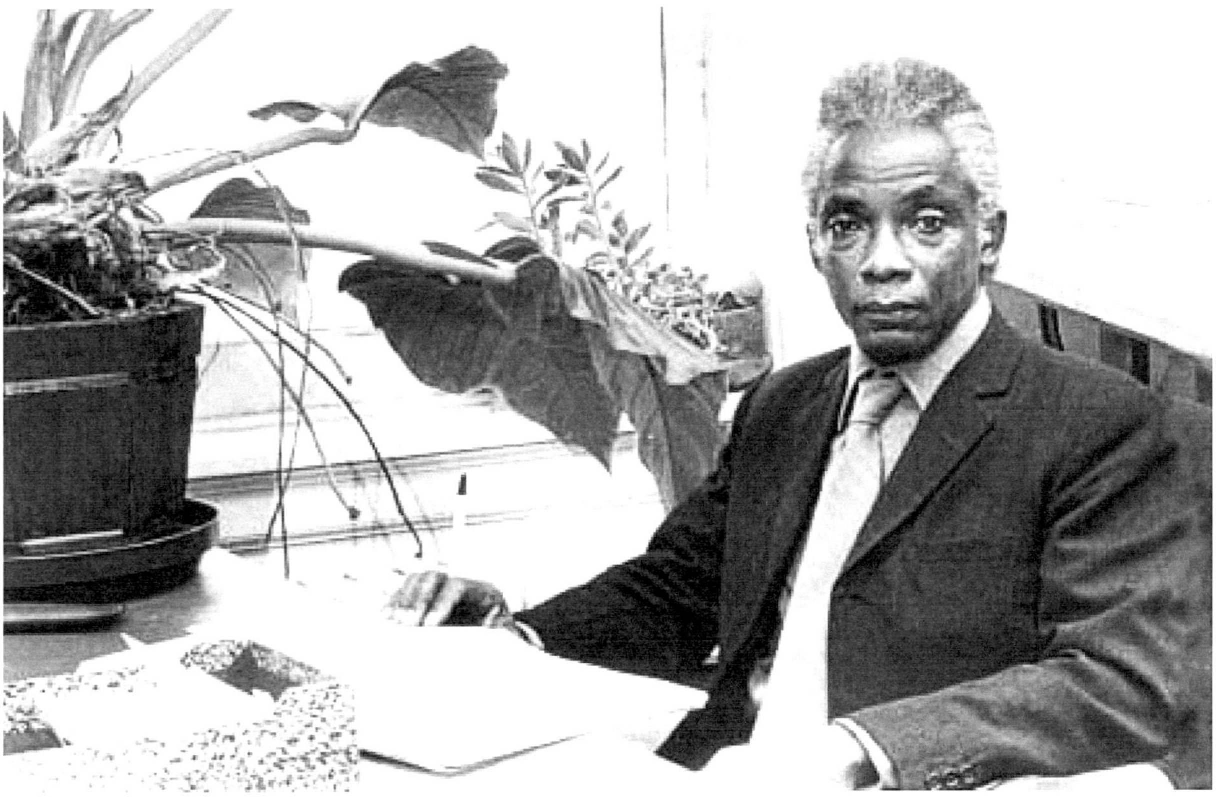

Denis Williams
1923–1998

Chronology

1923

1st February. Birth of Denis Joseph Ivan Williams in Georgetown, British Guiana.

1940–1943

Studies under the British colonial educational system and completes Cambridge Junior School Certificate.

Being tutored by pioneering art teacher Edward Rupert Burrowes.

Attends art classes organised by Golde White.

Completes Cambridge Senior School Certificate. Exempted from London Matriculation.

Exhibits work with the British Guiana Arts and Crafts Society.

1944

Exhibits work with the Guianese Art Group. Attends art lectures organised by the British Council. Establises a local reputation as a figure painter.

1945

Represented at The Institute of Jamaica – *Exhibition of West Indian Paintings*.

Works purchased for a national collection by the Joint Art Committee in Georgetown.

1946–1948

First British Council Scholar in Art from British Guiana.

Sails to Europe on the *Marine Marlin*. Compatriate Arthur. J. Seymour is also a passenger.

Studies at Camberwell School of Art where he is tutored by, among others, Claude Rogers, William Coldstream and Lawrence Golding.

1949

First London exhibition at the Berkeley Gallery with Kofi Antubam. He attracts the attention of Wyndham Lewis.

Exhibits works at the *Colonial Exhibition* at Marble Arch, London.

Meets Felix Giovanelli in New York *en route* during a visit to British Guiana.

Exhibits *The Plantations* in Georgetown to a hostile reception.

Begins the series of paintings which he will finish on his return to London.

Publishes essay "Guiana Today", in *Kyk-over-al*.

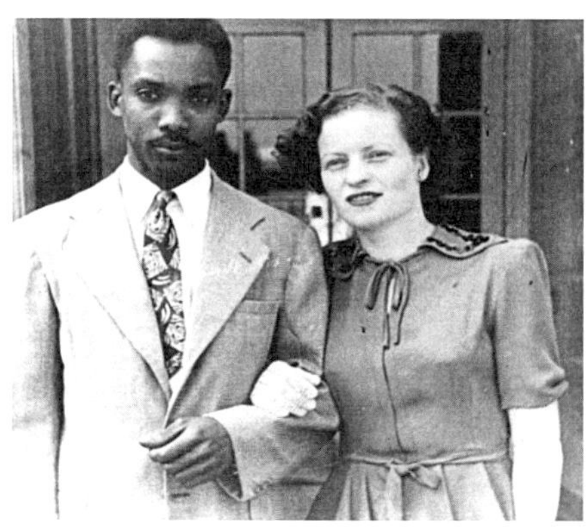

Marries Katie Alice in 1949.

1950

Becomes the *protégé* of Wyndham Lewis.

Exhibits at Gimpel Fils of Mayfair, London, with "Scottie" Wilson, showing *Human World* series.

Tate Gallery, London, reserves two works.

Features in *Time* magazine as "Newcomer from Guiana".

1950–1952

Exhibits *Hysteria* at the new premises of the ICA. Takes part in several of their subsequent mixed exhibitions of contemporary painting.

Teaches Life Drawing and Painting at the Central School of Arts and Crafts (Saint Martins). Associates include Alan Davie, William Turnbull, Keith Vaughan, Victor Pasmore.

Becomes visiting tutor, Slade School of Fine Art under William Coldstream.

Occupies studio space alongside Francis Bacon.

1952

Undergoes radical departure of approach in art practice.

Paints *Colour, Weight, Sound*.

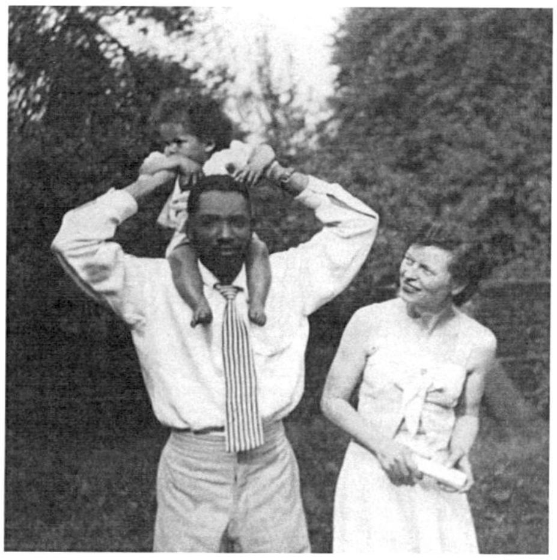

Visit to North Wales, home of Katie Alice.

1953

May. Exhibits in the third Fitzroy Street exhibition organised by Adrian Heath.

July to August. Exhibits at the ICA in *Eleven British Painters: Recent Work*.

July to August. Exhibits at Gimpel Fils of Mayfair in mixed exhibition, *Collector's Choice*.

For George Lamming: jacket design for his first novel *In The Castle of My Skin* (London: Michael Joseph) – the first book jacket design by a West Indian for a West Indian.

October. Exhibits at Galerie de France, Paris, in *Tendances de la Peinture et de la Sculpture: Britanniques Contemporaines*.

1954

April. Exhibits with Roger Hilton at Gimpel Fils of Mayfair showing *Plane Compositions*.

July. Exhibits at Gimpel Fils of Mayfair in mixed exhibition, *Of Light and Colour: An Exhibition of Recent Paintings and Sculptures*.

Experiments with wall painting in Chislehurst Caves, Kent.

For George Lamming: jacket design for his second novel *The Emigrants* (London: Michael Joseph).

Wilson Harris visits for a time with the Williams family at 21 Oxford Road, London.

1955

Prize-winner in the Daily Express *Young Artists' Exhibition* at the New Burlington Gallery, London, with Painting in Six Related Rhythms. Judges include Herbert Read, Graham Sutherland, Anthony Blunt.

Line drawings of Jan Carew, George Lamming and Denis Williams commissioned by *The Times British Colonies Review*.

Paints Portrait of *Katie Alice*.

1956

Human World arrives in Georgetown.

Participates in *This is Tomorrow* at London's Whitechapel Art Gallery. Two sketch pages by Williams feature in the iconic exhibition catalogue.

Commissioned to produce line drawings and

jacket design for *British Guiana: The Land of Six Peoples* by Michael Swan (London: HMSO).

1957–1962

Leaves London for Africa.

Teaches drawing and painting at the Department of Fine and Applied Art, Khartoum, Sudan.

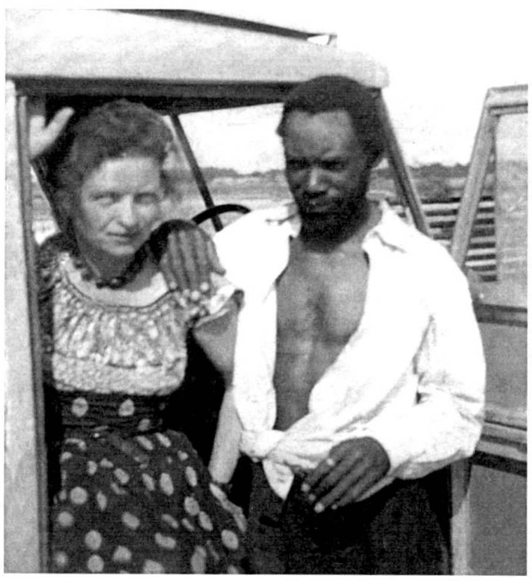

Desert excursions in Sudan.

In the rôle of artist–draughtsman he accompanies archaeological expeditions to Meroë, an ancient city and civilisation on the banks of the Nile on the borders of Egypt and Sudan.

1958

Exchange of letters with Arthur J. Seymour, reproduced in *Kyk-over-al*.

Begins in-depth research on the theme of "identity" which will eventually culminate in *Other Leopards*.

Paints *Self-portrait*, exploring origins and identity.

1959

September. Completes *Moulid el-Nabi*.

Begins compiling his *Africa Journal* of developing ideas on art and identity.

Undertakes extensive tours of Northern Rhodesia, Kenya, Uganda, Tanganyika and Zanzibar.

1960

"Hamilton of the Sudan", in *Kyk-over-al*.

Makes the acquaintance of Ulli Beier, a relationship that continues later in Nigeria.

June. For Jan Carew: jacket design for *The Last Barbarian* (London: Secker & Warburg).

1962–1966

Appointed as lecturer in the School of African Studies, University of Ife, Ibadan Campus, Nigeria.

1962

Is invited with Julian Beinart to conduct the first Oshogbo Art Workshop.

Begins compiling his research into classical African art, producing some 200 drawings and the material which will finally be realised as *Icon and Image* (1974).

Participant at the first African Writers' Conference held at the University of Makerere, Kampala, Uganda. Other participants include Wole Soyinka, Chinua Achebe and Rajat Neogy, founder of *Transition* magazine, of which Williams becomes an associate editor.

1963

January. *A Plastic Calligraphy.* Designs the catalogue for an exhibition of Arabic Calligraphy by Ahmed Mohammed Shibrain at Mbari, Ibadan.

June. "A Sudanese Calligraphy: A Contemporary Interpretation of Mohammedan Art", in *Transition*.

Other Leopards (London: Hutchinson). [Reviewed in the *Times Literary Supplement* in July].

Two chapters (3 and 4) from *Other Leopards* published in *Transition*.

Is invited with African-American artist Jacob Lawrence to conduct the second Oshogbo Art Workshop. Publishes his findings in "Second Experimental Art School" in *Ibadan*.

For Dennis Brutus: jacket design and illustrations for *Sirens, Knuckles, Boots* (Nigeria, Ibadan: Mbari Publications).

Recipient of grant from the International African Institute, London, towards the task of compiling *A Corpus of Yoruba Bronze Art*.

Recipient of research grant from the University of Lagos, Nigeria, for a study of traditional African iron metallurgy.

"Lost-wax Brass Casting in Ibadan", in *Nigeria* magazine.

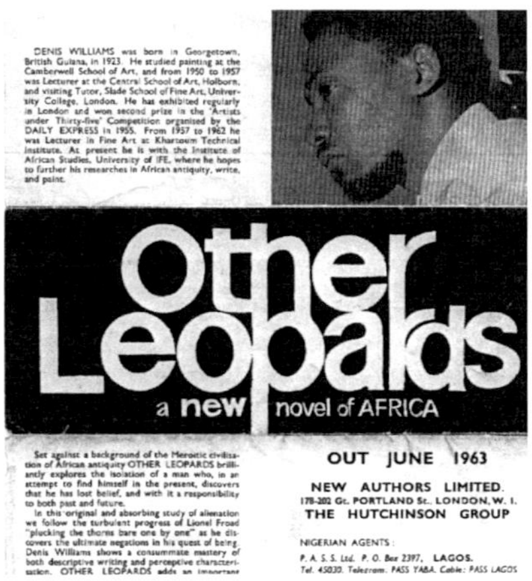

Publisher's flyer for *Other Leopards*.

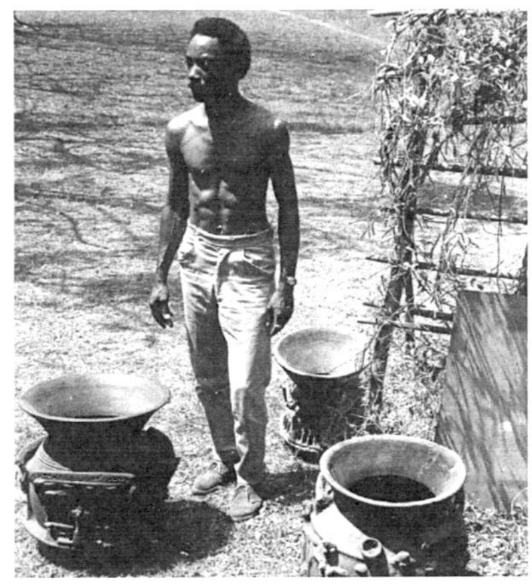
Examining ritual cult objects in Nigeria.

For Wole Soyinka: jacket design and illustrations for *The Swamp Dwellers, The Trials of Brother Jero, The Strong Breed* (Mbari Publications).

1964

February. Final visit to Khartoum for continuing research.

Designs large mosaic for University of Ibadan.

External examiner in African Art and Literature at Makerere University, Kampala, Uganda.

Recipient of research grant from the University of Ife for his fieldwork on Yoruba bronzes.

Recipient of grant from the University of Ife for his project on Yoruba bronzes in the British Museum.

Publishes "Iconography of the Yoruba Edan Ogboni", in *Africa: Journal of the International African Institute*.

"The Nigerian Image", in *Odu: University of Ife Journal of African Studies*.

A Long Long Pause [short story], in *Stories from the Caribbean* (London: Elek Books Limited).

Contributes to "The Arts in Africa". Studies in the report on a conference organised by the International African Institute, London, in *Africa*.

1966–1967

Lecturer in the School of African and Asian Studies, University of Lagos, Nigeria.

1966

February. Presented to HM Queen Elizabeth II on the occasion of her visit to British Guiana.

May. Invited by President Burnham to attend Guyana's independence celebrations as an honoured guest.

July. Visiting Professor and external examiner (African Art and Literature), Makerere University, Uganda. Gives seminar presentation entitled *The Traditional Theme in African Art and Literature*.

"An Outline History of Tropical African Art", in *Africa in the Nineteenth and Twentieth Century* (London: Nelson; Ibadan: Ibadan University Press).

"A Corpus of Yoruba Bronze Art: Report on Field-work", in *Africa*.

With Smith R. S. "A Reconnaissance Visit to Oyo-lle", in *Odu: University of Ife Journal of African Studies*.

1967

"Bronze-casting Moulds, Cores and the Study of Classical Techniques", in *Lagos Notes and Records*.

"Iron and the Gods: A study of the Sacred Iron Figurines of the Yoruba". [Seminar paper delivered at the School of Asian and African Studies, University of Lagos].

1967–1974

Returns to Guyana and settles at Issano on the Upper Mazaruni River, resuming his painting.

Commences research into the petroglyphs and the prehistoric record of the region.

1967

Sperm of God. Three short chapters, written in Nigeria, for his proposed "Caribbean novel", in *Transition*.

With A. J. Seymour initiates the *Edgar Mittelholzer Memorial Lecture Series*. Seymour delivers the inaugural Lectures.

1968

Publication of *The Third Temptation* (London: Calder & Boyars).

1969

"The Concept of the Ancestor", "The Complex Womb", "Image and Idea in African and Caribbean Literature", "Image and Idea in the Arts of Guyana". *The Edgar Mittelholzer Memorial Lectures,* Second Series (Georgetown: Ministry of Information, National History and Arts Council).

Appointed as Director of the National History and Arts Council.

"African Iron and the Classical World", in *Africa in Classical Antiquity* (Ibadan: Ibadan University Press).

1970

A Long Long Pause [short story, 1965], reprinted in *Island Voices* (New York: Liveright Publishing Company).

Aubrey Williams visits Denis Williams at Issano.

1972

Delivers a welcome address at first CARIFESTA.

The Sperm of God. Further "extract" from a novel, in *New Writings in the Caribbean*, edited by Arthur J. Seymour, (Georgetown: National History and Arts Council).

1973

Awarded the Golden Arrow of Achievement (AA) by the Government of Guyana.

Recipient of research grant from the Latin American Archaeology Fund of the Smithsonian Institution, Washington DC for archaeological investigations on the Mazaruni River.

"Art in Metal", in *Sources of Yoruba History*, ed. Biobaku, S. O. (Oxford: The Clarendon Press).

"Art and Society", in *The Literary Vision of Carifesta '72: The Rôle of the Artist in Third World Society*, in *Kaie*.

Giglioli in Guyana 1922–1972 (Georgetown: National History and Arts Council).

Returns permanently to Georgetown.

Urgently addresses the issues of national identity and initiates the process of local artists tendering for public commissions.

Paints *Portrait of Pauline*.

Preliminary studies for *Majestas*, commissioned by the Anglican Church.

1974

Appointed Director of Art in the Department of Culture of the Ministry of Education.

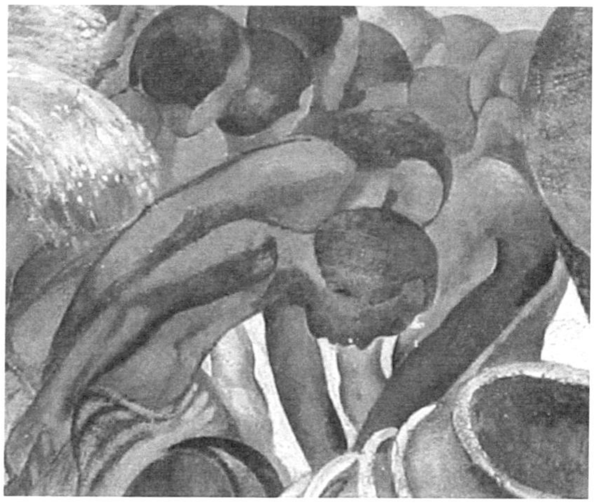

Embedded self-portrait in *Memorabilia II.*

Founds the Walter Roth Museum of Anthropology and Archaeology, Georgetown.

Majestas is consecrated at St George's Cathedral and taken to St Francis de Sales Church, Kamarang. Currently curated by the National Gallery in Georgetown.

Icon and Image: A Study of Sacred and Secular Forms of African Classical Art (London: Allen Lane; New York: New York University Press).

1975

Visits Mexico City to study mural art.

Establishes the E. R. Burrowes School of Art, Georgetown, and becomes its first Principal.

Completes *Memorabilia I*. (National Collection).

1976

Curates the touring exhibition, "Colonial Art to Revolutionary Art 1966–1976" and writes the text of the exhibition catalogue. (Georgetown, 1976).

Memorabilia II is unveiled on the occasion of the official opening of the National Cultural Centre in Georgetown on 16 May 1976.

May. "Review of the 1763 monument". Published for the unveiling of Philip Moore's Cuffy monument on Sunday 23 May 1976 to mark the tenth anniversary of the independence of Guyana.

July. "1763, Carl Blackman and all that ..." in *Kaie*.

Writes the introduction to Ivan Forrester's book of poetry *A Voice from Cuffy's Grave* (Georgetown: Office of the General Secretary, People's National Congress, and Ministry of National Development).

"Identity in Guyanese Plastic Art", in Hearne, John (ed.), *Carifesta Forum: An Anthology of 20 Caribbean Voices*.

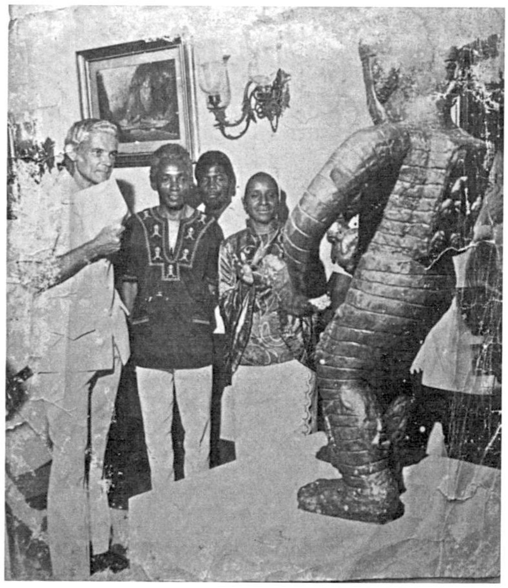

With Prime Minister Michael Manley and Minister Shirley Field-Ridley during Carifesta '76.

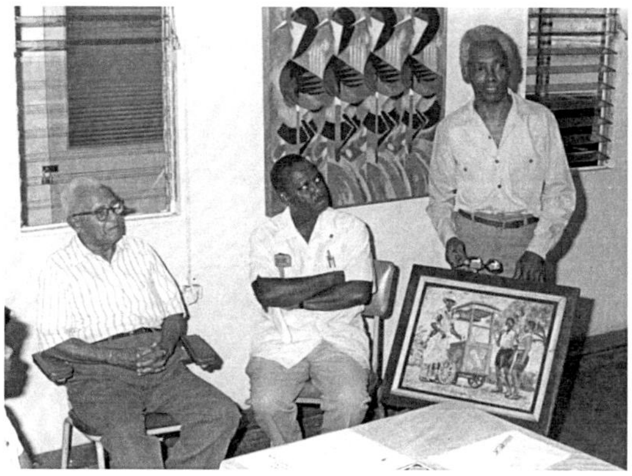

Promoting the "Guyana School" of artists. Hubert Moshett (far left).

Curates the touring exhibition "Contemporary Art in Guyana".

Writes the text of the catalogue for Republic of Guyana: Contemporary Art as part of Carifesta '76 in Jamaica (Georgetown: Bovell's Printery).

1977

Attends the second World Black & African Festival of Arts and Culture (FESTAC), Lagos, Nigeria, 15 January–12 February.

"Archaeological Reconnaissance on the Middle Mazaruni". Report to Smithsonian Institution on Grant for fieldwork. (Georgetown: Department of Culture).

His monument to the Enmore Martyrs is unveiled on 16 June 1977, to mark the 29th anniversary of the five deaths.

Officially appointed Chairman of the National Trust of Guyana.

1978

Founds *Archaeology and Anthropology*, the Journal of the Walter Roth Museum of Anthropology.

"Prehistoric Rock Art in Guyana and the Antilles". Paper given at the Tenth Conference of Caribbean Historians, US Virgin Islands.

"Petroglyphs at Marlissa, Berbice River", in *Archaeology and Anthropology*.

"Test Pits at Itabru, Berbice River", in *Archaeology and Anthropology*.

1979

"Archaeology and Anthropology". Transcript of radio discussion between Denis Williams and Ada Akai, in *Kaie*.

"Meso-Indian Fishtraps on the Upper Essequibo River". Report on a survey of unusual petroglyphs on the Upper Essequibo and Kassikaityu Rivers. (Georgetown: National Commission for the Acquisition, Preservation and Republication of Research Materials on Guyana, 1979).

"A report on Preceramic Lithic Artifacts in the South Rupununi Savannas", in *Archaeology and Anthropology*.

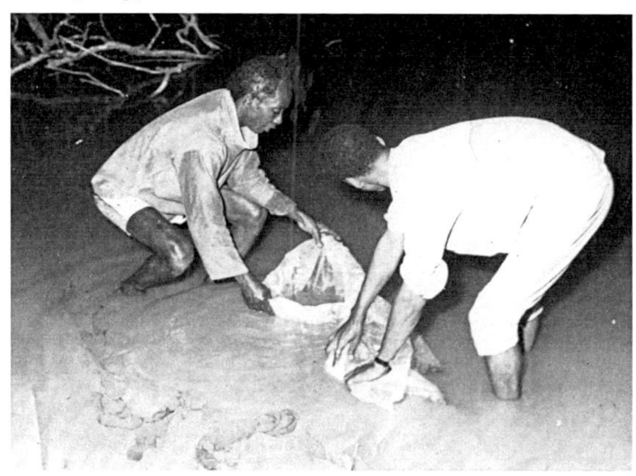

Swamp excavation in the interior.

"Controlled Resource Exploitation in Contrasting Neotropical Environments". Valcomonica Symposium III.

1980

Visiting Research Scholar, Department of Anthropology, Smithsonian Institution, Washington DC.

"Rock Tallies of Food Sources", in *Research Reports* (Smithsonian Institution).

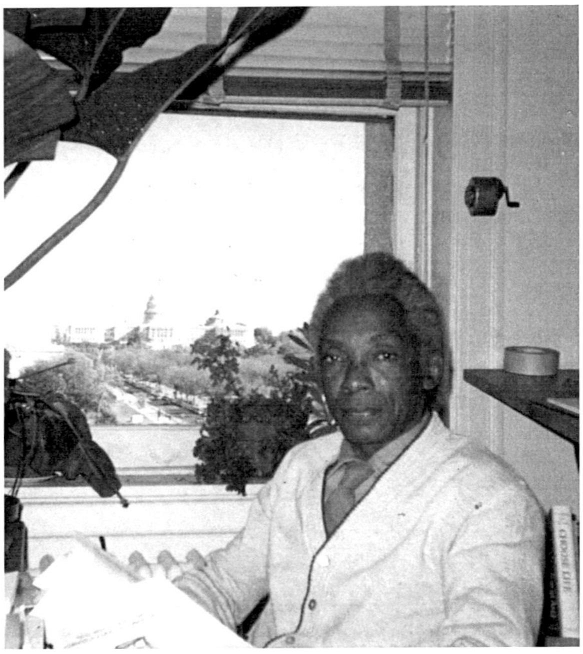
Study at the Smithsonian Institution, 1980.

1981

"Eine Lange, Lange Pause", in *Die Nacht in der die Hütten leer blieben: Erzählungen aus der Karibik*, edited by Peter Schultze-Kraft. [A German translation of *A Long Long Pause* (1965, 1970)].

"Archaeology and Anthropology", in *Kaie*.

"Excavation of the Barabina Shell Mound, North West District: An Interim Report", in *Archaeology and Anthropology*.

"Three Sites of the Taruma Phase in Southeast and East Guyana", in *Archaeology and Anthropology*.

1982

"Some Subsistence Implications of Holocene Climate Change in Northwestern Guyana", in *Archaeology and Anthropology*.

1983

Other Leopards reprinted by Heinemann in their Caribbean Writers series, with an introduction by Edward Baugh.

April. "Guiana Today" (1949) reprinted in *Kyk-over-al* (Nos. 33–34, "The Golden Kyk-over-al": an anthology drawn from Nos. 1–28).

1984

Curates Amerindian Heritage touring exhibition and writes text for exhibition catalogue: Guyanese Pre-history: "The Amerindian Heritage". UNESCO grant-aided. (Georgetown: Walter Roth Museum).

Delivers the ninth series of the *Edgar Mittelholzer Memorial Lectures*. (Georgetown, 19, 21, 23 and 26 November).

Review of *Heavensgate* (1962) in Critical Perspectives on Christopher Okigbo, edited by Donatus Nwoga, (Boulder, Colorado: Lynne Rienner Publishers).

1985

Participant in the International Visitor Programme of the United States Information Agency.

"Petroglyphs in the Pre-history of Northern Amazonia and the Antilles", in *Advances in World Archaeology* (New York: Academic Press).

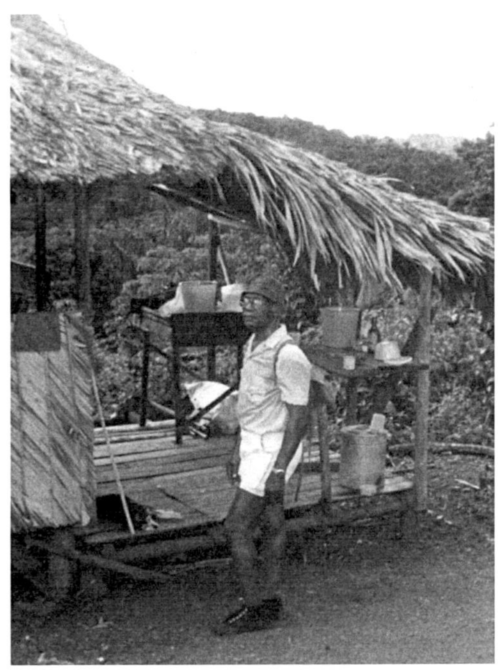
Remote logie camp in the Guyanese interior.

"The Tidal Swamps of the North West and Pomeroon Districts", "Intercontinental Hunters and Gatherers in the Rupununi Savannas", "Climate Stress and Subsistence Options in the Tropical Forest", and "The Specialized Coastal Adaptations of Horticulturalists". Revised texts of the 1984 *Mittelholzer Memorial Lectures*, published with a foreword by President Desmond Hoyte as *Ancient Guyana* (Georgetown: Department of Culture).

Founds the Museum of African Art and Ethnology (now the Museum of African Heritage) in the building gifted by Bertie Nicholson, who also donated his collection.

Amazonian Petroglyphs. [Unpublished typescript. In National Anthropological Archives, Walter Roth Museum of Anthropology, Georgetown].

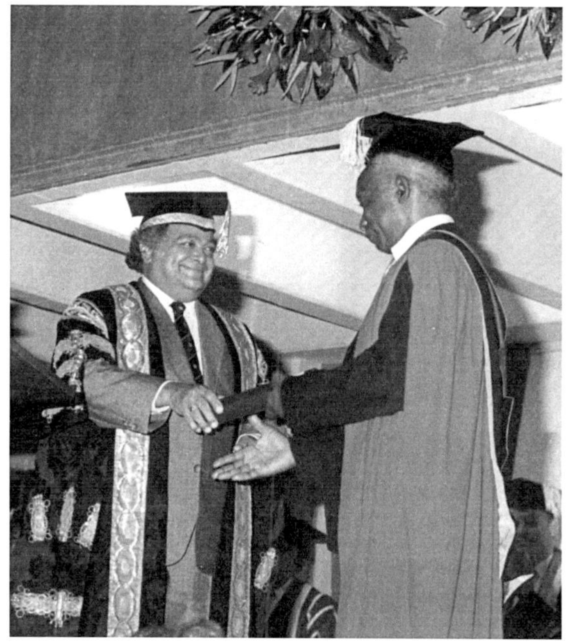

Degree ceremony with Sir Shridath Ramphal.

1986

Preliminary drawings for the *Human Evolution* exhibit (1986–1988): paints centerpiece and nine roundels for the Walter Roth Museum.

Paints final *Self-portrait*.

1987

March. "Achievements and Potentialities in the Guyanese Plastic Arts". A translation of the paper delivered in Cuba in November 1986. It forms the text of an Exhibition Catalogue accompanying items from the National Collection of Guyana exhibited in Caracas, Venezuela.

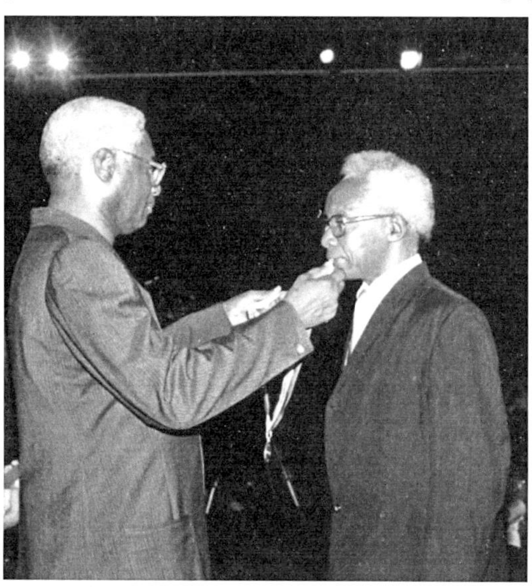

Receiving the Cacique Crown of Honour from President Desmond Hoyte

"The Visual Arts in the Cultural Evolution of the People of Guyana", in *The Caribbean Supplement* to the English Language Edition of the *UNESCO Courier.*

1988

Grant from RESCAN Environmental Services, Vancouver, for an Environmental Impact Survey at Omai, Upper Essequibo River, Guyana.

Pages in Guyanese Pre-history (Georgetown: Walter Roth Museum of Anthropology).

1989

Receives the title of Doctor of Letters (D.Litt) *honoris causa* from the University of the West Indies at the Trinidad campus.

Awarded the Cacique Crown of Honour (CCH) by the Government of Guyana.

The Archaic of North-western Guyana (Turkeyen: History Society).

1990

Grant from UNESCO Part-Participation programme for *The Arawak Language Project on the Upper Pomeroon River*, part 1.

Grant from RESCAN Environmental Services, Vancouver, for an Environmental Impact Survey of the Potaro River, Guyana.

1992

"The Columbus Quincentennial". Transcript of a Venezuelan Radio interview with simultaneous Spanish translation: cassette tape dated January 1992.

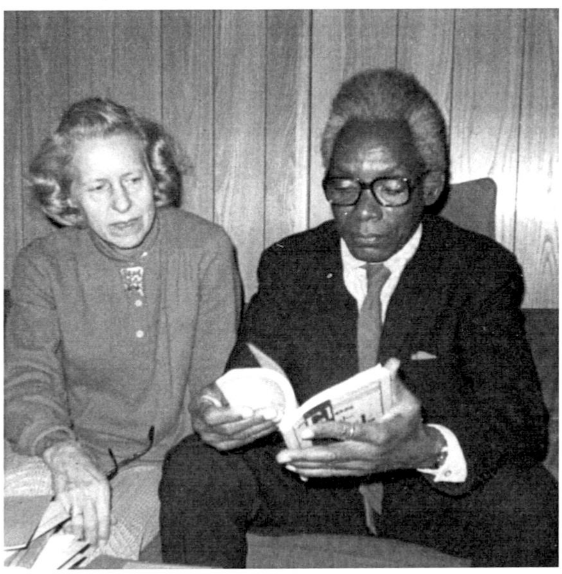

With archaeologist Betty J. Meggers.

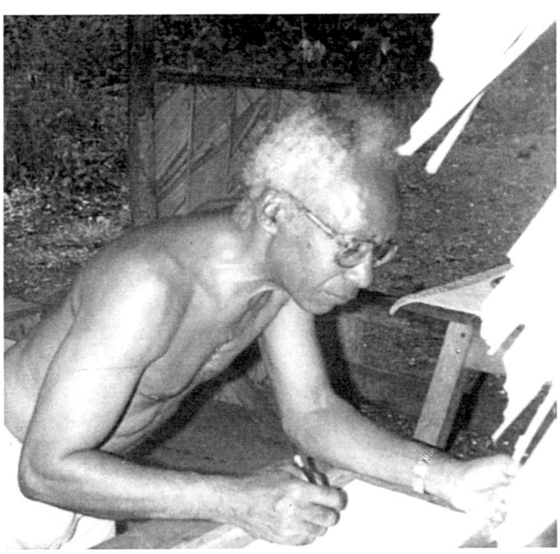

Working at a field camp desk.

"El Arcaio en el Noroeste de Guyana y los Comienzos de la Horticultura", in *Proceedings of the Symposium: Americans before Columbus* (Smithsonian Institution, Washington: Taraxacum).

1993

Grant from UNESCO Part-Participation programme for *The Arawak Language Project on the Upper Pomeroon River*, part 2.

"The Forms of the Shamanic Sign in Prehistoric Guyana", in *Archaeology and Anthropology*.

Catalogue notes for the inaugural exhibition of the National Collection at Castellani House.

1994

Grant from the Commonwealth and the Government of Guyana for an Environmental Impact Survey of the Iwokrama Rainforest Programme.

Iwokrama: The Commonwealth and Government of Guyana Rainforest Programme (Georgetown: Natural Resources Agency).

1995

Writes review of *Guyana Dreaming: The Art of Aubrey Williams*, (ed. Anne Walmsley) in *Stabroek News*.

1996

Smithsonian Institution Research Grant for the Archaeological Survey of the Aruka River, Guyana.

Prehistoric Cultures of the Iwokrama Rainforest Reserve (Georgetown: Guyana Natural Resources Agency).

"Archaeology in the Guianas", in *Society of American Archaeology Bulletin*.

"The Mabaruma Phase: Origin, Characterisation and Chronology", in *Archaeology and Anthropology*.

"Guyana", in Turner, Jane (ed.) *The Dictionary of Art*, 34 volumes (London: Macmillan).

Establishes *The Hamburgh Register for Anthropological Titles*, an initiative to bring together all the anthropological publications of the Guianas.

1997

"Early Pottery on the Amazon: A Correction", in *American Antiquity.*

"The Archaic Colonisation of the Western Guiana Littoral and its Aftermath". A paper prepared for the Smithsonian Institution Press.

1998

"Aubrey Williams in Guyana". Monograph (London: Institute of International Visual Arts (inIVA).

Death of Denis Williams on 28 June in Georgetown.He is buried at St Sidwell's Church.

SECURING THE LEGACY

The Cowrie Circle pin is awarded posthumously to Denis Williams by the president of the Commonwealth Association of Museums and accepted in trust by Jennifer Wishart (1999).

Publication of *Prehistoric Guiana* (2003).

The Wordsworth McAndrew Award for contributions to Guyanese Culture (2004).

Inauguration of the Denis Williams Summer School of Anthropology, and the return of *Majestas* to Georgetown (2007).

Evelyn Williams, "Denis Williams: Art, Blood and Heritage". *Edgar Mittelholzer Memorial Lectures*, Thirteenth Series (2009).

Peepal Tree Press reissue *Other Leopards* and *The Third Temptation* (2009, 2010).

Charlotte and Evelyn Williams co-edit *Denis Williams: A Life in Works. New and Collected Essays* (Amsterdam & New York: Rodopi, 2010).

Evelyn Williams, "Denis Williams in London: 1946–1957", in *Third Text* (25, 2, April 2011), pp. 157–168.

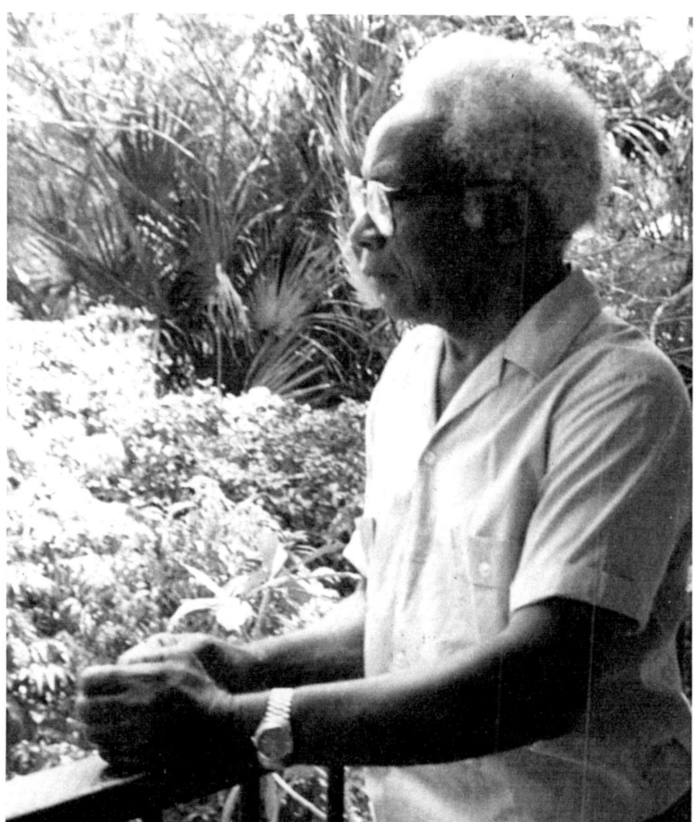

Relaxing at home at D'Urban Backlands, Georgetown.

BIBLIOGRAPHY

WORKS BY DENIS WILLIAMS

1.1 ON ART AND ARISTS – AFRICA

1.1.1 ARTICLES

"Second Experimental Art School, 27 April to 4 May 1963", in *Ibadan* (No. 17, November 1963), pp. 22–26.

"The Arts in Africa". [Studies in the report on a conference organised by the International African Institute in London], in *Africa: Journal of the International African Institute* (1, 1965).

"The Nigerian Image", in *Odu: University of Ife Journal of African Studies* (2, 1, Ife, 1965).

"An Outline History of Tropical African Art", in Anene, Joseph C. & Godfrey N. Brown (eds). *Africa in the Nineteenth and Twentieth Century* (London: Nelson; Ibadan: Ibadan University Press, 1966).

1.1.2 CATALOGUE NOTES

A Plastic Calligraphy. Notes for an exhibition of Arabic Calligraphy by Ahmed Mohammed Shibrain (Khartoum) at the Mbari, Ibadan, 25 January 1963.

"A Sudanese Calligraphy: A Contemporary Interpretation of Mohammedan Art", in *Transition* (No. 9, June 1963), pp. 19–20.

1.2 ON ART AND ARTISTS – GUYANA AND THE CARIBBEAN

1.2.1 ARTICLES, REVIEWS, LETTERS AND BROADCASTS

"Guiana Today", in *Kyk-over-al* (Vol. 2, No. 9, December 1949), pp. 9–10. Reprinted in *Kyk-over-al* (Nos. 33–34, "The Golden Kyk-over-al": an anthology from Nos. 1–28, April 1983), pp. 131–133, and in *Stabroek News* (*The Guyana Review*) on 28 May 2009.

Correspondence with Wyndham Lewis (1949–1950). Courtesy of Cornell University Library: Kroch Library, Rare Books department, archive no. 4612.

"Art in the Caribbean". Transcript of BBC Colonial Service broadcast, in *Caribbean Voices* (21 January 1951), pp. 1–3.

With Seymour, A. J. "An Exchange of Letters", reproduced in *Kyk-over-al* (24 December 1958), pp. 93–99.

"Art and Society", in *The Literary Vision of Carifesta '72: The Rôle of the Artist in Third World Society*, in *Kaie* (No. 11, August 1973), pp. 100–115.

"The Artist in Society", in *Timehri: Journal of the Guyana Museum and Zoo, South America* (No. 45, 1975), pp. 78–90. [Guyana Society Lecture Series, May 9, 1977].

"What image of ourselves?" in the *Review of the 1763 Monument* (Georgetown: Castellani House, 1976).

"1763, Carl Blackman and all that...", in *Kaie* (No. 14, July 1976), pp. 52–55.

Introduction to Ivan Forrester's poetry anthology *A Voice from Cuffy's Grave* (Georgetown: Office of the General Secretary, People's National Congress, and Ministry of National Development, 1976).

"Identity in Guyanese Plastic Art", in Hearne, John (ed.) *Carifesta Forum: An Anthology of 20 Caribbean Voices* (Jamaica: Institute of Jamaica, 1976), pp. 177–185.

Note on *Memorabilia II* in the First Performance Souvenir Programme for the National Cultural Centre (Georgetown: Guyana Printers Ltd., May 1976), pp. 14–15.

"Contemporary Art in Guyana". Text of catalogue for the exhibition *Republic of Guyana: Contemporary Art* as part of Carifesta '76 in Jamaica (Georgetown: Bovell's Printery, 1976), pp. 1–5.

Review of *Heavensgate* (1962) in Nwoga, Donatus (ed.) *Critical Perspectives on Christopher Okigbo* (Boulder, Colorado: Lynne Rienner Publishers, 1984).

"The Visual Arts in the Cultural Evolution of the People of Guyana", in *The Caribbean Supplement* to the English Language Edition of the *UNESCO Courier* (Vol. 1, No. 7, 1987), pp. 2–4. From an unpublished typescript entitled "The Cultural Heritage" (1976).

"Achievements and Potentialities in the Guyanese Plastic Arts". Translation of a paper delivered in Cuba in November 1986. [It forms the text of an Exhibition Catalogue accompanying items from the National Collection of Guyana exhibited in Caracas, Venezuela, in March 1987].

"The Columbus Quincentennial". Transcript of a Venezuelan Radio interview, recorded on cassette tape dated January 1992.

Review of Walmsley, Anne (ed.) *Guyana Dreaming: The Art of Aubrey Williams* (Sydney: Dangaroo Press, 1990), in *Stabroek News* (Georgetown, 5 February 1995), p. 27.

"Guyana", in Turner, Jane (ed.) *The Dictionary of Art* (34 volumes; London: Macmillan, 1996) Vol. 13. pp. 873–78.

1.2.2 CATALOGUE NOTES

This is Tomorrow. Notes and sketches in Exhibition Catalogue (London: Whitechapel Art Gallery, 1956).

"Colonial Art to Revolutionary Art, 1966–1976". Exhibition catalogue (Georgetown, 1976).

"Africa and the Origin of Man". Exhibition notes (Walter Roth Museum, 1988).

Catalogue notes for the inaugural exhibition of the National Collection in Castellani House, 1993.

"The sculpture of John Clowes". Exhibition catalogue (Georgetown: Department of Culture, April 1995).

"Aubrey Williams in Guyana", in Dempsey, Andrew; Gilane Tawadros & Maridowa Williams (eds) *Aubrey Williams* (London: inIVA, 1998), pp. 36–45.

1.3 LITERARY WORKS

1.3.1 NOVELS

Other Leopards (London: Hutchinson, 1963). Reprinted by Heinemann in their *Caribbean Writers* series, with an Introduction by Edward Baugh (1983) and by Peepal Tree Press, with an Introduction by Victor Ramraj (2009).

The Third Temptation (London: Calder & Boyars, 1968). Reprinted by Peepal Tree Press (2009).

1.3.2 SHORT STORIES AND FRAGMENTS

A Long Long Pause [short story] in *Stories from the Caribbean* (London: Elek Books Limited, 1965). Republished in *Island Voices* (New York: Liveright Publishing Company, 1970), pp. 218–222.

Sperm of God. Three short chapters of a novel, in *Transition* (28, 6, 1967), pp. 9–13.

The Sperm of God. Further "extract" from a novel, in Seymour, Arthur J. (ed.) *New Writings in the Caribbean* (Georgetown: National History and Arts Council, 1972), pp. 301–316.

1.4 PUBLISHED LECTURES

"The Concept of the Ancestor", "The Complex Womb", "Image and Idea in African and Caribbean Literature", & "Image and Idea in the Arts of Guyana", collected in *Image and Idea in the Arts of Guyana: The Edgar Mittelholzer Memorial Lectures*, Second Series (Georgetown: Ministry of Information, National History & Arts Council, January 1969), pp. 5–14; 15–22; 23–32; 33–39. [With an Introduction by A. J. Seymour].

1.5 BIOGRAPHY

"Hamilton of the Sudan", in *Kyk-over-al* (No. 7, 1960), pp. 87–93.

Giglioli in Guyana 1922–1972 (Georgetown: National History & Arts Council, 1973).

"Giglioli and the Redemption of Guyana", in *Sunday Chronicle* (26 January 1975), p. 6.

1.6 ARCHAEOLOGY – AFRICA

1.6.1 BOOKS

Icon and Image: A Study of Sacred and Secular Forms of African Classical Art (New York University Press, 1974).

1.6.2 ARTICLES, REVIEWS AND JOURNAL CONTRIBUTIONS

Review of Ulli Beier's *African Mud Sculpture* (1963) in *Ibadan* (No. 17, University of Ibadan, November 1963), pp. 31–32.

"Iconography of the Yoruba Edan Ogboni", in *Africa: Journal of the International African Institute* (34, 2, London, 1964), pp. 139–166.

"Lost-wax Brass Casting in Ibadan", in *Nigeria* magazine (84, Lagos, 1965), pp. 96–100.

"A Corpus of Yoruba Bronze Art: Report on Fieldwork", in *Africa: Journal of the International African Institute* (2, 2, 1966), pp. 204–205.

The Traditional Theme in African Art and Literature. Lecture given at Makerere University in July 1966. [Transcript].

With Smith R. S., "A Reconnaissance Visit to Oyo-lle", in *Odu: University of Ife Journal of African Studies* (3, 1, Ife, 1966), pp. 55–60.

"Bronze-casting Moulds, Cores and the Study of Classical Techniques", in *Lagos Notes and Records* (1, 1, University of Lagos, 1967), pp. 27–28.

"Iron and the Gods: A study of the Sacred Iron Figurines of the Yoruba". Seminar paper delivered at the School of Asian and African Studies, University of Lagos (1967).

"African Iron and the Classical World", in Ferguson, John & L. A. Thompson (eds) *Africa in Classical Antiquity* (Ibadan: Ibadan University Press, 1969).

"Art in Metal", in Biobaku, S. O. (ed.) *Sources of Yoruba History* (Oxford: The Clarendon Press, 1973).

1.6.3 ARCHAEOLOGY – GUYANA

1.6.4 BOOKS

Prehistoric Guiana (Kingston, Jamaica: Ian Randle, 2003).

1.6.5 ARTICLES, REVIEWS AND JOURNAL CONTRIBUTIONS

"Archaeological Reconnaissance on the Middle Mazaruni". Report to Smithsonian Institution on grant for fieldwork. (Georgetown: Department of Culture, 1977).

"Prehistoric Rock Art in Guyana and the Antilles". Paper given at the Tenth Conference of Caribbean Historians, US Virgin Islands (1978).

"Petroglyphs at Marlissa, Berbice River", in *Archaeology and Anthropology* (Journal of the Walter Roth Museum of Anthropology, 1, Georgetown, 1978), pp. 24–31.

"Test Pits at Itabru, Berbice River", in *Archaeology and Anthropology* (1, Georgetown, 1978), pp. 34–39.

"Schomburgk's Artist", in *Archaeology and Anthropology* (2, 1, 1979), pp. 87–88. A commentary on *Sketches of Amerindian Tribes 1841–1843* by Edward Goodall with an Introduction and Notes by M. N. Menezes (London: British Museum Publications Limited, for the National Commission for the Acquisition, Preservation and Republication of Research Materials on Guyana, 1977; reissued by Macmillan Caribbean, 2002).

"Archaeology and Anthropology". Transcript of radio discussion between Denis Williams and Ada Akai, in *Kaie* (16 July 1979).

"Meso-Indian Fishtraps on the Upper Essequibo River". Report on a survey of unusual petroglyphs on the Upper Essequibo and Kassikaityu Rivers (Georgetown: National Commission for the Acquisition, Preservation and Republication of Research Materials on Guyana, 1979).

"A report on Preceramic Lithic Artifacts in the South Rupununi Savannas", in *Archaeology and Anthropology* (2, 2, Georgetown, 1979).

"Rock Tallies of Food Sources", in *Research Reports* (Smithsonian Institution, 31, Winter 1980), pp. 1, 3.

"Archaeology and Anthropology", in *Kaie* (17 July 1981).

"Excavation of the Barabina Shell Mound, North West District: An Interim Report", in *Archaeology and Anthropology* (4, (1, 2), Georgetown, 1981).

"Three Sites of the Taruma Phase in Southeast and East Guyana", in *Archaeology and Anthropology* (4, (1, 2), Georgetown, 1981).

"Some Subsistence Implications of Holocene Climate Change in Northwestern Guyana", in *Archaeology and Anthropology* (5, (1, 2), Georgetown, 1982), pp. 82–94.

"The Amerindian Heritage". Text of UNESCO Exhibition Catalogue, *Pages in Guyanese Prehistory* (Georgetown: Walter Roth Museum, 1984).

"Petroglyphs in the Prehistory of Northern Amazonia and the Antilles", in *Advances in World Archaeology* (4, New York: Academic Press, 1985).

"The Forms of the Shamanic Sign in Prehistoric Guyana", in *Archaeology and Anthropology* (9, Georgetown, 1993).

Iwokrama: The Commonwealth and Government of Guyana Rainforest Programme (Georgetown: Natural Resources Agency, 1994).

Prehistoric Cultures of the Iwokrama Rainforest Reserve (Georgetown: Guyana Natural Resources Agency, 1996).

"Archaeology in the Guianas", in *Society of American Archaeology Bulletin* (14, 1, 1996).

"The Mabaruma Phase: Origin, Characterisation and Chronology", in *Archaeology and Anthropology* (11, Georgetown, 1996), pp. 3–54.

"Early Pottery on the Amazon: A Correction", in *American Antiquity* (62, April 1997).

The Archaic of North-western Guyana (Turkeyen: History Society, 1989).

"El Arcaio en el Noroeste de Guyana y los Comienzos de la Horticultura", in *Proceedings of the Symposium Americans before Columbus*, Smithsonian Institution (Washington: Taraxacum, 1992).

Pages in Guyanese Prehistory (Georgetown: Walter Roth Museum of Anthropology, 1995).

1.6.6 PUBLISHED LECTURES

"Habitat and Culture in Ancient Guyana". Four lectures in *The Edgar Mittelholzer Memorial Lectures*, Ninth Series (Georgetown, 19, 21, 23 & 26 November 1984). [See next entry].

"The Tidal Swamps of the North West and Pomeroon Districts", "Intercontinental Hunters and Gatherers in the Rupununi Savannas", "Climate Stress and Subsistence Options in the Tropical Forest", & "The Specialized Coastal Adaptations of Horticulturalists". Revised texts of the 1984 *Edgar Mittelholzer Memorial Lectures*, published with a foreword by President Desmond Hoyte as *Ancient Guyana* (Georgetown: Department of Culture, 1985).

ABOUT DENIS WILLIAMS

2. 1 ANONYMOUS ARTICLES

"Newcomer from Guiana", in *Time* magazine (18 December 1950), p. 46.

"Denis Williams of B. G. Styled 'Artist of Genius'", in *British Guiana Chronicle* (7 January 1951). [By a Special Correspondent].

"Exhibitions at the ICA", in *The Studio* (April 1951).

"Art in Guyana". (National History & Arts Council, 1971).

"Leading Yoruba dancers coming: Cuba to take big part in CARIFESTA", in *Guyana Graphic* (12 February 1972), p 8.

"The Rôle of the Artist in Third World Countries", in *Guyana Graphic* (9 September 1972), p. 3.

Guyana Participation at Second World Black & African Festival of Arts and Culture: Lagos, Nigeria, January 15–February 12, 1977 (Georgetown: National History & Arts Council, Ministry of Information & Culture, 1977).

"Guyana Report – Workshop on Museum Policy", in *CAM Bulletin Number 6* (February 2000).

2.2 LITERARY WORKS

Aiyejina, Funso. "The Backward Glance: Lamming's *Season of Adventure* and Williams' *Other Leopards*", in *African Literature Today* (14, 1984), pp. 118–126.

Akanji, Sangodare. Review of *Other Leopards* in *Black Orpheus* (No. 13, November 1963), pp. 61–62.

Ashcroft, B., G. Griffiths & H. Tiffin (eds). *The Empire Writes Back: Theory and Practice in Post Colonial Literatures* (London: Routledge, 1989), p. 148.

Baugh, Edward. Introduction to *Other Leopards* (Oxford: Heinemann: *Caribbean Writers* series, 1983), pp. v–xviii.

Breslin, Paul. *Nobody's Nation: Reading Derek Walcott* (University of Chicago Press, 2001), pp. 36–37.

Cambridge, Vibert. "Denis Williams and the New Novel: The Status of *The Third Temptation*", in Williams, Charlotte & Evelyn A. Williams (eds) *Denis Williams: A Life in Works. New and Collected Essays* (Cross/Cultures; Amsterdam & New York: Rodopi, 2010), pp. 111-123.

James, Louis. "Or the Hopeful Dawn". A review of *Other Leopards*, in *Public Opinion* (Kingston, Jamaica, 16 June 1965), pp. 14–15.

—. Introduction to *The Islands in Between* (London: Oxford UP, 1968), pp. 1–49.

—. "Denis Williams", in Lindfors, Bernth & Reinhard Sander (eds) *Dictionary of Literary Biography* (Vol. 117, Detroit, London: Bruccoli Clark Layman, 1992), pp. 313–316.

—. "'The closeness of profound curiosity': The Parallel Visions of Wilson Harris and Denis Williams", in *The Journal of Caribbean Literatures* (Vol. 2, Spring 2000), pp. 47–53. Reprinted in Williams, Charlotte & Evelyn A. Williams (eds) *Denis Williams: A Life in Works* (2010), pp. 77–87.

Kinkead-Weekes, Mark. "'Africa' – Two Caribbean Fictions", in *Twentieth Century Studies* (No. 10, 1973), pp. 37–59.

Lindsay, Andrew. "Preparing the Palette: The Artist in Words", in Williams, Charlotte & Evelyn A. Williams (eds) *Denis Williams: A Life in Works* (2010), pp. 125–141.

Locher, Frances C. (ed.). "Williams, Denis Joseph Ivan", in *Contemporary Authors, A Biobibliographical Guide to Current Writers in Fiction, General Nonfiction, Poetry, Journalism, Drama, Motion Pictures, Television, and Other Fields* (Detroit, Michigan: Gale Research Company, 1980). Vols 93–96, pp. 556–557.

Moore, Gerald. *The Chosen Tongue* (London: Longman, 1969).

Page, Malcolm. Review: "West Indian Writers", in *Novel: A Forum on Fiction* (Vol. 3, No. 2, Winter 1970), pp. 167–172.

Ramchand, Kenneth. *The West Indian Novel and its Background* (London: Faber & Faber, 1970), pp. 159–163.

Ramraj, Victor J. "Denis Williams", in Dance, Daryl Cumber (ed.) *Fifty Caribbean Writers: A Bibliographical Critical Sourcebook* (New York: Greenwood Press, 1986), pp. 483–492.

—. Introduction to *Other Leopards* (Leeds: Peepal Tree Press, 2009).

Rowe-Evans, Adrian. "Other Freedoms". Review of *Other Leopards* in *Transition* (3, No. 11, November 1963), pp. 57–58.

Seymour, A. J. "The Novel in Guyana", in *Kaie* (4, 1967), pp. 59–63, particularly p. 63.

Walcott, Derek. "His is the Pivotal One about Race", in *Sunday Guardian* (Trinidad, 1 December 1963), p. 23.

Wali, Obiajunwa. "The Dead End of African Literature?" in *Transition* (Vol. 3, No. 10, 1963), pp. 13–15.

Williams, Charlotte. "'A young man with a hope': Side Notes on the Novel *Other Leopards*", in Williams, Charlotte & Evelyn A. Williams (eds) *Denis Williams: A Life in Works* (2010), pp. 88–110.

2.3 ARCHAEOLOGY

Gore, Charles. See Picton, John.

Laughlin, Nicholas. "As it was in the beginning", in *The Caribbean Review of Books* (Trinidad and Tobago: MEP, August 2005). Reprinted as "'As it was in the beginning': A Commentary on Prehistoric Guiana", in Williams, Charlotte & Evelyn A. Williams (eds) *Denis Williams: A Life in Works* (2010), pp. 201–211.

Picton, John & Charles Gore. "Denis Williams in Africa: A New Approach to its Arts and Technologies", in Williams, Charlotte & Evelyn A. Williams (eds) *Denis Williams: A Life in Works* (2010), pp. 150–168.

Wishart, Jennifer & Evelyn A Williams. "The Island of Guiana", in Williams, Charlotte & Evelyn A. Williams (eds) *Denis Williams: A Life in Works* (2010), pp. 186-199.

Williams, Evelyn A. See previous entry.

2.4 ART

Beier, Ulli. "Demas Nwoko, Uche Okeke", Mbari Exhibition notes, July 1961.

—. "The Oshogbo Art Workshop", in *Twenty Years of Oshogbo Art* (Universität Bayreuth: Iwalewa-Haus, 1991). Reprinted in Williams, Charlotte & Evelyn A. Williams (eds) *Denis Williams: A Life in Works* (2010), pp. 143–151.

Bissember, Elfrieda. "Burrowes School retrospective", in *Guyana Review* (July 1996), pp. 38–39.

—. Correspondence with Rev. Canon John Dorman and Peter Dorman [about *Majestas*]. [Original file in Castellani House].

Bourne, D. L. "Painting in British Guiana", in *Kyk-over-al* (Vol. 1, No. 2, June 1946, and Vol. 1, No. 3, December 1946), pp. 26–27.

Burrowes, E. R. "Old Wine in New Wineskins", in *Kyk-over-al* (Vol. 2, No. 8, June 1949), pp. 18–19.

—. "Art in British Guiana", in *Kyk-over-al* (Vol. 5, No. 15, Year end 1952), pp. 41–44.

Dorman, Canon John and Peter Dorman. Correspondence with Elfrieda Bissember (q.v.).

Greaves, Stanley. *The Artist in a Developing Society*. Typescript. Feature address to the Convocation of Artists (University of Guyana: Division of Creative Arts, 25 April 1981).

—. "The Sustainable in Art", in *Sunday Stabroek* (Georgetown, 9 May 1999).

—. "Meeting Denis: A Mind Engaged", in Williams, Charlotte & Evelyn A. Williams (eds) *Denis Williams: A Life in Works* (2010), pp. 169–185.

Grieve, Alastair. "Charles Biederman and the English Constructionists 2: An Exchange of Theories about Abstract Art during the 1950s", in *The Burlington Magazine* (Vol. 126, No. 971, February 1984), pp. 67–77. [Special edition devoted to twentieth-century art].

—. "Towards an Art of Environment: Exhibitions and Publications by a Group of Avant-Garde Abstract Artists in London 1951–55", in *The Burlington Magazine* (Vol. 132, No. 1062, November 1990), pp. 773–781.

—. "'This is Tomorrow', A Remarkable Exhibition Born from Contention", in *The Burlington Magazine* (Vol. 136, No. 1093, April 1994), pp. 225–232. Reprinted as "This is Tomorrow, a group exhibition and publication, 1956", in Grieve, *Constructed Abstract Art in England: A Neglected Avant-Garde* (New Haven: Yale University Press, 2005), pp. 35–43, particularly p. 38.

Harris, Wilson. "Review", in *Kyk-over-al* (Vol. 2, No. 9, December 1949), p. 32.

—. "Two Periods in the Work of a West Indian Artist", in *Kyk-over-al* (Vol. 6, No. 20, 1955), pp. 183–187. Reprinted in Williams, Charlotte & Evelyn A. Williams (eds) *Denis Williams: A Life in Works* (2010), pp. 41–47.

—. "Denis Williams", in *Kaie*, 4, Special Expo '67 Issue (July 1967), pp. 21–22.

Hickey, William. "I Take Dalí to Look at the Art", in *The Daily Express* (London, 28 April 1955).

Hinds, Basil. "'New Art' in British Guiana", in *Kyk-over-al* (Vol. 9, No. 27, December 1960), pp. 113–118.

—. "Retrospect of Art in the Sixties", in *Kaie* (No. 6, December 1970).

Jefferson-Miles, Andrew. "The Unframing of the 'Indwelling': Self-Portraits", in Williams, Charlotte & Evelyn A. Williams (eds). *Denis Williams: A Life in Works* (2010), pp. 49–63.

Lewis, Wyndham. "The London Galleries", in *The Listener* (British Broadcasting Corporation, 14 July 1949), p. 68.

—. "A Negro Artist", in *The Listener* (British Broadcasting Corporation, 7 December 1950), p. 696. Reprinted in Michael, Walter & C. J. Fox (eds) *Wyndham Lewis on Art: Collected Writings* (New York: Funk & Wagnalls, 1969), pp. 423–424.

—. "Denis Williams". Notes for Gimpel Fils exhibition, 1950.

—. Letters. See Rose, W. K.

Meyers, Jeffrey. *The Enemy: A Biography of Wyndham Lewis* (London: Routledge & Kegan Paul, 1980).

O'Keeffe, Paul. *Some Sort of Genius: A Life of Wyndham*

Lewis (UK: Pimlico, 2003).

Romney-Towndrow, Kenneth. "Kofi Antubam and Denis Williams at the Berkeley Galleries", in *Venture: Journal of the Fabian Colonial Bureau* (Vol. 1, No. 7, August 1949), p. 11.

Rose, W. K. (ed.). *The Letters of Wyndham Lewis* (London: Methuen & Co. Ltd., 1963).

Townsend, William. *The Townsend Journals. An artist's record of his times 1928–1951*. Ed. Andrew Forge (London: Tate Gallery, 1976).

Wainwright, Leon. "Speaking to Contemporary Art History: Denis Williams and Guyana", in Williams, Charlotte & Evelyn A. Williams (eds) *Denis Williams: A Life in Works. New and Collected Essays* (2010), pp. 65–75.

Walmsley, Anne. *The Caribbean Artists Movement 1966–1972: A Literary & Cultural History* (London and Port of Spain: New Beacon Books, 1992).

—. "Bridges of Sleep: Continental and Island Inheritance in the Visual Arts of Guyana", in Maes-Jelink, Hena., G. Collier, G. V. Davis & A. Rutherford (eds) *A Talent(ed) Digger: Creations, Cameos and Essays in Honour of Anna Rutherford* (Amsterdam: Rodopi, 1996), pp. 261–270, particularly pp. 262–264 and p. 267.

Williams, Evelyn A. "Art, Blood and Heritage". *The Edgar Mittelholzer Memorial Lectures*, Thirteenth Series (Georgetown: Walter Roth Museum of Anthropology, Ministry of Culture, Youth and Sport, 2009).

—. "The 'Uncanny-Potency' of Art", in Williams, Charlotte & Evelyn A. Williams (eds) *Denis Williams: A Life in Works* (2010), pp. 1–24.

2.5 INTERVIEWS

Brewster, Errol R. "'A Given Dream' – Dr Denis Williams CCH in his own words". Transcript of a series of interviews. Dated 14 July 1998.

—. *A Given Dream*. Television documentary (1998) based on the interviews detailed above. DVD from VHS original (Georgetown: Walter Roth Museum of Anthropology, Ministry of Culture, Youth and Sport, 2010).

Harvie, Stephanie. Interview with Denis Williams. Georgetown, Guyana, 7 October 1991. [Included in MA dissertation on Aubrey Williams. University of Warwick, 1992].

Richards, Spencer A. Interview with Denis Williams. Georgetown, Guyana, 16 June 1997.

Walmsley, Anne. Interview with Denis Williams. Georgetown, Guyana, 26 & 27 November 1993.

Williams, Charlotte. Series of interviews with Denis Williams. Georgetown, Guyana: 20 March, 23 March, 24 March, 26 March, 31 March & 7 April 1998.

2.6 OBITUARIES AND BIOGRAPHIES

Brewster, Errol. "Related Rhythms: Denis Williams 1923–1998". Paper given as part of the Guyana Folk Festival, Columbia University, New York (4 September 2004).

—. "Denis Williams 1923-'98: An Appreciation", in *Caribarts*, July 2004. Available on-line at www.caribarts.org/newsletter/pdf/21jul04.pdf. Accessed 2 March 2008.

Hazlewood, Carl E. "Notes on a life: Denis Williams 1923–1998", in *Nka: Journal of Contemporary African Art* (9, Ithaca, NY, fall-winter 1998), pp. 14–15.

Lindsay, Andrew. "Denis Williams", in *The Literary Encyclopedia* (April 2007).

McDonald, Ian. "The last of the Renaissance men: Denis Joseph Ivan Williams D.Litt., C.C.H. 1923–1998", in *Sunday Stabroek* (Georgetown, 5 July 1998), pp. 19, 21.

Meggers, Betty J. "Denis J. I. Williams 1923–1998". Obituary in bulletin of the *Society for American Archaeology* (Vol. 17, No. 4, September 1999).

Walmsley, Anne. "Denis Williams: Icons of Identity", in *The Guardian* (4 July 1998), p. 17.

—. "He lived his life totally", in *Sunday Stabroek* (Georgetown, 5 July 1998), p. 21. Reprinted in Williams, Charlotte & Evelyn A. Williams (eds) *Denis Williams: A Life in Works* (2010), pp. 213–217.

3 ADDITIONAL READING

Braithwaite, Barrington. "The Arts in the 90s", in *Sunday Stabroek*, *Guyana Review* (Vol. 15, Issue No. 185, May 2008), pp. 5, 7.

Brathwaite, Edward Kamau. "Timehri", in *Savacou* (September 1970), p. 38.

—. "Doing it our way", in *West Indies Chronicle* (April 1974), pp. 104-105.

—. "Caribbean Man in Space and Time", (1975) in Hearne, John (ed.) *Carifesta Forum: An Anthology of 20 Caribbean Voices* (Jamaica: Institute of Jamaica, 1976), pp. 199–208.

Carter, Martin. "Is there a West Indian Way of Life?" Symposium in *Kyk-over-al* (Vol. 6, No. 20, 1980), pp. 193-194.

Cummins, Alissandra; Alison Thompson & Nick Whittle (eds). *Art in Barbados: What Kind of Mirror Image?* (Kingston, Jamaica: Ian Randle Publishers, in association with Barbados Museum and Historical Society, 1999).

Haniff, Nesha Z. (ed.). *60 Years of Women Artists in Guyana 1928-1988: A Historical Perspective* (Sponsored by the Guyana Women Artists' Association, 1988).

Lewis, Wyndham. "On Canada", in Woodcock, George (ed.) *Wyndham Lewis in Canada* (Vancouver: University of British Columbia, 1971).

McDonald, Ian (ed.) *AJS at 70* (Georgetown: Autoprint Ltd., 1984). [With frontispiece portrait by Denis Williams].

Parker, Kenneth. "To Travel...Hopefully?" in Glage, Liselotte (ed.) *Being/s in Transit* (Amsterdam: Rodopi, 2000).

Roopnaraine, Rupert. *The Primacy of the Eye: The Art of Stanley Greaves* (Leeds: Peepal Tree Press, 2005).

Roth, Vincent. "Graphic Art in British Guiana: A Collection of Works by Local Artists 1944–1948". Foreword in the *Guiana Edition* No. 14 (Georgetown: *Daily Chronicle* Ltd., 1949).

Salkey, Andrew. *Georgetown Journal: A Caribbean Writer's Journey from London via Port of Spain to Georgetown, Guyana, 1970* (Trinidad, Port of Spain: New Beacon Books, 1972).

Seymour, A. J. "Notes Towards the Definition of Culture", in *Kyk-over-al* (Vol. 2, No. 8, June 1949), p. 33.

—. "The Creation of Quality in the West Indies", in *Kyk-over-al* (Vol. 6, No. 18, mid-year 1954), pp. 43–53.

—. Foreword to "Image and Idea in the Arts of Guyana", in *The Edgar Mittelholzer Memorial Lectures* (1969).

—. *Art in Guyana* (Georgetown: National History & Arts Council, 1971).

—. *Growing up in Guyana* (Georgetown: Labour Advocate Printers, 1976). [First part of autobiography, 1946–1972].

—. *Family Impromptu* (Georgetown: Labour Advocate Printers, 1977). [Autobiographical].

—. *Cultural Policy in Guyana* (UNESCO, Paris: Imprimerie des Presses Universitaires de France, 1977).

—. *Pilgrim Memories* (Georgetown: Labour Advocate Printers, 1978). [Autobiographical].

--. *Thirty Years a Civil Servant* (Georgetown: Labour Advocate Printers, 1978). [Second part of autobiography, 1972–1978].

Singh, Rickey. "Artists told: Think as Caribbean Nation", in *Guyana Graphic* (8 September 1972), p. 3.

Swan, Michael. *British Guiana: The Land of Six Peoples* (London: HMSO, 1957).

Trotter, David. "A most modern misanthrope: Wyndham Lewis and the pursuit of anti-pathos", in *London Review of Books* (January 2001).

Vaughan, Keith. *Journal and Drawings 1939–1965* (London: 1966), p. 159.

Vieira, Philip. "Adventure in Art", in *Kyk-over-al* (Vol. 3, No. 12, 1951), pp. 166–167.

Williams, Charlotte. *Sugar and Slate* (Aberystwyth: Planet Books, & Kingston, Jamaica: Ian Randle, 2002).

Williams, Charlotte & Evelyn A. Williams (eds). *Denis Williams: A Life in Works. New and Collected Essays* (Cross/Cultures; Amsterdam & New York: Rodopi, 2010).

Williams, Evelyn A. "Denis Williams in London, 1946–1957", in *Third Text* (No. 109, Vol. 25, Issue 2, March 2011), pp. 157–168.

INDEX